Local empowerment
and business services

Local empowerment and business services

Britain's experiment with Training and Enterprise Councils

Robert J. Bennett
Peter Wicks
Andrew McCoshan

UCL
PRESS

First published in 1994 by UCL Press

UCL Press Limited
University College London
Gower Street
London WC1E 6BT

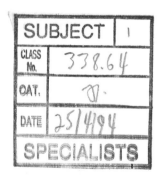

The name of University College London (UCL) is a registered trade mark
used by UCL Press with the consent of the owner.

ISBN: 1-85728-144-6 HB

British Library Cataloguing-in-Publication Data.

A catalogue record for this book is available from the British Library.

Typeset in Times Roman.
Printed and bound by
Biddles Ltd, King's Lynn and Guildford, England.

Contents

Dedicated to the memory of
Peter John Wicks,
who died tragically in a road accident
in May 1993
just as this book was completed.

Preface

This book examines one of Britain's major experiments to offer empowerment to businesses in local communities. The Training and Enterprise Councils (TECs) in England and Wales and the equivalent Local Enterprise Companies (LECs) in Scotland were set up over an 18 month period from April 1990 to October 1991. Their design developed over the period from 1987. The assessment given here complements and extends an earlier study which examined how local economic capacity could be built. This book and that earlier book should be read together: Bennett & McCoshan *Enterprise and human resource development: local capacity building* (Paul Chapman 1993).

Local empowerment is one of the key routes being followed within businesses to shift power and responsibility down the management hierarchy. It seeks to meet customer-driven needs through a stronger leadership vision that links the operational and strategic levels. The TECs and LECs are an attempt to apply this approach to an economy – to "UK plc".

Such an innovative approach is bound to experience many problems – and we evidence many of the difficulties in this book. But we also show some dramatic benefits that have been gained from the attempt to develop local empowerment. What we conclude, however, is that the initiative, by 1992 and 1993, was stalling and needing new vigour. We conclude that to empower means just that. There is no halfway house. The key impediments to business development in the UK is that not enough power has yet been given out to redress a century-long imbalance that has frustrated Britain's economic growth. The reforms we propose all seek to complete the mission that was given to TECs and LECs. But fully to empower also means to integrate development with other local business-led bodies. Hence we advocate the merger of TECs and LECs with Chambers of Commerce. We examine the potential and the difficulties of this proposal' and suggest a way forward.

The conclusions we offer are tough: the road to be followed will not be easy for government or local agents; the learning still required is considerable. But success will be achieved only by thinking long term and giving a sustained commitment to business leadership. Empowerment cannot be stopped halfway, otherwise it will lead only to disillusionment.

PREFACE

The analysis in this book combines a national coverage with local studies at various levels of detail. We seek to examine how the national issues relate to each other in different local circumstances. The assessment is based on a large number of original interviews and surveys collected specifically for this book. Where possible, we have sought to support comments and conclusions by attribution to sources, but this has not always been possible for reasons of confidentiality or sensitivity. Because of this need to preserve confidentiality, in what were frequently very candid interviews, most local responses are anonymous but are identified by TEC/LEC area through an anonymous code.

The book chiefly derives from a study financed by the Leverhulme Trust. We are most grateful to the Trust for its support. In addition the book has gained significantly from considerable subsequent research as well as the involvement of the authors in a number of the key policy studies that have been developed over its time of preparation and writing. We have also gained benefit from overlap of the Leverhulme study with other studies at LSE and would particularly wish to acknowledge the benefits of discussions with Günter Krebs and John Sellgren as well as the excellent secretarial support of Christine Gazely and cartographic support of Jane Pugh, Mike Scorer and Mina Moshkeri.

The book is based on a wide range of surveys and interviews. We acknowledge an immense debt to many organisations and individuals who have given their time to help our work. We would particularly like to express our thanks to: the TECs and LECs, to other local interviewees, to the Department of Employment, Training Agency (now TEED), the Department for Education, the DTI, the CBI, Association of British Chambers of Commerce, Business in the Community, and to all the other individuals and organizations in each area who, unfortunately, are too numerous individually to mention. Despite our debt to these bodies this book is independent of any organization and we remain responsible for its conclusions and any errors or omissions.

July 1993
London School of Economics

Abbreviations and acronyms

ABCC	Association of British Chambers of Commerce
ACE–HI	Association of Community Enterprises in the Highlands and Islands
AFE	Advanced Further Education
AONB	Area of Outstanding Natural Beauty
APL	Accreditation of Prior Learning
AZTEC	TEC for Wandsworth, Merton and Kingston-upon-Thames
BET	Business Enterprise Training
BGT	Business Growth Training
BIM	British Institute of Management
BITC	Business in the Community
BOTB	British Overseas Trade Board
BS	British Standards
BSC	British Steel Corporation
BSI	British Standards Institute
BTEC	Business and Technician Education Council
CAG	Comptroller and Auditor General
CALLMI	Computer-aided Local Labour Market Information
CAT	City Action Team
CAT	Credit Accumulation and Transfer
CBI	Confederation of British Industry
CENTEC	Central London TEC
CEWTEC	Birkenhead and Wirral TEC
CILNTEC	City and Inner London North TEC
CITB	Construction Industry Training Board
CMED	Charter for Management Education
CSE	Certificate of Secondary Education
CSO	Central Statistical Office
CTC	City Technology College
DBRW	Development Board for Rural Wales
DE	Department of Employment
DES	Department of Education and Science (up to May 1992)

ABBREVIATIONS AND ACRONYMS

DFE Department for Education (from May 1992)
DLG Derelict Land Grant
DMC District Manpower Committee
DOE Department of the Environment
DSS Department of Social Security
DTI Department of Trade and Industry
EA Employment Action
EAS Enterprise Allowance Scheme
EBP Education–business Partnership
EC European Community
EDG Employment Department Group
EDU Local authority Economic Development Unit
EEA Enterprise and Education Adviser
EHE Enterprise in Higher Education
EITB Electrical Construction Industry Training Board
ELTEC East Lancashire TEC
ENTA Enterprise Agency/Trust
ERA Education Reform Act (1988)
ESF European Social Fund
ET Employment Training Programme
EZ Enterprise Zone
FAM Financial Appraisal and Monitoring system
FE Further Education
FEFC Further Education Funding Councils (for England, Wales and Scotland)
G10 National group of regional TEC Chair representatives
GCSE General Certificate of Secondary Education
GDP Gross Domestic Product
GNVQ General National Vocational Qualification
HE Higher Education
HEFC Higher Education Funding Council
HIDB Highlands and Islands Development Board
HIE Highlands and Islands Enterprise
HMI Her Majesty's Inspectorate
HNC Higher National Certificate
HO Home Office
HRM Human Resources Management
HTNT High Technology National Training
ICI Imperial Chemical Industries (until May 1993)
IIP Investors in People
IM Industry Matters
IMS Institute of Manpower Studies
IPM Institute of Personnel Managers

IT	Information Technology
ITB	Industry Training Board
ITO	Industrial Training Organisation
JTPA	Job Training Partnership Act (USA)
JTS	Job Training Scheme
LA	Local Authority
LAMB	Local Area Manpower Board
LAWTEC	West Lancashire TEC
LCU	Large Companies Unit (ET) or Large Contractors Unit (YT)
LEA	Local Education Authority
LEAG	Local Enterprise Agency Grant
LEAP	Local Enterprise Agency Project
LEC	Local Enterprise Company
LEG	London Employment Group
LETEC	London East TEC
LEN	Local Employer Network
LIF	Local Initiatives Fund
LMI	Labour Market Information
LMS	Local Management of Schools
LSE	London School of Economics
LTU	long-term unemployed
MCI	Management Charter Initiative
METROTEC	Wigan TEC
MSC	Manpower Services Commission
NACETT	National Advisory Council for Education and Training Targets
NAO	National Audit Office
NATFHE	National Association of Teachers in Further and Higher Education
NCC	National Curriculum Council
NCVO	National Council for Voluntary Organisations
NCVQ	National Council for Vocational Qualifications
NDP	National Development Project
NEDC	National Economic Development Committee
NEDO	National Economic Development Office
NETT	National Education and Training Targets
NIC	Newly Industrializing Countries
NMA	National Managing Agency
NORMIDTEC	Central Cheshire TEC
NROVA	National Record of Vocational Achievement
NSTO	Non-statutory Training Organization
NTTF	National Training Task Force
NVQ	National Vocational Qualification
OECD	Organisation for Economic Cooperation and Development
ORF	Output-related Funding

OPL Open and flexible learning
OSS One Stop Shop
PES Public Expenditure Survey
PIC Private Industry Council (USA)
PICKUP Professional Industrial and Commercial Updating
PRF Performance-related Funding
PYBT Prince's Youth Busiess Trust
ROA Record of Achievement
SACETT Scottish Advisory Council for Education and Training Targets
SCIP School Council Industry Project/School Curriculum Industry Partnership
SCOTVEC Scottish Covational Education Council
SDA Scottish Development Agency
SE Scottish Enterprise
SEAC Schools Examination and Assessment Committee
SEM Single European Market
SERC Sheffield Economic Regeneration Committee
SEO Senior Executive Officer
SFS Small Firms Service
SME Small and Medium Sized Enterprise
SO Scottish Office
SOLOTEC South London TEC
SPRINT Strategic Programme for Innovation and Technology Transfer
STEP South Thames Enterprise Programme
SQW Segal, Quice Wickstead
SVQ Scottish Vocational Qualification
TA Training Agency
TAP Training Access Point
TC Training Commission
TEC Training and Enterprise Council
TEED Training, Education and Enterprise Directorate
TF Task Force
TFS The Field System (of TA budget management)
TFW Training for Work
TNPU Tecs and National Providers Unit
TOPS Training Opportunities Programme
TPO Teacher Placement Organiser
TQM Total Quality Management
TSAS Training Standards and Advisory Service
TTWA Travel to Work Area
TVEE Technical and Vocational Educational Extension
TVEI Technical and Vocational Education Initiative
UBI Understanding British Industry

ABBREVIATIONS AND ACRONYMS

UDC Urban Development Corporation
UPA Urban Programme Area
VAT Value Added Tax
VET Vocational Education and Training
WDA Welsh Development Agency
WG Working Group
WO Welsh Office
WRFE Work-related Further Education
YOP Youth Opportunities Programme
YT Youth Training
YTS Youth Training Scheme

Chapter 1
Why TECS and LECS?

Introduction

Local empowerment is the central theme of this book. Empowerment is a force
of reform developed primarily in business management to devolve more power
down the management hierarchy. Through devolution it is sought to enhance
the quality of services through a closer relation of products and services to
customer needs.

Local empowerment as we interpret it here is concerned with government's
attempt to bring customer requirements to the field of national policy on enterprise and training. Local empowerment is thus a specific means to introduce
new management concepts into these government programmes. How can empowerment help "UK plc" through these programmes? We assess in detail the
experiment that has been developed since 1988 with Training and Enterprise
Councils (TECs) in England and Wales, set up by the Government to tackle the
problems of Britain's training and wider local economic development problems, and Local Enterprise Companies (LECs) in Scotland.

TECS and LECS have sought to empower business leaders by giving them
responsibility for developing a strategy for government's training and enterprise programmes. This empowerment has been sought at a local level within a
network of 104 new local bodies across Britain led by business. TECS and LECS
were announced by the Government in two separate White Papers in December
1988. The first were established in April 1990 and all were in place by October
1991. They have the purpose, through a contract with government, "to plan and
deliver training and to promote and support the development of small businesses and self employment within their area" (Employment for the 1990s: DE
1988: 40). The core of TEC/LEC activity is the training and business assistance
programmes previously run by the Department of Employment (DE), the most
important being Youth Training (YT) and Employment Training (ET), Business
Growth Training (BGT), Small Firms Counselling, and Enterprise Allowance
Scheme (EAS). But it is also intended that "the TEC will be a catalyst for change
within its community. It will serve as a forum for local leaders . . . develop new
projects and activities . . . work with schools and colleges to raise skill levels

1

and smooth the transition from education to work. And it will play a vital rôle in promoting the importance of training as a business strategy" (TECs Prospectus 1989: 1).

The TECs and LECs thus have the ambitious aim not only of administrating training schemes, but also of empowering business to play a major rôle in the wider economic development of their areas: "the fundamental aim of every TEC will be to foster economic growth and contribute to the regeneration of the community it serves. Its special focus will be on strengthening the skill base and assisting local enterprise to expand and compete more effectively" (TECs Prospectus 1989: 1). The wider economic development rôle was reaffirmed in 1992 by Gillian Shephard – "what we are about is local economic development" – and the President of the Board of Trade, Michael Heseltine, as "economic development in the widest sense" (TECs conference, July 1992).

Much of the concept of TECs and LECs developed from thinking around the structure of Private Industry Councils (PICs) in the USA. Indeed one of the leading directors of a US PIC, Cay Stratton, has been special advisor to all Secretaries of State for Employment between 1989 and 1993. But also drawn upon were models of European Chambers of Commerce, as in Germany or France, regional labour boards as in Sweden, and Japanese government–industry relations. Despite these examples, the British approach was fundamentally different from PICs or other models.

It is clear that the government was stimulated to look at foreign examples, not only to harness experience, but also because of its concern to increase the international competitiveness of the British economy, not least in preparation for the Single European Market. A concept has emerged that British institutions designed to support the local economy should be at least as good as those in Europe. Michael Heseltine called for them to be of "world class standards" (TECs conference, July 1992). This has motivated the 1993 development of One Stop Shops.

At the same time the Government has seen TECs and LECs in the context of its mainstream agenda to improve management of the public sector attuned to the needs of the economy. TECs and LECs can be seen, therefore, as particular vehicles which seek to improve the management of employment and training programmes through giving the private sector the lead in their management. They are one form of what Osborne & Gaebler (1993) term "reinventing government" through introduction of private sector management methods.

It is also clear that the Government hoped to take advantage of the special opportunity offered by the demographic downturn since the late 1980s and the tight labour market that this was expected to induce. This seemed to offer the opportunity in the 1990s both to stimulate business to place training and local community involvement higher on its agenda, and also to stimulate to enter jobs those minority and "disadvantaged" sectors of the population which have previously found greater difficulties of gaining access. Whether these stimuli will prove strong as Britain comes out of its 1990–93 recession remains to be seen.

The foundation of TECs and LECs has some close similarities with a growing body of opinion that has called for increased "local empowerment" and "local capacity building" in the British economy. An earlier LSE study has examined how the political developments of the 1980s emphasized the need for a supply-side reform (Bennett & McCoshan 1993). In practice this has usually meant enhancing institutional capacity to respond to economic needs. Much of this development is needed at national level. But a major part of the institutional fabric exists at the local level: this is where the individual or firm is located and from which it draws most institutional links. The changing emphasis can be summarised by the increasing recognition that more resources alone may change nothing: indeed more resources may make matters worse by strengthening the power of institutions allocating the resources from which change is required. This can mean that giving out resources alone often actually makes matters worse – the so-called *perverse policy syndrome*. Local capacity building requires the institutions to change and adapt, not be reinforced in inappropriate practices. TECs and LECs represent an attempt to lever such change through the development of a new local institution.

TECS/LECS: the essential features

The TECs and LECs offer ambitious objectives, substantial funds, seconded civil service staff and other support, and a new institutional framework which has the potential to make significant improvements in the relations between businesses and local communities. The key elements of the development of TECs and LECs are:

- 104 TECs and LECs covering the whole of Britain (see Figure 1.1);
- Important differences of power and responsibilities between:
  - 12 Scottish Enterprise (SE) LECs,
  - 10 Highlands and Islands Enterprise (HIE) LECs,[1]
  - 82 England and Wales TECs;
- Substantial public funds, over £2.3 billion in 1993/94;
- Organised as companies limited by guarantee;
- Business leaders have a majority of two-thirds of the Board members;
- Staffed primarily by former civil service personnel;
- Geographical coverage relating mainly to counties/Scottish regions and metropolitan district boundaries;
- Funding on average in 1993/94 of £20 million (£18 million in England and Wales, £32 million in SE LECs, and £3.6 million in HIE LECs);
- Most funding related to unemployment training programmes (74%);
- Additional minor funding external to government resources.

Much of the early phase of TEC/LEC development has been concerned with adapting former Training Agency programmes that have been transferred to

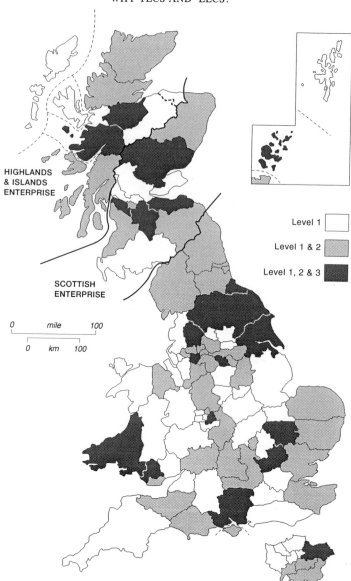

HIGHLANDS
& ISLANDS
ENTERPRISE

Level 1

Level 1 & 2

Level 1, 2 & 3

SCOTTISH
ENTERPRISE

0   mile   100

0   km   100

Figure 1.1 The map of TECs in England and Wales and LECs in Scotland showing the coverage of SE and HIE. One LEC (Moray, Badenoch and Strathspey) is in both HIE and SE areas. The levels of analysis refer to the research framework of this book, and are defined in the text.

4

them. In summary, their main responsibility has been for the former programmes titled:

- YT (Youth Training programme);
- ET (Employment Training programme);
- BGT (Business Growth Training);
- Enterprise Allowance Scheme (EAS);
- Small Firms Service (SFS);
- Trainer training development;
- Training Access Points (TAPs);
- A proportion of the government funds allocated for WRFE (Work-Related Further Education);
- Careers Service involvement through Careership Partnerships;
- Contract holders for the development of Education–Business Partnerships (EBPs) and Compacts;
- In addition, LECs have additional responsibilities for physical development and infrastructure programmes transferred from the former Scottish Development Agency (SDA) and Community Development Action transferred from the former Highlands and Islands Development Board (HIDB).

Despite the diversity of program funding, the main budget of the TECs and LECs is for training programmes that were formerly part of YT and ET. This constitutes 74% of the total for TECs and 38% for LECs. An important secondary budget is for enterprise, which is 20–37% of the budget. There are small sums for education as well as an element for WRFE. In addition, there is a local initiative fund (LIF), which varied in size between TECs from £100,000 to £500,000 in year one, with annual sums of about 10% of that level in later years. Because of these relative resource levels we would argue that *TECs are necessarily driven by training priorities, concerned closely with enterprise development, and have to work closely with other local agents in other areas of education and economic development activity.* The ordering of priorities is not necessarily a bad thing: indeed we argue that to make this prioritization clearer would be a major advantage both for TECs and the other agents with whom they deal.

The *LECs, in contrast, are also driven by training and are concerned with economic development, but because they have major environmental and physical development resources, they are key animators of more general economic development in their areas.* The contrast in power and impacts of TECs and LECs is an important part of our analysis. From this analysis we draw major policy conclusions about the needs in England and Wales for TECs to collaborate closely with other agents (particularly local authorities and Chambers of Commerce).

Assessing TECs and LECs

The TEC/LEC initiative is a major and innovative development which has sought to change the fabric of local economic development in Britain. Assessing its contribution to achieving improvement in the fields in which it is targeted requires similarly large scale and innovative study. This book uses a mixture of extensive and intensive methods of analysis. The research on which it is based has been undertaken at four levels of analysis.

Level 1 involves a complete coverage of all TECs and LECs, investigating the key elements of: objectives, staffing, budgets, area coverage, economic characteristics, etc. This information was gathered from published and other sources, and postal surveys of all TECs and LECs.

Level 2 involves a face-to-face detailed interview survey which was undertaken with the majority of TECs and LECs. These interviews in virtually all cases involved the chief executive. In some cases there were supplementary meetings with programme managers in specific fields. The sample included most "early" TECs and LECs that were operational by April 1990 as well as many later ones. In all, 62 out of the 104 TECs/LECs (60%) were surveyed. The coverage was kept approximately the same across each area: 44 in England (59%), 4 in Wales (57%), 8 in Southern Scotland (67%) and 6 in the Scottish Highlands and Islands (60%).

Level 3 involves 20 areas which were studied in greater depth to assess the interfacing of TECs/LECs with other agents and to gather detail on specific programmes or issues. The chief areas included in this way were chosen for their contrasted characteristics of economy, geography, social and local institutional structures, and size of TEC/LEC area. The study also sought to have a balance of England (15%), Wales (29%) and Scotland (SE: 33%; HIE: 30%). The smaller areas of Wales, SE and HIE are overrepresented in order to obtain a large enough sample size of each area. The areas included can be seen in Table 1.1.

In each of these areas the face-to-face interviews with TECs/LECs were supplemented by at least two further interviews, in many cases by three, four or more. These interviews always included the major existing local business organization (Chamber of Commerce, enterprise agency, etc.) and the local authority (officer and/or councillor). Additional interviews normally covered key business leaders (TEC Chairs, TEC Board members, or other significant figures) or other key local agents. In seven of these areas we were also able to draw on the earlier in-depth study reported in Bennett & McCoshan (1993). Greater detail of the survey methods is given in the Appendix (p.315). The national map of TECs and LECs, shown in Figure 1.1, exhibits the coverage of areas by each level of the analysis in this book.

Level 4 of our analysis involves, in addition to the structured interviews through the three levels outlined above, a further range of interviews undertaken both on a more ad hoc basis and as part of other structured studies. One of the most important of these additional sources has been a study with all London TECs, involving interviews with all TEC Chairs and chief executives, as well as many programme managers. As a result of these additional interviews a further

Table 1.1   Areas included in the analysis of TECs and LECs.

England	Wales	Scotland
Teesside	Mid Glamorgan	SE
Sheffield	West Wales	Tayside
North Yorkshire		Renfrew
Manchester		Lothian
Birmingham		Lanarkshire
Cambridgeshire		
London East		HIE
Hertfordshire		Lochaber
Hampshire		Inverness and Nairn
Humberside		Orkney
East Lancashire		

30 TECs and LECs have been examined. This, combined with the national surveys of TECs and LECs undertaken at Level 1, means that all TECs and LECs have provided information in one form or another. In particular, these further interviews have emphasised comment from TEC Chairs and business directors. As a result 23 Chairs and 34 business directors have been interviewed directly.

It should be noted that although this book is based on an enormous number of face-to-face interviews (over 400 in all), we cannot reflect all of the detail in the text. In addition, all interviews were given in confidence and we refer in the text to TEC/LEC areas by an anonymous number and to the office holder by title, not name.

In the rest of the book we address the assessment of TECs/LECs as follows:
- Specification of the gaps and needs that TECs/LECs seek to fill (Chapter 2);
- The process by which TECs and LECs were developed (Chapter 3);
- The management structure of TECs and LECs (Chapter 4);
- The variation between TECs/LECs in different areas, assessing how far their differences meet the needs of different local situations and their relation to other agents and institutions (including local authorities and educational bodies, Chambers of Commerce, enterprise agencies, training agents and labour unions – Chapter 5);
- How TECs and LECs relate to government, the Treasury and the nature of public accountability (Chapter 6);
- Assessment of the contribution made by TECs/LECs to improving Britain's capacity in training (Chapter 7);
- Assessment of the impact of TECs/LECs on school education and WRFE (Chapter 8);
- Assessment of the contribution of TEC/LEC programmes to enterprise development (Chapter 9);
- Assessment of the differing contributions of TECs and LECs to the more general economic development of communities, and how TECs/LECs inter-

face with other agents within local economies (Chapter 10);
- How the present structure and activities of TECs/LECs might be developed to improve future performance (Chapters 11 and 12).

Summary

This book seeks to put TECs/LECs into the context of other national and local institutions with which they collaborate or sometimes conflict. A major part of the discussion concentrates on the institutional development that TECs/LECs themselves represent, and seek to stimulate in other institutions. The book also places strong emphasis on the contrasts that exist between TECs and LECs in different places. Perhaps the major innovation that they can make to Britain's institutional fabric is to become the powerful local *agents* in their areas that was their original mission. The extent to which they have developed an authority and local flexibility appropriate to local needs is, therefore, a major aspect of the assessment we present.

The book is not partisan to a particular political position. Rather it seeks to cut through the political mists that have surrounded TECs/LECs. It has been natural for central government and its civil servants in the Employment Department and the former Training Agency (now termed Training, Education and Enterprise Directorate – TEED) stridently to defend TECs and LECs. Similarly TECs and LECs themselves have concentrated on publicity of positive outcomes. Other interests, such as the opposition parties and their related research institutions have naturally been critical. More dispassionate analysis has been rare, and this book seeks to provide it.

The book concludes that TECs and LECs represent a major development of British local institutions and that they offer considerable benefits in helping to overcome many of Britain's specific and long-running economic problems. However, we also caution on expecting too much from TECs and LECs, and against complacency that other, even deeper, institutional reforms of Britain are not still required. We generally conclude with positive support for the achievements of TECs and LECs and their potential. But we also argue for major and fundamental further development.

These arguments are developed at length in later chapters. The main specific conclusions are itemized at the end of each chapter. In summary, our chief assessments of TEC/LEC effectiveness, which are detailed in Chapters 11 and 12, suggest that:
- The LECs have performed significantly better than the TECs. This is as a result of having a single central government office to deal with (the Scottish Office), having intermediary bodies at a regional level (Scottish Enterprise and Highlands and Islands Enterprise), moving faster to recruit staff with specialist skills, and developing a business-led mission;
- There are fundamental deficiencies in the structure of TECs and to a lesser

extent the LECs as a result of unclear mission, inadequate empowerment, conflicts in local leadership, gaps in personnel skills to deliver and ability of the Boards to manage, cost inefficiency and budget uncertainties;

– There are also fundamental questions about the size and geographical coverage of TEC/LEC areas which we conclude are key stimuli to reform and merger;

– Despite major improvements in programmes there are still significant gaps in all the main fields of TEC/LEC activity: training, education, enterprise, and economic development.

From this assessment we derive the following key conclusions on how developments should take place in the future:

– We argue that Britain needs to seek truly world class targets for its economy, and this means seeking to overcome some of the most deeply entrenched barriers to change, not least within government and ministries themselves;

– That fully developed local business empowerment means that government must give up considerable power;

– That local agents can be educated to assume that power in a stage-wise process of learning over time;

– This development requires TECs and LECs to be primarily acting as purchasers and facilitators, rarely if ever as providers;

– As strategists TECs and LECs can develop meaningful local missions only if they are owned by local stakeholders who will act on the mission;

– To have ownership by local employers, the vision of TECs and LECs must be merged with the mission of Chambers of Commerce, but with significant enhancements of both agencies;

– But merger alone is only one of the first steps towards a wider empowerment by which government lets go of major elements of the TECs and LECs and shifts to a body founded on the concept of "business self-administration", with which government can contract, to which it delegates regulation, and from which it can derive a proper partnership relation. This, we argue, requires that government give not only power to merged TEC–chambers, but also a general revenue resource.

Chapter 2
Britain's need for change

An institutional gap

The TECs and LECs are primarily an institutional development. They are first and foremost a reorganization of the way government is seeking to allocate its resources in training and enterprise programmes. They also reflect government's intention to establish an employer-led body in each local area. Thus the aim for TECs and LECs has been to draw closer together two distinct cultures, one centring on business requirements and the other focusing on government-funded providers. The importance of institutional change in the 1990s was recognized at the outset in the White Paper (DE 1988: 60):

> We stand at a parting of the ways. In one direction lie the behaviour and attitudes, the short term planning and the easy options that have so bedeviled our performance in the past. In the other direction lie the new approaches, the new systems, the long-term planning, investment and professionalism which this White Paper has described.

In this chapter we assess the argument for institutional reform in Britain. We discuss in turn the system problem; the need for institutional reform; and how TECs and LECs can help.

A system problem

Britain's economic performance on all of the major indicators has given continued grounds for concern since at least the 1950s. Although much of the period of the 1980s recorded some notable improvements in many areas, high inflation, increasing unemployment and economic slowdown after 1989 have confirmed that long-term improvements in economic capacity have still fully to be realised. The rest of the 1990s will evidence whether or not the changes that occurred in the 1980s were long term.

Economic growth and employment

Figure 2.1 shows the long-term rates of growth of GDP in Britain compared to the average of OECD economies since 1950. Based on these long term averages,

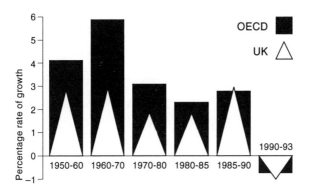

Figure 2.1 Average rates of growth of GDP of Britain compared to the rest of OECD countries. *Source:* OECD and CSO.

it is only for the brief period of 1985–90 that the British economy has equalled or exceeded the growth rate in the other industrial economies. GDP is a measure of the total national wealth and income available for distribution. It is, there-fore, the crucial measure of the bottom line of "UK plc".

Compared to the USA and Germany, Figure 2.2 shows one key element of GDP, the profitability in manufacturing. Again Britain's performance has been

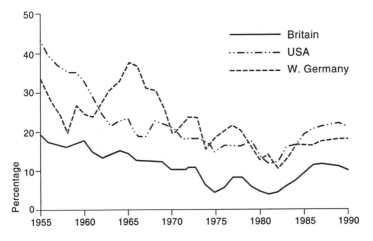

Figure 2.2 Profitability in manufacturing (measured as net rates of return to fixed capital) in Britain, USA and West Germany, 1955–87. *Source:* British Business.

11

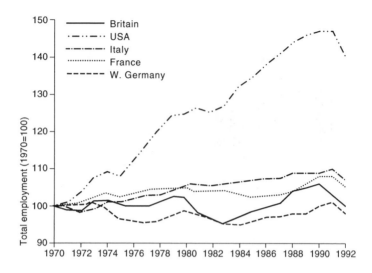

Figure 2.3 Total employment, main OECD countries. *Source:* OECD.

poorer, over the long term, than in our major competitors. The ability of the economy to deliver jobs depends on its wealth (GDP) and profitability. Figure 2.3 shows that in the field of jobs, too, Britain has had a declining level of employment relative to many countries, though Figure 2.3 also brings out the sluggishness of job growth in Europe as a whole compared to the USA.

The converse of jobs is the unemployment record. Figure 2.4 shows that Britain has moved from a relatively low unemployment rate in the 1950s, to

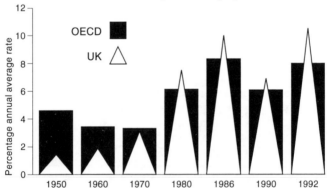

Figure 2.4 Unemployment rates in Britain and OECD countries, 1950–92. *Source:* CSO and OECD, 1950 for the six main industrialized countries only.

12

progressively equal, and then substantially to exceed the OECD average. Concern about the sensitivity of the British economy to register high rates of unemployment earlier than most other economies has returned in the 1990–92 recession.

Education and training

These trends all point to an historically poor, and in a number of areas, deteriorating economic performance of the British economy. It is natural, therefore, that a major emphasis should have been placed on one of the crucial factor inputs to business, the quality of education and training. As shown in Table 2.1, the UK is bottom of the league of the five main OECD industrial economies in terms of the staying-on rate in full-time education and training of 16- to 18-year-olds as well as higher education participation. Its average rate of staying-on for the 16–18 age group is less than one-half of that in the USA, Japan or France and is also less than half of the higher education participation rate of Japan, Germany and France. A large part of this low participation derives from the very rapid decline in staying-on at ages 17 and 18. For example, Britain's 18-year-old participation rate is approximately one-third of that in most of the other countries listed. Low staying-on to 18 inevitably also feeds into low staying-on in higher education.

TECs and LECs have been given a primary focus on tackling the problem of raising the level of 16–19 participation in education and training. If people are not in the training system then skills will not be enhanced. However, as well as the quantity of training, there have also been concerns about its quality. The 16–19 staying-on rate is thus probably only part of a more general deficiency in Britain's human resource development that applies across the board – to education, to vocational training, to managerial capacity, to entrepreneurialism, to innovation and to the capability properly to apply human resource inputs.

Quality is difficult to compare across countries because definitions of qualifications and course content vary. But Table 2.2 gives strong evidence for Britain's qualitative deficiencies. In terms of highest qualifications received Britain has a far lower proportion of its population receiving higher or intermediate

Table 2.1 Participation in full-time education and training (including YT) of 16–18 year olds (percentage of total population by age cohort).

	16 years	Average 16–18 years
United States	95	81
Japan	96	79
France	88	77
Germany	100	92
United Kingdom	93	70

Source: FEFC (1992).

Table 2.2   Highest level of qualification of school leavers in Britain, France and Germany.

	Britain	France	West Germany
No qualifications	10	10	10
Low level school leaver			
(below 1 C grade at GCSE)	35	–	–
Intermediate level			
(1 'A' level and below)	40	55	60
Higher level (university entrance)			
(2 or more 'A' levels)	15	35	30

Source: CBI (1989a) from a variety of sources.

qualifications. There has also been concern, recently highlighted in the Higginson Report (1988), that the main intermediate and higher-level qualification obtained, "A"-Levels, is singularly inappropriate to the needs of business. Below intermediate level, Table 2.2 shows that the low-level school leaver with grades below C in GCSE makes up a large proportion of the British school leavers' highest qualifications – a group which does not exist in France or Germany. These estimates are backed up by recent detailed comparisons by NIESR that only 27% of English 16-year-olds in 1990/91 reach the equivalent of GCSE grades A to C in mathematics, the national language and one science, compared to 50% in Japan, 62% in Germany and 66% in France.

Research and development

Some of the other defects are evident in Figure 2.5, which shows the R&D expenditure of the main OECD economies. Britain has maintained a fairly level expenditure as a proportion of GNP since 1970 whereas the commitment of GNP in all the other countries listed, and in the OECD as a whole, has rapidly increased. The comparative rates of growth of R&D as a proportion of GNP are 20% for all OECD countries, 41% for Japan, but only 5% for the UK between 1970 and 1988. Thus Figure 2.5 shows the UK steadily losing ground. Moreover, compared to other countries, a larger proportion of the UK R&D expenditure is for defence rather than civil R&D: approximately 22% of all sources in 1989, and 91% of government funds.[1] The impression of the decline of Britain in R&D is further reinforced by the relative decline in rate of patents registered in the USA, shown in Figure 2.6. Between 1970 and 1989 UK companies maintained a virtually constant level of new patents registered in the USA, compared to significant growth by German companies (an increase of 100%) or Japanese companies (an increase of 700%).[2] Total world patent applications by UK companies have remained fairly constant over time (24,300 in 1965, 19,700 in 1980, 20,700 in 1988). This can be compared for example with the growth by Japan from 60,800 in 1965 to 175,700 in 1980 to 308,800 in 1988.[3]

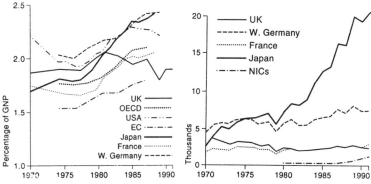

Figure 2.5 R&D expenditure as a proportion of GNP. *Source:* UK CSO Annual Survey; other countries, OECD and *Financial Times* (3 December 1990).

Figure 2.6 Patents granted in the USA to non-US companies. *Source: Financial Times* (3 December 1990; 9 June 1993).

As a result of these changes British export markets have been continuously eroded in manufacturing in particular. The strongest effect has been on high technology trade. The trends in this sector, shown in Figure 2.7, make clear that Britain has been losing its share of world trade to Japan and the NICs faster than all the other countries listed, except the USA.

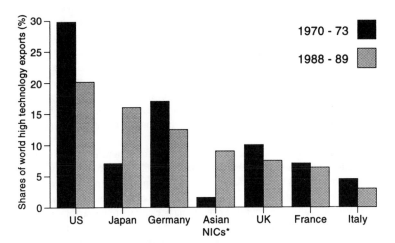

* Hong Kong, S. Korea, Singapore, Taiwan

Figure 2.7 Shares of world high technology exports 1970–73 and 1988–89. *Source:* Tyson (1992).

The difficulties of improving Britain's economic capacity would be easier to tackle if they were confined to the specific programme areas. However, it is clear that Britain's difficulties stem from the total system and network of relations that interconnect deficient programmes of supply with the poor indicators of the demand they are seeking to meet. Each area of deficiency is both the cause and product of deficiencies in other areas. Hence improvement cannot be sought from reforming programmes one at a time. It is this that has led some commentators to argue that Britain suffers from a system failure that needs a system-wide solution.

The need for institutional reform

The system-wide problem that is influencing the poor performance of the British economy arises chiefly from the way in which resources are applied to problems. If resources continue to be applied in routine ways when needs have markedly changed, then the new resources will not meet needs. They may even make matters worse. This is the *perverse policy syndrome*.

The perverse policy syndrome in an economy arises from the system of relations between its people and its institutions. No modern economy is a pure market of atomistic individual decision making. Instead it is often chiefly shaped by organizations, institutions and other intermediaries – companies, interest groups, government, trade unions and other organizations. These institutions link individuals together and support networks of exchange of information and incentives. A country's economic system is a complex combination of its individuals and its institutions. The assessment of a country's economy therefore depends not only the relationships of macroeconomic and microeconomic indicators, but also on the performance of its institutions in relation to its economic goals. It has only recently been recognized that strong government is often needed to assure as close as possible an approximation to market allocation decisions, because only strong government can keep the power of other institutions in check in order to allow economies to work better. Such strong government must also be a government that works to stimulate economic forces, not to conflict with them.

Mancur Olson (1982) was one of the first to recognize that institutions, including government, are subject to a perverse policy syndrome. His argument is that no economy can maintain a position in which all groups and organizations have equal power. As a result, economically efficient outcomes will not be achieved through comprehensive bargaining because more powerful groups will always assert their interests over weaker groups. A powerful interest group "will have little or no incentive to make any significant sacrifices in the interests of society; it can best serve its members' interests by striving to seize a larger share of society's production for them" (Olson 1982: 44). As a result, over time, economic efficiency is reduced because institutional interests, monopolies and oligopolies seek to prevent change or to extort higher prices than are justified by their productivity.

Stable societies accumulate more organizations over time. Hence the longer that time progresses, and the more stable a society is, the greater will be its accumulation of special interest groups and organizations, the greater will be the control by cartels, and the greater will be the distortion of decision making away from economic objectives. The development of the perverse policy syndrome is the result of this accumulation of interests. Top management groups and the country's elite defend the interests of their organizations, and a smaller and smaller range of views thus enters economic management decisions. A form of bargained "consensus" emerges. The concentration of power limits an economy's adaptability and flexibility, and thus its capacity for economic growth. The perverse policy syndrome may also have long-term cyclic structures. Middlemas (1990) has identified a political cycle, covering the period from 1918 to the 1970s, in which the interest groups of industry, labour, government and the financial sector grew in maturity and learnt to work with each other: "corporatism". This cycle of accumulation was linked to a particular cycle of industrial practice dominated by large-scale industries, centralization and narrow management elites.

The effect of suboptimal performance in one sector also spills over into other sectors. A major industry does not go out of business if it is an inefficient monopoly. Instead, as observed by Malinvaud (1977), its allocatively inefficient rules will contribute to either underemployment or excess capacity in another market. When prices are completely out of line with market conditions, inefficient factor utilization in one area leads to inefficient product outputs in others, until the point is reached where the whole economy becomes inefficient. This is a special form of "crowding out", which has been associated with excess public sector activity reducing the extent of private action. As observed by Porter (1990: 506):

> The British case illustrates why it is so hard to turn around an economy once it starts to erode. There was no shock or jolt to reverse the cycle; indeed a victory in the war bolstered confidence, and lingering market positions and customer loyalties may have allayed a sense of urgency about the need to change.

Detailed appraisals have been made of the history of many British industries in comparison with competitors. Each of these demonstrate the British problem of poor business strategy, poor management, sluggishness and slow innovation.[4]

An earlier study (Bennett & McCoshan 1993: Ch. 4) has argued that the key elements of the perverse policy syndrome derive from five main areas: business strategy, employment and the labour market, education and training, economic policy and the welfare compromise, and central–local government relations.

17

Business strategy

Business strategy relates product development to markets, strategic management and R&D. Compared to leading competitors, recent studies have demonstrated Britain's often myopic approach to business innovation.[5] Technological activities are too frequently treated just like other activities in response to market demand and price stimuli, with similar discounting for risk and time. This undervalues long-term R&D and explains Britain's tendency to produce yesterday's products better. Dynamically innovating businesses, in contrast, treat technological products as occasions to change their organization and commercial approach, which require an entirely different appraisal of risk. At the same time business R&D in Britain has often been divorced from the research R&D of the state-funded research institutions. The result has been that "like a chef cooking a meal, a German company has at hand most of the ingredients it needs to innovate. In contrast, British companies have to reach a long way for what they need, whether it is technology, staff or finance. Their cooking has to be constantly interrupted by visits to shops to get ingredients".[6] As a result, not only is response sluggish but, in a period of accelerating technological change, whole industries will be left floundering with out-of-date core technologies and products. Perversely, simply putting more resources into R&D will not alone solve the problem, because the institutional gaps will prevent the resources being properly applied. R&D has to be better linked to economic needs and enhanced management.

Employment and the labour market

Also at the core of Britain's poor economic performance is the way in which its human resources are applied. The institutional structures of the labour market have tended to slow down revisions in work practices, skills and management that the economy has needed in order to adjust to change. The effect of trade unions is only part of a wider institutional resistance affecting industrial performance.[7] Also important are the rôle played by unemployment, management, and industrial relations. Britain has long possessed an "unnaturally high natural rate of unemployment" (Meade 1982). Olson (1982) explains this by arguing that high unemployment results both from worker demands that set wages above the market level, so that it is uneconomic for employers to hire more workers; and from employers attempting to control competitive pressures that limit their long-term market expansion. Olson argues that Britain has sought to maintain an uncompetitive position through protection of markets, and co-operation between institutional interests in order to maintain their interests (of employers, or of groups of workers). For "the worker . . . the productive process, let alone success in the market, was no responsibility of his"; this "degree of motivation explains the performance; the performance demonstrates the degree of motivation; and the nature of the historical experience of the working class accounts for both . . . it determined their human quality – their all-round capability and effective intelligence, their aptitude for more and sophisticated tasks" (Barnett 1986: 191–2).

Among managers Wiener (1981) notes that already, by the mid-19th century, there was a strong desire to keep trade at arm's length: that it was a scarcely respectable activity. This tended to cultivate a national perception that "the pursuit of wealth was vulgar". This position had only slightly changed by the early 1970s so that there has been, over the long term, a lower status accorded to business careers compared to the civil service, military, clerical or purer academic activities.[8] A long-term degeneration of industrial relations has resulted from these institutional separations of the interests of workers and employers. A strong demotivation of the workforce developed, which gave little stimulus to the acquisition of skills or adaptation of working practices; management increasingly pursued objectives irrelevant or perverse to the needs of the economy, and developed a passiveness and complacency about the growing need to adapt and deliver products to rigorous performance criteria of delivery time or quality. As a result, the British labour market has been a major example of the perverse policy syndrome: simply applying more resources will normally make matters worse rather than better. As noted by Ball (1989: 45), "With extreme rigidities in the process of adjusting the price of labour, simply pumping money into the economy (along Keynesian lines) resulted not in the creation of more jobs, but more inflation". In such a situation, Keynesian demand management cannot work. Emphasis must instead shift to factor supply through adjusting the set of regulatory and institutional forces that affect innovation, workforce, skills and capital.

Education and training

Education and training is a crucial ingredient of Britain's systems failure. Recognition of the problem is not new, but has been understood at least since the 1870s. The recent concern dates from Prime Minister James Callaghan's speech at Ruskin College Oxford in 1976: "There seems to be a need for a more technological bias . . . that will lead towards practical applications in industry . . . there is no virtue in producing socially well-adjusted members of society who are unemployed because they do not have the skills".[9] The OECD (1975: 74) had also castigated Britain for a lack of balance of the rôle of "technological development and the rôle of the state, and of the place of education and science in the process of production".

The problems of the British education and training record are part cause and part effect of the perverse policy syndrome. The educational system had certainly been allowed to develop almost totally independently of the needs of the economy. The 1950s and 1960s have been seen as: "the golden age of teacher autonomy" over the curriculum when an "ideology of teacher professionalism" became dominant. This excluded all other interests. The curriculum was routinely seen as a "secret garden" which was not open to extended appraisal by noneducationalists. The OECD had highlighted the Department of Education and Science (DES) as "passive" and "secretive". After a highly critical House of Commons Select Committee report (DES 1976: 10) the DES was forced to admit that it had "erred in encouraging schools to prepare pupils for 'social' rather than their 'economic' rôle". Moreover this perverse separation from the needs of the economy appeared to be driven by the close symmetry of the interests of the teachers' unions and the DES who had developed a very close relationship of mutual support in their own exclusiveness and concern as the producers of education. Sarup has called the relationship between the NUT and DES "a cosy symbiotic relationship" from 1944 until the mid-1970s.[10] As a result "DES officials were . . . hopelessly tainted".[11] The situation up to the 1970s was therefore the most vivid portrayal of the perverse policy syndrome.

However, it is a mistake to see deficiencies of education and training in isolation from the deficiencies in the rest of the economy. In a situation in which productivity was scorned, business strategy and management was deficient, and skills and training undervalued in companies, it is not surprising that the education sector became isolated. Businesses, too, bear a responsibility for neglecting their demand-side impact on the education and training sector. This has led to a vicious circle in which low management targets have led to low investment in skills, low technology and low output and low quality levels. Britain's poor education and training record is both product and cause of the country's poor economic performance; what has been termed a "low skills equilibrium".[12]

The rôle of education and training's interaction with the economy is thus not only a vivid portrayal of the perverse policy syndrome. It is also indicative of the difficulties of finding a solution: that merely producing more highly educated or skilled people alone will not overcome the deficiency. *It is not possible to succeed with a skills-led strategy alone.* This is one reason why the MSC training initiatives since the 1960s have mostly met with, at best, halfhearted success. To be effective, skilling must be linked to systematic change also in business strategy across the whole field of management culture, product development and marketing, and innovative R&D. This has profound implications for the rôle of TECs and LECs.

Economic policy and the welfare compromise

Economic growth, education and training inevitably involves a crucial rôle to be played by government. This rôle concerns both priorities for regulation and public expenditure. But also important is how government balances its economic rôle with its social and other policies. This affects the balance of the state and private sector. It also concerns how government affects the environment within which economic decisions are made. It is in this sense that Britain's welfare compromise assumes a central relevance.

The form of the post-war development of public services can be seen as a compromise which sought to balance economic and social needs through bargaining between institutional groups. The resulting settlement of the compromise is argued by Corelli Barnett to have given success to Beveridge's social policy, founded on a "romantic idealism" of "dreams and illusions", over Kingsley Wood's (the then Chancellor) economic "realism" concerning how everything could be paid for. Barnett argues that it was inevitable that a sentimental view of the worker should develop. For Himmelfarb, as well as Barnett, the precursors that institutionalised a welfare state were the assertion of the concept of social responsibility over that of individual responsibility. The "poor" were separate, identifiable and a class created by society to whom a social responsibility was owed. For Himmelfarb this represents the ascendancy of moral puritanism over individualism. Greenleaf has extensively chronicled how this ideology of collectivism then became institutionalised as the government's social responsibility.[13]

There has now been extensive rethinking of these ideas of the welfare state across all OECD countries. But the British welfare compromise has a strong effect on the overall institutional structure and training tradition that, in the words of one of the system's most extreme critics, provided the "incentives to fail" (Murray 1984: 1989); and from incentives for individuals to fail comes the failure of the economy. Thus, increasingly, the welfare compromise has been seen as another example of the perverse policy syndrome.

Foremost among the perversities was that stable employment, through Keynesian management, became a claim of "rights" against society that had to be provided by the state. Employment, even in the private sector, almost acquired the character of a public "service". As a result, economic policy became largely subordinated to social policy. As a result, industrial policy in the period up to the late 1970s variously followed strategies on spotting and supporting *strategic industries* and *national champions; nationalization; selective* channelling investment and support through subsidies, tax privileges and protection; *regional policy selection* to prevent growth or divert industries from the congested South East focusing on compensatory and "worst first" policies rather than investing in success – between sectors and between regions; and increasing use of *inflation* solutions rather than limiting investment to the resources available, which stimulated a culture of paying more than the labour product. In general, the government responsibility for the economy stimulated a system based more on patronage than performance: "private industry . . . was increasingly dependent on government favours" (Sampson 1982: 182). The result was "pluralistic stagnation" (Middlemass 1990).

One of the key aspects of these developments was "corporatism" in industrial policy. For a significant period this was dominated by a tripartite structure: a centralised corporatism run by negotiation between government, the TUC and the CBI. The idea developed that highly centralised bodies could decide everything for the whole economy. In the words of John Banham, Director-General of the CBI in 1989, the idea was: "that somehow the great and good, or the not so great and the not very good, sitting in the middle of London could somehow determine what happened. It was always a fraud and that was exposed."[14] From the 1964 Industrial Training Act a tripartite Central Training Council was constituted (the precursor of the Manpower Services Commission) and tripartite Industrial Training Boards (ITBs) which exacted a training levy on business. By 1966 there were 13 ITBs covering 7.5m workers in most of the key manufacturing sectors, and thus having a profound influence on the economy as a whole. In this structure it is not an unfair caricature to see government as primarily concerned with its welfare objective of full employment, the unions as mainly preoccupied with wages, and craft unions with exclusion of the "unskilled masses" and demarcation, and the employers as concerned to control wages.[15] No-one focused very hard on training or the strategic development of industry as a whole, and year-on-year wage agreements systematically eroded job differentials and hence the returns to skilling. This has proved a key handicap to human resource incentives, as we shall see in Chapter 7.

Central–local government relations

The importance of local government to the national perverse policy syndrome is that it is one of the key institutions through which much public policy has been organized and administered. Central government has had few direct service delivery functions. Most activity has been delivered by local government or other agencies in the health, social security or employment ministries. As a result even when a problem has been diagnosed at national level, and a priority and resource allocated for its solution, the implementation has usually been handed to local government. The response will then be very variable locally, and may frequently be perverse to the defined goals. This has been because the traditional pattern of central–local relations has given considerable autonomy to local government, both in guidance and in resources.

Traditionally local government has found substantial resources for its policies from central government. Since 1974, the majority of local government expenditure has been supported by a general grant which local authorities could use fairly freely in developing their own priorities. The level of this general grant (the Revenue Support Grant) rose from 38% to 51% of current expenditure in 1974. By 1993/94 local government taxes supplied only 16% of local government spending.[16] This has divorced local accountability from its financial consequences and has separated central government policies from their local delivery. The result has been hit and miss. Thus, for example, the result of the 1944 Education Act

> offered not so much an executive operational framework as an opened
> gate to an empty construction site on which local authorities might or
> might not (depending on their zeal and the effectiveness of the ministry's

22

nagging) build the technical and further education system that Britain so desperately needed. Yet even the most zealous local education authority would have to work within government limits on expenditure. What therefore followed in the next forty years was yet another halting, spasmodic, spotty advance like those following the *Technical Instruction Act* of 1889 and the *Education Act* of 1902.[17]

The 1988 Education Reform Act is the latest milestone in this evolution and, as we shall later argue, it still remains to be seen whether it has successfully overcome the key criticisms of the need to rebalance the needs of "cultural" against "practical" teaching.

The implementation of national policies depends on local priorities. Since the electorate for local government is its people, local political priorities tend to be heavily dominated by residence-related services, not the needs of the business community. Geraint Parry and colleagues in their 1992 study have found the business community to be the group most separated from the agenda of local council leaders. Although council leaders are closely in tune with citizens, they are distant from the needs of the economy which implies a strategic gap between the management of a local authority and its economy. This separation is further reinforced by the structure of local government management in Britain, which is unique in the world. It has a dominance of government by committee with the responsibility for the functions to be borne by the elected council as a whole. As a result it is difficult to have a unified executive, or single corporate structure of management, either administratively or politically. Attempts at corporate management are thus more difficult and the chief executive and officers are separated from the committees. The local economy as an issue is, therefore, usually left to a single committee and officer, usually isolated from the rest of the council: "frequently at odds with the more entrepreneurial approach needed".[18] The Widdicombe Committee in 1986 reaffirmed most of these characteristics, and the Audit Commission has suggested that the only way to get attention to the needs of the local economy into a sufficiently central rôle is to locate the economic development function in the chief executive's office which can ensure that it receives top level support.[19]

These problems have been further compounded by the rôle of local government in the welfarist and corporatist state. For example, elected members who are also council employees or municipal trade unionists in Inner London boroughs comprise between 33% and 50% of the council members, with 61% in the former GLC.[20] As a result they have found it difficult to distinguish their rôles as politicians, employees and trade unionists.

These developments have interacted with the processes of social filtering in the inner city areas.[21] Poor housing, low educational attainment, high youth unemployment and high public service costs and inefficiency have each contributed to further social filtering. The process has been set amidst decline in the economic structure of the inner city economies as a whole. This has made dependent groups more dependent and less able to participate because of inappropriate training or labour skills. It has often been difficult, therefore, for inner city councils to break out of a circle of higher taxation and dominance for the concern of social problems over the more fundamental economic issues which are their cause.

How TECs and LECs can help

This chapter has sought briefly to demonstrate and explain Britain's poor and degenerating economic performance in the period up to the 1980s. It has argued that the explanation is to be found chiefly in institutions. Because of its long period of political stability, Britain's institutions have inexorably increased in number, their power has come to dominate economic decision making, and objectives at odds with economic performance have come to direct more and more activity away from the needs of the economy. The result has been an institutional structure that will often subtly pervert the objectives of economic policy. This "perverse policy syndrome" has the consequence that more resources alone will change nothing; indeed *more resources may make matters worse* by strengthening the power of the institutions allocating those resources. Moreover, substantial resources become tied up in avoiding problems or limiting the damage caused by the barriers that prevent change. The only way to break out of the perverse policy syndrome is to *break away from the institutional priorities and economic values of the past and to develop new institutional goals and systems of economic support.*

TECs and LECs were designed to contribute to this institutional break with the past, as the opening quotation to this chapter demonstrates. To achieve this they were designed to offer:
– new leverage (financial and non-financial);
– new leadership;
– a focus on the performance of programmes;
– emphasis on customers over producers;
– a shift from subsidy and compensation to stimulating individual effort and employer involvement;
– local flexibility for government programmes within a national strategy; and
– work in partnership with local communities empowering them to develop change.

TECs and LECs were not alone in this mission. A wide range of other government initiatives have sought similar stimuli to local agents through central action. And the reforms of polytechnics, further education colleges, schools and hospital finance have all also sought to stimulate greater local involvement. In the following chapters we turn to an assessment of how far the design of TECs and LECs has allowed them to achieve the level of sustained change required.

Chapter 3
Establishing the TECs and LECs

Central government's lead

The system of TECs and LECs was announced in two White Papers in December 1988, separately for Scotland and for England and Wales. Phased introduction allowed the first to become operational in April 1990, with the last becoming operational in October 1991. The TECs and LECs grew from a firm supply-side perspective in which labour market constraints, in particular, were argued to be key limits on economic growth. The most important constraint identified in the White Papers was the influence of an ageing workforce. As a result of the demographic downturn, the number of people aged 16–19 declined by 1.2m, or 32%, between 1983 and 1993. As a result, 97% of the year 2000 workforce were already in employment in 1985. This focuses attention on upgrading the skills of the workforce already in employment. The White Papers also recognized as major constraints the low level of self-employment in Britain, improved but still hesitant industrial relations, and a lack of flexibility in wage bargaining. But above all the White Papers recognised the opportunity offered by the demographic downturn to place a greater emphasis on the emerging gap between skill levels and the new industrial demands of the 1990s.

The TECs and LECs were, however, a very special supply-side solution: to achieve change through institutional engineering and local decentralization. It is this focus which we treat as the key aspect of our analysis. In this chapter we analyze how TECs and LECs have developed across four dimensions:
- Local capacity building;
- Responding to ambitious targets;
- Institutional development; and
- Getting started through a local bidding process.

Local capacity building

TECs and LECs have been given a major focus on building a new local institutional capacity. The development of Britain since the 19th century, we have argued in Chapter 2, has produced a separation of interests, while corporatist politics has produced cohesion of the state but a fragmentation of the economy. The "perverse policy syndrome" was the consequence of a separation in which the wider objectives of the economy were left unaddressed within each separate field of activity. From this national syndrome derived local consequences. Yet it is at the local level where most real decisions are taken, where incentives directly bear upon individuals, schools, and most firms. This has led to a realization that a major part of the national solution to Britain's economic ills lies at the local level. The establishment of TECs and LECs has been one of the most important attempts to address this issue. It can be argued to be concerned with empowerment, leverage and leadership. We examine each below.

The attempt to rebuild the economy through local initiative has two different loci: one concerns individuals, the other concerns local institutions. The focus on *individuals* has been part of a general shift in western society away from welfare and "social rights" approaches that emphasise "compensation" and "subsidy", towards incentives for individual responsibility. The focus on *local institutions* has also been reflected in a wide range of initiatives in western society to "decentralise". Both thrusts emphasise *empowerment* – of people, of localities – as part of a shift of responsibility away from the state at national and particularly local level.

The rhetoric surrounding the launch and early development of TECs and LECs more than fully reflected this emphasis. Norman Fowler, Secretary of State for Employment during the launch of TECs called for "a local focus – what works in one area may not work in the next . . . We want people with the power to create change in their communities . . . Everyone who has a stake in their community has a stake in the TEC".[1] The Highlands and Islands launch document of 1989, entitled *Spread your Wings* and intended primarily for business people, argued that "It's good to know that the people who sit around the boardroom table of your new LEC share the same local issues as you". More broadly it was argued that "Employers need to be given a sense of *ownership* of the system of training and enterprise creation" as stated by the Industry Department for Scotland launch document (Industry Department Scotland 1988: 9).

The specific emphasis on the concept of empowerment derived chiefly from Cay Stratton, special advisor to each Secretary of State for Employment since 1989: "Our starting point must not be to fit TECs into well established Training Agency patterns. Rather it must be to begin from a position that *empowers*, that encourages . . . real choices about the way public funds are invested".[2] Empowerment was further seen as a means of reorientating from the producer to the consumer: it was intended to be a clear break with corporatism. Again Cay Stratton led the conception:

> TECs will take the labels off, will start to design programmes from the outside in; from the standpoint of the consumer, not the producer . . . they will conceive of holistic packages of services that meet consumers' total needs, not as discrete products . . . on an organizational chart.

Neither the client nor the employer care about complex administrative rules, programme boundaries or ministerial turf. What they want is quality services tailored to their specific and *individual* needs . . . I think TECs will be powerful advocates for such an approach.[3]

The same concepts carried throughout the system. Even in the Scottish launch the earlier experiences of the SDA, HIDB and Urban Programme were used to argue that "experience shows that the effective initiation of enterprise tends to start by the motivation of the individual".[4]

TECs and LECs were, therefore, part of a general thrust by government to enhance the interests of the consumer over those of producers, to tackle issues as strategic wholes, and to emphasise local initiative within a national strategy. Whether this was realistically or immediately possible in a British society where many still advocated welfarism, where many employers actually wanted producer control, and where TEC/LEC staff were dominated by civil servants, is a question we seek to answer in later chapters.

The central government's emphasis on local initiative in the setting up of TECs and LECs is also reflected in other programmes. The shift of central government policy from subsidy and compensation policies to an emphasis on incentives and enterprise has led to many initiatives directly from central government into local areas (Enterprise Zones and Urban Development Corporations (UDCs), City Action Teams and Task Forces); joint central–local activity (mainly through Urban Programme Areas); and a strong emphasis across all fields on collaboration of public initiatives with the private sector. This has led to a strong refocusing of central government support away from national and regional policies to very localised policies. A strong emphasis of this approach has been on the concepts of leverage and stimulating new local leadership.

Leverage has often been narrowly applied to the attempt by government to use public money to encourage private sector investment. Certainly UDCs and other initiatives have sought this type of financial leverage. But leverage has also been applied in a more subtle and potentially more significant way to encourage local action that otherwise would not have occurred. TECs and LECs fundamentally exemplify this concept of leverage. "We look to the TECs . . . for mobilization of the whole employer community . . . Their task is to consult, involve and lead the whole local community" stated Norman Fowler in the launch phase.[5] It was all about "achieving a sea-change in attitude and practice" in Cay Stratton's view.[6] Leverage in this sense confronted the perverse policy syndrome head on: the TEC or LEC was to be a source of institutional refocusing, as well as an "inspiration" to others in the local economy.

Local leadership is an important related aspect of stimulating local empowerment. "We must get the right people as TEC Directors" stated Cay Stratton. "They must be acknowledged leaders whose presence will give the TEC instant prestige and influence. Accepting second best will kill TECs before they start",[7] . . . Without the top level leaders on TEC Boards, we have little chance of achieving a sea-change in attitude and practice".[8] The Scottish White Paper (Industry Department Scotland 1988: 1) referred to those "in the top ranks of private sector businesses". New leadership, therefore, was seen as the crucial ingredient of achieving institutional change. The new leaders were to be the custodians of the message and the source of stimulus for the refocusing of local institutions.

Local capacity building is, however, a broader issue than leverage and leadership. If any initiative is to be more than a short-lived fillip, it has to build a self-sustaining structure that can reproduce its message and diffuse its ideas, through its influence in local networks, across the whole of a local economy. This is the central dilemma of TECs and LECs – as new institutions they can be custodians of the desired creed of change, but to sustain local development requires that existing local institutions come on board and develop new positions. The dilemma was nicely summed up by Linbert Spencer in the launch phase:

> It is simply not sufficient to identify new means of delivery when, in fact, we do not have the capacity on the ground . . . We tend to think that somehow if we make a programme available, organizations will arise to be able to take the programme, and yet if we spent a little bit more money around the programme we could enable the programme to develop.[9]

In an earlier study (Bennett & McCoshan 1993) local capacity building has been identified as "a learning process". To achieve a long-term reversals of the perverse policy syndrome requires harnessing the talent and energy of the people and key organizations anchored in the local community. Local people and key agents must not be just used, marginalised or merely left to maintain accustomed practices separated from the economic development process. For system-wide changes to occur they have to be fully involved, particularly at the outset, in the development of strategy and its implementation. But this takes time and requires learning.

This learning process requires a shift from reactive to proactive modes of response locally. Figure 3.1 shows the main characteristics required for a sustained shift to occur. The success of TECs and LECs depends on an architecture that emphasizes the proactive over the reactive. The TEC and LEC agenda recognized this: for example in the Scottish launch document it was noted that:

> A way has to be found of encouraging the private sector to take more responsibility . . . a shift is required from a bureaucratic system within which the private sector has a purely advisory rôle to one which is led by the private sector . . . as a powerful agent of change.

Hence local leadership by business was seen as intertwined with the need to empower and decentralise the public sector. But the extent to which this empowerment has really been achieved is still being tested. As we shall see, the dilemma for the TEC/LEC mission, between *exerting* leadership and *developing* local leadership, remains the key issue for the future.

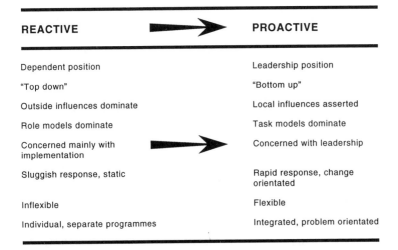

REACTIVE	PROACTIVE
Dependent position	Leadership position
"Top down"	"Bottom up"
Outside influences dominate	Local influences asserted
Role models dominate	Task models dominate
Concerned mainly with implementation	Concerned with leadership
Sluggish response, static	Rapid response, change orientated
Inflexible	Flexible
Individual, separate programmes	Integrated, problem orientated

Figure 3.1 The learning process in local capacity building: the development of the learning needed to move from reactive to proactive responses at a local level (after Bennett & McCoshan 1993: Figure 9.3).

Ambitious targets

The publicity and rhetoric surrounding the start-up of TECs and LECs was unprecedented. The Prime Minister launched the initiative in Newcastle with video links to London, Manchester and Plymouth. Subsequently large-scale newspaper advertisements were run, particularly in the business press. Important further launches occurred at the 1988 and 1989 CBI conferences, and through other business organizations such as Business in the Community and the Chambers of Commerce. A Business in the Community conference in December 1989 (BiTC 1989) was also important, as were a large number of well-resourced events around the country. There was considerable razzmatazz. Expectations were raised very high. Support was stimulated, and an overwhelming business response was stimulated from almost all the traditional quarters, as well as many new sources.

The focus of the launch was "putting employers in the driving seat". The solutions to overcoming supply constraints was argued by the government to be the delivery of a private sector-led approach to training and enterprise development. The TECs/LECs were the local mechanism to achieve the institutional change through new business leadership. The White Paper argued that only employers could "link training plans with business plans" (DE 1988: 30):

Employers themselves must assume active leadership in preparing and maintaining a skilled workforce and in creating a climate conducive to business development, self-employment and job creation (DE 1988: 39). Planning and management of enterprise and training need to shift from the public to the private sector. Employers are best placed to identify key skill needs and to ensure that the level and quality of training and business services meet those needs (TECs Prospectus 1989: 4).

Thus TECs would empower business leaders to express employer demand for training, represent employer interests, and build on the commitment business had already shown in a variety of other initiatives. The supply-side improvements were to be achieved by giving business a dominant voice in skills training provision.

This policy was fed by previous TA analyses and programmes, which we assess further in Chapter 7. These had attempted to bring employers into partnership with providers of training through a series of earlier initiatives. The major early attempts were the Local Area Manpower Boards (LAMBs) and ITBs. More recent attempts followed the 1984 White Paper *Training for Jobs*. This led to the development of plans for local FE colleges and removed 16% of the Education Block Grant for Work-Related Further Education from the DES to the MSC. The WRFE plans were intended to be associated with Local Employer Networks (LENs) that sought to bring *local* employer organizations directly into the FE planning process, but such arrangements never developed beyond informal and ad hoc links in practice.

These approaches had all failed to achieve what was sought by the MSC and TA, namely an improvement in supply–demand relations for training through a local strategic mechanism. The Area Manpower Boards had no local powers and made few attempts to change local delivery. Following the 1984 reforms there was still little reorientation of private training providers or of LEA WRFE programmes to reflect the closer relation to local labour demand that the MSC conceived as being desired. The WRFE Plans had been a useful innovation for LEAs. Indeed they introduced planning for this sector for the first time in most LEAs. But despite major changes to training delivery, plans did not contribute substantially to changes in delivery or to LENs (Wicks 1990; FEU 1989). Moreover, the LENs initiative significantly failed to get a strong employer influence over training supply decisions, partly because of the inadequacy of funding of LENs, partly because of weak management of the initiative which allowed it to drift over too wide an agenda, but mainly because LENs were not powerful enough in their relations with LEAs in the local economy – they were easily ignored (Bennett et al. 1990b).

The TECs and LECs were intended to be altogether more powerful bodies than LAMBs or LENs. LAMBs had no budget control or dedicated staff. TECs and LECs have an annual budget of £18–32m each (as opposed to LENs' £20,000), a local and experienced staff averaging 50 (as opposed to LENs' single local manager), and direct control of the contracts for a wide range of training programmes. Unlike LAMBs and LENs, therefore, TECs and LECs could not be ignored. But they were also a break with the corporatist past, by putting employers in the dominant leadership position.

These developments alone would have been enough to make the TEC initiative important. But added to their responsibility for training are a number of other programmes in the fields of business links with school education and enterprise. This led to highly ambitious claims for the rôle TECs should seek to develop: "The fundamental aim of every TEC will be to foster economic growth and contribute to the regeneration of the community it serves" (TECs Prospectus 1989: 1).

They had to be visionary and enterprising organizations "born of the enterprise culture, with a bold vision that stretches beyond existing programmes, institutions and traditional methods of delivery" (TECs Prospectus 1989: 4).

Hence TECs and LECs were established not merely to improve training programmes, not even just to work within the other programmes for which they had responsibility; they also had a missionary purpose as key agents for change in local economies. "A TEC will have as its foundation the training and business assistance programmes previously run by the Employment Department . . . but managing existing programmes is only the start. A TEC will be a catalyst for change within its community" (TEC Operating Manual 1989: introduction). This was to be achieved not just with direct programme delivery, but by using leverage: "Relatively small investments by the TEC may be able to influence larger amounts of money, whether from the private sector or other bodies" (DE 1991: 27).

In the less formal comments of those closely involved in the development of the programme, the long-term missionary purpose was reiterated. Norman Fowler stated in the launch period that "TECs are a serious business . . . They are not a quick-fix solution or the latest flavour of the month. We are developing a network that must stand the test of time . . . This is a once in a generation opportunity".[10] Cay Stratton echoed the same words and saw the TECs with "goals that will require serious and sustained effort over the next decade".[11] David Main, the TA TECs project team Director saw the early TECs as *pioneers . . . The message is quality. We are making no concessions. . . . "TECs are a once in a lifetime opportunity"*.[12]

As a result of this ambitious vision, the guiding aims of TECs and LECs at the launch covered a wide field (DE 1988):
- To contribute to business success and economic growth;
- To encourage employees and individuals to accept greater responsibility and costs for training;
- To work within government frameworks and funds for the unemployed;
- To encourage recognised standards of competence, industry-led, across all occupations, nationally validated through NCVQ;
- To seek to ensure that qualifications for all young people and adults were based on these standards;

- To facilitate a process by which responsibility for delivery of training was, as far as possible, devolved to local areas;
- To allow the flexibility to shape delivery by enterprises, individuals and local communities.

By the November DE (1991: 10) paper *Strategy for Skills* these aims had become "the Government's six priorities for the 1990s at the centre of a national strategy". The six targets set for 1992/93 were:

- Employers must invest more effectively in the skills their businesses need;
- Young people must have the motivation to achieve their full potential and to develop the skills the economy needs;
- Individuals must be persuaded that training pays and that they should take more responsibility for their own development;
- People who are unemployed and those at a disadvantage in the jobs market must be helped to get back to work and to develop their abilities to the full;
- The providers of education and training must offer high quality and flexible provision which meets the needs of individuals and employers;
- Enterprise must be encouraged throughout the economy, particularly through the continued growth of small business and self-employment.

These six priorities have a greater significance than mere government statements of intent. Each year they are translated into a set of specific targets which in turn are calculated for each TEC. These targets are then used as the basis for calculating part of the TEC budget which is linked to performance in meeting targets. This Output-Related Funding (ORF) element has been increasing in significance over time (see Chapter 6). Since 1993/94, the targets have also been defined in terms of National Education and Training Targets (NETTs).

The 1993/94 *strategy* paper maintained the momentum (DE/DTI 1992). But it made the important innovation that the paper was a joint guidance from the two Secretaries of State, for Employment and Trade and Industry. This represented the first government commitment to joint departmental rôles for TECs and LECs. It also represented a shift in the emphasis of the enterprise programmes towards established and growing business and away from micro-businesses and self-employment. This did not change the general statements of priorities from those listed above for 1992/93. But it made important innovations in detail. First, the priorities were related to the National Education and Training Targets (NETTs) which set percentages of the workforce to be at specified levels of qualification by 1996 and 2000. Second, these targets drew heavily on the system of National Vocational Qualifications (NVQs). These targets were also more specific and detailed than before, allowing them to become the basis of TEC/LEC ORF (see Chapter 6). This becomes an important context for funding from 1993/94 onwards.

The key innovation from 1993/94, however, was the shift in emphasis from a training-led approach to business enterprise programmes, and away from micro-towards small and medium-sized businesses. Whereas the 1992/93 Priority Six had expressed the need to develop a strategic focus for enterprise, the 1993/94 priority was to work with other bodies and enhancing the quality of all local business support services. Whereas 1992/93 stated as a priority to assist survival and growth of small businesses and the growth of self-employment, the 1993/94 priorities state an emphasis on existing small and medium-sized businesses and do not mention self-employment at all.

From this new emphasis followed a further implication; that: TECs were explicitly to work with other agents in the field of enterprise. From the co-ordination of the Departments of Trade and Industry and Employment was to flow a new local system of enterprise support through "One Stop Shops". This initiative is evaluated in detail in Chapters 9 and 11. Its thrust, however, ran quite counter to the way in which many TECs and LECs had been developing themselves as *providers* of business services. There was no doubt of the need for a change in emphasis of TECs and LECs in the mind of Michael Heseltine, President of the Board of Trade: "I see TECs rôle . . . as the enablers: a driving force in bringing local players together to work as partners to a common goal . . . I do not, however, see TECs as the direct deliverers of business support services where these are available from others such as Chambers of Commerce and Local Enterprise Agencies" (DE/DTI 1992: 5).

An evolution has thus occurred in TEC/LEC development. But the political ambitions for the system have remained very high. An important question for our analysis in this book is how far these ambitions have been, or are capable of being, achieved by the design of the TECs and LECs that has been put in place.

Design of the new institution

The TECs/LECs are primarily an *institutional development*. They were not intended primarily to deliver new programmes, although they have modified, sometimes radically, old programmes and are also developing some new ones. The importance of institutional change has been clear from the outset:

Above all TECs are about a new institutional framework . . . a vision for the future . . . that is on offer to employers, individuals and communities ready to accept the challenge (TECs prospectus 1989: 3).

The new framework chosen established TECs/LECs as companies limited by guarantee with their own Memorandum and Articles of Association. They are controlled by a Board of up to 15 members, or up to 10 in the smaller HIE LECs. The Board members must act as individuals, not as representatives of their organizations. Hence, TECs and LECs seek to be independent institutions, not representative bodies. The Board is a strategic body which seeks to develop its own view of what is required and, although normally seeking co-operation and support with other bodies, it does not necessarily have to work through consensus. TECs and LECs are thus a major step away from corporatism.

To reinforce these attributes, the Board has to be constituted from members two-thirds of whom are drawn from private sector businesses. The remaining third is drawn from public sector companies, local authorities, education, research institutions, community and voluntary bodies, trade unions, and other bodies. From a Board of 15 in maximum size, there will be thus a maximum of five people from outside the private sector. This has been mandated, and strongly defended, by central government in order to assure a focus on economic objectives by putting employers in the driving seat. Thus TECs "place the responsibility for local business growth squarely in the hands of the people best qualified to organise it: the successful leaders of the business community" (TEC newspaper advertisements 1989).

The staffing of TECs was drawn initially almost exclusively from the former Area Offices of the former Training Agency. In Scotland staff from the old TA area offices were combined with former SDA and HIDB staff and all are employed by SE and HIE and are seconded to LECs. These staff began as civil servants seconded to TECs. The staff size averages approximately 50 in TECs, 15 in HIE LECs and 90 in SE LECs. Those not wishing to be seconded in some cases were able to take "gardening leave" (paid normally, but with no new working rôle). The only significant early appointments outside of the civil service were usually the chief executive, who could be appointed competitively from normal advertisements. In late 1991 43% of chief executives had been appointed from outside either the former Training Agency or SDA/HIDB in Scotland (see Table 4.4). But this proportion has now substantially increased. After the TA staff transferred, as TECs became operational, the old Area Offices were wound up. The DE Regional Offices in England and Wales, and the Scottish Office in Scotland, then assumed responsibility for local liaison and for various contractual monitoring.

The TECs work to a contract from TEED, and the LECs with the Scottish Office through SE and HIE, to deliver specific programmes subject to their agreed Corporate Plan and various performance targets on the programmes themselves. For the training programmes, quality has been sought by focusing on outputs of qualified trainees at certain specified levels. The contract with TEED/SE/HIE specifies a geographical area of coverage and key objectives that must be met. These are derived from the agreed 3 year Corporate Plan. In return the government agrees to pay a level of resources from public funds.

In addition to the public money that is allocated, the TEC/LEC is expected to raise additional resources for itself, and also to lever other agents into better deployment of their own resources. The concept of *public leverage* is, therefore, a crucial one underpinning the hopes for TECs/LECs. The chief resources which it is sought to lever are:
- Direct cash contributions, donations and fees for services;
- Membership subscriptions;

- Other public sector sources (other government department funds, EC grants, etc.);
- "Efficiency gains" from cutting the costs of existing programmes;
- Increasing and improving employers' efforts in employee training;
- Increasing employer commitment to management education;
- Working with other agents to develop enterprise support services to stimulate small firms or self-employment;
- Reprioritizing of resources allocation in related fields of education, local authority economic development, etc.

In practice no significant private sector finance has been obtained by TECs and LECs, but significant public sector money for the EC has been obtained and other means of leverage have also been deployed. Hence, it is important for TECs/ LECs to be seen not only as focusing on their own training programmes, but also to have impact on the training, education, enterprise and physical development strategies of other agents in their areas. Crucial to their success, therefore, is the extent to which they can lever or encourage these other agents.

Institutional development since 1992

The early policy developments around the TECs and LECs were chiefly related to getting them going. For the last group of TECs, particularly those in London, getting started proved a troublesome and difficult process. From the budget year 1992/93, however, major developments in their objectives occurred (see, e.g., DE 1991: 31–2). Particularly important was the use of a range of more specific outcome measures through which TEED/SO is to measure progress towards achieving its strategic objectives. The measures include:
- Job placements from TEC-funded programmes;
- NVQ Level 1, 2, 3 and 4 targets for TEC/LEC-funded programmes related to the CBI national Education and Training Targets (NETTs);
- Other positive outcomes for TEC-funded programmes (e.g. number of people who, 3 months after leaving programmes, are in self-employment, full-time training or full-time education);
- For business starts, survival rates at 26, 52 and 78 weeks;
- Number of local businesses making a commitment to become Investors in People by size bands (above and below 200 employees);
- The number of organizations recognised as Investors in People by size bands (above and below 200 employees);
- Changes in percentage rates for young people staying-on in full-time education at 16;
- Changes in the numbers of 18-year-olds entering Higher Education;
- Targets for participation from disadvantaged groups.

In addition the Government pressed more strongly for "progress in generating income from external sources and targets for raising external funding" for the following 3 years of the Corporate Plan. TEED also asked for specific plans "to develop membership schemes to increase accountability and responsiveness to the local community".

The new targets were subject to a marking or points system that were used to assess the quality of the TECs' Corporate Plans. In addition, these points were also linked to subsequent performance measures that could be used, as in the 1991/92 year, to award additional performance bonuses (see below).

Subsequent to the April 1992 General Election the immediate future of TECs and LECs became assured. The Labour opposition had committed themselves to TECs and LECs, but wanted to change the balance on Boards to at least 50% non-business members. Some parts of the Labour opposition also want much more radical change, including their employment spokesman (see McKleish 1991). With uncertainties removed the government has set about two immediate changes which chiefly affect the 1993/94 year onwards.

First, a restructuring has occurred to give greater emphasis to the Regional Offices of TEED. In part this reflects the results of the Styles Report, an internal review, that the rôle of the regions should be enhanced (DE 1992a, discussed further in Chapter 6). It also represents a response to the growing demands from Europe for some form of regional entity. EC grants require applications to be made on a regional basis which can be done in England only through special arrangements between local authorities, central government regional offices and other bodies. The TECs also looked jealously at Scotland's LECs and felt that SE and HIE played a more effective rôle in partnership with LECs than TEED did with TECs. As a result TECs felt themselves disadvantaged in some areas by the lack of scale economies, particularly with respect to promotion of inward investment, and access to the EC. The NTTF (1992a: 5) concluded that "without an appropriate regional framework TECs and other partners may well be missing vital opportunities".

The most fundamental regional change to occur was that the Welsh Office was given oversight of Welsh TECs with the loss of almost all powers for Wales by TEED. But more subtly the Regional Offices of TEED have also been enhancing their rôle. In some cases this has led to major reorganization, with a smaller number of staff but with higher seniority, as in London. In other cases it also reflects an attempt by the Regional Offices to play a greater rôle in partnership with TECs. Probably the most successful region in this respect has been the Northern Region. Beyond this, preparations are also being made for a restructuring of the rôles and links between government regional offices and agencies, particularly DE and DTI, and also the DOE. In part this has been stimulated by the Audit Commission's (1989) conclusion that government needed better to coordinate its local programmes. The extent of devolution of power from TEED to these offices remains as yet uncertain. It will depend for its development less on TEED (whose internal review offered only modest change – DE 1992a) than on the political priority attached to enhancing the rôle of the English regions.

The second change since 1992/93 has been the shift in responsibility for TECs to become shared between the DE and DTI. A reorganization of the government departmental responsibility for small firms support occurred in the summer of 1992 with the enterprise responsibility being transferred back to DTI, from where it was removed in 1985. This mainly affected the old Small Firms Service budget as well as some other programmes. It represented about £45m in 1993/94. The remaining small firms budget in DE is focused on allowances to individuals to move from unemployment to self-employment (termed Enterprise Allowances in the past). The first major manifestation of the cultural change that has resulted is the announcement by Michael Heseltine, President of the Board of Trade, that TECs could obtain their funds that had been transferred from DE to DTI only through a competition process for the support of One Stop Shops. We discuss this initiative in detail in Chapters 9 and 11. What it seeks to do is to stimulate TECs to develop a new agenda for their enterprise budget, in *partnership with* other local agents. The One Stop Shops also apply in Scotland and Wales. This initiative represents a cultural change for TECs. Now they have to deal directly with two central departments which have separate cultures, different emphases on objectives, and different accounting rules and conventions.

Beyond the 1993/94 financial year a wider set of changes are likely to affect TECs and LECs. At the time of writing these could go in a variety of directions. We evaluate the alternatives in Chapters 11 and 12 and conclude on where the preferred path of development should lead.

Getting started

The December 1988 White Papers defined a procedure for TECs and LECs to be set up largely from the "bottom up" by a bidding process. In Scotland the process differed in that "bottom-up" local bids responded to a plan for the layout of the network developed by the Scottish Office through the SDA and HIDB who played a much greater rôle in "managing" the bidding process.

The bidding process initially covered finance for a development phase. The development funding granted was up to £100,000 plus the support of TA staff. The application for development funding had to address six key elements:
- The geographical area covered;
- The initial Board to oversee development;
- The support of the business community;
- The chief priorities for change in the labour market;
- New initiatives and activities that were required;
- An outline budget requirement; and
- A timetable for the development phase covering 6–12 months.
From the start, therefore, issues of boundaries, critical mass, local support and initiatives were prominent.

Much of the thinking derived from analogy with the American Private Industry Councils (PICs) as well as the existing administrative structures of the MSC/TA. The TA laid down some clear guidelines on TEC size. These covered the following criteria:

- A "labour market of some scale" (DE 1988: 42) defined as an "average working population of 250,000", and normally at least "100,000 unless there are exceptional circumstances" (TECs Prospectus 1989: 11);
- An area possessing "its own sense of identity" (DE 1988: 42);
- A budget range of £15–50m in England and Wales;
- A total number of TECs, about 100 for the whole of Britain, that should not "exceed the number that can be reasonably supported and monitored for performance" (DE 1988: 42);
- Boundaries would not be prescribed but would reflect "the diversity and local relevance that TECs are bringing to managing the delivery of training, enterprise and education services" (DE, TEC Report 1990/91: 7);
- A staff complement sufficient to justify at least one grade 7 and one SEO equivalent post (regional office guidance notes).

These criteria gave British TECs and LECs a working population size similar to USA PICs, where a similar 200,000 criterion was employed, but a budget that was much larger: there was only £1.5m ($2m) for the average PIC in 1992/93. However, compared to Germany TECs and LECs appear rather small. The working population size is about two-thirds and staff about one-half of that of a German Chamber of Commerce or Craft. The TEC/LEC budget is about one-tenth of the German Chambers' non-client budget that is retained as a central management resource (not passed to trainees) (see Bennett & Krebs 1993).

Despite fairly firm criteria, the government stated that the process of formation should be chiefly "bottom up", with bids emerging from business groups and leaders: the growth of TECs "must be carefully paced" and "must emerge through employer leadership and broad community support" (DE 1988: 43). Despite this bottom-up commitment, it is clear that major efforts went into stimulating business involvement through the CBI, Business in the Community, the Chambers of Commerce and other bodies. And in Scotland the networks were negotiated largely at a national level. The process was, therefore, a highly orchestrated grass roots movement!

The individuals who were carefully selected in each area by the leading national and local agents were often "fingered" in a special way. There were implicit rewards of recognition within local or national organizations, or through the honours system. This very special "recruitment process" has led to its own difficulties since rewards could not be delivered to *all* the 1,000-plus private sector Directors involved. In effect, the main appeal was to the altruism and social responsibility of individuals who felt they could contribute to getting the job done. The launch of TECs and LECs and their mission excited many business leaders who felt that, for perhaps the first time, there was going to be a sustained commitment to a proper private sector rôle in the development of "UK plc".

On the other hand, a number of significant local businesses stayed outside the Boards, despite considerable attempts to woo them. Interview evidence suggests that, in general, these appear to have been composed of four categories. First, many foreign companies were anxious to protect their own management skills and training base' and were unconvinced that sharing it with others through a TEC or LEC was to their advantage. This applied to a number of areas in North East England, South Wales, Scotland and South East England. One German business leader of a firm located in Britain interviewed saw the whole TEC approach as so deficient in design that it would degrade best practice, hence contributing to increases in labour poaching from his firm. Second, a large group of firms could not see the relevance to their businesses of being heavily involved in developing strategy for bodies which they perceived as dominated by government unemployment programmes, particularly in a period of skills shortage where the unemployed were largely becoming a residual category. This applied particularly to central London and the South East. Third, many small firms did not feel they had the senior managerial time to devote to TECs and LECs. Fourth, a number of firms were too myopic to see the benefits of enhanced training. These were the firms that were perhaps most in need of hearing the TEC/LEC message, but there was no reason why they should listen.

The reasons for not joining a TEC/LEC Board became the same reasons for resigning at a later date. The issue of motivation of Directors is therefore a key part not only of establishing the system, but sustaining its quality over time. This has combined with the lack of a representational legitimacy to make it difficult for TEC/LEC Boards to move beyond the criticism that they are self-appointed, self-perpetuating cliques.

England and Wales

In England and Wales TEED was the central control of TEC development, together with the National Training Task Force (NTTF). This was a government appointed group of largely private sector business people who replaced the former Commissioners of the MSC. They scrutinized each bid and advised the Secretary of State (see also Chapter 6). During the development phase the primary objective was to prepare a business plan which would be the basis for the contract with TA/TEED for the final operational phase. The business plan had to include:
- A vision for the area;
- Labour market analysis and assessment;
- A stock-take of existing training and enterprise provision;
- 3-year objectives and a 1 year detailed plan;
- Management structure;
- Proposed Board members and Chair;

– Detailed operational budget request.

The development phase therefore continued the pressure for missionary zeal but brought this down to essential dimensions of assessing need and existing provision, and the key elements of Board structure.

The bids for both development funding and operational contracts were scrutinised by the TA, as well as by the NTTF. The NTTF was particularly exercised by the problem of the quality and balance of the Board and the general quality of the proposals.

The evolution of both the development and operational phases was extremely rapid. Originally envisaged to take 3 to 4 years, all TEC/LEC areas were in development phase less than 2 years after the 1988 White Paper, and all TECs were operational in less than 3 years. Despite the success of a much more rapid start-up than originally envisaged, there is some evidence that speed was achieved at the expense of quality or long-term sustainability. The pressure from politicians and the sheer enthusiasm for the start-up process tended to bowl along many of the key actors, particularly some local business leaders and TEED. In this sense the pressure to get started fast mirrors the LENs initiative, which experienced similar problems of accepting some less satisfactory bids.

Some of the issues that arose are evident from Figure 3.2. An early group of bids received rapid development funding and an early operational contract: 50% of TECs were in development less than one year after the December 1988 White Paper, and 50% were operational in just under 2 years. The early rush

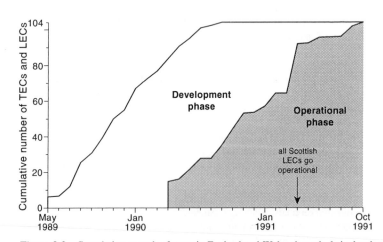

Figure 3.2 Cumulative growth of TECs in England and Wales through their development and operational phases, with development of Scottish LECs shown only by related time points of development.

shows three aspects. First, it made it difficult for the TA and NTTF to take a strategic view. In only two areas, the Northern region and Scotland, was a coherent approach possible which produced a systematic structure. For example, all five of the Northern region TECs went operational in a short period of time over the first 6 months of operational funding, three at the outset. The TA regional office was benefited by a history of close co-operation at local level and put considerable effort into encouraging an outcome which produced TECs of sufficient size to satisfy the original TA criteria. Its main concerns were to ensure that Northumberland and Sunderland (Wearside) produced viable entities. In part it achieved this by reallocating resources within the region to favour these smaller areas; in most significant part, however, it worked hard to ensure that a single Tyneside TEC developed covering four local authority districts (three of which were very small).

Secondly, a strategic approach does not appear to have been possible in other areas. The result was that some leading local groups were able to make pre-emptive strikes. This allowed them to carve out parts of the map at an early date. This created problems for other areas in adjusting to their presence, leading to a problem of a possible "Swiss cheese effect" – where pieces of the map had developing TECs, but interstices were left out and became difficult for other TECs to cover, or the opportunities for more rational groupings were lost.

Pre-emption fragmented many metropolitan areas, particularly Oldham, Rochdale and Wigan (Metrotec) in Greater Manchester, and in London. In London, for example, Wandsworth was carved out of inner London to give to AZTEC in order to make its focus on the relatively small centre of Kingston viable. This undermined a lot of inner London development having the knock-on effect of later requiring the Central London bid to include Camden in order for its area to be large enough. This in turn affected the City-based CILNTEC which raised an unsuccessful campaign to obtain Camden. The "Swiss cheese" problem also arose in other early bids, such as Milton Keynes, North Nottinghamshire, and South and East Cheshire, which carved out parts of non-metropolitan counties.

A third aspect was that many small areas emerged whose case for being a TEC area was too easily accepted. This often related to pre-emptive strikes. Some of the smallest TECs in terms of staff and budget were those created in the early months. Ten out of the smallest 20 TECs were in the group to go operational in the first 6 months (excluding Wales and Scotland). Many of these are in metropolitan areas, particularly in North West England. Thirteen of the smallest 27 TECs in England correspond to single metropolitan districts or small groups of London boroughs. The NTTF appears to have accepted these bids either because they found it difficult to turn down a well presented case urged with considerable force by influential local business and community leaders, or because they felt the need to keep the momentum of TEC development alive. Interview evidence suggests that the NTTF were under political pressure to keep up the pace. They also felt reluctant to become embroiled in local parochial disputes, which would have been required to put many separate local TEC bids together to produce larger entities. As a result local negotiations were left largely to TA regional offices, with support from TA Moorfoot, who seemed unable or unwilling to hold back development to satisfy the original criteria of size.

The result has been an outcome in which, in England and Wales, 41 TECs (50%) did not reach the 1991/92 minimum budget criterion of £15m, 8 TECs did not reach a staffing level of 30, and 9 TECs have working populations of less than 100,000 (see Chapter 5). Of the smallest TECs it is not clear how many have the "exceptional circumstances" envisaged in the TECs Prospectus. Of the smallest 20 by staff size, only 4 arguably have special circumstances either because of their rural or island location, e.g. Powys, Isle of Wight, Wiltshire, and Hereford and Worcester. For the rest it is not clear why a single small metropolitan district, small part of London, or division of a county should have been accepted in what are small parts of much larger labour markets. It is clear that the start-up phase of TECs faced a mixture of short-term political pressures, local parochialism and an inability or reluctance to appraise and argue the benefits of economies of scale and critical mass. The result has been a TEC structure that contains many local, economic and financial tensions for long-term sustainability.

A different problem beset some of the very last areas to enter the development and operational phases. One aspect was the special difficulties of starting TECs relates to London. Six of the last 12 TECs to go into the development phase were in London, and the last 5 TECs to become operational were all in London. There were special problems experienced in getting TECs underway in London as a result, in part, of the special aspects of London businesses' and in part of protracted boundary disputes. A second aspect of the late TECs was experienced by at least five of the last non-London TECs to go operational. These suffered from the pre-emptive activity of early TECs. Greater Nottingham, North Derbyshire, CEWTEC (Birkenhead and Wirral), Normid TEC (central Cheshire) and LAWTEC (West Lancashire) all suffered to differing degrees from the "Swiss cheese" effect, of having part of their potentially wider catchment already removed. A third aspect of the late TECs was the special difficulty of finding leaders and balancing local interests in areas with widespread rural catchments. This characterizes Powys, Lincolnshire, Humberside and Sussex. Finally, running across each of the previous issues, most of the late TECs had a weak or very low presence of other key animators from the business sector. Most early TECs drew heavily in their early and development phases from existing local business organizations, particularly Chambers of Commerce, but also enterprise agencies, LENs, regional CBIs, employer groups and group training associations. Where these organizations provided little pre-existing business infrastructure there were special difficulties for TECs in generating a business commitment and leadership. This explains the slowness of most of the last twenty TECs, including many parts of London.

Scotland

The pattern of development in Scotland was different in many important respects. We have already noted that a much more strategic approach was developed. This delayed Scottish LECs so that all became operational together at one point in time, April 1991, when over 60% of England and Wales TECs were already operational, some having been operational since April 1990. Scotland's approach allowed what can be argued to be a more sustainable system to be developed, although the situation differs considerably between the SE and HIE areas.

Scotland's approach was also fundamentally different in having an intermediary between the LECs and government (represented by the SE and HIE). This difference, we will argue, is one of the most fundamental elements which has allowed the LECs to become more effective than TECs and has provided a much greater level of empowerment. The extent of local power differs significantly, however, between SE and HIE. As measured by budget allocation, HIE is a much larger intermediary than SE. In 1992/93 HIE retained 27% of the budget and significant scrutiny over expenditures. Any environmental expenditures in a LEC over £15,000 had to have specific HIE approved. In contrast, SE retained only 14% of the budget centrally and the LECs are free to spend up to £250,000 without consulting SE.

The origin of the thinking for Scottish Enterprise (SE) and Highlands and Islands Enterprise (HIE) was, in part, separate from that in England and Wales. Bill Hughes, the Chairman of the CBI in Scotland, had floated in June 1988 a plan for merger of the TA and SDA budgets in Scotland to produce a single body. It seems certain that Hughes' initiative was with the sanction of the Prime Minister to whom he had earlier presented his proposals at a Chequers weekend gathering. It seems that the early floating of the idea in Scotland was specifically orchestrated partly to allow a longer period of public debate, which was stimulated by Scotland's more open and consensual approach to policy developments. But it was also timed to separate the debate from the December launch planned for England and Wales so as to preserve a sense of "Scottishness" about the LEC proposal. It was also convenient to be able to portray the Scottish developments as led by business. Certainly this was how the CBI subsequently portrayed Hughes' initiative.[13]

The initial floating emphasised the benefits of drawing the TA and SDA together, but the details of local delivery and the rôle of the HIDB were not fully addressed. A difficult internal debate and battle ensued as to the rôle of the HIDB which resulted in its eventual and reluctant inclusion in reform. Not all SDA commentators were enthusiastic either. For example, a former SDA operational Director, Peter Carmichael, noted that "there is nothing wrong in principle with the Hughes proposal for local agencies, but what was missed . . . was the need for a strategic set of national objectives . . . which could founder in a sea of parochialism".[14] The result for both SE and HIE was a two-tier structure that sought to balance these concerns with the overarching desire to move to a predominance of local delivery.

The SO did not seek to be as clear as the TA in laying down guidelines for the size of LEC areas. It emphasised the "advantages in choosing reasonably compact areas" and suggested aggregations of Travel to Work areas (TTWAs), many of which were "too small" or "too narrow an economic base to be able to support viable agencies" (Industry Department Scotland 1988: 17). The initial proposal, therefore, was a balance between the 60 TTWAs and the former national-scale bodies of SDA and HIDB.

The proposed number of LEC areas was 22 for both SE and HIE areas. This is exactly equal to the final outcome, but the layout was profoundly different. The map proposed by the Industry Department Scotland (1988: 30) envisaged only 6 HIE LECs and 16 SE LECs and was based exclusively on TTWA boundaries, ignoring local authorities.

The original proposed map ran into difficulties on four counts. First, it failed to recognise the importance of LEA provision of FE college training programmes which offered the bulk of training in Scotland, as south of the border. This was especially significant since no WRFE funds had been removed from LEAs in Scotland as they had in England and Wales. Similarly local authorities are the main planning and environmental body in each area. Hence, a basis on TTWAs produced an awkward map with regard to negotiation and "partnership" with other key agents. Second, the original LEC map was seen by many critics as being part of a "hidden agenda" for redrawing the local authority map of Scotland. This may indeed have been the case, since there was much talk in central government and the TA even in 1988 of planning for the era where there would be no LEAs. But to do this through the development of LECs would lead to the alienation of many of the key supporters the government needed, not only in local government, but also because local business leaders were also not ready for radical change of local government. The third problem was the issue of size and viability. This had not been fully thought through, particularly for HIE. The attempt to get areas with large working populations resulted in very large aggregations which proposed only 3 LECs for the Mainland and Inner Hebrides, and one each for Orkney, Shetland and the Western Isles. This was in conflict with local delivery in an area where it could take at least a full day to travel by surface transport between many parts of the proposed Highlands LECs. Fourth was the issue of changed philosophy in the SE area. The former SDA had only 8 regions within which most of its local activities had been highly targeted through "projects". The LEC structure required a complete coverage. In order to safeguard many of the former SDA projects, areas were initially proposed that maintained a local focus. This was particularly true for Dundee, Alloa/Falkirk, Bathgate and Inverclyde/Greenock. Subsequent merger of these focused areas into the larger LEC regions has indeed been subsequently criticised as "dilution".[15] One chief executive (57) commented that this has led to LECs being looked at as a "band aid for places in need" with "a major difficulty of squaring the business focus with a social dimension".

The consequence of the more open debate in Scotland, on set-up and boundaries, was a more strategic approach; first to maintain national strategic resources in SE and HIE, and second, to prescribe the map of SE LECs to which local bids would then be addressed. Hence, the subsequent 1989 White Paper was phrased as "an invitation . . . your opportunity to participate" for business leaders; "an opportunity for those in the top ranks of private sector business in Scotland to contribute". The map was not, therefore, a major issue in the bidding process in Scotland. This did not stop some rival bids for subdivisions of parts of SE LEC areas. Most notable amongst these was for Perth (the old "Perthshire") and Dundee/Angus to be separate from the Scottish Office proposal for Tayside as a whole. This reflects longstanding tensions in Tayside.[16] Despite vigorous lobbying in this and a few other areas, the original SE LEC map withstood all pressures.

In HIE the debate over the local map was more protracted with the old HIDB leadership fighting a rearguard action, right up the launch of LECs, on the scale and functions of local LECs. The HIDB had had no significant local presence. There were only a few local HIDB promotional offices which had no local management or administrative discretion. The TA had no local offices at all; everything was managed from Inverness, which itself had little independence of the Scottish Office and TEED. Hence the LEC mission required a major cultural change away from centralised administration in the HIE area.

For the Highlands and Islands the 1988 Scottish White Paper had been ambiguous, with three alternative proposals for the HIE area: (i) the body actually constituted, combining TA and HIDB functions, (ii) HIDB continuing and with SE managing the local LECs for training and some devolved HIDB functions, and (iii) HIDB continuing and with SE managing only local training. Even the final launch document (HIE 1989: 27) also left the issues of local powers ambiguous: "HIE will have a strong strategic rôle and . . . will design, develop and secure the implementation of projects with an applicability across the area; approve major projects which fall outside the LECs' delegated authority." Although giving a clear and transparent formula for allocation of funds to each LEC, the scale of resource was to be heavily constrained at the centre – only 40% was proposed to be available to the LECs without recourse to HIE, and in 1991/92 only 30% was actually made available, increasing in 1992/93 to the 40% level.[17] The majority of this derived from the TA budget for YT, ET and EAS. The implementation of the HIE network, therefore, de facto maintained HIDB at the centre with the main local devolution chiefly affecting former TA programmes.

The outline of the map was prescribed by HIE, but with more ambiguity and a "lack of central commitment". It appears that "until the end HIDB did not take seriously the need for local delivery and was more concerned to safeguard itself than commit enough management time to the local framework".[18] Development bids were initially based on the original 6 LECs planned in the HIE area. But at a late stage these large LECs were resisted by HIDB, reportedly at Chairman level, and the larger number of smaller LECs were defined based on a strategy of "divide and rule" that allowed HIDB to retain more central control. The mid-Highland LEC in particular was seen as "too big and too powerful" compared to HIDB.[19]

The early phase of LEC development therefore used a more strategic approach than England and Wales. The rôle of SE and HIE has been regarded jealously south of the border as a preferable relationship to that existing between TECs and TEED. Undoubtedly the LECs have gained compared to TECs through having an effective body that stimulates them to work together with each other. They have been able more fully to respond to the needs of developing a national strategy for Scotland. However, tensions remain. As we shall see, these tensions operate at three levels.[20] First, between SE/HIE and the local LECs the development of local flexibility and independence has been slower than hoped for. Second, in SE considerable tensions still exist within some LEC areas which result from the "dilution" of targeting and the need to balance between areas. Local substructures have only gone part way to overcoming this difficulty. Third, in HIE there is still a major tension about whether any of the LECs can develop enough critical mass and "clout" to make enough impact in their areas. We address these issues more fully in later chapters.

Assessment

The establishment of TECs and LECs involves a supply-side initiative focused on institutional change. Their establishment is a response to demands to address Britain's perverse policy syndrome by changing the delivery mechanism. Redirecting attention to the local level has provided an opportunity to bring in new *leadership*, primarily sought from the private sector. It was also sought through this means to direct more responsibility to those who had the ability to respond. This was seen by some of the key designers as "empowerment" of people and localities. Most of all, however, it was directed at empowering businesses and put them "in the driving seat" of local training and enterprise policy as far as central government was concerned. To this end central government sought to use its public money and leadership to *lever* change at a local level.

The targets were highly ambitious in the launch phase, and have been reaffirmed by each successive Secretary of State and Scottish Secretary. They have been broadened since 1993/94 to include DTI as well as DE ministers. A momentum has been built up from a Prime Ministerial launch to cover a wide range of business issues at the local level.

The set-up phase successfully brought the necessary business leaders forward. Most are indeed of high calibre and have allowed a creditable start to be made on tackling some of Britain's most intractable problems. Considerable flexibility has been allowed to the new bodies, although there are significant differences in relationships with central bodies between England, Wales and Scotland.

However, it was clear at the outset that the TEC/LEC mission contains a central dilemma. They are the new institutions that were designed to lead and lever change. But as independent bodies their capacity to achieve change depends on working with other local institutions. TECs and LECs do not fill the whole policy space, let alone meet the full market demand for training, enterprise and business services. As recognised by Brian Wolfson (Chair of the NTTF) "the TECs will not be a panacea by themselves, however good they are".[21] They have to work with other agents.

Recognizing this central dilemma between *exerting* leadership or *developing* local leadership is the key to our assessment of TECs and LECs in what follows. This chapter has already demonstrated some of the tensions resulting from the size and geographical layout of the system. First there was a lack of clarity, or capacity to assert it, in TEED/NTTF, SO and the HIDB as to the extent of local power and hence the size of TECs/LECs required to assure a local critical mass. Second, there has been the tension between the central bodies and the new local agencies. How far the TECs and LECs have got the flexibility and autonomy they need is one of the key issues in their ongoing debate with government. Third, has been the gap between rhetoric and reality in the mission. Far from empowering local business leaders to address their skill needs, almost all the emphasis has been placed on training of the unemployed. Businesses have much to contribute in this area, but that was not what most believed they were embarking on when TECs and LECs were launched. Finally, there has been a further gap with regard to personnel. Local "empowerment" of businesses has been undertaken by giving them strategic control of bodies largely staffed by former civil servants. We turn in the following chapters to assessing how these tensions are undermining the capacity of TECs and LECs to deliver on their mission statements.

Chapter 4
Managing the TECs and LECs

Management objectives

The ambitious designs for TECs and LECs led to the specification of a very highly prescribed organization and management structure. Indeed the management structure was a key part of the objective to introduce business empowerment into government programmes. The TECs Prospectus (1989) specified five major principles which had to govern organization and management:
- Employer-led;
- Achieving a focused approach to the range of training and enterprise fields;
- An emphasis on performance targets;
- Developing an enterprise organization, setting targets and managing delivery;
- Local management structure.

To achieve this an *incorporated structure* was employed. Each TEC or LEC is an independent company, subject to company law, operating as a company limited by guarantee. Each is managed by a Board of Directors which operates under a performance contract with the government. Any activities outside the scope of the contract with the government must be managed by a subsidiary company.

In this chapter we assess the local management of TECs and LECs. In Chapters 5 and 6 we assess how local management relates to central management by TEED and the Scottish Office, SE and HIE. The discussion below is developed across eight broad aspects:
- The rôle of corporate status;
- Board Directors;
- Composition of the Board;
- Wider community links – partnership;
- Personnel;
- Chief executive;
- Management substructure;
- "Membership".

Corporate status

The use of a Company limited by guarantee offered a number of advantages over alternative structures for TECs and LECs. The major alternatives are use of a local host organization (such as a Chamber, local authority, etc. as was done for Local Employer Networks LENs), setting up a quango run by representatives like the previous Local Area Manpower Boards (LAMBs), or constituting the TEC/LEC as an advisory committee. The advantages of corporate status were seen to be:

- Establishment of a strong management structure capable of developing the private sector lead of government programmes;
- Use of an established legal framework for which no special legislation was required;
- Independence of the TEC or LEC both from government, to which it is contracted, and from the delivery organizations, to which it offers contracts;
- Introduction of a private sector style of managerial approach in which individual Directors are responsible and accountable for their programmes, overcoming the perceived ineffectiveness of LAMBs and weakness of LENs;
- Providing an integrative structure which allows a wide range of additional activities to be added, thus offering the potential to link previously disparate initiatives – both private and public, both national and local.

There was considerable legislative advantage and simplicity for the government to be gained from using an established legal framework. However, in the longer term there might have been considerable benefit to be derived by looking at alternative legal structures. Of these a public law status is the major alternative, as used for example in Germany, Austria or France. This has the advantages of ensuring (or compelling) a wider membership from business, hence assuring representativeness. It also helps to ensure that an organization meeting minimum standards will exist everywhere, and it allows revenue to be raised from business through fees or taxes. It is understandable that a Thatcher government was reticent about a statutory approach, but this would have offered the major long-term benefits of a sustainable and national *system*. This approach is still open now that TECs and LECs have been developed, and we evaluate it further in Chapter 12.

The corporate independence of the TEC or LEC has been important. It has given the potential to direct local activities and to choose contractors as training providers on the basis of performance. There is otherwise a danger of conflict of interest and external interference in award of contracts. The corporate status provides a necessary condition for independence and was supported by the experience of those few USA PICs which became independent companies. The majority of PICs in the USA are not independent and are strongly influenced by City Mayor or State Governor's Offices (Bennett 1993c). However, corporate status is not a sufficient condition for success since also required is the discretion and financial resources to set local standards and to hire and fire staff. Under the system that developed, independence has been severely limited in practice by:

- The majority of staff being derived from the TA;

- A lack of financial resources and flexibility to hire and fire staff based on needs;
- The imposition of national criteria on training programmes, such as YT, which limit the capacity to tailor to local needs;
- The use of nationally defined, rather than local, performance targets to assess outputs sought, cost-effectiveness, etc.;
- The intrusion of TEED/SO and Treasury restrictions into how a TEC or LEC can act.

It is clear from USA experience with PICs that problems are created by central performance targets which are too tightly drawn.[1] There is a strong tendency to maximise on the performance indicators rather than truly tailoring programmes to local needs. The US experience shows that the tighter the funds and the less freedom there is over management and staffing, the more the vehicle (PICs or TECs and LECs) is driven by the programme (JTPA[2] or YT) rather than by broader objectives. As a result, US PICs have tended to become more concerned to "defend the turf" of their training programmes, rather than develop new fields of activity. This will be the more evident the tighter are funds, as is becoming apparent with TECs and LECs as their orientation is focused towards output-related funding (ORF) (see Chapter 6).

The Board of Directors

The clear priority for TECs and LECs is for them to be business-led. Not only was it desired that they should be business-led, however, their Boards had to be drawn from "the nation's top business leaders"; "the cream of the local community".[3] A strong restriction was placed on Board members that they had to be chairs, chief executives or Directors of companies. Above all other elements in TEC/LEC design this demand was adhered to by the NTTF. In fact some commentators would say that it was the only criterion that NTTF ultimately defended. The thinking was based on using company leadership to transmit change through companies and employers, but also that key business leaders were also the potential change agents in the economy as a whole. John Banham (1992: 6), Director-General of the CBI, backed this. The Board members "are not employers' representatives drawn from personnel, training and other service departments of a firm, nor are they middle managers who can be spared. If you want something done properly, you must look to . . . the one who most knows what time management is about".

The rôle of the Management Board was to "set strategic policy and evaluate overall performance of programmes" (TECs Prospectus 1989: 12). To maintain the status and accountability of the Board:

- each member is treated as an individual, not a representative of an organization;
- no substitution of attendance or Directors is allowed in order to maintain

personal accountability;

- each member has equal voting power; there are no block votes or shares, thus the business majority is assured if all attend;
- any personal interests of Directors have to be declared and they must refrain from voting on matters related to their interests.

These rules were chosen partly as a result of evidence of the drift in quality of US PICs allowing lower-level business personnel to participate. Partly they were also chosen with the memory of the old Local Area Manpower Boards (LAMBs) in mind.[4] TECs and LECs were designed to prevent corporatist structures impinging through union or local authority pressure.

Majority control by private sector business Directors was argued in the TEC/LEC launches to offer key advantages:

- Businesses should best know their own needs, they are the "customers" for training, and can articulate these directly on the Board;
- Business leaders are more capable of making rapid adaptations to needs as they develop and change over time, and are not limited by complex problems of social equity;
- Private sector control tends to emphasise performance, "the bottom line", rather than process; it was hoped this would lead to more cost-effective training provision;
- "High-level" business leaders offer "strategic" direction and may be those best able to lever other local firms.

However, there have been severe limitations on the empowerment of business leadership. There is a contradiction between the statements about the levels of power in the TEC/LEC Articles of Association, which state that the TEC – "shall be managed by the Directors" and the TEC operating Agreement which limits the Boards rôle through specific contractual obligations on treatment of civil service staff secondees, finance and programme delivery. These contractual obligations have been more onerous each year as ORF has come to play a larger rôle.

The characteristics of the Directors has also caused difficulties. Specifying that the business leaders on Boards should be of high calibre is clearly important. But the experience of both TECs/LECs and PICs indicates they need not come from large companies: "Business leadership has nothing to do with company size." The condition for success is the quality of individual Board members as well as their "network of contacts" so that they can "act as ambassadors" for the message which is being developed. Board membership of the TEC or LEC, therefore, could be viewed from a "value-added" perspective: value-added by individual members because of their personal qualities or because of their local influence on other businesses, as well as the value-added by the TEC/LEC to the members of the Board by the expansion of their influence.[5] The TECs Prospectus was not sufficiently clear on these broader concepts. The criteria to be used in vetting Board membership by the National Training Task Force

(NTTF) were similarly unclear. There was thus a danger of local activities becoming dominated by large businesses and senior business people who might know nothing of the problems of training and enterprise that TECs and LECs have to address. It is now clear that the prescription was mistaken. Board membership is better based on the personal effectiveness of members, not on company size or personal status. How this effectiveness is assessed is a key question. The rôle of DE, CBI and ministers "fingering" individuals who then become a self-perpetrating clique has been strongly criticised. The Boards would be greatly strengthened if a system of election from the business community were to be developed.

Another difficulty for Board membership is that to keep high-level business leaders interested they need something significant to do. It was clear from the outset that the training programmes themselves would not generate a long-term commitment. These programmes were already well developed, there was too little discretion over them, and funds were already small and too rapidly diminishing to provide major scope for innovation. Experience of the US JTPA also showed that key business leaders began to lose interest once the training programmes were set up: they then needed flexibility to do further work. A key issue for TECs and LECs therefore has been to keep Directors interested by allowing them to develop new initiatives and by giving them more power and control over programmes. This was recognized at the outset. Norman Fowler as Secretary of State for Employment noted that "no Chairman or chief executive of any calibre will be content with administering detailed bureaucratic rules and systems" (CBI National Conference 1989). This has largely been prevented, as we shall see, by TEED methodologies and Treasury limitations.

There is mounting evidence of disillusionment among many Directors with the character of TECs/LECs and their lack of flexibility. The private sector lead depends on the commitment of Board members which itself draws a great deal from personal altruism and the parent company's commitment to social responsibility activities. This contrasts with the staff of a representative body where people are involved as part of their mainstream job. This is a strong contrast between TECs/LECs and Chambers of Commerce. The commitment required to TECs and LECs is considerable. In interviews, TEC Chairs estimated that they needed at least 2 days per week, particularly in the start-up phase. "Our Directors are spending between one and two days a week, and that is at the weekends as well, to work out a vision and undertake teambuilding" (Richard Field, Chair of Sheffield TEC, in BiTC 1989). Indeed interviews indicated that those few Chairs that were de facto full time concluded that this is the only way that the job could be done. TEED guidance was that TEC Board members require a minimum of two days per month, but many have found this inadequate for them to play an effective rôle. The 1993 *Financial Times* survey of TEC Directors (10 May) found that 40% were giving 1–3 hours per week, 29% 3–6 hours, and 27% over 6 hours. Among the private sector members 62% were giving over 3 hours per week (compared to 43% from the public sector), both proportions being considerable increases from 1992 (of 52% and 33%, respectively).[6]

To influence the public sector negotiations with TEED on the one hand, and consider local interests on the other hand, has required immense time input by Directors to achieve the flexibility required. Also because of other commitments to their businesses, the TEC/LEC business meetings often have to be at relatively unsocial times over breakfasts, evenings or weekends. These time commitments have been compounded by the problem of managing Boards in which "local authority and voluntary sector people want to talk a lot . . . a committee culture is developing, controlled by the TEC staff and their civil service culture" (London TEC Chair 45). It is not clear that these demands are realistic expectations for a sustainable structure of private sector commitment to be supported over the long term.

The level of commitment required for Board members to be as effective as they need to be has created a particular tension for business leaders, since TEC/LEC commitments compete with their full-time jobs. It is not surprising therefore that attendance of many Board members at meetings has tended to fall off,[7] and that a high turnover of Board members has occurred through resignations. This tends to mirror the pattern of PICs in the USA (Stratton 1989, and in BiTC 1989). The turnover of TEC Directors has increased markedly in the early years. For the early TECs, from April to October 1990, there was a turnover rate of 9.3%.[8] By the end of 1991 the annual turnover rate had increased to 27% among TEC Directors and 22% among TEC Chairs.[9] Over the year to the end of June 1992 19% of Directors had resigned (*Financial Times*, 20 August 1992). By June 1993 the turnover was 16% and over the 5 months April–August 1993, the loss of Chairmen was 10%. The reasons for the Director resignations relate mainly to pressure of time (32%) or job changes (42%). The "pressure of time" indicates a level of downgrading of the level of commitment to TECs by both individuals and companies compared to other needs. The chief reason for the rest of resignations was company closure or liquidation (16%) which demonstrates the problem of impermanence for private-led bodies relying on direct inputs from business personnel. For the later resignations the proportion arising from pressures of time and company closure has risen. The most notable element is the resignations due to lack of time since these cover those Directors that are disillusioned. The high overall turnover rate tends strongly to undermine the credibility of a system that sought to produce a sustained sea change to Britain's training and enterprise system.

The experience of Scottish LECs is a little better. Over the 18 months from their foundation up to October 1992, SE LECs experienced an annual turnover of Board members of 8.9%, whereas in HIE LECs the turnover was 12%. Among Chairs the annual turnover in SE LECs was 17% and in HIE LECs was 13%.[10] The reasons for resignation are available only for SE LECs: 54% "left" or were "replaced", 25% "retired from business", 13% moved jobs, and 8% were local councillors who lost their seats.[11] This suggests a higher level of disillusionment among those who left in Scotland, although the total turnover rate is lower than in England. It is also worthy of note that turnover tends to be concentrated in a few LECs. In SE, two LECs account for 40% of the turnover, and in HIE 2 LECs account for 42% of the Board turnover. Where things go wrong they tend to go badly wrong. In the worst 2 cases nearly half the Board has left. This contrasts with England and Wales where the pattern of turnover has been more even between TECs, except in London, where none of the founding Chairs were in place by the end of 1993.

The lack of power and flexibility, on the one hand, and the extensive time commitment required on the other hand, is likely to continue to erode the level of interest of key business leaders. The result is an accelerating drift of interest which tends to erode the capacity of the Board to take a meaningful strategic view, and to place more power in the hands of TEED/SE/HIE and TEC/LEC full time staff, or both. The DE has argued that the "turnover level of busy senior executives represents a perfectly reasonable rate of natural wastage" (*Financial Times*, 20 August 1992). But the problem was recognized at the outset: "why should a thrusting entrepreneur or wealth creator who is any good in a Thatcherite society spend his (sic) spare afternoons sitting on enterprise councils? He must be a fool" (Lord McCarthy, *Hansard*, 5 April 1989: 1149–50). The outcome is not a system that can be argued to be producing a strong business-led, stable, reliable and quality system.

Composition of the Boards

The Directors of the TECs and LECs are appointed as individuals who receive no remuneration and seek to reflect the local mix of industries. As well as maintaining a balance of two-thirds majority of private sector businesses (including the Chair), the TECs Prospectus also required the Board to develop "links with the community" and "broadly reflect the whole of its area".

It has been sometimes difficult for TECs and LECs to balance their small number of Directors across the wide set of interests they are supposed to cover. Business Directors should "broadly reflect the mix of commerce and industry in their area . . . including small firms" and "should command the support of the business community across the whole TEC area"; and for the non-business Directors they "must also be selected as individuals in their own right who bring expertise, commitment an credibility to the TEC" (TECs Prospectus 1989: 11). This has led in practice to selecting business people with a spread across the main sectors, with at least one representing small firms. Where a TEC area is geographically dispersed across several significant settlements, generally it has been sought to draw members from each place, e.g. in Tayside to balance Perth, Dundee and Angus; in Humberside to balance Hull, Grimsby, Scunthorpe, Goole and Bridlington. However, problems emerge with areas covering a very large number of different places, e.g. in London East it has not been possible for each of the six boroughs to have representatives, even though that TEC pressed very hard to allow the Board's size to be increased to allow this. In the case of Sheffield an approach was made to the minister to allow an equal number of business and non-business Directors, but this was turned down by the Secretary of State (Field 1990: 58).

The TEC and LEC Boards have up to 15 Directors in England and Wales, and 10–12 Directors in SE and HIE. The Board sizes have generally been close to the maximum. The balance of the Boards that has developed in practice has given slightly more than two-thirds of the Board seats to the private sector – approximately 71%, as shown in Table 4.1. The higher proportion is partly a result of deliberate policy in some TECs, partly a result of not filling all available places on the Board, and partly a result of the rapid rate of turnover which often leaves at least one place vacant at any one time.

The spread of other categories of Board members if fairly diverse. Trade unions account for about 5% of members, local authorities for 8.6% (almost all are chief executives in England and Wales, but in Scotland a slightly larger proportion are elected councillors),[12] local education authorities (LEAs) (mainly the Chief Education Officer) account for 4.5% and other education bodies 2.5%

Table 4.1 Proportion of TEC Board members originating from different organizations (excluding TEC chief executives).

Date of survey	April 1990	Sep 1990	Oct 1990	Jun 1991	Jul 1991
PQ	7 Jun 1990	1 Nov 1990	27 Nov 1990	26 Nov 1991	19 May 1992
Private sector employers	72.2	69.6	69.5	70.9	70.1
Employer organizations	1.2	N/A	1.5	1.0	0.9
Trade unions	5.3	5.3	5.3	5.1	5.4
Local authorities	8.9	9.7	9.2	8.5	8.6
LEAS	3.6	3.3	N/A	4.2	4.5
Other education organizations	3.0	N/A	N/A	2.4	2.5
Voluntary organizations	3.6	2.9	3.7	3.7	3.8
Other	2.2	9.2	10.8	4.2	4.0
Women	N/A	10.1	N/A	10.7	10.7
Ethnic minorities	N/A	N/A	1.4[1]	N/A	3.5
Number of TECs	13	36	41	82	82
Average size of Board (excluding chief executive)	13	13.5	13.3	13.8	13.9

Source: Parliamentary Questions (*PQ*), at dates given: except Note 1 which is derived from a CLES (1990) sample of 15 TECs.

(mainly principals of FE colleges, polytechnics and universities). Voluntary organizations account for 3.8%. There is a surprisingly low and declining proportion of employer organizations represented (only 1%) who are chiefly from Chambers of Commerce. However, this figure undoubtedly understates the reality since in a large number of interviews, in some TECs and LECs it was clear that some private sector Board members often de facto represent the interests of Chambers, enterprise agencies, the CBI or other significant local employer bodies.

Table 4.1 records some of the development steps over time of the TECs. There is surprisingly little change in the overall proportions of the different types of Board members from the first 13 TECs established in April 1990 to the full system completed in October 1991. This is indicative of the strong guidance given by the NTTF and TEED on the composition of the non-private sector category. An additional feature of NTTF/TEED guidance has been pressure on TECs to recruit a significant number of women and ethnic minorities onto the Boards. This has proved difficult. The proportion of women is just over 10%, and the ethnic minority percentage has risen from 1.4% in mid-1990 to 3.5% in the completed system. Of these only 0.3% represent ethnic business organizations (*PQ*, 26 November 1991).

The composition of the private sector businesses on the Board has proved difficult for TECs to balance. They have been directed by NTTF to have a sectoral spread and at least one small business representative. Analysis of the first 20 TECs has demonstrated a strong bias to manufacturing compared to services (CLES 1990). On the Board of these TECs 48% came from the manufacturing sector and 38% from services, compared to average proportions of employment of 27% and 63% in their local economies. The bias to manufacturing is borne out in more detailed analysis of 33 TECs shown in Table 4.2. This demonstrates that the largest sectors supplying TEC Board members are metals manufacturers with 24%, and other manufacturing with 15%. After these comes chemicals manufacture (9%), which are particularly strongly represented in non-metropolitan areas, construction (7.6%) which is strong in the rather small London sample, and food and drink manufacture (7.3%). The high level of representation of these sectors relates more to the rôle of nationally leading companies that are present in the particular TEC areas than to their relative importance within the economy as a whole.

A similar problem of representing the diversity of small firms' interests is also recognized. An analysis of all business Directors in 1993 showed that 15% came from companies with under 50 employees (*PQ*, 4 May 1993), whereas 11% of TECs had no Director from firms with under 24 employees (Vaughan 1993). Analysis of the 33 TECs reported in Table 4.2 shows that only 3.6% of Directors came from firms with fewer than 20 employees. In a survey of TECs in mid-1992 only 20% of the 46 responding TECs had a good spread of Board members from the small business sector (*Financial Times*, 30 June 1992). There remains, therefore, a problem for TECs and LECs to be representative of sectors,

Table 4.2 Proportion of 275 private sector TEC Board members in 33 TECs originating from different industrial sectors.

SIC sector	Non-metropolitan areas (%)	Metropolitan areas (%)	London (%)	Total (%)
Extractive industries and primary processing	4.1	5.8	–	4.4
Manufacturing				
Construction	6.7	5.8	36.4	7.6
Chemicals	11.3	4.3	–	9.1
Metals and engineering	23.6	27.5	9.1	24.0
Food & drink	6.7	8.7	9.1	7.3
Timber, paper, rubber	5.1	7.2	–	5.5
Other manuf.	13.3	20.3	9.1	14.9
Wholesale and retailing	4.6	8.7	9.1	5.8
Hotels, catering, cultural and recreational	3.1	1.4	–	2.5
Transport and communications	5.1	–	9.1	4.0
Banking, insurance and ancillary	7.7	4.3	–	6.5
Business services and other	2.6	4.3	–	2.9
Law, accountancy and advertising	1.5	–	9.1	1.5
Utilities	2.6	1.4	–	2.2
Other services	2.1	–	9.1	1.8
Number of TECs	22	9	2	33

Source: Analysis of LSE sample of 33 TEC Development Funding Bids, June 1990.

areas, firm sizes or any other criteria. With the constitutional structure of their Boards as the only representational vehicle that they initially could develop there are major limitations: 15 people can represent only a small cross-section of an area. The issue of representational legitimacy is discussed further in relation to "membership" below.

Wider community links – "partnership"

The TECs and LECs are locally-based organizations led by business. But they cannot be independent of other local interests. Partnership was envisaged from the outset: "a partnership that is forged to pursue benefits for the whole community, whether inner city, rural, industrial or commercial" (TECs Prospectus 1989: 4). Effective local links are essential to the success of TECs and LECs if they are to meet the needs of developing local capacity that we have argued to be crucial to the development of the economy.

But TECs and LECs have a special design of partnership in which the private sector is given a majority voice on the Board. It seems entirely consistent with the government's priority to tailor the strategy of provision to employers' needs that it should give private sector business leaders majority control of such programmes. However, effective links and support from other non-private employers, public providers, local business bodies such as Chambers, interest groups or unions are also critical to success. This requires effective representation on the Board and general networking within the locality.

Many business leaders and local business organizations have criticised the TECs and LECs for not giving enough control to the business sector: "a business service organization should be fully led by business, not by a quango staffed by civil servants" (interview comment with leading CBI member, 1990). However, the unequal balance of partnership has been criticized by some commentators as not giving a strong enough voice to local educationalists, unions, public sector funders, etc. This concern has ebbed as TECs have developed. Certainly in other countries, such as Germany, the Chambers largely operate through such a system for contracted training and this does not undermine effective partnership with local government or unions. In the USA the PICs also have a private sector lead and it is argued there that this is essential in order to assure that businesses' needs are satisfied: they state that "the public sector already has so many voices, and indeed the programme is all public money". Thus "there is no need to worry about getting the public sector 'on board' – they are already there" (interview with David Lacey, Chairman of Philadelphia PIC 1989; Bennett 1993c).

Ironically, the partnerships may be stronger in Scotland as a result of the wider powers of LECs. As a consequence the LECs are less dominated by training programmes. HIE LECs have a wider community budget as well as the environmental and business promotion programmes which are also available in the SE LECs. From the outset, therefore, LECs have had to work through stronger partnership particularly with local authorities. As TECs have developed, local links have also had to grow stronger. But the lesser budget and more limited responsibility of TECs in the environmental and community development fields has fundamentally constrained both their capacity to influence others, as well as affecting their own strategic outlook.

Early LSE surveys in 1990 and 1991 showed that TECs were well behind LECs in widening their programmes. Later surveys show that they had not caught up in 1992 (see Chapter 10). This was particularly true of developments involving environmental improvements, physical economic development and strategies linked to innovation and R&D strategy. Our subsequent analysis of the different fields of TEC/LEC activity, in Chapters 7 and 10, outlines the generally slower development of the TEC vision compared to LECs.

TEC/LEC personnel

The initial staff of TECs was derived almost exclusively from secondees, on 3 year secondments, from the former Training Agency (TA). This was subsequently extended to secondment up to 1996. The main staff came from previous TA Area Offices in England and Wales. But in Scotland a larger scale transfer from the *central* offices of the TA, SDA and HIDB to the LECs took place. The Scottish staff contracts also differ in that all staff are not LEC direct employees, but are employed by SE and HIE and are seconded to the LECs. The transfer of TA staff in England and Wales was launched as providing the specialist expertise that business leaders needed to support the TEC Board strategy. "The staff of the Training Agency . . . can be the executive arm" said Norman Fowler.[13] Or in the words of Cay Stratton (in BiTC 1989): "sound management will combine policy direction and performance oversight, by the TEC Board, with day-to-day operational control by the TEC chief executive and staff. We believe this brings together the best of two worlds: private sector entrepreneurialism and management expertise, with public sector skills."

The staff available for transfer to TECs and LECs from the former TA allowed for about 50 personnel per TEC/LEC. But the SE LECs also gained further staff from the SDA. In the HIE LECs a more centralised delivery structure was initially maintained with 70% of staff remaining at the former HIDB offices in Inverness and an average of only 9 staff per LEC going to local LEC offices. From April 1992 some staff from HIE have been reassigned so that now there are 13–14 per LEC, although numbers vary widely between LECs. The LECs also received a higher proportion of the former TA staff than did the central SE or HIE offices. This reflects a stronger influence of the former SDA and HIDB in the changes, staff from these former bodies being dominant at the centre of each system.[14]

TEC staff contracts have been a significant source of tension between the TECs and government and between TEC Directors and TEED. We would argue it is the most crucial design failure of the TECs. Many staff did not want to be transferred, and "gardening leave" was extended to some of those who refused. The TECs therefore received a workforce with a mixed level of commitment. To overcome the perceived gaps in staff quality and commitment a few TECs/LECs went to considerable lengths to control which staff they did accept as secondees. But there was stiff resistance from the TA/TEED. In at least one case this resulted in a TEC going to an industrial tribunal over a post it did not wish to fill with a TA secondee. In Scotland the tension for LECs is that all employment management of staff ultimately resides with SE and HIE from which almost all staff are seconded.

Most TEC/LEC Boards have felt that they have had insufficient freedom to develop personnel policies. Although the TECs/LECs were free to establish their own incentive pay and bonus schemes and recruit direct employees, these have to be paid from external funds. Thus the TECs/LECs could not perform as normal companies hiring and firing staff and setting pay and conditions in line with their product development. Initially, the only flexibility over conditions, pay and appointment had to come from privately raised funds or from efficiency

savings in the management budget. In theory this was a source of discretion for
TECs and LECs – a secondee could accept a new offer or retain normal pay and
conditions. But in practice no real discretion was available since, first, insufficient private funding sources were available, and second, "whatever choice is
made [by a secondee], staff will be able to remain civil servants on secondment
to a TEC" (TEC Operating Manual 1989: para 6.13). A strong line was taken that
"public funds should not be used to meet the salary costs of other TEC employees who replace civil servants" (TEC Operating Manual 1989: para 6.21) unless
exceptionally, and with TEED Regional Office approval.

In practice some flexibility on pay has been possible through efficiency savings. This has allowed improvement in pay of many existing TEC/LEC staff. But
significant resources have not been available to appoint new staff. Hence by
early 1992 approximately 70% of TEC staff were still seconded civil servants.

It is understandable that few staff opted for changed status. As TEC secondees
they received pay directly from the same EDG Central Pay Office, received their
normal civil service pension rights, and the same generous overtime payments
and leave entitlements. For LECs all main employment conditions are determined by SE and HIE to whom all employment contracts are devolved. The
guidance to staff on their transfer to the TECs makes clear the difference in
culture envisaged compared to the upbeat rhetoric of the TECs Prospectus, newspaper advertisements and the other efforts to raise the commitments from business. Far from "putting employees in the driving seat", staff were informed
that minimal changes would affect them (DE 1989, emphasis added):

- "The intention is that TECs should be staffed by Area Office personnel on
  secondment";
- "Secondment will be for a period of three years . . . The initial three year
  period of secondment will be renewable, and there will be no maximum
  duration";
- "You will be eligible for promotion in the same way as all other [non-TEC]
  staff . . . If you are successful at a promotion panel, the TEC *will be required
  to release you*";
- "You will stay on the same terms and conditions of service as you had
  before . . . you will retain membership of the Principal Civil Service Pension Scheme";
- "In most cases your line managers and your countersigning officers will
  themselves be civil servants";
- "TECs will be expected to welcome TA Area Office staff . . . If a TEC does
  not wish to take someone whom the *Regional Director deems suitable*, the
  Regional Director will be able to *reduce the TEC's management budget* accordingly . . . There will be safeguards to prevent a TEC from recruiting
  non-civil servants who would replace suitable secondees";
- "If you have a grievance . . . you will have access to the normal Employment Department group procedures. TEC management will deal with any

problems . . . but they will not be able to take formal disciplinary action against you";

"You will remain in every way a member of the Employment Department group with access to the group's career opportunities".

Thus TEC and LEC Boards could only with difficulty develop proper line management and effective control of their staff. "They are just the same people, doing the same job, looking out of the same windows" (LEC 100, local enterprise trust contractor). The Board was de facto closer to a committee managing a quango than an effective strategic body. In the words of one senior DE commentator "they were only intended to be Local Area Manpower Boards with new paint". And if they returned staff to the DE the cost was borne on the TEC budget. Opinions differ on how the staffing culture has actually developed. Many TEC and LEC chief executives echoed the claim of one that the "style has changed spectacularly". Norman Fowler as the Secretary of State launching the initiative (CBI National Conference 1989) stated that "never before has government offered employers, at government's expense, a fully experienced back-up staff to achieve industry's needs". But the Boards and those who have dealt with TECs/LECs as partners and contractors have been far from happy: 96% of external agents by mid-1992 still saw the civil culture of TECs and LECs as a major or minor problem in their dealings with them as partners or contractors; 71% of respondents thought there were too many tiers or layers of staff structure (see Table 4.3). In Scotland the criticisms of LEC staff are generally more muted than in the TECs, probably because the former SDA and HIDB staff had more experience of a proactive approach. However the criticisms of Scotland's former TA staff are at least as vigorous as in England. The criticisms of staff are generally most negative with respect to the TEC/LEC main field of training contracts (see Chapter 7).

As the TECs and LECs have become established a number of developments in staff conditions have been announced that have increased flexibility. From mid-1992 it was agreed that the costs of a reduced management budget by a TEC returning civil servants to TEED was to be removed if the former civil servant secondee could be found a job in the rest of the civil service. This has allowed a number of staff who could not be accommodated in the TEC culture to be replaced.

Table 4.3 Perception of TEC/LEC staff structure by partners or contractors to TECs and LECs. Percentage of respondents.

Issue	Major problem	Minor problem	Not a problem
Civil service culture of staff	60	36	4
Too many tiers/layers of staff structure		71	29

Source: LSE survey of other agents in 20 TEC/LEC areas in early and mid 1992: $N = 45$.

The most crucial change, however, was the announcement in December 1991 that, from January 1993, the TECs could recruit outside of the civil service and could move to the direct employment of the staff seconded to them. TECs and LECs were asked to move to direct employment of all staff by the end of their fifth operational year (by April 1996). To allay fears over who would be liable for any future redundancy payment costs, particularly pension rights, the government had to agree to cover the costs of past civil service employment if the lay-off occurred within 5 years of a former secondee's employment with a TEC (*PQ*, 16 December 1991). This decision was related to a similar, and retrospective agreement, to pay the civil service redundancy and pension liability of staff made redundant from the former Skills Training Agency when its privatised owner, Astra, issued new employment conditions in late 1991. Under the TECs/LECs arrangement, no civil servant was compulsorily transferred, they were free to choose whether to become employed by the TEC/LEC or return to the civil service. Despite these changes, by mid-1993 43% of TEC/LEC staff were still seconded civil servants and many TECs had given a commitment to employ secondees until 1996. Even with direct employment of former civil servants, we believe that the resulting inertia from the former Area Offices and the link of staff culture back to TEED is one of the fundamental brakes on development. It is also far from clear that the government will honour its commitment to take back all remaining secondees in 1996. We return to this in Chapters 6 and 11.

The chief executive

Similar tensions to those relating to TEC personnel emerged over the appointment of the Chief Executive. The appointment was highly constrained: "TECs should first consider appointing the Training Agency area manager" (TEC Operating Manual 1989: para 6.10). If this appointment was made it would be on the same terms of secondment as other staff, with the same dilemmas as noted above. Annual appraisal is undertaken by the Chair "who will be invited to consult with the Regional Director before setting pen to paper" (DE 1989). If a TEC Board did not wish to appoint the local area manager, they could advertise but had to form a selection committee of the TEC Chair, a TEC Director and a TA senior official, and the appointment was subject to endorsement by the Secretary of State. If an appointment outside of the TA was made, the salary could be covered from public funds only up to the average of the relevant civil service grade.

As a result of these controls, it is not surprising that the TEC/LEC chief executives came predominantly from the public sector. Table 4.4 shows that over 70% came from previous public sector employment, with a slightly higher proportion of 73% in Scotland. Of this group the majority came from the previous former bodies: 55% from the former TA in England and Wales, and 64%

Table 4.4 Previous employment of TEC/LEC chief executives: proportion of all 104 TECs and LECs as at August 1991.

	England and Wales %	Scotland %	Total %
Training agency	55	9	45
SDA	-	23	5
HIDB	-	32	7
Local Authority	9	-	7
Other public sector	6	9	7
Trusts, etc.	6	4	6
Private sector	24	23	24

Source: Original survey.

from the TA, SDA and HIDB in Scotland. In Scotland the SDA and HIDB are the predominant former employers of chief executives. This reflects the balance of power of the various bodies (see Chapter 6). Other public sector former employers are more diverse, with local authorities the main category accounting for one-half.

It is not completely clear, from the information that could be obtained, from what level in their former public sector organizations these chief executives came. From the data available on 20 England and Wales TECs 20% were from the Employment Department or TEED, 25% were former area managers and 10% former regional managers, whereas 45% came from below manager level in (mainly) area or regional offices. The former area offices had limited discretionary or management responsibility. Hence, although it is the quality of the individual rather than their former status that is the most important issue, it is probable that the majority of chief executives from the former TA came with little experience of proactive management or previous skills of exercising significant discretion. This has made it more difficult for TECs to break away from top-down methodologies used by TEED.

A surprisingly small presence of chief executives derives from Trusts; surprising given their widespread presence in most economies and their experience in many fields of TEC activity. The Trusts that are represented are a diverse group of Youth Enterprise, Skillnet, Royal Society of Arts, Groundwork, a training consortium and an enterprise agency.

The private sector chief executives are 24% of the total overall, and are a very similar proportion in England, Wales and Scotland. The size of this group is surprisingly large given the early rules constructed by TEED. The size of this group has also been increasing, with a number of former TA chief executives in England either leaving or being dismissed. The origins within the private sector appear to show a balance of approximately one-third from SMEs, one-third from large firms, and one-third from consultancies.

It is difficult to be confident in assessing whether a TEC/LEC has been advantaged or disadvantaged in the development of its mission by the way it has pursued its chief executive's appointment. Undoubtedly too large a number of former TA staff found their way into these posts. It would be surprising if so many entrepreneurial senior leaders had been present in the former TA Area Offices given the lack of discretion these officers had. In its most extreme form in HIE, several business Board members interviewed expressed extreme scepticism that 6 out of 10 HIE local LECs chief executives, plus one from the TA, could be found from sufficiently well-qualified people from the single old area office in Inverness from which they all initially derived.

However, it is also clear that the TECs/LECs gave some former TA staff a new opportunity to develop the necessary qualities. A few TEC and LEC Chairs with private sector chief executives felt that some former TA staff could have been better suited for the chief executive post in the initial phase since "they know better how to play the Moorfoot game". There are, however, probably only two or three of these highly entrepreneurial former TA chief executives in England and Wales.[15] This amounts to only 5% of the former TA staff. Also, as time has progressed, the benefit of having former TA experience has reduced. In Scotland the situation is more complex to assess since many former SDA/HIDB staff came from recent private sector backgrounds.

In contrast to the TA former employees, recruits to chief executive posts from the private sector have often had to struggle to understand the system. Three contrasted scenarios appear to have developed. The first and most common scenario is where the externally appointed chief executives has had to rely on the former TA local managers. The effectiveness of this has depended on local staff quality, morale and personal relationships. The outcomes have varied from very good to poor. A second scenario applies in the few cases where a private sector chief executive has been able to confront the previous management style head-on and radically to change it. This has needed strong and extensive TEC Chair/Board support and an ability to effect a strong management line. In interviews and visits we have seen this achieved effectively in only 3 out of 62 TECs and LECs.

A third scenario has been where a chief executive has come from another local agency and has facilitated the "capture" of the TEC/LEC by the other local agency. This has been widely associated with one of the early large city TECs which had a chief executive from a local authority. The result is claimed by many agents in the area and some Board members to be that the TEC is in the local authority's pocket. This scenario is not common. But attempts have been made by local agents to use other means to influence the local TEC/LEC, e.g. through their Board members, or through key external appointments within the TEC. This probably applies to parts of the programme activities of most TECs and LECs, and may not be a negative outcome. Indeed in some cases it has clearly helped to prevent the TEC/LEC making some crucial mistakes.

In contrast to the appraisal of staff, the appraisal of chief executives by

Table 4.5 Perception of effectiveness of TEC/LEC chief executive by partners and contractors to TECs and LECs. Percentage of respondents.

	Very effective	Effective	Ineffective	Don't know
Chief executive	43	38	11	8

Source: LSE survey of other agents in TEC/LEC areas in early and mid 1991: $N = 45$.

partners and contractors to TECs and LECs shows that most felt that the appointment was effective (see Table 4.5). At the most senior level, therefore, differences in background have not been of such significance to effectiveness in the job.

Management substructure

Because of the size and complexity of their task, all TECs and most LECs have established substructures. These structures have allowed the establishment of "Action Groups" and "Task Forces" to cover specific areas. The substructure was seen at the outset as a means of bringing wider groups into contract with TECs:

'its substructure must provide ample opportunity for interest groups to participate in policy formulation and programme design . . . the TEC Board will have 15 Directors. That is a minuscule sliver of any patch. If it is to achieve its share of the national goals the TEC will need to engage the commitment of the people and organizations throughout the community . . . Each TEC must establish effective ongoing channels of communication that both inform and comment' (Cay Stratton, in BiTC 1989).

Substructures were seen therefore as both a consultation mechanism and a management tool. All TECs appear to use a substructure based on divisions of training, enterprise, education and internal management/external marketing policy. Beyond this, however, there is great variety in the forms of substructure. In a survey of 68 early TECs and all 22 LECs in 1990/91 nearly half of all TECs and LECs had substructures based on either industrial sectors and/or geographical sub-areas (see Table 4.6).

Industrial sector substructures are attractive to those TECs/LECs that have major focuses of their economies which they want to stimulate, or need to respond to. Many of the TECs in large manufacturing areas have such substructures, e.g. in Birmingham across a wide range of sectors where the sector structure mirrors that in the LEN, Chamber of Commerce and, to a lesser extent, local authority economic development focus such as the Milan car industry network (see Bennett & McCoshan 1993, Ch. 11). In other areas sector substructures represent the importance of one or two key parts of the economy, e.g. in ELTEC (North East Lancashire) for engineering; or in some London TECs for financial services and hotels/catering.

Table 4.6 Substructure of TECs and LECs: in existence or planned (late 1990 – early 1991). Sample includes all 22 LECs and 66 TECs operational at date of survey (80% of all TECs).

	Industrial sector		Geographical subareas	
	No.	%	No.	%
TECS	32	48.5	34	51.5
All LECs	9	40.9	8	36.4
SE	2	16.7	3	25.0
HIE	7	70.0	5	50.0
Total with substructure	41	46.6	42	47.7

Source: Original survey; see Bennett et al. (1993b).

Table 4.6 shows that sector substructures are most highly developed in the Highlands and Islands, where there is frequently a particular focus on important local industries, e.g. agricultural products, tourism, natural resource industries, etc. The very low number of sectoral substructures of Scottish Enterprise LECs appears to derive from their more integrated approach to development. However, it has also been influenced by the early date at which the survey was undertaken, the more integrated framework within which SE works deriving from the earlier SDA. Subsequently SE LECs appear to have developed sector substructures to a greater extent.

Geographical subareas are an important means for TECs/LECs to develop different actions appropriate to different parts of their areas, as well as managing a sense of equality of treatment to each place. Some elements of this equity strategy are surprising for a business-led body which could be expected to concentrate resources in the areas where they would yield the greatest returns. The stated reasons for TEC area substructures evident from interviews vary from (i) a strategy to keep all areas perceiving an equal treatment, even though a concentration of resources is taking place, and (ii) a response to TEED performance measures that encourage a concentration of resources in areas yielding the quickest returns, to (iii) a genuine sense of needing to give all areas an equal share, particularly those areas with greatest problems which might yield the greatest returns.

It was clear from interviews that whatever the real motivation, all TEC/LEC actors (staff and Chairs/Board members) felt they had to keep the appearance of equality of treatment "because TECs and LECs are public bodies using government money".[16]

One-half of all TECs and the LECs have developed area substructures, but these are again least developed in the SE area. For SE the explanation for this lesser development is different to that of sectoral substructures. It appears to derive from the relatively small geographical size of a few of the SE LECs. Generally, area substructures are more highly developed for larger LECs and TECs and for those which cover more dispersed or more rural areas.

Membership

Membership is one of the crucial issues facing the TECs and LECs because it relates to the core focus of empowerment. The way in which TECs and LECs were set up had nothing to do with "membership": it varied between relatively spontaneous "bottom-up" groups of business leaders who have come together, and local individuals who had been "fingered" to take part by external agents such as the CBI, Chambers, BiTC and even local authorities. Whichever method led to the original TEC/LEC bid, the Board of Directors, even on the non-business side, cannot be claimed to be other than a self-appointed group. They have no legitimacy or representational relationship to the local community, other than their position in their companies or organizations and their personal standing. The Board is not empowered by, and it does empower, the local business community.

The problem of the TEC being divorced from the local community was recognized at the outset. The TEC/LEC substructure was seen as the primary mechanism for consultation: if such participation "is not central the TEC will soon be perceived as an elite club, largely white and largely male, out of touch with a good share of its customers. In a market-driven system that is an absolutely fatal error" (Cay Stratton, in BiTC 1989). Despite valiant efforts, such as those in Sheffield where "every single family in our city will be touched at least once" (Richard Field, in BiTC 1989), substructures have not proved to be an effective means of reaching businesses. Substructures reach agencies and representative organizations, but not clients directly. In the fields of training and education, and in fields dominated by the public sector, substructures work well. But for links to business this approach has failed. TEC/LEC membership was an attempt to overcome this problem: "a stimulus to more effective communication with business", in the words of one senior TEED commentator.

At the simplest level membership has been interpreted as widening the contact networks and action subgroups of the TEC/LEC. Beyond the TEC Board it is possible for the TEC to have other members, but the Directors remain those who are personally and legally responsible. As a result, it is not at all clear what being a "member" of a TEC means. In Sheffield, membership has been interpreted as part of a wider local partnership organization (Sheffield Economic Regeneration Committee – SERC) of which the TEC is a part (see Field 1990). SERC pre-dated TECs and has provided a mechanism for the TEC to have a wider network of consultation and community involvement. In this sense the SERC and others are "members" of the TEC. This has been an effective vehicle to give the TEC a wider legitimacy and consultation route in the community. But there is still no doubt that it is the Directors who control the TEC. Membership does not constitute any means of control as it would in an elected local authority council or Chamber of Commerce council.

Other examples of membership schemes vary greatly. Some are no more than mailing lists. Indeed TEED advice has focused mainly on this development: "mailing lists can be seen as membership as they do give contact" (senior TEED commentator). Other schemes go as far as seeking a constitution for the TEC Board. In SOLOTEC (South London) a system of "associate membership" has been established with rates varying from £50 to £250 which has as its purpose "to increase accountability of the TEC, wider membership, involve those with influence in the area and produce new Directors". From members, a Council will be drawn who "will retain residual powers to vote on, and decide, major issues . . . [they also] have the power to appoint and remove Directors" (SOLOTEC, January 1992).

A debate has emerged on the possible interpretations of membership. Although specified in the original TEC Operating Manual, most developments followed *A Strategy for Skills* paper (DE 1991) which placed membership as a target for the 1992/93 corporate plans. Although this guidance was removed in the guidance for 1993/94 (DE/DTI 1992) TEC/LEC membership schemes are still being developed.

The motives that lay behind the TEC Operating Manual (1989) and DE (1991) membership schemes are not clear. Some of the possible benefits that might accrue are:

- Strengthen TECs/LECs in their dealings with government;
- Help TECs/LECs build a stronger and more representational base among their local employer community;
- Help TECs/LECs communicate and transmit their vision;
- Help generate income for TECs and LECs;
- Help reach new markets and develop linkages and networks;
- Help TECs/LECs to manage succession on their Boards.

Each of these can be taken at face value (cf. *Full Employment UK* 1992). Since some senior TEED commentators have argued that data bases and mailing lists are enough to act as membership, there may indeed be no competition with other bodies. Chambers of Commerce, however, have been highly critical of TEC/LEC membership schemes. Chambers have, probably correctly, been suspicious that membership is a spoiling strategy thought up by DE senior civil servants to undermine Chambers of Commerce, which have been becoming stronger local agents and offer an obvious challenge to TECs/LECs as the legitimate business bodies in their areas.

It is certainly the case that a membership base would help TECs and LECs in their dealings with government. It could also help to build a stronger business involvement to transmit the vision and to reach out to new markets. However, membership alone does not guarantee this, since many businesses either have not heard of the TECs and LECs, or have heard, and do not want to know. A perception in the DE appears to exist that TECs/LECs could be better "branded" and marketed through membership schemes. However, this is clearly naive and falls at the same hurdle as membership of Board Directors. Our interviews with

TEC/LEC Boards demonstrate that most businesses want to know, and to pay for, only those things which offer them direct benefits. They are doubtful as to whether TECs/LECs offer them any benefits and believe it is mostly the reverse – that the benefits flow to the TECs/LECs, to the civil servants, and perhaps to other participants. Most businesses are unconvinced that they need many of the products that TECs/LECs feel would do them good. This particularly applies to IIP, MCI and some NVQ standards (see Chapter 7). Hence, it is clear that many businesses feel that many of the TEC and LEC products are a cocktail concocted at TEED which are distant from the realities of their everyday needs. We confront the degree to which these business views are valid criticisms in later chapters.

The extent to which membership schemes could generate extra income depends on what the schemes provide. Most TECs/LECs conceive of membership arrangements as starting with entry to a mailing list for disseminating TEC/LEC information: this is arguably not membership at all and costs public money for usually little measurable return. The next level of membership charges businesses a token fee, say £25, probably in exchange for discounts on services. This fee level would be equivalent to Chambers of Trade. It would cost TECs/LECs at least this whole sum to administer a membership scheme (unit costs for Chamber membership are of this order, Bennett 1993e). Moreover, discounting of services is a useful marketing strategy only if TECs and LECs have a product that businesses want to buy.

There might be some greater saleability of membership as part of a local business club, to encourage local networking of businesses. A number of TECs and LECs are going down this route, but again it is not clear why they should do this when many Chambers of Commerce or Trade already organise such events.

A more realistic possibility exists for TECs/LECs to develop a specific segment of high quality business services and charge realistic fees. However, it is not clear why the TECs and LECs should be participating in this market. On the one hand, a substantial and rapidly growing private sector market exists for contracted business services (see, e.g., *Financial Times*, 20 February 1992). The entry of TECs and LECs into this market could be merely a waste of public money or constitute a crowding out of private sector activity. On the other hand, there exists a range of public and collective business services which are currently provided by local government, Chambers of Commerce, enterprise agencies and other bodies. Entry of TECs and LECs into this market could be beneficial, but would have to be sensitive, again, to prevent either crowding out or duplicating existing private sector resources. The quoted services in this category are "health checks" and training needs assessments. One Stop Shops are seeking to take the range of services further by focusing on business counsellors. We appraise this development further in Chapters 9 and 11.

The development of a membership scheme on its own therefore seems a rather insensitive instrument; when linked to the crowded market for business services it appears as yet another government initiative linked more to civil service departmental ownership than to rational market assessment, which crowds out the market or other organizations. Being sensitive to these problems, some TECs have developed combined membership with local Chambers of Commerce, e.g. SOLOTEC, North West Wales. In the cases of South and East Cheshire, Northamptonshire and Barnsley and Doncaster, a possible merger of a TEC and Chamber is being discussed with the likely initial outcome being a joint service company. In Kent and Humberside an integrated service structure among all the key agents is being attempted. But in each of these cases it is not membership of the TEC/LEC which is the crucial question, but linking the TEC or LEC to other local business agents in order to present a greater coherence to the market.

The key issues which membership does address for TECs and LECs are those relating to empowerment, legitimacy and succession of the Board Directors. A proper membership scheme should mean that the members are "owners" of the company who, like shareholders, can vote for the Board, ensuring both a turnover and tenure related to perceived quality of performance. This would ensure accountability and legitimacy of the Board in the local community thus overcoming the valid criticism that TECs and LECs are presently a self-appointed and self-perpetuating group. The DE would wish to assert the qualification of chief executive/Managing Director status for Board members; indeed they are quoted as "being prepared to go to the stake on this issue above all others". But, if that constraint is sensible (and we have criticised it earlier) it could be used as a qualifying criterion for the candidates for election.

A 1992 LSE survey shows the extent of development of memberships schemes amongst TECs and LECs. Table 4.7 shows that membership schemes became popular in England and Wales and in the Highlands and Islands, but were least developed in 1992 among SE LECs. One-third of TECs were already operating membership schemes (by mid-1992), compared with one-quarter of both HIE and SE LECs. However, when future plans are taken into account, these differences become even more apparent. Whereas 61% of TECs intended to run or already ran membership schemes, and 75% of HIE LECs planned to or already did so, no SE LECs, beyond the existing 25%, planned to adopt a membership scheme in the future.

The membership schemes can be either independent or joint with local Chambers of Commerce. Table 4.7 shows that nearly twice as many TECs were running their membership schemes independently (68%) than were doing so jointly with Chambers of Commerce (32%) or other bodies (6%). All SE LECs were running their schemes independently, and 50% of HIE LECs who indicated their approach were running membership independently. The entry of the publicly-funded TECs/LECs into membership schemes previously dominated by private and voluntary-sector bodies confirms our other findings (Chapter 9) that TECs/LECs have instinctively behaved as providers rather than as partners in enterprise initiatives. This has led them into competition with existing local institutions.

Table 4.7 Membership schemes being developed by TECs and LEC. Percentage of TECs/ LECs with different schemes (multiple responses allowed).

	England and Wales	SE	HIE	Total
Membership scheme in existence:				
Yes	33.9	25.0	25.0	31.6
Planned	26.8	0.0	50.0	25.0
Yes + planned	60.7	25.0	75.0	56.6
Sample size	56	12	8	76
Joint or independent scheme:				
Independently	67.6	100.0	50.0	67.4
With a Chamber	32.4	0.0	16.7	27.9
Other	5.9	0.0	16.7	7.0
Objectives of scheme				
Recruitment to Board	29.4	66.7	50.0	34.9
Help meet IIP targets	32.4	66.7	16.7	32.6
All major firms as members	76.5	66.7	50.0	72.1
Sample size	34	3	6	43

Source: LSE survey (Bennett et al. 1993b).

The competition with Chambers is evident when the objectives of membership schemes are analyzed (Table 4.7). TEC and LEC target numbers sought for membership schemes by 1994 show that three-quarters of TECs targeted all major firms, while less than one-third each specifically aimed at businesses holding the Investors in People (IIP) kitemark (32%), or at recruitment to the TEC board (29%). Only two of the three SE LECs with a membership scheme were able to indicate their objectives; both viewed all three of these purposes as equally important to their membership targeting. HIE LECs showed more interest in targeting all major firms and potential board recruits (both 50%) than IIP firms (17%).

The target size of recruitment by 1994 (Table 4.8) from the sample of those TECs/LECs developing membership shows that over two-thirds of responding TECs, and all SE LECs, were seeking memberships in excess of 500; one-third of TECs and two-thirds of LECs were seeking memberships of 1,000 or more. This focus on developing TECs and LECs as large-scale membership organizations, rather than for recruitment to TEC/LEC Boards or IIP, directly competes with Chambers. Only HIE LECs differ from this pattern, with the majority aiming at no more than 200 members by 1994, 40% seeking a membership of only 50. In part this must reflect the small size of most of the catchments in HIE LEC areas.

Table 4.9 shows the average subscriptions sought for the membership schemes. TECs were seeking annual subscriptions at an average level of £32, with a range from a minimum of zero per member to a maximum as high as

Table 4.8 Number of members sought by TEC/LEC membership schemes. Percentage of TECs/LECs with targets for recruitment by the end of the 1993–94 financial year ($N = 38$).

Target for membership numbers	England and Wales	SE	HIE	Total
50	10.0	0.0	40.0	13.2
200	10.0	0.0	20.0	10.5
500	33.3	33.3	20.0	31.6
1,000	26.7	66.7	0.0	26.3
2,000	6.7	0.0	0.0	5.3
All major local businesses	6.7	0.0	20.0	7.9
Other	6.7	0.0	0.0	5.3

Table 4.9 Subscriptions sought for membership to the TEC or LEC in 1992–93 ($N = 37$).

Subscriptions	England and Wales £	SE £	HIE £	Total £
Minimum	0	0	0	0
Maximum	200	200	0	200
Overall average	32	30	0	31.67

£200 per member. SE LECs were seeking an annual subscription averaging only £30 per firm, and no HIE LECs intended to charge a subscription at all. 35% of TECs, and 40% of LECs (36% of the total sample) with membership schemes had no subscription at all, yet had large recruitment targets. The average subscription for members of Chambers of Commerce in 1992 was £131 (British Chambers of Commerce Annual Census) so that TECs, and particularly LECs, were clearly undercutting the private sector. An example, which is typical of most TEC membership schemes, is provided by Staffordshire TEC (Press Release, November 1992). This is seeking "to ensure that local businesses were well represented and influence decisions made by the TEC . . . Benefits of joining include free health and safety information, assistance with training existing employees, regular fact sheets, participation in pilot projects, and invitations to attend specially organised seminars . . . discounts on certain items and events . . . a chance to meet up with other business people on a social or professional basis".

Interview comments also show a strong level of misunderstanding by TECs and LECs over what membership means. Some TECs quote membership that is derived from purchase of Yellow Pages, other data bases, or enquiries and contacts rather than actual subscribing members. These findings demonstrate that most TECs are very confused about what they mean by membership. If 36%

of TECs and LECs make no charge, and many quote members merely from enquiries and data base listings, it has to be questioned whether this constitutes "membership" at all. Data bases do not constitute membership. Many TECs/ LECs therefore seem very confused about both why they are developing membership, and what it constitutes.

Membership schemes and TECs/LECs are not incompatible. They could yield benefits if developed sensitively. The detailed evaluation of possible mergers with Chambers in Barnsley and Doncaster, Northamptonshire and South and East Cheshire is demonstrating that a vehicle can be constructed to satisfy both TEC and Chamber demands, although developments are desperately slow. This is allowing the drawing together of the TEC/LEC and the Chamber concept. But it is clear that major constraints presently stand in the way of this strategy, most of which derive from the sense of impermanence of TECs and LECs and the extent of their control by TEED/SE/HIE/treasury independent of their Boards which gives a significant chance of membership of TECs being seen by business as a "con". We turn to this in later chapters.

Assessment

The TECs and LECs were designed to be employer-led, focusing previously dispersed and programme-driven activities, enhancing performance and networking with other local agents. This chapter has shown that concerns on each of these issues exist as a result of their management powers.

The employer lead has been undermined by the need to counterbalance private sector demands with the more general equality of treatment of different areas, to prioritise special needs, and to give emphasis to many social needs that influence a number of TEC/LEC programmes (particularly those affecting the training of the unemployed). The private sector Board members have also found it difficult to maintain the time and commitment required, particularly given the nature of the entity as it has evolved.

The move away from a programme-driven focus for TEC/LEC activities has been inhibited by rigid TEED/treasury guidelines, accounting practice and performance targets. The extent of detailed guidance targets has inhibited flexibility and given many Board Directors the feeling that they were acting as a committee of a quango rather than on a business-driven entity in which they were "in the driving seat".

The sense of running a quango has been significantly reinforced by having to work with a staff of former civil servants. Although training could have been applied to improve the performance and "culture" of staff, the fact that each member of staff was encouraged "in every way to remain a member of the Employment Department with access to the group's career opportunities" has undermined retraining or major reorientation. Some improvements in detail have been made since 1993, but the dominance of the civil service staff structure remains one of the severest handicaps to the Board lead.

The success of local networking varies greatly between areas, as we shall see in the following chapters. But some systematic difficulties undermine the capacity of TECs and LECs to be the change-agent desired. First, the method of recruiting the Board has undermined their legitimacy in local communities. There is no clear rationale for appointment or succession. As turnover of the Board has occurred, some areas have drifted from an initially self-appointed group with some local legitimacy into a self-perpetuating clique. In two or three areas the Board, after only 12 to 18 months, has lost all local legitimacy by shifting to a group of business Directors who had little local relation to other bodies or interests. More typically the sense of mission has been lost by the leading local figures, both those on and off the Board. Second, the development of membership schemes and attempts to compete in business service provision has brought TECs and LECs into conflict with private sector suppliers and other business-led agents such as Chambers of Commerce. This has demonstrated the considerable insensitivity by TEED and many TECs and LECs to the real needs of the market. Experiments with membership have sought local empowerment of the Board but at the same time have demonstrated how far TECs and LECs have to go to achieve a proper legitimacy.

Chapter 5
Local Fit

New localism

More than any other innovation introduced by the development of TECs and LECs, it is the intention that they become local agents of change that is perhaps most innovative. This is a fundamental underpinning to the concept of empowerment. Previous attempts to develop training through the Industrial Training Boards (ITBs) had been based on industrial sectors, and Local Area Manpower Boards (LAMBs) had been local only in the context of a strong national top-down structure which kept all significant decisions at a national corporatist level between the CBI, TUC, and government. There has not previously been a powerful, government-led entity developing national training and enterprise programmes at a *local* level.

As stated by Brian Wolfson (Chairman of the NTTF):

> what we are trying to do with the TECs is to get the people living in a community to focus on their local balance sheet of their problems and opportunities . . . The ability of the TEC to respond to its local problems with local solutions is the critical differential.

Or in the words of Cay Stratton:

> It is at the local level, where people live and work, where their children go to school, where jobs are created, and where there is a civic culture, that either inspires risk taking and innovation or inhibits economic change and economic investment.[1]

This was a critical ingredient of what Stratton saw as local empowerment. In this chapter we focus particular attention on how this new local basis has been developed. We assess not only how TECs and LECs have developed locally, but also how they interrelate with the existing major local agents that already occupy part of the domain that TECs and LECs have sought to fill. We discuss in turn:

- Boundaries;
- Contrasts between TECs and LEC areas;
- Interfacing between TECs and LECs;
- Relations with other local agents;

75

- Enhancing local capacity;
- Assessing success.

Boundaries

In Scotland the LEC boundaries were developed by negotiation with a strong lead from the Scottish Office and SDA/HIDB. A complete pattern was defined from the start (see Chapters 3 and 4). The boundaries of the TECs, however, were developed in the same way as their other elements: they emerged from the interplay of bottom-up bids, that sought to cover certain geographical areas, with TEED/NTTF controls through acceptance of the final bid. The stated aim was for bottom-up evolution to play a leading rôle. To allow this to happen the evolution of TECs was to be gradual, over three to four years, which "must be carefully paced" to ensure that it "must emerge through employer leadership and local community support" (DE 1988: 43).

In practice a series of other institutional constraints on the boundaries fundamentally undermined the bottom-up process, the careful pacing, and the structure of employer/community support. First, the pace of change accelerated with the result, as stated earlier, that many bids for small areas were allowed that carved off parts of the map, pre-empting a more strategic view of boundaries. Second, because of the importance of building links with local authorities, particularly LEAs, their boundaries, or aggregations of them, came to dominate the debate. Although early advice from TEED/NTTF suggested that boundaries could be drawn anywhere to reflect the sense of local business community or local labour market, the tension of such boundaries with local government and key education providers proved too strong to resist in most cases. Particularly in Scotland the "free" boundary notion received vociferous resistance from local authorities where it was seen as a hidden agenda to restructure and take over local government functions. Subsequently, in 1992, the setting up of a Local Government Commission for England and the announcement of SO and WO plans for unitary councils has cast long-term doubt on the emphasis put by TECs and LECs on existing LEA boundaries.

Third, the concept of the local labour market as a strong source of guidance was effectively abandoned. It was recognized very early that the national map of Travel to Work Areas (TTWAS) was virtually useless for TEC purposes. For example Bennett et al. (1989a; 23) argued that the TTWAS were largely irrelevant:

- They were based on Census data which were very out of date (1981);
- They were based on a 'normal' self-containment criterion that 75% of the population both live and work in an area; areas that result are very small labour markets, compared to that desired for TECs, with most contained in the range from 3,500 to 20,000;
- There was no ready means of aggregating TTWAS without extensive further analysis which would in any case be based on out-of-date data.

Interview comments from senior TA officials and Regional Directors confirm the sense of exasperation that developed over the absence of *useful* definitions of local labour market areas.

Even if up-to-date statistics had been available, there was in any case major resistance to use of the local labour market concept. One TA Regional Office document commented that there is "no easy way of determining a discrete labour market or local economy. Travel-to-work patterns differ for men and women and for different occupations and levels of skill. . . . It follows that it may be impossible for any TEC to make a completely reliable assessment" of the skill demand for a particular area.

Hence, because of the rapidity of change in the British economy since 1981, the impossibility of ready aggregation of TTWAS, and the inherent impossibility of defining self-contained labour markets, any use of local labour market definitions by TECs had to be very limited.

A fourth constraint on boundaries was that from the pre-existing TA area structures. The White Paper stated that "the government do not intend to prescribe boundaries . . . but in general they are likely to be based on subdivisions or, in certain circumstances, aggregations of the existing 57 Training Agency areas [in England and Wales]" (DE 1988: 43). This was in direct conflict with the TEC Prospectus (1989: 6) that "there are no predetermined geographical boundaries . . . the prospective TEC should consider what boundaries best reflect the economic, geographical and travel-to-work patterns of the local labour market and the size of the local population to be served". The result was a number of disputes between the TA and local TEC bids which sought to divide TA Area Office patches. These disputes were particularly vigorous where a TEC bid wanted to bridge across a TA Regional Office boundary. As a result no significant regional boundary crossing occurred, despite major attempts to do so, particularly between London and the South East regions, between the South East and East and West Midlands regions, between the North West and West Midlands regions, and on the Welsh boundary. An exception is the amalgamation of the High Peak (East Midlands) with Stockport (North-West region). The general rigidity of the regional boundary reflected the seemingly innocent phrasing in the TECs Prospectus (1989: 11): "it is for the prospective TEC to determine its geographical coverage, in consultation with the Regional Director of the Training Agency".

The geographical boundaries of TECs and LECs have predominantly followed those of LEAs, i.e. metropolitan districts, London boroughs, shire counties in England and Wales, and regions in Scotland. As shown in Figure 5.1, where there has been a deviation from these boundaries, this has normally been only a minor element to include an adjacent district, or to amalgamate two counties. Amalgamations affect Devon and Cornwall, East and West Sussex, Dyfed and West Glamorgan, and Berkshire and Buckinghamshire. However there are five important divisions of counties into fairly equal-sized parts: in Cheshire, Nottinghamshire, Derbyshire, Lancashire, and Cambridgeshire.

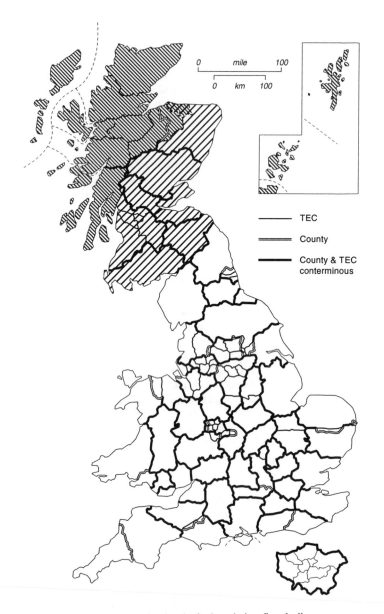

Figure 5.1 Map of TEC and local authority boundaries: fine shading HIE area; coarse shading SE area.

Table 5.1 Relationship of TECs and LECs to local authority boundaries.

	% of TECs/ LECs with one local authority	% of TECs/ LECs with more than one local authority	% of all TECS/LECS	Average. no. of local authorities for those with > 1	Average no. of LEAs per TEC/LEC
London	0	100	8.6	3.7	3.7
Metropolitan areas	76	24	24.0	2.7	1.4
Non-metropolitan areas: county/					
regional level	93	7 ⎫	67.3	2.0	1.1
district level	1	99 ⎭		6.0	0

Despite these important local deviations, the great majority of TECs/LECs follow local government boundaries or aggregations of them. But there is considerable variation between areas in the number of local authorities that TECs/ LECs include. This greatly affects the structure of their local negotiations and the complexity of their management and substructures. Table 5.1 shows that the metropolitan areas outside London have the simplest pattern. In these areas 76% of TECs/LECs have only one local authority to deal with, but those with more than one local authority have an average of 2.7. This simple structure is reproduced at the county level in non-metropolitan areas where 93% have only one county to deal with, although 36% of all TECs/LECs have some form of split across a metropolitan district/London borough/county/Scottish region boundary. The relatively small number of local authorities that have to be negotiated with at metropolitan district and non-metropolitan county/Scottish region level is particularly beneficial for developments in the fields of education policy and physical planning.

However, this relatively simple structure is not reproduced in London, across all fields of activity, or within counties when negotiating with local districts. London TECs have an average of 3.7 local authorities to negotiate with, all of which are also LEAs. In the case of London East the number reaches 6, the largest number of LEAs that any TEC has to deal with.

Similar problems of complexity arise at the district level in the case of the nonmetropolitan areas, where TECs/LECs have to develop relations with an average of 6 districts. The number rises to 16 in Devon and Cornwall; with 14 in Essex, Sussex and Kent; 13 in Hampshire, 11 in Surrey; and 10 in Hertfordshire, Thames Valley and West Wales. The relations with districts/London Boroughs include physical planning, infrastructure and enterprise development. Given not only the number of these districts, but also considerable variation in their political complexion and economic development priorities, TECs have experienced considerable difficulties in developing coherent strategies. As we have seen, the solution of area-based, local substructures and other methods of developing outreach, have usually been employed. This has allowed approaches to be developed which are sensitive to the issues of equity and the needs of local districts. But diffusion of funds has undoubtedly occurred, area committees have proliferated, and overcomplex consultation structures have been required. Hence the spread over a range of local authority areas has not necessarily enabled either the development of a strategic system or the delivery of value for money through effective targeting of funds. We return to these issues in our concluding chapters.

Contrasts between TEC and LEC areas

Although they form national networks, individual TECs and LECs differ considerably between one another in a wide variety of aspects. These differences have a major impact on the size of their budgets, the problems they have to face, the strategies they need to develop, and the way in which they have evolved. We outline here their main differences with respect to:
- Budget and staff;
- Population size;
- Area and population density;
- Unemployment;
- Workforce;
- Sectoral concentration;
- Size concentration of business.

Budget

The budget variation between TECs/LECs in the launch period is shown in Figure 5.2. This demonstrates that in 1991/92 most budgets lay between £8m and £25m, with an average of £17.4m. The total range is extreme: from £1m to £82m. The 10 smallest TECs/LECs by budget are all LECs in Scotland, all in the HIE area. The next smallest TECs are the Isle of Wight, Powys, Rochdale, Milton Keynes and Central and South Cambridge. These small budgets indicate the special characteristics of the HIE LECs and the effects created by subdivided areas in England. The HIE LECs and to a lesser extent SE LECs do, of course, gain benefits from additional resources dispersed centrally from HIE and SE, but the smallness of the HIE area budgets is still extreme. The largest LEC budgets by decreasing size are Glasgow, Lothian, Lanark, Renfrew and Ayrshire. The largest of the TEC budgets are for Merseyside, Devon and Cornwall, Birmingham, Tyneside and Humberside.

Significant changes in budget allocation occurred in 1992/93 and 1993/94. These affected both regional allocations, as a result of the rapid increases of unemployment in London and the South East, and also reflected a shifting funding regime which emphasised participation levels in programmes and output-related (ORF) funding. We report, and assess, these changes in Chapter 6.

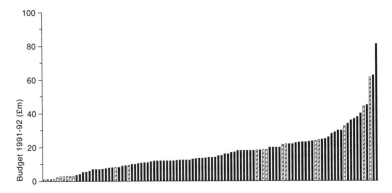

Figure 5.2 TEC/LEC budgets in 1991/92: solid shading TECs; cross-hatch LECs.

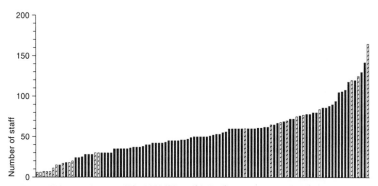

Figure 5.3 TEC/LEC staff in 1991/92: solid shading TECs; cross-hatch LECs.

Staff

The size of TEC/LEC staff varies very much in line with budget, see Figure 5.3 (the correlation is $r^2 = 0.84$ in 1991/92). For the five smallest areas, which are all HIE LECs, staff varied between 3 and 7 in 1991/92, although their numbers increased in 1992/93 to a minimum of 9 to 10 following further decentralization from HIE. These are, however, very small resources to draw on. The fifteen smallest TECs/LECs in 1991/92 all had 25 staff or under. The largest staff compliment reaches 165, with 10 TECs/LECs having over 100 staff. Most TEC staff compliments in 1991/92 varied between 30 and 75 with a mean of 60. In 1992/93 there has, in most areas, been a contraction of staff as TECs and LECs have enhanced payment levels to develop flatter structures, have sought to attract more highly qualified staff and have coped with budget retrenchment. However, a few areas have increased staff: chiefly those LECs gaining as a result of greater decentralization from HIE, and a few smaller TECs, particularly in southern England, that have gained from budget reallocation as a result of increased unemployment levels or have sought to use their own staff as the main means of increasing programme activities. The extreme example is AZTEC which has increased staff from 18 to 50 between 1991 and 1992 through use of all of its management fee, most of the LIF, and TEED/ESF project finance. AZTEC's argument has been that only by staff increases can the TEC deliver the management required to make its programme links effective. It remains to be seen how far increasing TEC/LEC staff size, rather than use of funds in programmes, staff restructuring or local partnership, are the most effective approaches.

Population

The budget allocated to TECs and LECs is chiefly based on residential population and local unemployment numbers. Hence the variation in the populations of TECs and LECs shown in Figure 5.4 is closely related to budget and staff sizes. The 10 smallest areas by population are all LECs, 9 in HIE and 1 in SE. All have less than 100,000 people. The smallest population sizes for TECs are Powys, Isle of Wight and St Helens, all with less than 200,000 people. The largest populations are all in England. They exceed 1m for the cases of Sussex, Hampshire, Essex, Kent, Devon and Cornwall, London East, Manchester, South London, Staffordshire and Surrey.

Area and density

The geographical area of TECs and LECs are one of the most extreme sources of differences (see Figure 5.5). All the smallest areas are in London or metropolitan areas; CILNTEC and CENTEC are the smallest. In contrast the largest areas are all rural. Devon and Cornwall and North Yorkshire are the largest, and most of the other large areas are in Scotland and Wales.

The relation between area and population is measured by density. This provides a simple measure of accessibility, shown in Figure 5.6. The 12 lowest density areas are in Scotland or Wales. The highest densities are in metropolitan areas. CILNTEC and CENTEC are the highest; 9 of the highest 12 are in London; the other high density areas are Birmingham, Glasgow and Sandwell. The extreme variations in density demonstrate the variety of accessibility problems with which TECs and LECs have to cope.

Unemployment

Unemployment levels are crucial determinants of TEC/LEC budgets. There is considerable volatility over time in unemployment. Figures 5.7 and 5.8 show the statistics for 1989/90 for absolute numbers at the foundation stage of TECs

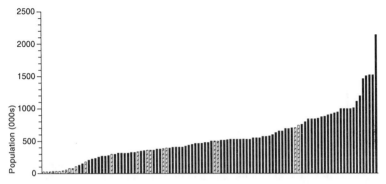

Figure 5.4 TEC/LEC population (1991): solid shading TECs; cross-hatch LECs.

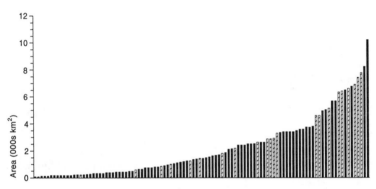

Figure 5.5 TEC/LEC areas (in km²): solid shading TECs; cross-hatch LECs.

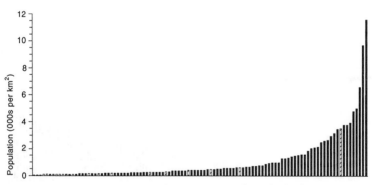

Figure 5.6 TEC/LEC population density (people per km²): solid shading TECs; cross-hatch LECs.

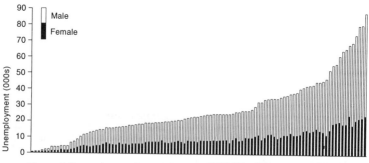

Figure 5.7 TEC/LEC total unemployment (1989/90). *Source:* DE statistics.

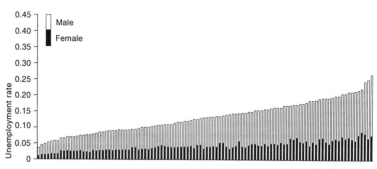

Figure 5.8 TEC/LEC unemployment rate (1989/90). *Source:* DE statistics.

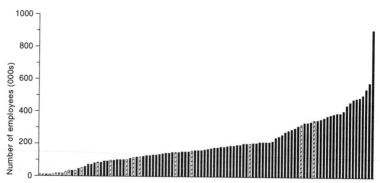

Figure 5.9 TEC/LEC size of local workforce: solid shading TECs; cross-hatch LECs. *Source:* Census of Employment (1989).

and LECs. Considerable restructuring and absolute changes have since occurred as a result of the 1990–93 recession. The largest numbers are generally associated with central city locations; e.g. Merseyside, Birmingham, Manchester, South Thames, Glasgow, Tyneside and London East. But the next largest categories more reflect TECs' absolute size, by population: Devon and Cornwall, Kent, Humberside, Essex and Hampshire. The smallest unemployment levels are all in the small LECs.

Unemployment rates are a more sensitive measure of the extent of local problems. Here the rankings differ considerably. In ranked order they were in 1989/90 at the foundation stage of TECs and LECs: Merseyside, Wearside, Western Isles, South Thames, Dunbartonshire, Glasgow, Teesside, St Helens, Barnsley, Skye and Lochalsh. Long-term unemployment rates tend to be more focused on the inner cities, with the highest ranked being Merseyside, Glasgow, St Helens, Birmingham, CILNTEC and CENTEC; but Orkney and Ayrshire also ranked very high. The lowest ranked unemployment rates were Milton Keynes, Surrey and Powys in 1989/90.

The effects of recession in 1990–93 have shifted the relative unemployment rates considerably, as well as absolute numbers which have doubled over the period since the inception of TECs and LECs. We return to the effects of this shift in later chapters.

Workforce

The workforce of a TEC or LEC is one of the criteria most relevant to business, although resident population is the criterion used in budget allocation. The size of workforce was also the criterion used in the initial set-up phase where an average of 250,000 and a minimum of 100,000 was set in England and Wales. The overall average for TECs does just match the 250,000 criterion, but Figure 5.9 shows that 24 TECs and LECs do not even meet the 100,000 criterion. Fifteen of these are in Scotland, including all 10 in the HIE area, where this criterion was not employed. The smallest TECs, ranked upward in size, are Isle of Wight, St Helens, Rochdale, North West Wales, Rotherham, Oldham, Northumbria, Wigan and Wearside. As commented early, perhaps only 3 of these have genuinely exceptional circumstances. A further 46 TECs are below 250,000. Therefore, only 27 TECs and 2 LECs exceed the average of 250,000 set as desirable in the White Papers.

Sectoral concentration

The variation in concentration in different sectors of industry by TEC/LEC areas is quite marked and can be expected to be an important influence on local policy. Figure 5.10 shows that 12 areas have less than 15% of employees in manufacturing: in ascending order CENTEC, CILNTEC, Shetland, South Thames, Inverness, Caithness and Sutherland, Argyll, Orkney, South Glamorgan, West-

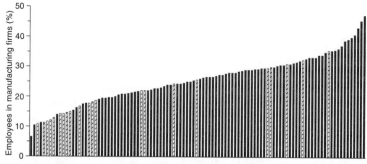

Figure 5.10 TEC/LEC percentage of employees in manufacturing firms: solid shading
TECs; cross-hatch LECs. *Source:* Census of Employment (1989).

ern Isles, Moray and Lochaber. The 12 areas with the highest concentrations of
manufacturing, exceeding 35% of employees, are all TECs: in descending order
ELTEC, Sandwell, Oldham, Calderdale, Walsall, South Derbyshire, Leicester,
Rochdale, Staffordshire, South and East Cheshire, Dudley and Coventry. Service industry concentrations are in inverse order to the manufacturing rankings.

Size concentration

The importance of small firms in overall economic growth has been increasingly recognized. Many TECs and LECs claim to be dominated by small firms.
This is understandable since nationally 97% of firms have less than 20 employees. The pattern of employment is, however, different: 64% of employment is
in firms with more than 20 employees. The rate of growth of employment in
small firms has been the most rapid: between 5 and 30% in firms of 1–20
employees, compared to 3 to 10% in firms of over 20 employees between 1979
and 1987.[2]

The variations between areas are not, in most cases, extreme (Figure 5.11).
Almost all TECs and LECs have between 20 and 30% of their employees in firms
with less than 20 employees.[3] Only 2 areas have markedly low levels of small
firms: CILNTEC and South Derbyshire. The next lowest concentrations, all hav-
ing under 20% of firms less than 20 employees, are North Derbyshire, West
London and Birmingham. The 15 areas with higher concentrations, exceeding
30% of firms with less than 20 employees, are very varied and are mainly in
Scotland. In descending order they are: Argyll, Moray, Lochaber, Ross and
Cromarty, Orkney, Caithness and Sutherland, Powys, Isle of Wight, Dumfries,
North West Wales, Borders, Devon and Cornwall, Western Isles, Dorset and
Shetland. These rankings are undoubtedly biased by the source of data, but
nevertheless do evidence the relatively small degree of variation between areas
in firm size concentration.

86

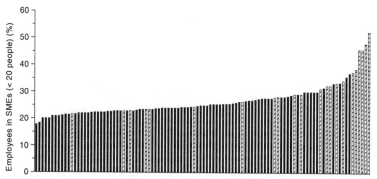

Figure 5.11 TEC/LEC employees in SMEs of less than 20 employees as percentage of total employees: solid shading TECs; cross-hatch LECs. *Source:* Special tabulations of Census of Employment (1989).

Interfacing between TECs and LECs

TECs and LECs were conceived as independent entities, each contracting separately with TEED/SE/HIE. No account was taken in design, and no account has been taken in funding, for interfacing with other TECs or LECs. However, because so many TECs/LECs are small, and because local labour markets could provide only a weak guide to boundaries, the cross-flows of trainees, workflows and business relationships can be very large. The concept of TECs and LECs as independent entities has, therefore, needed considerable reinterpretation in practice. The reinterpretations have not yet all fully occurred.

There are four main issues of TEC/LEC interfacing. First, is training. In general terms, the smaller the TEC/LEC the more likely it will be that it has to interface with other areas for training. Interactions with other TECs and LECs are most significant in metropolitan areas, especially London where some colleges import up to 70% of their students from outside of their area. In one South London college £4m of its £14m budget came from other London boroughs and the South East region in 1992/93. There are also significant flows in many rural areas, e.g. Central Wales and Highland Scotland where there are few local training or FE facilities and long-distance travel is required out of one TEC area to another. Before TECs and LECs there were already important instances in most urban areas of competition for students between FE colleges in different LEAs. With TECs and LECs this has become to some extent competition between TECs. Since 1993/94 the shift of college funding to the FE funding councils has significantly alleviated the budget problem caused by flows as far as the colleges are concerned, but it has left a problem for TECs and LECs. We return to this in later chapters.

A second issue of interfacing is that TECs/LECs also experience flows once training is completed. Once trained, it is common for employees to move outside the area in which they received their training, especially over their later steps in a career. This is not a major concern for colleges. But for TECs and LECs, flows of trainees raise the problem that groups of employers in one TEC or LEC end up training workers for groups of employers in other TECs or LECs: the poaching problem between employers is shifted to a different geographical level and to the institutional level. This issue clearly raises important questions about who pays for training, how TEC/LEC budgets are determined, and what is the motivation for TEC/LEC Board members. The shift of FE funding to funding councils goes a long way towards solving these problems, although the effect of flows remains important within London, other metropolitan areas, at the London–South East boundary, in Central Wales, and in Highland Scotland.

Third, is the relation of TECs and LECs to other business organizations and the local economy. The emphasis of TEC/LEC boundaries on the public sector administrative boundaries of local government has no ready fit with the labour market and trading interactions of businesses, which may be radically smaller, or larger, than TEC/LEC boundaries. The concept of a business Board engaging the business community has therefore suffered considerable stress because the area covered is often not seen as relevant by businesses. The One Stop Shop initiative in 1993/94 has been an attempt to bring some aspects of business advice closer to businesses at a more local level, but this has introduced its own tensions (see Chapters 9 and 11). For local business organizations, such as enterprise agencies and Chambers of Commerce, the problem is similar. Because enterprise agencies and trusts have been very localised, they have had to adjust to TECs and LECs by forming groupings, companies and consortia. In some cases this has worked well (e.g. Kent and Tayside). In other cases the TEC or LEC has had to walk delicately between strategic interests and those of often rival local bodies. For Chambers the TEC/LEC relationship has often been even more difficult since their size and coverage is usually larger than the TEC/LEC area. The Chambers have thus had to face the problem of trying to get two or more TECs or LECs to work together. The difficulties of doing this are evidenced by the fact that only two first-round One Stop Shop (OSS) bids for 1993/94 covered more than one TEC/LEC area, and one of these, for inner London, was a "feasibility study".

The fourth issue of interfacing is at the more strategic and *regional* level. Where local economies are strongly integrated into a regional structure of economic interdependence the local scale of a TEC/LEC may prevent effective tackling of the strategic economic problems if all TECs and LECs act independently. In Scotland this was recognized at the outset by retaining a core central budget in SE and HIE. This amounted in 1991/92 to 17% and 69% of the budget, retained, respectively, in SE and HIE. This proportion fell to 23% in HIE by 1993/94 with the SE proportion staying approximately constant. Indeed the level of regional control was particularly criticised in the case of HIE as too centralised for the LEC local vision to have chances of success and a further decentralization of HIE staff and budgets occurred in 1992/93. The Scottish developments reflected the positive evaluation of the importance of a level of regional co-ordination deriving from the experience of the former SDA and HIDB. This had allowed a coherent regional focus for promotion of inward investment, links to the European Commission, strategic planning, financial management and accounting, many elements of which were retained, albeit on a smaller scale, in Scotland.

The regional element has not been very prominent south of the border, however. Recognising this, from 1992/93 the WO took control of TEC budgets from TEED. But developments of effective regional co-ordination in Wales have been slowed by continued uncertainty (and tension) between respective rôles of the TECs and the WDA. In England the rôle of the regions has purportedly been enhanced as a result of the Styles Review (see Chapter 6). But regional co-ordination is still weak. Even in the most effective regions for co-ordination (usually credited to be the Northern Region and the South East Region), actions mainly concern joint meetings, teambuilding between TEC chief executives and a few joint bids to the EC. In most other regions the TEED Regional Office has not been able, as yet, to exert effective coordination and has been undermined by the contract and methodology of TEC funding which puts almost all emphasis and individual TEC targets. TEED has given no incentives to inter-TEC cooperation. In some cases it has stimulated competition, for example by awarding National Development Projects for one TEC to compete with another (as has occurred in London for data base construction).

The worse case of strategic gaps at the regional level has been London, where the 9 TECs have yet to agree fully a method of effective co-operation beyond the exchange of papers, joint lobbying of G10/TEED, monthly meetings of chief executives and quarterly meetings of Chairs. A detailed study of options for inter-TEC collaboration has resulted in significant improvements in London.[4] But most of these developments involve small groups of TECs working together rather than, as yet, the 9 TECs as a whole taking an effective strategic view for London which they then operationalize. This local fragmentation was recognized as a danger from the outset. A National Training Task Force London Employer Group report (NTTF LEG 1989) had called for "a London-wide employer-led Board . . . [with] a key longer term rôle, to ensure that London's strategic needs be properly considered and taken account of". In the event a consultative body, the London Strategy Group, mainly composed of TEC Chairs, was set up in 1991 which was abolished in 1992. The impact of the fragmentation of TECs is made worse because the other business, training and educational agents in London are also fragmented.

There are two views on how to cope with TEC/LEC interfacing in the future. One is that it is right to treat each TEC or LEC as an independent body. This inevitably means that some competition between TECs, at their margins, should be accepted. Such competition could generally be expected to have desirable outcomes in that it should permit each TEC or LEC to concentrate on matching the profile of labour market requirements and the profile of labour market recruits. Local flexibility was the key objective in the TEC/LEC mission. But if this view is accepted it suggests that TECs and LECs should have been given a more flexible framework of boundaries. It was suggested at the outset[5] that TECs could have been defined for a definitive set of *core areas*, but that this should have been *complemented by the freedom to develop flexible links and overlaps* at their margins. Experience in the USA supports this view. US PICs have developed placement relationships for trainees with firms outside their boundaries, although they cannot (strictly) offer training to non-residents of their areas, even though some do. Fixed boundaries create an unnecessary rigidity, creating some perverse incentives that undermine the ability of TECs and LECs to offer a proper labour market coverage.

A second view is that the desire by TEED for independence in treatment has diverted some TECs and LECs into wasteful competition, reinvention of the wheel, and confusion of brands in an already fragmented market. In the extreme case of London:

'The present situation can be compared to a supermarket with a range of similar products on nine different sets of shelves. The labels of each product may be similar but may sometimes contain oil where the customer expected vinegar; in other cases the similar oil is in bottles labelled differently. Sometimes they may indeed be called oil, but on other occasions they may be called something that is not oil, even though they contain oil. While each product may be attractively labelled and might have immediate appeal to the customer, reading of the small print of the ingredients and price shows that their characteristics are often different from the impression of the superficial glance. Indeed the small print shows that there are often complex tradeoffs made by the manufacturers between cost and quality, or cost and lifespan/duration of the product'.[6]

This may seen an extreme analogy. Certainly there have been some efforts to coordinate branding of some London TEC products in the case of IIP, YT and ET. But even in these programmes there are local differences, and for ET and Employment Action the differences can be extreme. In most of the enterprise fields the number of differences in products has often outweighed the similarities.

It is clear that in London and elsewhere the organization, funding and TEED contract methodology is sometimes perverse in not encouraging effective cooperation. Specific problems that arise are:
- Residence-based funding for TECs encourages, in the field of YT, ET and WRFE, a focus on *local* FE colleges to the detriment of a free flow of students to the most appropriate centres of excellence;
- This, combined with pressures driving down the unit price of WRFE, stimulates a fragmentation of provision and reduction of quality or breadth in

some locally or nationally strategic courses (see also Chapter 7);
- Fragmented, and sometimes competitive, approaches with different "brand-ing" of service provision which is confusing to the individual and business client alike. This particularly affects enterprise support, EBP, Employment Action, ET, aspects of YT, and links to firms through IIP and other pro-grammes;
- Duplication of marketing and management budgets and loss of economies of scale resulting in a waste of public funds;
- A loss of any sense of region-wide action, strategy and momentum; instead a reinforcing local parochialism and balkan villages rather than world class standards.

We return to these problems later and assess possible solutions.

Relations with other local agents

Links with other agents were a key part of the TEC/LEC mission. For training and education a successful TEC/LEC needs not only a meaningful geographical area containing potential customers to train, but also a client group of *busi-nesses* interested and motivated by the TEC/LEC to offer placements and work experience. Similarly for enterprise programmes, the TEC/LEC needs to be able to relate to other agents and the community of businesses in its area.

TECs and LECs experienced a major difficulty in their foundation because both the concept and reality of *local* business communities in Britain are very weakly developed. While there are a few areas where a strong business commu-nity can be identified, particularly in the major cities, there was no *general* existing structure with which TECs and LECs were able readily to link. Indeed, in many cases, previous research by the authors has demonstrated the fragmen-tation and negative aspects of parochialism among business communities at a local level in Britain.[7]

This weakness is in marked contrast to many other countries, notably the USA, Germany, France and Japan, where strong local business communities exist. These local business communities have been stimulated in the USA, and to a lesser extent in Germany, by the existence of a strong State/Länder level of government. Business has organised itself to address this level of government, and this has also stimulated local business commitment and community identity.

In Germany and France, as well as some other countries, a further stimulus has also been given by an effective organization of local Chambers of Com-merce. These have been stimulated by public law status, compulsory member-ship, and an ability to levy fees from members. They normally cover an area roughly about twice the size of an average English county (in Germany, the *Kreis*).

In Britain there is no general counterpart to the Chambers of Commerce in Germany or France, although the Association of British Chambers of Commerce is developing British Chambers into a stronger national system. Other local business organizations also populate the territory, many of which are rival or seek to pull off some market segments. As a result of this history, Britain has a confused and highly complex network of business organizations. The outcome has been an overpopulation of agencies, with clutter and overlap in some places, and significant gaps in others. Michael Heseltine, the President of the Board of Trade, has called for "integrated service by organizations which are co-located, share a common strategy and have developed enduring partnerships for the benefit of the local business communities" (in DTI 1992).

The evolution of TECs and LECs has been fundamentally affected by, and has itself affected, the number and composition of other organizations in each area. In general, there are a large number of organizations of relevance to TECs and LECs:

- Private sector agents such as banks, business legal and accountancy advisors, etc.;
- The WDA/DBRW in Wales and the rôles of SE and HIE in Scotland;
- Chambers of Commerce;
- Regions of the CBI;
- Enterprise agencies;
- Business in the Community (BiTC) and its local Business Leadership Teams;
- UDCs, TF and CAT;
- Rural Development Commission;
- Local government, especially LEAs;
- Group training associations and other training providers.

The relative strength of the major of these organizations can be captured by the comparison, in Figure 5.12, of the main agents by the size of geographical area that they cover and the size of their budget. Included in this are Chambers of Commerce both at their existing scale and within their new national network (see below). Many of the other data derive from original surveys.[8]

Figure 5.12 shows a wide range of diversity in size between agents. Generally the greatest mismatches between the size of resources and *geographical area* are for the private-led bodies which have large areas and small resources. In geographical area, local government is medium to large in size (local authority counties/regions or boroughs and districts). Central government local agents are usually very small and focused (EZs, UDCs, CATs, TF). TECs and LECs in comparison are the largest centrally-funded local body and they are the only network that covers the whole country. Private sector bodies are intermediate or large in area (Chambers and Enterprise Agencies). However in *expenditure*, local government bodies are very large (except non-metropolitan districts) whereas private sector bodies are small, and central government local agents are intermediate.

Apart from a confusing range of scales of agents, their specific geographical focus is also very variable. Local government and TECs/LECs are present every-

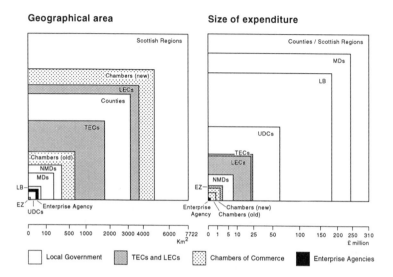

Figure 5.12 Average geographical area and average expenditure by different agents on economic development activities (in 1990/91).

where, but there is often confusion because of the division and lack of co-operation between tiers in non-metropolitan areas. In contrast, most central government local agents are very focused on specific places and, when their programmes are undertaken through local authorities, support is not uniformly available everywhere. Important differences of support and resources apply in Urban Programme Areas (UPAs), TF, CAT and UDC areas. EC Structural Funds criteria add further dimensions of selectivity to the local areas eligible for external support.

The general confusion of size, responsibility and geographical coverage by different agents led the Audit Commission (1989: 1) to recognise the problem of "a patchwork quilt of complexity and idiosyncrasy" at local level in which "it is hard to escape the conclusion that at the level of the individual city there can be programme overkill with a strategic vacuum" (1989: 32). The result is fragmentation, overlaps, gaps, complexity, and a producer rather than a customer focus.

The fragmentation of programmes between both government and other agents is a major constraint on the development of TECs and LECs. Indeed it can be argued that TECs and LECs have to be very sensitive if they are not to contribute to further fragmentation within the local patchwork quilt. A crucial issue for TECs and LECs is, therefore, how they work with other agents.

Enhancing local capacity

Despite the already crowded territory of local agents, TECs and LECs were
nevertheless created as a new agent, thus potentially adding to the confusion
already existing. But, from the outset, it was recognized that the TECs and LECs
had to build links with the other local bodies. Sensitive contexting to the local
community was seen as essential: "while employers will play a preeminent
rôle, they must do so in the context of a partnership that is forged to pursue
benefits for the whole community".[9] But throughout the TEC launch and subsequent development there has been the assumption that local communities needed
new bodies that would do something to them: that TECs/LECs "would do them
good".[10] "The TECs will be a missionary . . . we go out there to sell a message".[11] Hence there was always a deep-seated ambiguity between partnership
and enhancing local capacity on the one hand, and changing local systems and
introducing new local leadership on the other hand.

This ambiguity is evident in the TECs Prospectus's language which suggests
that the TEC "will serve as a forum for business and community leaders to
identify problems, set priorities, define strategies for change and direct available resources accordingly",[12] i.e. it is assumed that this is not already occurring and that ultimately "each TEC will shape its own agenda to reflect the
special economic and social needs of the area".[13] The level of TEC autonomy
from existing partnerships was clear from the examples offered in the Prospectus: "to *match* training and opportunities"; ". . . to *select* training contractors";
". . . to *decide* the level of payment"; "to *change* the *design* and content of
programmes"; and ". . . to *switch* funds between activities" (all emphases
added). This is very much the methodology of initiative creation prevalent in
the former MSC and TA (which we discuss further in Chapter 6).

The belief that pre-existing local community bodies were deficient is also
reflected in the 1991 TECs Conference comment by Geoffrey Holland, then
permanent secretary at the DE, that there is still the need "to create a quality
infrastructure and produce quality performance".[14] There has thus been a strong
top-down view of what a TEC should be seeking to achieve, and a strong encouragement to them to act autonomously to take up the leadership of their areas. As
we shall see in later chapters, outside the training field this has proved to be
totally unrealistic for TECs, although more possible for LECs.

The experiences of TECs and LECs working from this starting point differs
considerably between different places, depending upon the existing strengths of
other agents. We examine local experiences in later chapters. But some measure of the general potential of TECs and LECs as local leaders can be developed
by comparing their budgets with the strength or weakness of other agents in
their areas. We evaluate these relationships in more detail in later chapters,
particularly in Chapter 10 where we assess TECs' and LECs' contribution to the
general economic and community development of their areas. Here we make a

more general statistical comparison of the strength of TECs/LECs and that of other agents.

Tables 5.2–5.7 make these comparisons. They show that in general there is no statistically significant relationship between TEC/LEC budget sizes and the strengths of the two main private sector bodies of Chambers of Commerce and enterprise agencies (Tables 5.2 and 5.3). This means that there is no pattern of complementary support through general strong/weak matchings. Thus TECs and LECs have not emerged as general gap fillers. Instead there is a wide variety of outcomes in each area, as sometimes TECs/LECs have to take the lead whereas in other areas they can draw on other bodies or will conflict with them. The need on the part of TECs and LECs to be sensitive to the variety of key local private sector agents of Chambers and enterprise agencies is further confirmed in Chapters 9 and 10.

Turning to the public sector local authority situation there is a different pattern. There is some complementarity between large TEC/LEC budgets and weak local authority Economic Development Units (EDUs), and conversely small TEC/LEC budgets and strong local authority EDUs (Table 5.4). A similar complementary relationship holds for the relation of TEC and LEC budgets with UPA powers (Table 5.5).

For the case of education a different pattern is evident; Table 5.6 shows a pattern of TEC/LEC budgets being generally largest in the same areas as those in which EBPs are already strongest, and TEC/LEC budgets being smallest where EBPs are weakest. Less prominently the same strong/strong and weak/weak matching characterises the relation between TEC/LEC strengths and school staying-on rates post-16.

All these relations are general statistical patterns. The local experience in developing leadership and change will depend as much on personalities as budgets. But for the fields of *enterprise development, education links,* and general *economic development* TEC and LEC resources are constrained (in comparison to their training budgets). The effect of small budgets is to allow only small staff resources to be applied. As a consequence in each of these fields, the TEC/LEC is often small, and is dwarfed by the local authorities and LEAs. Thus the budget measure applied in Tables 5.2–5.7 is a realistic measure of the possible leadership that TECs and LECs can offer. It shows that:

– There is a mixed pattern of TEC/LEC strength compared to the private sector bodies, Chambers and enterprise agencies. As a result no single model of leadership by local agents is likely to emerge to cover the country; rather there will be different leadership models to fit different situations. This particularly affects enterprise development but also influences all other programmes. In some cases a Chamber lead may be required, in other cases a TEC/LEC lead, and in other cases a variety of forms of *shared* leadership (see Chapter 9).

– There is a complementary pattern of TEC/LEC strength compared to local

Table 5.2 Comparison of size of TEC/LEC budget with strength of local Chambers of Commerce.

TEC/LEC budget	Chambers of Commerce				
	Strong	Medium	Weak	Very weak	Total
Lowest 25%	-	1	10	13	24
		(1.0)	(9.6)	(12.5)	(23.1)
Middle 50%	4	16	22	13	55
	(3.8)	(15.4)	(21.2)	(12.5)	(52.9)
Highest 25%	7	11	3	4	25
	(6.7)	(10.6)	(2.9)	(3.8)	(24.0)
Total	11	28	35	30	104
	(10.6)	(26.9)	(33.7)	(28.8)	(100)

Source: Chamber data: Bennett (1991). *Note*: No. of TECs or LECs in each category (percentage in brackets out of 104) (Spearman rank correlation 0.002; $t = 0.02$; not statistically significant.

Table 5.3 Comparison of size of TEC/LEC budget with strength of local enterprise agencies.

Budget	Enterprise agency				
	Strong	Medium	Weak	Very weak	Total
Lowest 25%	1	3	8	12	24
	(1.0)	(2.9)	(7.7)	(11.5)	(23.1)
Middle 50%	2	15	37	1	55
	(1.9)	(14.4)	(35.6)	(1.0)	(52.9)
Highest 25%	4	12	8	1	25
	(3.8)	(11.5)	(7.7)	(1.0)	(24.0)
Total	7	30	53	14	104
	(6.7)	(28.8)	(51.0)	(13.5)	(100)

Source: Enterprise agency data: Bennett & McCoshan (1993). *Note*: No. of TECs or LECs in each category (percentage in brackets out of 104) (Spearman rank correlation 0.12; $t = 1.26$; not statistically significant.

Table 5.4 Comparison of size of TEC/LEC budget with strength of local authority EDU.

Budget	Local authority EDUS			
	Strong	Medium	Weak	Total
Lowest 25%	5	7	12	24
	(4.8)	(6.7)	(11.5)	(23.1)
Middle 50%	12	26	17	55
	(11.5)	(25.0)	(16.3)	(52.9)
Highest 25%	9	14	2	25
	(8.7)	(13.5)	(1.9)	(24.0)
Total	26	47	31	104
	(25.0)	(45.2)	(29.8)	(100)

Source: Data on EDUS: Sellgren (1987, 1989); Bennett & McCoshan (1993). *Note*: No. of TECs or LECs in each category (percentage in brackets out of 104) (Spearman rank correlation –0.27; $t = 2.84$; statistically significant at 99% level).

Table 5.5 Comparison by size of TEC/LEC budget with coverage by UPA Status.

Budget	UPAS				
	Most of area	Significant part of area	Minor part of area	No UPA	Total
Lowest 25%	3	2	2	17	24
	(2.9)	(1.9)	(1.9)	(16.3)	(23.1)
Middle 50%	10	13	4	28	55
	(9.6)	(12.5)	(3.8)	(26.9)	(52.9)
Highest 25%	8	7	4	6	25
	(7.7)	(16.7)	(3.8)	(5.8)	(24.0)
Total	21	22	10	51	104
	(20.2)	(21.2)	(9.6)	(49.0)	(100)

Note: Number of TECs or LECs in each category (percentage in brackets out of 104) (Spearman rank correlation –0.30; $t = 3.23$; statistically significant at 99% level).

Table 5.6 Comparison of size of TEC/LEC budget with level of development of Education–Business links in 1989–90.

Budget	EBPS			
	Level 3–4 and above	Level 3	Level 2 and 2–3	Total
Lowest 25%	–	6	18	24
		(5.8)	(17.3)	(23.1)
Middle 50%	4	24	27	55
	(3.8)	(23.1)	(26.0)	(52.9)
Highest 25%	2	17	6	25
	(1.9)	(16.3)	(5.8)	(24.0)
Total	6	47	51	104
	(5.8)	(45.2)	(49.0)	(100)

Source: Links data: CBI & Bennett (1992). *Note*: Number of TECs or LECs in each category (percentage in brackets out of 104) (Spearman rank correlation 0.35; $t = 3.75$; statistically significant at 99% level).

Table 5.7 Comparison by size of TEC/LEC budget with staying-on rate in education post-16.

Budget	Staying-on rate in education post-16				
	High	High/mixed	Low/mixed	Low	Total
Lowest 25%	12	2	7	3	24
	(11.5)	(1.9)	(6.7)	(12.9)	(23.1)
Middle 50%	13	7	17	18	55
	(12.5)	(6.7)	(16.3)	(17.3)	(52.9)
Highest 25%	5	5	7	8	25
	(4.8)	(4.8)	(16.7)	(7.7)	(24.0)
Total	30	14	31	29	104
	(28.8)	(13.5)	(29.8)	(27.9)	(100)

Source: Data: Bennett & McCoshan (1993: Figure 3.17), from DES and SO data. *Note*: No. of TECs or LECs in each category (percentage in brackets out of 104) (Spearman rank correlation 0.19; $t = 1.99$; statistically significant at 95% level).

government EDUs. This suggests that a pattern of gap filling may emerge in which, for the field of local economic development policy, TECs and LECs can take a new lead where local authorities have been reluctant to do so. Elsewhere mixed partnership solutions will be required (see Chapter 10).

- There is a close similarity of strengths in the field of education links and education staying-on rates. This suggests that TECs and LECs will generally have to work closely with existing EBP bodies, LEAs, schools and colleges in areas where they are strongest. But in areas where these bodies most need support or new leadership, TECs and LECs commonly will also be most stretched for resources (see Chapter 8).

Assessing success

This chapter has assessed how TEC and LECs have evolved as local institutions. The discussion has shown a number of impediments to future development:

- The bottom-up approach to defining boundaries has led to many small TECs and LECs emerging and many unusual and awkward fits with the economic geography of the community.
- Considerable complexity affects a number of TECs and LECs that cover a large number of local authority areas. This particularly affects London, and to a lesser extent all other metropolitan areas;
- There is a great range of contrasts between TEC/LEC areas in terms of size of budget, staff, population, unemployment, sector strengths, workforce and firm size. The result is a considerable variety of TEC/LEC areas and econo-mies: this should lead to a major range of variation in programmes and strategic approaches, but the extent of local flexibility will be determined by the flexibility of central guidelines.
- Because of the smallness of many TECs and LECs, as well as other factors, interfacing between them is required on a fairly extensive scale; but this rarely occurs in practice and there are disincentives to effective interfacing.
- The relations with other agents are complex locally. There are, we feel, only a few cases where TECs and LECs can realistically and genuinely expect to follow their mission of becoming the "key agents for change in their areas". In almost all areas, in one field of activity or another, it is essential that TECs and LECs develop effective relationships and partnerships with other agents. Failure to do so will result not only in a failure of TECs and LECs to achieve useful progress, it will also undermine other agents, resulting in a deteriora-tion in local economic capacity. This issue is most sensitive in the case of private sector agents since they have no alternative sources except their ca-pacity to trade and develop markets. TECs and LECs can undermine this through undercutting, crowding out or spoiling strategies. This danger par-ticularly affects: private sector trainers, private consultants, advice and in-formation agents, Chambers of Commerce, enterprise agents.

ASSESSING SUCCESS

This chapter forms a background to the next chapters in which we assess the success of TECs and LECs in different areas adapting their programmes in each field to the local requirements. In Chapter 6 we assess how far the relations between the Treasury, TEED and the SO and WO is capable of allowing effective local flexibility. In Chapters 7–10 we examine the local rôle of TECs and LECs in relation to other agents. In the case of *training* (Chapter 7), TECs and LECs are dominant players. Their policies as oligopolists are crucial to the quality of, and market for, publicly financed training. In the case of *education* (Chapter 8), TECs and LECs are minor players in a complex and confused field. Their rôle has not only to be one of partnership, but is likely to have to change radically as schools opt out, LEAs become less important agents, and the FE Funding Councils develop. In the case of *enterprise* (Chapter 9), TECs and LECs are important players, but only one of many with similar size and resources. Moreover the fit of TEC/LEC strength with the strength of other players is complex. This requires very sensitive development of their enterprise strategies: in different cases to be leaders, partners, or supporters. With respect to broader *local economic and community development* (Chapter 10) LECs are powerful bodies, but TECs are often minor players. Both, however, suffer from small resources in comparison with their different mission statements. Many TECs and LECs see their way forward in the fields of economic and community development policies through gaining greater resources. However, an effective rôle in local economic development depends less on resources than on the capacity of TECs and LECs to act as an effective partner with others. We assess in later chapters how far this is occurring.

Chapter 6

TECs, LECs and Government

The tension of institutional change

The foundation of TECs and LECs was argued at their launch to be primarily an institutional development, required to overcome what we have identified as the perverse policy syndrome through empowering new local leadership, emphasising business customer needs and using the leverage of public funds. Inevitably there are tensions created by such a reform. We examine in this chapter the overall success of the centrally-inspired sea change. Can the new local structure take up the challenge? What are the consequences for the implied loss of power at the centre? How have TECs and LECs been able to reconcile their mission's demand for autonomy and a market lead with the requirements of working with government and maintaining public accountability? It is these areas in which most tension has been evident, where TEC and LEC Directors have felt trammelled and misled, and where future reform needs to be focused.

Tensions are inevitable in any attempt at institutional change. These are the tensions between attempting to *lead* change, and seeking to *develop* a self-sustaining local base. We look in turn at seven aspects of this tension:

- The process of institutional reform;
- The attempts of the former Manpower Services Commission (MSC) to institute change;
- The central–local structure for TECs;
- The central–local structure for LECs;
- The budget allocation process;
- Public accountability;
- Continuing reform since 1993.

The process of institutional reform

TECs and LECs have not been alone in their attempt to exert new leadership at a local level. The 1980s in Britain have seen a wide range of other initiatives to empower local business-led organizations as a process of seeking to develop change. Other important cases have been the Urban Development Corporations

(UDCs), the development of Funding Councils for higher, further and school education, and the introduction of budget-holders and local trusts for health and hospital administration. These reforms have all had the common objective of developing a new business leadership, injecting and/or improving managerial efficiency in public administrative systems. Davies and Powell (1993) (Davies being the Director-General of the CBI since 1992) has highlighted, with others, the fact that the stimulus to greater decentralization to self-governing units for schools, colleges, GPs or hospitals has, paradoxically, required greater central control. This has led to the concept of a "tight–loose" structure dominating many reforms:[1] tight central control of standards and financial procedures, loose and decentralized power to local units.

New institutions can be created in a variety of ways. The TECs and LECs are fundamentally local institutions intended to be "loose" in terms of powers, but created and maintained by a "tight" centralised process. The central creation of local entities can proceed by a variety of routes. The analysis of these routes has not moved far beyond Selznick's assessment over 40 years ago (1949). He suggested that there were two dimensions of institutional development:

1. The balance between co-option and recruitment

Co-option allows the working together of local and central bodies in a form of partnership. The central body seeks to use local agents to host or manage programmes, it entrusts or empowers them. *Recruitment* uses central norms to guide specific local agents. The central body defines and works to a model to which local agents are recruited to run central programmes, albeit with limited local discretion.

2. The content of relationship

Formal relationships require sharing of executive, administrative and financial functions but with power concentrated at the centre. The central body exerts detailed control through its contracts down to the level of programme delivery. Financially this means a very specific contract relation with detailed performance targets, earmarking and "specific grants".

Informal relationships require accommodation between local and central sources of power. The central body allows "hands-off" local decisions at executive and programme delivery levels. Financially this means a broad contracting relation or "block grant". In terms of strategic management informal relations are required if local "empowerment" is to be achieved.

The relation between these two dimensions allows a variety of formal/informal and co-opted/recruited structures between central and local agents. The reference to Selznick's (1949) line of thought is particularly relevant to TECs and LECs, since there is considerable evidence in the guidance materials produced by DE of the influence of the American thinking inspired by the Tennessee Valley Authority (TVA), and similar more recent US federal government attempts to stimulate local development, particularly the PICs. The prime source of this direct influence became Cay Stratton (1989 and in BiTC 1989), formerly Director of the Boston PIC, who has been retained as the full-time advisor to the successive Employment Secretaries of State, Norman Fowler, Michael Howard and Gillian Shephard (see Bennett 1993c).

In Selznick's models the most autonomous structure is *informal co-option*: local decision makers act as hosts within a loose framework of monitoring and central accountability. This was the structure of Local Employer Networks (LENs) which were a small-scale attempt in the period 1986/89 to use local agents to develop local training plans. LENs were one of the most poorly funded of all MSC initiatives and were assessed as unsatisfactory by the MSC because they were patchy (depending on the strength of local hosts). If they were effective they involved a loss of central control over what happened. They relied on trusting local hosts which the MSC, believing in a British "system failure", was ultimately not prepared to give.

Informal recruitment offers local autonomy to a newly-recruited local body. Arguably it is this model which is *empowering* in nature. The individuals are new and they are given autonomy over their strategy. This was what the Directors of TECs and LECs *believed* they were being drawn into, given the launch emphasis on "putting business in the driving seat" with control over the allocation of a general budget with few strings attached.

Formal recruitment was the structure that TECs and LECs *actually inherited*. The central bodies of TEED, and to a lesser extent SE and HIE, exert control down to the programme level, through the TECs and LECs, to their subcontractors. Public accountability does not stop at the TEC/LEC level, but also goes right down to subcontractor level. Funds are largely "specific grants" for programmes since only 5% virement between programmes has been allowed. Formal recruitment was also the model for the pre-existing Local Area Manpower Boards (LAMBs). Although TECs and LECs have clearly gained a level of discretion over funds and greater strategic control, they still fit into the same broad category as the LAMBs. The rôle of Industrial Training Boards (ITBs) from 1973 to 1981 also followed a form of formal recruitment. They became "advisers charging a fee for services"[2] co-ordinated and part-funded by the MSC.

The fourth category, of *formal co-option* has been used in the British labour market field in a number of ways. The development of Non-Statutory Training Organizations (NSTOs) in the period following the 1981 Employment and Training Act is one key example. The NSTOs were initially largely based on ITBs whose statutory functions had been abolished, but later came to be widened to Chambers of Commerce, FE colleges, and group training associations through the mechanism of "managing agents" that followed the MSC's 1981 launch of the New Training Initiative. Other key examples were those of Compacts, which set specific goals for school leavers and which were managed by local employer lead bodies in conjunction with schools and LEAs.

The tensions which these approaches each address is how to achieve a centralized goal of change with a local implementation and delivery system. Formal models maintain central control, informal models truly empower the local level. Co-option is used where a suitable local agency exists, recruitment is needed where there is no suitable base to build on. With the exception of the weak LENs and the later form of ITBs, why has the informal route to true local empowerment been so little followed? There appear to be three chief factors.

First, and most obvious, the informal model challenges the power at the centre. Once a centralized body exists it is difficult to overcome the bureaucratic mechanisms of self-defence. With TECs and LECs there was the formidable power of the old MSC to overcome, which at its peak in the 1970s had been employing 22,000 people. Until 1989 the MSC/TA in Sheffield also directly administered programmes in Scotland. The MSC had a strong culture of independence. As an administrative agency it had been able to operate largely at arms' length of government. The culture it developed became "initiative-driven", parcelling out money to lever local change. It was accustomed to rapid change and extensive executive control. Rapid change itself maintained power to the centre by continually resetting local goals, allowing the MSC to maintain and switch control over contractors virtually arbitrarily. In the words of an employer "change has been a dominant characteristic of my working environment, but I question whether it would have been adequate preparation for employment by the MSC".[3] Or in the words of a trade union leader "dealing with the MSC has been like chasing some supernatural animal lifted straight out of Celtic mythology. No sooner do you get hold on one leg than it is shed, and two others are grown in its place".[4] Even Geoffrey Holland, Director-General of the MSC from 1981 to 1986 and then DE permanent Secretary until early 1993 admitted that "we have an unnerving tendency to dig up tender plants, and lots of the building blocks are very new and very tender indeed".[5] One independent researcher has likened the MSC in Moorfoot to:

> a kind of menagerie where every room you enter, every corner your turn, opens up a new group of individuals labouring to create a new initiative to sell to the MSC management who in turn could sell it to ministers. All this undertaken quite independently of the consequences for the local agents who would first be recruited and then subsequently dropped when the money ran out and a new initiative was invented.[6]

Not only did the central bureaucracy of the MSC gain from resistance to local empowerment; a second feature is that government also benefited from centralization. Secretaries of State at Westminster, Edinburgh or Cardiff and all leading politicians like to feel in control, to be able to claim personal and party successes from policies, and are also accountable for their programmes (politically accountable to parliament and financially accountable to the Comptroller and Auditor General (CAG) and to the Treasury). True local empowerment thus has the formidable barriers of the central "constitutional" and ministerial ambition to overcome.

A third factor limiting the implementation of informal models and local empowerment has been the problems of the "perverse policy syndrome" (see Chapter 2). To the extent that it is the failure of systems of institutions and incentives that are preventing change, then giving trust to these institutions at the local level runs the risk that nothing will improve. Many analyses of organizational change and the rôle of the MSC have demonstrated how effective resistance to change can be.[7] The failure to change behaviour can usually be explained by the effect of one or more of four factors:

- There are *collective benefits of stability* which derive from distaste for change and uncertainty, and the strategic advantages of defenders of existing institutions;
- There is *calculated opposition to change* which seeks to maintain prevailing advantage (perceived or real), protects existing "quality", and resists the costs of adjusting mental attitudes;
- There is *inability to change* because of "mental blinkers" such as programmed training systems, fragmentation of decision making, and perverse incentives deriving from historical precursors; and
- There are *system obstacles* arising from resource limits, accumulated constraints deriving from fragmented regulations, and limitations due to inter-organizational agreements.

The result is that change is often inhibited by divisions of power between the top and bottom, or central and local levels. The capacity to block unwanted action usually increases the longer an organization exists without major change. This suggests two implications. First, if there are no major changes to an organization, power inevitably gravitates downwards. Second, the number of tiers of administration tends inexorably to increase.

The dilemma of developing change in the massive and complex organization of a society the size of Britain is that, without giving out local power, nothing will really change. The commentary on all the energetic years of the MSC's activities tends to support this view that nothing has changed. In the case of training one leading employer doubts whether "many more craftsmen or technicians are now employed in the engineering industry as a result of YTS".[8]

We turn below to assessment of the MSC and why it failed to achieve lasting change. Understanding the failure of the MSC leads us to an assessment of the chances of success of the system of TECs and LECs.

The MSC's attempts to institute change

The MSC was formed in 1973 to oversee the former Employment Service and Training Skills Agency. The structure is shown in Figure 6.1. A tripartite Commission at national level developed in 1975/76 a network of 125 local District Manpower Committees (DMCs), 15 of which were in Scotland. In 1983 these were nationalised into Local Area Manpower Boards (LAMBs). There were 58

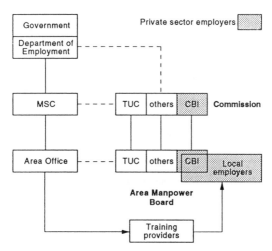

Figure 6.1   The organizational structure of Area Manpower
Boards and the MSC.   (After Bartlett 1989.)

of these, nine of which were in Scotland. Each LAMB was supported by a local
Area Office which contained the field delivery of MSC services and was run
exclusively as part of the civil service. There were 57 Area Offices, eight of
which were in Scotland, one office for Argyll serving two LAMBs.

The LAMBs were the first serious attempt in Britain to constitute a locally-led
delivery system. But they were relatively weak entities. Their main rôle was,
like the former DMCs, to comment on contracts between the delivery of the new
training products of YTS and the Community Programme developed following
the new Training Initiative launched in 1981. They also had a more ambitious
objective of becoming "planning bodies covering the whole spectrum of local
training needs and provision". However the participation was "generally token
and LAMBs were essentially there to implement MSC policy".[9] In effect MSC
Sheffield developed the programmes, the Area Office negotiated the contracts
for local delivery, and the LAMB approved the local projects. But where there
was conflict between a LAMB and MSC headquarters the MSC almost invariably
overruled the local Boards.[10] The system was thus strongly centralized both in
England and Wales, and in Scotland. Any pressures from the LAMBs to obtain
stronger executive powers were firmly rejected by the Chair of the MSC because
"gains would be marginal".[11]

The constitution of the LAMBs themselves also occasioned criticism. Each
LAMB had five employer representatives, five trade union representatives, and
further representatives of local authorities, the education service, voluntary or-

ganizations, co-option of non-voting members, representatives of interested parties (often HMI) and a right of attendance for Principal Careers Officers. The Boards were encouraged to develop substructures to widen the involvement of interested parties. In some cases these structures were quite extensive, particularly in the education sector.[12] Employers tended to see the LAMBs as a "talking shop dominated by educationalists and vested interests". Although they frequently felt that something was gained by "firm talking and exchange of positions . . . no significant influence"[13] or change could be discerned as a result of the commitment of their time. Similar views were expressed by the trade unions, although they greatly appreciated the fact that they were involved and received a lot of information. Information diffusion was also one of the benefits most valued by LEAs.[14] However, a senior TEED view was that they were "an expensive failure".[15] Others have argued that the LAMBs were "swamped with paperwork" and "distracted by continual changes in the operation of MSC schemes".[16]

The LAMBs seemed to be accepted as a failure almost as soon as they were established and it is surprising that a reforming Conservative government held back in 1981 from more radical reform. The maintenance of tripartism and the lack of employer control are all strong contrasts to the setting up of the UDCs, which began in 1981. The explanation is probably to be found in a continuing government uncertainty in the early 1980s about which way their education and training policy should go. Although the 1981 New Training Initiative established the goals that were to be sought of 16–19 and adult training – and these have not substantially changed since – there was in the early 1980s no clarity about the mechanisms by which the goals were to be achieved.

The resulting lacuna was filled by the development of the MSC's own conceptions. Two significant reports appeared in 1984 and 1985: *Competence and Competition* and *A Challenge to Complacency* (NEDO/MSC 1984; MSC 1985). These chronicled Britain's training malaise compared to the USA, Germany and Japan and suggested that government interventions through ITBs and FE colleges was simply reinforcing the tendency for employers to believe that training was someone else's responsibility. The reports mark a turning point because they identified the need to simplify the training system, remove the "alphabet soup", institute a single system of qualifications, and develop a market for training in which individuals and businesses each responded to incentives to invest in the training that is needed. Subsequently the three original objectives for the 1981 New Training Initiative (standards of youth qualifications, all young people in training or education, and upgrading of adult skilling) have been built into the system of NVQs/SVQs, the National Education and Training Targets (NETT) and training credits system, discussed in Chapter 7. But the choice of agents to institute change was left unresolved until the establishment of TECs and LECs.

The reform of the MSC was particularly difficult because it was in the vanguard of government responses to rising unemployment, in which the MSC executive acted as government agent in contracting for YTS and other training schemes, with decreasing attention paid to the concerns of the Commission's corporatist partners. A tension therefore developed between the formal status of the MSC as a corporatist body and its actual practice, which was as a largely autonomous agency. This would sooner or later require restructuring if its brief and activities were to be brought together. The abolition of the MSC in 1988 and its rebirth, called successively the Training Commission (TC), and then Training Agency (TA), partially addressed this need. But the problem remained that, as a public sector agency, it was driving the system of training and vocational education provision from the supply side. From 1988 there was no direct central employer input at all. The effect of this structure was to create a disjuncture between employers' requirements and public training provision. This disjuncture was particularly strong at the local level since most training was funded through national programmes, with no means of meeting local needs. This problem was exacerbated by (i) a system of college provision led by the education service under a separate department, with a different set of objectives, dominated by adherence to traditional norms of the academic year and course structures, (ii) a chronic failure on all sides to gather and articulate sound data on employers' skill needs, and (iii) a confusion between the aims of the national training programmes as to whether they should primarily be driven by the skills needs of businesses or government's need to manage unemployment.

The Conservative government in the later 1980s and early 1990s can be seen as torn between its long-term agenda of decentralizing power to individuals and firms, and the available structure of agencies whereby most existing provision was still administered through LEAs and the MSC. The long-term agenda for public sector reform of FE, HE and schools was already clear in the minds of key politicians, civil servants and the CBI at least as early as 1987. This was to decentralize power to self-governing schools, colleges, former polytechnics and universities with central funding councils distributing resources. But none of these new institutions was in place. Thus the reform of the training system had to find a different solution. The TECs and LECs were that solution. But they have had to wrestle with the dying phase of a previous system inherited from the MSC.

The central–local structure for TECs

The relation of TECs to central bodies is based on a formal contract of the TECs with government, on the one hand, and formal contracts of the TECs with providers on the other hand. The TECs are overseen by the regional branches of TEED but there is no counterpart of SE or HIE. Since 1992/93 the WO has taken oversight of Welsh TECs. Thus the TECs were in practice designed to follow a formal recruitment model and differed little from MSC Area Offices. Central norms, performance targets and contracts are the key guides to local agents. In practice the relations have proved "tight" down to the level of programme performance, with control of unit costs in contract negotiations between TECs and TEED. Practice differed from the understanding at the outset of a "tight-loose" relationship in which performance was to be measured by the achievement of measurable outputs rather than by attempting detailed control of processes.

The setting up of TECs was led strongly by TEED in conjunction with the National Training Task Force (NTTF). The NTTF were used by the government as a quality control on TEC bids – a control which was little exercised in practice, as we have seen in Chapters 4 and 5, except with respect to the criteria for status of Directors. After TECs were established the NTTF maintained an advisory rôle with government until the end of 1992. An attempt was made to maintain the NTTF in a rôle of (i) assessing TEC performance, (ii) advising the DE and Secretary of State, (iii) convening groups to address long-term developments, (iv) helping the development of IIP, and (v) R&D. This was to be covered by three NTTF groups for IIP, R&D and TECs.[17] Some initial reports were prepared on education and local economic development. Government wanted to see the NTTF as the conclusion of its transition from the TC and MSC in a rôle "to advise government on national and strategic issues related to training, vocational education and enterprise development, and on the development of TECs" (DE 1992a: para 1.5). But the NTTF became unsustainable now that TECs controlled most local actions and TEED contained all the practical staff expertise. The NTTF was wound up in October 1992.

Government was forced to turn increasingly to the TECs themselves rather than NTTF from the middle of 1991 onwards. This was where the chief business leadership and knowledge lay, and where the dynamic for further reform of TEED and its programmes could be levered. Government wanted the TECs to constitute a representative body with which government could enter into dialogue. Initially this was G10, a grouping of Chairs of TECs and LECs each of whom was nominated as the representative of one of the 10 regions (Scotland included). The DE sought to use this as a single body which it could talk to in order to disseminate information to each TEC and LEC and to get representative views back.

The split purposes of G10, as independent representative of the TECs and as sounding board for government, led to increasing tensions through 1991 and 1992. The original membership of G10 was carefully chosen by TEED and invited to join by the Secretary of State. The original group contained many who had been on the inside of TEC development from early in 1988. The early view was well summarised by Eric Dancer, the first Chair of G10: "there is a clear need for a body which can represent the TEC movement as a whole . . . to provide a forum for representing a cohesive view on matters of common interest". The same view of the centrality of G10 was echoed by the subsequent G10 Chair, Edward Roberts "G10 will play a significant rôle in representing the views of the TEC movement . . . and in bringing forward initiatives and recommendations".[18]

This self-claimed representative rôle of G10 was deeply resented in many TECs. One of the more flamboyant comments, from a London TEC Chair (42), sums up the feelings of many: "They are taking away the things which we all joined TECs to do", "it is not acceptable", as G10 informed the 1992 TECs Conference, that "with your agreement, we will tell the minister"'. The G10 group was perceived as being run by the DE: "they are a bunch of self-appointed people working to a rule-less regime. There is no constitution for G10. No-one knows how its Chair is appointed. There are no elections. These Herberts then go to the Minister and talk on behalf of me, and I do not know what they are saying". The early meetings of G10 certainly had crowded agendas, prioritised by the DE "to legitimise what they had decided already".[19] Judith Donovan, for a time G10 member for Yorkshire and Humberside region, and Chair of Bradford TEC, resigned from G10 calling it "a cosy male dominated talking shop which had been far less effective than it should have been in dealing with government".[20] Another TEC Chair (93) described his G10 meetings as "controlled by Caxton House. It is like the scribes and pharisees. Entry to G10 is controlled so as to keep the supplicants at arm's length. It is a patronage system organised to keep the civil servants in business". A Yorkshire and Humberside TEC Chair (32) felt that Eric Dancer, the first G10 Chair, "had been used as a DE stooge who only realised too late that he was being controlled by the civil servants".

After an often vitriolic debate between the TECs and DE during 1991 and 1992, the structure of G10 was reconstituted in April 1992 as a TEC-owned body. The restructuring of G10 itself was a *cause célèbre*. A small Secretariat for G10 was established early in 1992 which initially sought to take more power to itself as a representative body. Its first design showed the Secretariat mediating all relations between TECs and outside bodies (see Figure 6.2). This was unacceptable to TEC Chairs. Many felt that the new Secretariat "was getting out of control" (e.g. TEC Chair 93). The form of G10 National Council operating since April 1992 shows the Secretariat chiefly servicing inter-TEC groups on

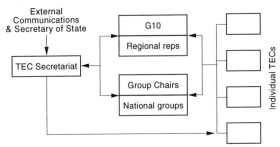

Figure 6.2 The TEC Secretariat view of how TEC–G10 relations should develop. *Source*: G10 (24 March 1992).

different issues ("groups") with the G10 Chairs and representatives doing the direct talking with government (Figure 6.3). The constitution of G10 was changed following a decision at the July 1993 TECs conference to a National Council with part time Executive Chairman. But many uncertainties remain. Different regions apply different approaches to finding their representative Chairs (most appear to allow the existing G10 representative to nominate the successor), and the relation of G10 to government remains unclear.

We take further the discussion of these developments at the end of this chapter where we assess the TEED structure. At this stage we highlight the key issues identified so far:

– The TECs have not developed the autonomy and flexibility they were promised. Their Directors have been and continue to be systematically misled by a mission statement in conflict with reality.
– The structure of NTTF and G10 has effectively suppressed criticism and allowed the DE/TEED to maintain maximum control.
– There was considerable continuity of thought process from the MSC/TA into the approach adopted by DE/TEED. Initiative-driven, programmatic budgets with low levels of virement and with control down to the subcontractor level have been the order of the day.

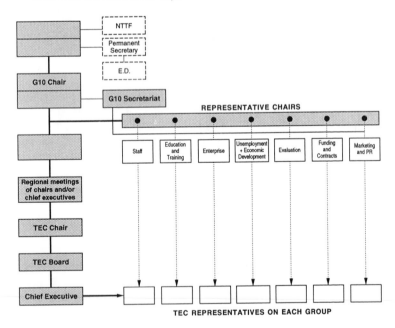

Figure 6.3 The agreed structure for G10-TEC relations since 1992, that also governs the TEC National Council since September 1993. *Source*: G10, April 1992.

The contrasts between the TECs' view of themselves and that of TEED are clearly evident in the diametrically opposite views depicted in Figures 6.4, 6.5 and 6.6, derived from TEED and TEC sources.

Figure 6.4 depicts the TEED conception, involving strong central control, exercised by itself, with the TECs being regarded as a weak periphery – "out there". TEED plays hub to the system's "wheel", providing the driving force through the "spokes" of its regional offices. This is a *formal recruitment* model.

The TEED view shows the TEC system as a slightly modified continuation of the pre-existing TA arrangement, with TECs fulfilling essentially the same rôle as did the former Area Offices, which indeed they directly replaced, often with most of the same staff and frequently in the same premises. The relationship between TEED, the regional offices and the TECs is hierarchical, with TECs following a central lead through a system imitating line management. In this view G10, the TECs' national body of regionally representative chairs, now

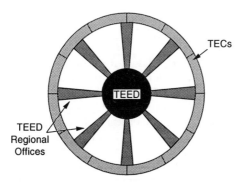

Figure 6.4   The TEED view of TEED–TEC relations as illustrated by Marquand & Murphy (1990).

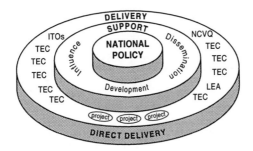

Figure 6.5   The relation between TECs and TEED as envisaged in the DE (1992a: 8). This has subsequently formed the structure for TEC–government relations since 1993. –

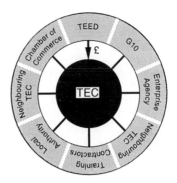

Figure 6.6 The TEC's views of TEED–LEC relations derived from interview comments.

called the TECs National Council, fulfils an advisory rôle to TEED and the Minister, complemented by the former NTTF. The whole structure represents a single system in which responsibility has been devolved without an equivalent decentralization of power.

The centralized view of the TECs at the periphery is echoed even in the Styles Report (DE 1992a), which has led to some restructuring of TEED since 1993. This represented the TECs as just one rather extensive set of agencies, amongst others, with which TEED had to deal. Figure 6.5 shows the Styles Report view, which places the government at the centre, an advisory ring of non-contractors who act as partners with government (chiefly the employer bodies of CBI, ABCC, NCVQ, and EC), and an external ring which are the contractors for carrying forward policy (the TECs, enterprise agencies, NCVO, and sector ITOs). The rôle of the advisory ring has subsequently been the focus for discussions of possible establishment of a TECs Funding Council.

The TECs' conception of themselves is quite different from these centralized views. They have seen themselves not as mere branches of a parent organization, but as free-standing companies with independence, commercial Boards and Memoranda and Articles of Association and policies of their own (shown in Figure 6.6). Their conception is closer to the *informal recruitment* model suggested in the original TECs Prospectus (1989).

In their view the TECs and G10 are an independent system, which operates at national and local levels and contracts with a central bureaucracy, treating TEED as a separate system rather than as a parent body. Though their contracts are individual, all TECs stand together on the same side of a contractual divide, and sponsor G10 to operate in their joint interests. The relationships between the TEC system and the Employment Department are perceived as akin to the relationships between individual TECs and their subcontractors – formalized, subject to scrutiny and review, but voluntary and open to negotiation and locally-inspired change.

The TECs had every reason to believe that their conception of their mission was the correct one. Not only the rhetoric, but their mission statement was drawn to suggest this. The TECs Prospectus (1989: 4) stated quite clearly that "Planning and management of enterprise and training need to shift from the public to the private sector". But the reality of a public expenditure programme was never likely to allow TECs strong control. In the event, as we shall see, the combined influence of TEED's vested interest to retain control, of the Treasury's concern to control the public accounts audit trail, and of the political/ economic pressure to reduce expenditure while maintaining unemployment support, has inevitably led to the formal recruitment model dominating over the TEC conception that they had been entrained to run a relationship based on a partnership of centre and locality.

The central–local structure for LECs

the relation of SE and HIE with Scotland's LECs differs significantly from the situation in England and Wales. SE and HIE were set up in Scotland as a result of the success of the former Scottish Development Agency (SDA) and the Highlands and Islands Development Board (HIDB). These bodies have acted as important intermediaries between LECs and governments and this has allowed the separation of aggregate resource allocation and distribution, which in TEED/G10 negotiations have been mixed together. There is also a stronger tradition in Scotland of working in partnership and there is much less development of "the TEED disease of saying you are inventing something new" (comment by Scottish Office senior spokesperson). Thus the central management of LECs was able to build on existing experience.

The SDA's brief involved the development of the Scottish economy, and the improvement of its physical environment. Its activities included rehabilitation of land, the provision and improvement of industrial property, and integrated projects with a physical dimension, but it had no major rôle in business development or training. The MSC in Sheffield managed the Scottish training system. It operated through a regional structure, centrally administered from its Glasgow headquarters, where more strategic, Scotland-wide activities were conducted. The HIDB's remit was to promote the economic and social development of the Highlands and Islands region. Its principal aim was to stimulate the depressed economies of the remote and sparsely-populated regions of the country, and to help alleviate social hardship through community development projects.

Replacing and reflecting these institutions, the LEC-based structure involved responsibility being devolved by the SO to SE and HIE. While they are accountable to the Secretary of State, the SO has taken a more hands-off approach regarding day-to-day affairs than TEED. In the words of one LEC chief executive (57), "SE has helped the Scottish Office by being a buffer so that it does not have to see everything".

The development of LECs involved a redistribution of some former SDA powers to HIE (such as international promotion) and the addition of a business development brief to SE such that both the new organizations have become fully responsible for policy in their geographical areas. Neither have any jurisdiction in each other's territory, unlike the previous situation in which the SDA had a brief covering the whole country, with HIDB concentrating upon its own area. The statutory position following restructuring is that SE may exercise its powers in the Highlands and Islands only at the invitation of HIE, or at the direction of the Secretary of State after consultation with both bodies.

The LECs themselves, like the TECs, are not statutory. Although SE and HIE are required to subcontract powers to the local bodies, this is handled in the form of a contract with each LEC which must be regularly renewed. The administrative link from government to locality sees the LECs account to SE or HIE, which in turn account to the SO, and the SO to the Treasury. The NAO cannot scrutinize the accounts of LECs directly, only SE and HIE. All civil service employees are employees of HIE and SE, not of the LECs. The DE is only involved, through the SO, principally in overseeing the major national training programmes. Perhaps the key aspect of the development of the LECs was that, for the first time, they drew the old TA programmes together with other economic development programmes. The LECs were the force for local integration, whereas the SO took over the old rôle of the Sheffield MSC.

As with TECs, the financial relationship between the central bodies and the LECs is somewhat stricter than the early proposals suggested: SE and HIE dispense money to the LECs and authorise how they spend it. There are strict guidelines as to the levels of spending permitted in each area, which is closely scrutinised by the SO, and the Treasury. For LEC Board members, like their TEC counterparts and for essentially the same reasons, early expectations of extensive budgetary discretion have been frustrated in practice. Linked to this is the more specifically Scottish issue of the balance of powers and responsibilities between centre and locality in each network. The precise division of responsibilities was left open by the 1988 White Paper (Industry Department Scotland 1988: 13):

A balance will have to be struck between local and central powers which enables the retention of present strengths as well as the desired improvement of local delivery. The government have not yet come to a conclusion as to where the balance should lie.

A subsequent statement made by the Secretary of State for Scotland, in July 1989, indicated a government intention that there should be a balance between "local discretion" and "strong national coherence", though again the interpretation of this as a specific policy was left to the discretion of SE and HIE. Both organizations were originally envisaged by the SO as enablers, supportive of an independent set of local companies, and a conduit for their funding. In practice, the extent to which powers have been devolved in each network has disappointed many LEC Board members, even though it is much stronger than for TECs.

A high degree of continuity exists between the old and new structures in Scotland. Despite LECs having been promoted as a quite new initiative, the policies and responsibilities are very often being developed by the same functionaries as before. This may be considered a strength or a weakness, but many commentators have viewed this as a potential impediment to achieving significant change. An effect which has certainly followed is that much control over policy has been retained at the centre, resulting in a contrast between the perceptions of LECs and SE/HIE as to the proper balance of powers within the system. As with the TECs, LEC Directors believe they should be entrusted with more powers than the central bureaucrats seem prepared to allow them.

There are important contrasts between SE and HIE. The SE LECs are larger and, although still carefully overseen by SE as well as guided firmly by the SO, and to some extent by TEED on training matters, are rather more autonomous than LECs under the jurisdiction of HIE, which takes a more interventionist rôle in their affairs and has retained considerable powers at the centre. In HIE, there has been a bias towards the shedding of the administrative burden of the smaller schemes at the centre, while retaining the significant projects which require less administrative labour per unit expenditure. This has reinforced the impression of devolution of responsibility without equivalent power. The way HIE views itself reflects this centralised approach. Its literature describes a "network", in which the LECs are depicted as "branches" on the HIE "tree", or "doors" through which clients may access the network. The logos for HIE LECs display a unified branding which was imposed upon individual LECs, and their documents carry the message of HIE much more prominently than that of the individual LEC Boards. Part of the reason is that HIE LECs, particularly those in the Islands, are very small and the pool of expertise from which their directors is drawn is limited. This initially raises doubts about the adequacy of their experience. Also to be borne in mind is the dominant rôle HIDB had played in the region for 25 years, a rôle it was reluctant to hand over. HIDB initially sought the establishment of a single, Highland and Island-wide LEC covering its existing area, but the central policy for decentralization, and local enthusiasm for taking up the reins, demanded a subdivision within the Highlands and Islands. HIDB's preferred solution was to limit change and retain for itself de facto much of the budget and staff that it had previously held as de jure responsibilities. Since 1992/93 further decentralization has occurred.

Despite the continuing centralised rôle of HIE and SE, Scotland's LECs have undoubtedly benefited from a looser central oversight than in England and Wales. This oversight has also been characterised by a greater sense of partnership in which a strategic approach is developed. However, in Scotland there is a tension similar to that evident in England and Wales, between Board members keen to exert local autonomy who feel limited by overseeing agencies which have been keen to retain centralized control. In other words, there is a local desire for an *informal recruitment* model instead of the *formal recruitment* pursued by the centre. Whereas there are strong arguments in favour of HIE, in particular, retaining a greater degree of central influence, it is notable that these developments contradict both the initial expectations of LEC board members and the stated policy of central government.

An important debate developed in 1992 which envisaged the introduction of a body like SE for England and Wales to replace or work with TEED. So far no change in this direction has developed or is likely, but we comment further on this debate further below and in Chapters 11 and 12.

The budget allocation process

The budgeting process for TECs and LECs is part of the complex Public Expenditure Survey (PES) round that all publicly-funded agents have in their negotiations with government. The resulting uncertainties and associated methodology immediately brought home to Directors that they were not dealing with the "entrepreneurial" and "enterprising" organization they had been led to expect. It was judged by some as a suitable christening to becoming managers of a quango and the culture of dealing with government. In particular, cuts in the total budget for TECs and LECs in the launch phase, as a result of public expenditure restraint, and threatened cuts each year created an air of uncertainty.

The general budget discussion for TECs and LECs got off to a bad start. After the announcement of outline funding levels for the whole system and draft totals for each TEC and LEC, each year's allocation has seen threatened cuts in funding. In the sensitive set-up phase for the 1991/92 budget the threats were extreme, starting with a threatened 30% cut in total funds, later revised to 20% and eventually being about 13%. This undermined the text of empowerment from the outset. John Banham, then Director-General of the CBI, wrote in 1992 that

any TEC chairman operating in the real world of conflicting demands, finite resources and hard decisions is going to find life less than Utopian . . . [but] . . . penny pinching or death by a thousand cuts by government in the funding of TECs just will not do . . . TECs Board members' standing in the community is likely to be considerably damaged.[21]

The funding level, and its certainty, is thus a critical issue underpinning the credibility of the TEC/LEC mission to empower business leaders.

Further difficulties affect the allocation of funds within the TECs and LECs. The PES allocation is made by main programme area. Up to 1992/93 this was translated into funding blocks for TECs and LECs. A major limitation on the TEC/LEC mission has been the restrictions on virement between blocks. Up to 1992/93 only 5% of funds could be moved from one block to another. Since 1993/94 virement has been eliminated altogether except between IIP and business start-ups. Instead a method of Output-Related Funding (ORF, see below) has been instituted which ties expenditure to targets in each programme area. John Banham (1992: 8) called for an increase in the flexibility of funds to satisfy the mission so that Boards could "decide their priorities just as they would do in their business life. This requires that TEC funds should come in the form of a single block". Since 1993/94 the funds have been in a single block, but the ORF targets allow the Treasury to exert a continual control on TEC/LEC Board decisions.

A further implication of the funding regime is that increases in budget, and the restrictions on virement, closely derive from the origin of the funds as satisfying the Employment Department's responsibility to run unemployment programmes. Just as the MSC was trammelled by this political priority, so have TECs and LECs been. Just as YTS and then YT became unemployment relief programmes from which trainees migrated as soon as they had a job, so TEC/LEC training has again filled the Department's needs to ameliorate unemployment. In 1993/94 this has been focused through the new "Community Action" and "Workstart" programme, announced in the 1993 Budget, and run jointly between DE and TECs and LECs. The tying of the funding regime to the parliamentary commitment to the unemployed has, therefore, been a further fundamental conflict with the mission statement of enhancing skills of the employed workforce.

Nowhere is this more evident than in recognising the shift in philosophy that occurred from the launch to the main operational phase after 1991. The *Financial Times* headlined the change as "Conceived in good times, born in bad" (2 April 1991). The 1988 White Papers talked of the demographic downturn and skill shortages. The period of implementation in 1991/94 has covered a time of unprecedented labour surplus of *skilled* people, both as a result not only of recession, but also of structural changes in employment created by new technology and the "peace dividend". In London and the South East, in particular, highly skilled people with craft, engineering and management skills were readily available; no skills revolution was required. TECs and LECs have thus been thrust back to the old MSC staple of training the unemployed which, although an important issue, has undermined the commitment which Boards signed up for.

Once the total budgets are allocated, the distribution between TECs and LECs first occurs at regional level. In Scotland this is between the SE and HIE networks and closely follows historical levels in the two systems. In England and Wales the chief funding, which is for YT, ET and enterprise, has been by formula based on a 80/20 rule: 80% of the budget is historically determined and 20% is based on a formula. In the formula, local unemployment totals, size of the resident population, and the number of VAT registered businesses are the chief determinants.

The formula is used only for allocation between regions. It has led to three main problems. First, where the relative concentrations of unemployment have changed very rapidly since TECs and LECs were established, some anomalies have appeared. The South East and London, in particular, gained after a one-year lag some of the additional resources they needed for their rapid growth in unemployment in 1991 and 1992. Second, the use of historical funding traps those TECs where local training provision has been poor and hence historical funding levels low. This is a special problem for inner London where it has been estimated that the 9 TECs were collectively underfunded by £48m in 1991/ 92.[22] A third problem of the formula is its emphasis on the supply side of the labour market which reinforces the unemployment focus. TECs were supposed to focus on employer demand which would require the working, not resident, population to be given a higher weight. The emphasis creates a poor psychology, since it conflicts with the TEC mission statement. It also penalises a region with a high degree of commuting. This affects London which is a large net recipient of workers from the South East.

Once the regional budgets are fixed, the allocation to individual TECs is determined by TEC regional offices or SE/HIE in negotiation with the LECs. The power and direction of the regional offices increased significantly after the launch phase of TECs. In general the regional offices, SE or HIE have sought to reward efficient TECs in terms of their presumed output. But they have also sought to protect small TECs and LECs. There has been a significant swing of resources in some regions to support the higher management costs of smaller TECs and LECs. This is mainly registered in their Block 5 management fee. In the set-up phase this was particularly important. For example, in the Northern region, the small Northumberland TEC has gained 20% more than its original planned budget, mainly in 1991/92 at the expense of Tyneside and Teesside. In Scotland, SE gave greater protection from the 1991/92 spending cuts to their smallest LECs of Borders and Dumfries, mainly at the expense of Glasgow, Lanark and Tayside. And in the London region, AZTEC and North West London TECs have been benefited mainly at the expense of the larger of the seven other TECs. As time has progressed the scope for regional office arbitrary discretion has been reduced by the emphasis on ORF (see below). This is likely to affect adversely the smaller TECs in the future.

Allocations to TECs and LECs are made one year at a time. Since 1993/94 there has been an improvement in England in that a minimum level of funding for programmes has been set 3 years ahead and the Operating Agreement between TECs and the Secretary of State has become "evergreen" – it continues until terminated by either party. However, the advantages of this development are minimal since prices, specifications and volumes are renegotiated annually. Thus the TECs are still set in an annual budget framework.

Each annual negotiation is unique and has usually been shrouded in secrecy until all TECs or LECs in a given region have agreed their contracts with the regional office. Generally in Scotland this process has been more open and speedier than in England and Wales. The annual cycle is further delayed by the need for TECs to base their negotiations with TEED upon the outcomes of draft contractual agreements with local providers. In the start-up phase this resulted in considerable delays which put some training providers out of business (see Chapter 7). Even by 1993/94 the delays were considerable and showed little relation to the needs of the commercial provider. The whole process is typical of a quango and not of a business-led commercial organization.

TECs and LECs negotiate with the regional office, SE or HIE on the basis of a 1 year contract for trainee weeks and other outputs, within the context of their rolling 3-year Corporate Plan. Since 1993/94 the minimum funding commitment over 3 years given by the Treasury has not significantly changed the annual process of negotiation.

Once the allocation has been received by the TEC or LEC little virement is allowed and strict accounting procedures are imposed by Treasury/TEED/SO that potentially go right through the TEC/LEC accounts to the subcontracting provider. This further greatly impedes the opportunity for TECs and LECs to act as commercially-managed entities.

The annual allocation to a TEC or LEC may be supplemented during the year. National Development Projects (NDPs) are one aspect of this. These maintain the style of the MSC for TECs to bid for relatively poorly funded initiatives that may be marginal to local strategic objectives (maximum usually £100,000; individual and projects average approximately £20,000, and a total budget average of only £140,000 per TEC in 1992/93; see, e.g. Ernst and Young 1993). Training credits and Employment Action were also allocated through a quasi-competitive process of bids for TECs and LECs. One Stop Shops are developed through a highly competitive process, only 6–15 TECs receiving funding in 1993/94. In 1993/94 there has also been a "TEC Challenge" for TECs to compete for programmes to help the unemployed.

Since 1993/94, *Output-Related Funding* (ORF) has taken over as the main mechanism for incentivizing TECs. In 1990/91 only 10% of budgets was allocated through ORF, but in 1991/92 and 1992/93 this grew to 25%. In 1993/94 it varied from 25 to 40%, and in 1994/95 rises to 100%, depending on negotiation between the TEC and the Regional Office. The ORF targets derive from the six specific priorities listed in the *Strategy for TECs* issued for each year since 1992/93 (see Chapter 3).

In addition to ORF, there is the Performance-Related Funding (PRF). This resulted in a series of bonuses being paid to TECs, which in 1990/91 amounted to £12m, rising to £27m in 1991/92. PRF is based on bonus points calculated with reference to seven specific criteria.

PRF is allocated in terms of "bonus points" ranging in half points from 0 to 4. The focusing of these bonuses has increased from 1990/91, when all 34 TECs that were eligible got some points and 11 (32%) got the maximum score of 4. In 1991/92 33 TECs received points, of which only 3 got the maximum. However the concept of bonus points is recognized as imperfect. It allocated only 2% of the budget in 1991/92. And it reinforced TEED's scrutiny. The incentive effect of PRF is also reduced because the funding is transferred to TECs only 12 months later. The wide range of criteria from which PRF is calculated also means that any one criterion gets low emphasis.

PRF has had some impacts on TECs. One of the top-ranked TECs in 1991/92 (as well as in 1992/93), for example, claimed in a press release "It's official! Dorset has one of the most effective TECs in the country, and as a result will be awarded additional training funds from central government".[23] In the early years TECs and TEED both saw PRF as a means of winning "brownie points" and this allowed many of the old MSC methodologies of rating local agents to surface again. Often quite arbitrary decisions and highly unreliable data are used in these PRF allocations. There is also a more philosophical issue as to whether PRF is an appropriate mechanism at all. It creates winners and losers whereas TECs are supposed to be supporting all relevant programmes that meet a speci-fied standard for community development. From 1993/93, also, a shift in budg-etary control has been sought emphasizing ORF rather than PRF. This is attempt-ing to change the method of public accountability within which TECs and LECs have to operate. We turn to this below.

Public accountability

From the outset of TECs and LECs it was recognized that a cultural shift in accountability was required as far as the DE was concerned. In the days of the MSC, as we have seen, oversight of public funds, through the field network of Area Offices, was maintained right down to the level of the smallest training provider. This is captured in Figure 6.1. Despite this close scrutiny, however, the system was open to gross as well as minor abuse. The contracts for training providers, in particular, allowed considerable scope for claiming MSC funds even when little happened on the ground. Places for training were funded even when they were not filled (see Chapter 7).

These difficulties have caused the Comptroller and Auditor General (CAG) to qualify the DE's accounts in every year since 1989–90. The CAG has had five areas of concern:
- Inadequate supporting evidence of claims by providers. In 1991/92 this was estimated to cover £19m.
- Duplicated payments, estimated to be at least £3.5m in 1991/92.
- Incorrect payments or overpayments to managing agents (and TECs) of £3.5–5.5m in 1989 and 1990.
- Incorrect payments to training participants of £5.7–8.3m in 1989/90 and £11.9–25m in 1991/92. Further overpayments involve the Employment Serv-ice as well as training budgets; these were estimated at £9.7m in 1991/92.
- Fraud, for which no accounts are available.
In aggregate the CAG questioned the propriety of £55m of payments by DE in

PUBLIC ACCOUNTABILITY

1989/90, £24.5m in 1990/91 and £40m in 1991/92. From 1990/91 these errors interrelate with the TEC/LEC structure. The estimates for incorrect payments to TECs for ET and YT are shown in Table 6.1.

Scotland has not been immune from these problems. In 1991/92 the CAG also qualified the Scottish accounts. In SE it found 11 LECs that had not arranged

Table 6.1 Estimates of incorrect payments to TECs in 1991/92. These are based on the sampling of training providers, TEC and TEED accounts.

	ET £million	YT £million	Total £million
Payments to TECs for training weeks:			
– which were ineligible (i.e. the trainee had ceased training or the training scheme did not qualify for funding)[2]	1.1	2.2	3.3[1]
– where the provider, and hence the TEC, had failed to abate for periods of unauthorized absence[2]	0.5	1.2	1.7
– where the TEC had failed to abate for unauthorised absence, despite having been notified of that absence by the provider[2]	–	0.1	0.1
– for which the TEC had already been paid	0.1	0.3	0.4
– where the TEC had claimed the incorrect amount (e.g. used wrong rates or made arithmetic errors when compiling its claim)	0.1	0.4	0.5[1]
Incorrect payment subtotal:			6.0
– which were not substantiated by adequate documentary evidence of trainee attendance[2]	0.3	15.3	15.6
– where there was no individual Training Plan for the trainee	3.0	–	3.0
Uncertain payment subtotal:			18.6
Payments to TECs for outputs:			
– which were ineligible	–	2.1	2.1
– where the TEC had claimed the incorrect amount (e.g. used wrong rates or made arithmetic errors when compiling its claim)	–	0.3	0.3[1]
– which were not substantiated by adequate documentary evidence	0.6	2.3	2.9
Incorrect payment subtotal:			5.3
Overall total:			29.9

Source: Report of the Comptroller and Auditor General, Appropriation Accounts 1991/92, Vol. 5, Class VI, Vote 1: v. *Notes*: [1] Included in these figures are underpayments totalling £0.6million. [2] Only these aspects, totalling £20.7 million in 1991/92, featured in the findings of the 1990/91 examination.

an internal audit to be carried out in the form required by the rules, and in HIE it found that half of the LECs had not implemented proper financial controls. Propriety of training funds was in question, largely because of the systems inherited by SE and HIE from the Training Agency.

Scotland does differ from England and Wales in the rôle of the CAG. Whereas the CAG can directly inspect the TECs and their contractors, in Scotland the CAG has no right to go beyond SE and HIE which are expected to undertake the auditing of the LECs and their contractors. This has been a key part of the greater empowerment of LECs in Scotland. It has allowed a stronger development of trust and given a greater psychological sense of independence.

The results of these qualifications have inevitably led to a tightening up of auditing procedures by the DE. These in turn have enforced a centralised budget control by TEED, SE and HIE on the TECs and LECs which has further reinforced the bureaucratic dimension of TEC/LEC relations – upwards to their central bodies and downwards to their contractors.

The CAG Reports serve not only to evidence the MSC's inheritance: the impression given is of a system that has been out of local control, with the centre dominated by a rate of innovation and intervention that swept away the capacity of its field staff to cope. The CAG reports also demonstrate the onerous nature of public accountability. A commercial organization that made incorrect payments might "sigh", write it off as a bad debt, and improve its accounting system next time. It would not take years to respond to a problem raised by its auditors. Similarly, a commercial organization would stop the audit trail at the point of its contract with other providers. It would rarely, unless fraud were suspected, be able to pursue the audit trail through the accounts of its contractors (training suppliers and managing agents) to its customers (the trainees). Public accountability therefore produces an onerous burden on the TECs and LECs and their suppliers.

The resulting outcome has been strongly criticized as undermining the whole mission of the TECs and LECs. On the one hand the directors can talk of partnership with empowerment of local community bodies. On the other, their local managers confront anyone who walks into a TEC with a contract that is 10 to 20 pages long, onerous and costly on accounting requirements, and allows auditors as well as TEC staff to inspect their commercially confidential accounts. In an LSE survey of contractors to TECs and LECs in 1991 and 1992 only 42% felt that it was appropriate for there to be scrutiny of their accounts in terms of commercial information on unit costs and surpluses, although 93% accepted that scrutiny of their accounts was acceptable to determine overall financial viability (Table 6.2). Among contractors, public sector contractors were the most resistant to commercial scrutiny compared to Chambers of Commerce and the private sector. The whole process of detailed public accountability therefore tends to squeeze out any commercial culture, and can usually be coped with only by agents working in a similar culture or who have subsidized finance to manage

Table 6.2 Acceptability of scrutiny of the accounts of contractors to TECs and LECs, in terms of viability and commercial information.

	Private sector providers and Chambers of Commerce %	Local government and FE college providers %	Total %
Accept need for TECs and LECs to scrutinize commercial information (unit costs and surpluses)	46	39	42
Accept need for TECs and LECs to require a business plan and assess viability	100	86	93

Source: original survey of 27 contractors to TECs and LECs (1991 and 1992).

the lengthy negotiation process. This inevitably means that TECs and LECs have increasingly dealt, in their training contracts, with other public sector providers (predominantly FE colleges) or agents that were bound-in to the system by altruism, commitment to the local economy or had voluntary time inputs (predominantly Chambers of Commerce and voluntary organizations).

One London TEC Chair (56) represented the problem as shown in Figure 6.7. He felt that "the whole process of public accountability is hamstringing the TECs". The culture of detailed tracking of public money was an incursion on the very incentives TECs were supposed to be developing. It "smacks of public intervention down to the level of the employer's own commitment to training. What right have these civil servants got to tramp around in these areas?". The contrast of TEC/LEC funding methods has been made with that of hospital trusts and the funding councils for FE and HE. In these latter cases the detailed external tracking of public money ceases at the institution level. It is then up the trust, college or university to keep its accounts in a proper form subject to external *independent* audit. The lack of trust implicit in the system of accountability of TECs and LECs is therefore a crucial constraint on development.

Some attempt to overcome this difficulty has been made through the development of ORF. It has been argued that the Treasury can be convinced to reduce the level of detailed scrutiny of TEC budgets if they can be assured that the money has been better spent than in the past. This should also help to remove the hand of TEED's bureaucratic control or intervention of initiatives. An ORF approach was envisaged at the outset. Cay Stratton noted (in 1989: 72–3) that TECs would not be

> converting public funds into unrestricted grants. Government can, and should, set clear programme objectives and rigorous performance standards. But accountability should be measured against outcomes, not inputs and process. . . . Since the earliest days of TEC development, officials in

When does public money cease to be public money?

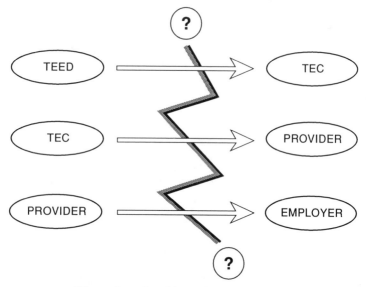

When does tracking of money cease?

Figure 6.7 The problem of detailed financial tracking and public accountability. The views of one TEC Chairman (56).

the Employment Department and the Training Agency have argued vigorously on behalf of TEC flexibility with our colleagues at the Treasury.
ORF is, then, a mechanism to assure that training places are actually filled and that payment is linked to actual results. It has also been tried in US PICs. The difficulty with ORF is that it is still a central managerial system. The targets to be met do not give a general budget empowerment, but are specifications centrally specified, even if they are negotiated with each TEC/LEC. These targets then have to be translated into specific goals for each TEC and LEC taking account of the different capacities of each area to meet the goals. These targets are then built into the contracts of providers. This all reinforces rather than diminishes the rôle of central control, albeit through a delegated structure. It is reminiscent of line management methods in businesses, and is not dissimilar to the Soviet 5 year plans which set targets and prices for each trading relationship between producers: a process that was termed "democratic centralism".

At the provider level ORF tends to impose arbitrary limitations. In the case of YT, for example, there is little incentive for trainees to stay on a course if they actually get a job. Such an absence is positive for the individual (and for

124

the economy), but for ORF it is an unfilled place and a cause of funds being lost to the contractor and the TEC. The bias to a "bums on seats" methodology has been addressed in part by focusing on the value-added by training courses, e.g. through qualifications obtained. But this also has social discriminatory problems resulting from the "creaming" of those who are easy to train. To redress this issue has required a further panoply of negotiations between providers, TECs and TEED for differently-priced contracts for special needs. Again the problem is not that the issue is not being addressed, but that it is being dealt with through a public planning and budgetary system that has no relation to commercial practice and disempowers rather than empowers business leaders.

Continuing reform since 1993

The 1993/94 financial year represented a turning point for TECs and LECs for a number of reasons:

- The system was now up and running. All TECs and LECs had at least 18 months experience, most, including all Scottish LECs, had at least 2 years. Inexperience was no longer an excuse.
- A substantial transition to ORF had occurred, ranging from 25 to 40% for 1993/94, and up to 100% in 1994/95, which was supposed to change the system of public accountability and allow more freedom.
- A minimum 3-year funding commitment was now being given by the Secretary of State to each TEC and LEC, even though each contract was still financially limited to 1 year at a time.
- The G10 dispute had settled down with the establishment of the TECs National Council and its position of being owned by TECs was no longer in major dispute.
- The NACETT council for TECs was established; this removed some of the tensions between G10, TEED and TECs by having a body which appeared more independent of government and the civil service for the setting of standards.
- A new system of One Stop Shops was being established which seemed to be bringing the DE and DTI approaches together thus putting to rest previous tensions.
- The education sector was experiencing major reform which appeared to be bringing it into a position of more closely satisfying the mission of TECs and LECs and meeting the NETT objectives.

The TECs conference in July 1992 had been an acrimonious affair dominated by tensions between the centre and the TECs. The July 1993 conference was more harmonious and a new sense of collective mission among TECs appeared to be being established. However, considerable uncertainties still surround the central–local structure for TECs, which still leaves large questions over how far the original mission will be met. We examine this through the two key developments of the restructuring of TEED following the Styles Report and the development of the NACETT.

The Styles Review of TEED was set up in 1991 and reported in February 1992 (DE 1992a). This report marks an important watershed and was the first concerted post-TEC attempt to unravel the former MSC internal structures. It recommended a less directive, more strategic rôle for the centre, with "maximum local discretion" allowed to TECs. TEED would become a slimmer organization (its staff reduced at the centre by a third), concerned with ministerial objectives, the national targets proposed by the CBI, and the evaluation and dissemination of good practice. It would relinquish detailed programme design and administration. It would "deliver through contracts, not procedures or instructions", "listen to TECs, and other stakeholders", and "avoid interference". A proposal to implement a long-term "culture-change", in which staff would become "increasingly output-focused and more consultative in their approach", indicated a recognition of problems caused by the continuation of the MSC/TA culture when it had ceased to be appropriate. The review might be said to have been long overdue, except for the fact that the TEC and LEC system was established much more rapidly than anyone had initially anticipated.

The Styles Report has led to reorganization of TEED, the most important aspects of which are:

- Restructuring of the regions and some enhancement of their rôle and powers in negotiations with TECs. From 1993/94 they have become the key decision makers on contracts within overall regional budgets set from the centre by formula.

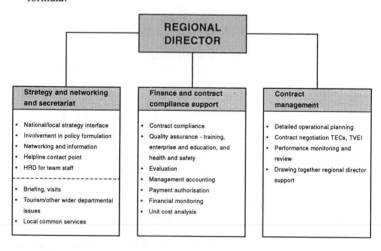

Figure 6.8 The organization of the Regional Divisions of the TEED Operations Division (after DE 1992a: Figure 7).

– The new regional responsibilities are shown in Figure 6.8; however, the criteria the regions use in budget allocation are still not explicit nor transparent.

– The restructuring of TEED into two substructures: one, a set of divisions for training, standards and enterprise, shown on the right-hand side of Figure 6.9 which is related to NACETT; second, an Operations Division linked to the regional teams, shown on the left-hand side of Figure 6.9.

The Operations Division of TEED has been discussed as the potential core area for a new TECs Funding Council or counterpart of SE, but no reform along these lines is yet envisaged. It covers the links of TECs to the PES round, contract pricing, operational policy, performance monitoring and accounting. It is linked to quality assurance but this is seen as also requiring a separation to ensure the independence of assessments. Some attempt has been made to allow quality assurance and monitoring to be redesigned for subcontracting outside of the civil service, following models for inspection of schools. A KCMG study in mid-1993 has assessed how far TEED operations can be subcontracted. But so far very little progress has been made (see also Chapters 11 and 12).

On the right-hand side of Figure 6.9, the Training Standards, Young People, Adult Learning and Employers, and Enterprise divisions are ripe for amalgamation with other government departments in a future reorganization. They stand incongruously in Figure 6.9 separated from the operational core. Simi-

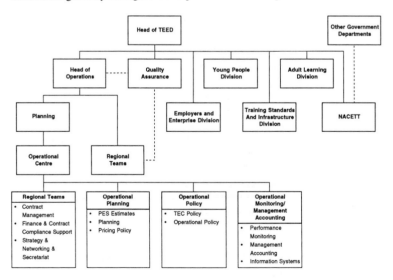

Figure 6.9 The restructuring of TEED as an Operational Division and a training, standards and enterprise division and its relation to NACETT. *Source*: Adapted from DE (1992a: Figures 5 and 6).

larly the independence of the Operations Division from any business lead is a major gap. These are the survivors of the MSC that once sought to act as an integrative body over the whole training, education and enterprise field. They continue to exist for historical reasons and await a more major interdepartmental reform.

NACETT (National Advisory Council for Education and Training Targets), established in April 1993, covers most of the divisional areas on the right of Figure 6.9. NACETT's Brief is to liaise closely with NCVQ and the Schools Inspectorate to advise the Ministers of DE, DTI and DFE on the progress towards the NETT objectives. A parallel council, SACETT, covers Scotland. Both bodies have a 60%/40% dominance of employers with a TEC or LEC representative appointed ex officio (initially this is the Chair of G10). Most of the business members have associations with TECs or LECs.

The NACETT and SACETT have been set up to monitor progress on targets and provide leadership on raising skill levels and increasing employer commitment. In many ways these mirror the NTTF in having no effective levers, relying on TEED, TECs and providers for monitoring, and TECs for increasing employer commitment. They have not satisfied the demands for a powerful intermediary between TEED and TECs, and in Scotland SACETT looks like an English transplant which is unnecessary given the rôle of the Scottish Office, SE and HIE.

In addition in mid-1993 Investors in People (IIP) has been set up as a further national body under Sir Brian Wolfson as Chairman. It has a budget of £1.8m and is to work with others to carry out research and assessments of national training organizations, including TECs and LECs, in order to enhance the prominence of NVQs. Both IIP and NACETT/SACETT are focusing on putting a new national policy at the centre of training, to replace the NTTF, as shown in the centre of Figure 6.5.

Whatever the two councils and IIP may achieve in monitoring targets, they offer little operational benefit to the TEC–government interface and reproduce many of the organizational problems of NTTF. At best the councils may be a bridging mechanism pending a more thorough restructuring of government departmental responsibilities between DE and DFE.

The restructuring of TEED and its relations with TECs and government was the subject of a G10 document (1992a) which assessed options following the demise of NTTF. The options assessed were: (i) The status quo (revival of NTTF); (ii) Zero option (no replacement for NTTF); (iii) Scottish model (a funding council, with or without a substructure); (iv) A national body.

These options were assessed against the TECs' desire to have a greater influence on policy and PES priorities; to have greater autonomy; to move to a more commercial relationship with TEED (simpler contracts, financial flexibility and greater virement, simplified accounting, freedom for carrying forward surpluses); and to have direct employment of staff. Against these desires options (i) and (ii) were non-starters. Option (iv) was used by the G10 Secretariat as its leading option. This was for a National TEC – NTEC – that would also be responsible for quality and strategy, *not* funding. This could have been resourced separately from TECs and take over the functions of TEED with an employer-led Board appointed by the Prime Minister. Option (iv) could have been a final abolition strategy for the MSC/TEED. Although favoured by G10, it was not adopted. Instead a form of option (ii), the zero option but with enhancement of G10, has developed.

Option (iii) was argued for by G10, following the model of Scotland. SE and HIE were seen as having the advantages of being business-led, setting strategy, having independence, pulling together other bodies at the regional level, and drawing together groups of TECs in manageable sizes. Its disadvantage was that it created an extra layer of management, because of the size of England and Wales would require separate provision for Wales and a regional structure for England. Crawford Beveridge, the chief executive of SE, argues that the result in Scotland has been "a much more pragmatic relationship with the Scottish Office than the TECs have with TEED". Whereas TECs dealings with TEED are often legalistic, LECs refer to their contracts only "as a last resort". Also the great benefit for SE of being able to get its 13 LEC chief executives "in a room together once every three months is a very powerful management tool".[24]

A slightly stronger regional element has developed. This was facilitated by separate treatment of Welsh TECs from 1992/93 under the WO. The remaining 75 TECs have been divided between the 10 English regions. The DE regions themselves were restructured, mainly to enlarge the former East Anglian region and reduce the size of the South East, so that more equally-sized regions would emerge. The new regions have also been developed to produce a close relationship to those adopted for the FEFC. The strong interrelation between FE funding and the TEC training budget has become an increasing driving force for reform, although no proper integration of management has yet occurred (see Chapters 7 and 8).

The development of slightly greater regional office powers and the development of G10 into a National Council do not satisfy the needs of the system. A TECs Funding Council was trawled by John Banham (1992: 11), to develop the system. This could "assume the responsibility of being the intermediary between the minister and the TECs . . . negotiate funding, strike contracts, hold TECs accountable for fulfilling them and provide a direct and effective auditing service". The absence of such an intermediary has restricted TECs' demand for independence. It has disadvantaged them compared to Scotland's LECs. They still have to deal independently with several government departments, not a single office like the SO. There is an unresolved rival rôle of the TECs and the FEFC which, although having some cross-membership, relate to different ministries with important differences in agendas. But the chief difficulty of the zero option is that there is no business lead to control TEED. The agenda is still set from the centre with targets and ORF still the central control mechanism. Thus

TECs have not been allowed to become the fully empowered business-led, local entities that the launch mission statement envisaged. Also, given the continued existence of TEED, albeit in a slimmed down form, the old methods of the MSC still have a strong capacity to make incursions. A CBI 1993 survey of TEC Boards showed the concerns on the form of development that has occurred. A more fundamental root-and-branch reform is awaited, to which we return in our concluding Chapters 11 and 12.

Assessment

This chapter has examined how the relations of the local TECs and LECs with the central bodies of TEED, SO and HIE/SE have developed. Clearly changes have not been an easy process. The developments in the future could go either way in terms of strengthening central or local powers. Many have sought to maintain a rearguard position for TEED. The new structures developing since 1993 seem to suggest that, for the moment, the minimal change option is developing. Hence, there are still formidable impediments to development of the TEC/LEC mission which the new structures of the TECs National Council and NACETT hardly addresses.

We examine these tensions in the following Chapters 7–10 through each of the main programmes of training, education, enterprise and community development. However, it is already clear from our discussion here that some fundamental issues remain to be resolved:

- How far will the public accountability rules and ORF allow the TECs and LECs to pursue a local strategy truly derived from flexibly-defined local needs rather than being made to fit to a central bureaucratic framework?
- How far can they develop a sustained strategy independent of the pressures experienced by the old MSC and TEED of having to focus on unemployment and "having to invent new initiatives to win Treasury money and keep ministers entertained"?[25]
- How far will ministers actually allow redesign of national programmes? Already some TECs and LECs have been prevented from making the changes to ET that they wanted to, just as LAMBs were held back.[26]
- How effectively can the new form of the TECs National Council and NACETT/ SACETT change the bureaucratic culture of training provision? Already the emphasis on "the importance of securing early tangible gains" (DE 1992a) is reminiscent of the results-tomorrow culture of the MSC. And the relations to the management and the bureaucratic price-setting of FEFC are unclear.
- The relation between the FEFC, NACETT/SACETT and the TECs is also still largely unresolved and can be made effective only through a more radical restructuring of government departments that reallocates to others TEED's training, standards and enterprise divisions. This leads to a particularly difficult question of the relation of TEC Boards to the FEFC Regional Committees.

Each of these concerns suggests that a major dilemma still exists for TEC management. There is much less of a problem for LECs because of the more effective mediation of HIE and SE and the more pragmatic and integrated structure of the SO. But even the LECs, like the TECs, have the same central clash between the TEC mission statement, to "put business in the driving seat" and to develop a truly "commercial organization" with a structure of state bureaucratic planning at best likened to reformed soviet-style "democratic centralism". The problem is recognized in Gillian Shephard's 1992 observation that "there is a tension between trying to give these tremendously motivated business people as much freedom as we can in a way which is consonant with the use of public funds".[27] We note that without a satisfactory resolution, the 1992 warning of Edward Roberts, Chair of G10, is likely to be realised: that Board members will give up in disillusionment: "there will be no mass protest, but their effectiveness will drain away into the sand of inertia".[28] Only when business is effectively empowered will this tension be resolved. We return to this issue in Chapters 11 and 12.

Chapter 7
Training

The goal of human resource management

Training is the core activity of TECs and LECs and dominates a large part of their budgets: 74% in England and Wales, and 38% in Scotland. TECs and LECs have been given ambitious goals to seek change in both national training strategy and its delivery. Training is also viewed as a means of stimulating a wider change of thought process within firms to seek longer-term goals and a greater emphasis on quality. Training is thus a key part of stimulating higher economic growth through human resources management (HRM). Thus the training emphasis of TECs and LECs is founded on the theory that business development can be training-led.[1]

The concept of training-led business development, like the emphasis of TECs and LECs on training, reflects the thinking of the former MSC and TA. It is thus founded more upon priorities which pre-date the TECs and LECs than upon the mission promulgated at their launch. Nonetheless, within the sphere of training itself the goals set for TECs and LECs are ambitious, aimed at transforming British training practice in terms of both strategy and delivery. Such priorities reflect training as the medium for changing the mindset of British managers towards a greater concern with quality in general and the pursuit of longer-term goals. Past policies aimed at tackling this deep-rooted national problem have met with successive failures. The training challenge for TECs and LECs is thus whether the tools they have been given to tackle such a daunting task are likely to be effective.

In this chapter we assess the success of TECs and LECs in tackling the new training agenda. We conclude that they are subject to crucial design defects that will lead them inevitably to significant failures unless the design is changed. We discuss in turn:
- The training market;
- The wider context;
- National training standards;
- Negotiating contracts;
- Youth training;

- Adult training;
- Assessment of change;
- Identifying the gaps.

The training market

The TECs and LECs are a bold step to rebalance the control of training in favour of the private sector. In particular it has been sought to change the strategic management of that training for which public sector funds are most crucial. In the words of the White Paper (DE 1988: 43), TECs

will give leadership of the training system to *employers*, where it belongs . . . TECs will ensure that training provision is more relevant to employers' needs and so improve the skills and enterprise of the workforce. By promoting training arrangements that are clearly linked to business success, TECs will generate more private investment in training.

Hence TECs and LECs have a prime training objective of adapting supply-side decisions on training provision to meet the demands specified by employers. This assumption led directly to the employer lead on TEC/LEC Boards, the control of training contracts for YT and ET, and an evolving rôle in FE and tertiary provision for the post-16 population.

But the government also hoped that TECs and LECs would stimulate much wider changes not just in the public sector supply and provision of training, but also in the way in which employers developed their internal training programmes, and in the way that individuals responded over their working lifetime. Indeed this was in many respects the central mission of TECs and LECs. It is in this sense that the training agenda set for TECs and LECs seeks the highly ambitious goals of stimulating a much wider emphasis on HRM within firms and a process of "lifetime learning" by individuals. As TECs and LECs are finding, no more ambitious targets could have been set.

Figure 7.1 depicts the key agents and interrelationships involved in training that the government has sought to change. Employers (both public and private sector) are the sources of demand for training, much of which is done in-house or subcontracted to external training providers. The HRM target seeks to use training activity as a means of improving the quality of workforce skills which in turn should lead to increased productivity and therefore increased output, profits and wealth creation. In this sense, training should be treated as an investment, the benefit of which employers and individuals recoup, respectively, in greater profits, wages or job security. Thus, stimulating the development of businesses' own training commitment was seen as the central TEC/LEC objective:

"Employers large and small must undertake a massive training effort . . . Employers as both providers and consumers of training have the primary responsibility for ensuring that our labour force has the skills to support our expanding economy" (DE 1988: 59).

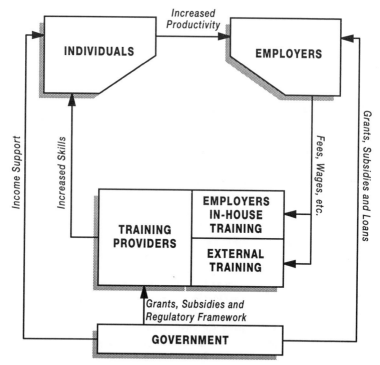

Figure 7.1 Interrelations between individuals, employers, training providers and government.

Individuals also play a key part in this process of change. They receive the investment, the benefits of which are shared between increased wages and profits. The government sought as much a sea change in individuals' as in employers' commitment to training and to adapting their skills and work practices:

> *Individuals* . . . will need to be committed to adapting their skills and, if necessary, acquiring new ones, throughout the course of their working lives. For individuals, investment in training is the best way to ensure both greater job security and enhanced earnings over the course of their working lives (DE 1988: 59).

So TECs and LECs had to seek to be key influences on mainstream business practice and on the working population at large. To achieve these ambitious goals the TECs and LECs were given some tools through controls over government training programmes and regulatory support. The White Paper suggested that the key rôle for TECs and LECs was to help government perform its rôle in the training market:

> *The Government* . . . can help to ensure that training opportunities are
> available for unemployed people . . . [and is] responsible for helping
> establish a framework both at national and local level which will ensure
> that training is carried out on the scale and to the quality our economy
> will require in the 1990s (DE 1988: 59).

The TECs and LECs are therefore part of an institutional framework aimed to
"ensure that training is carried out". The problem for TECs and LECs has been,
however, that the control and resources they possess affect only a minority of
the training programmes undertaken in the UK.

The extent of leverage of TECs and LECs is clear from Table 7.1.[2] The main
TEC/LEC programme expenditure is for YT and ET. This represents 17.5% of
the government's expenditure on training; and government expenditure in total
is only approximately 21% of all national expenditure on training. The YT/ET
programmes, therefore, represent only about 3.7% of total training expenditure
in Britain. TECs and LECs also have a level of influence over part of the WRFE
budget. But the total WRFE spend accounts for only a further 33% of government training expenditure, or 6.9% of total training expenditure in Britain.
Moreover the TECs and LECs currently control only about one-quarter of WRFE

Table 7.1 Training expenditure (1986/87).

	%		%
1. Government: £7billion (21%)		*of which:*	
		· Grants and fees/	
YT/ET	17.5	core costs	21.0
WRFE/AFE	33.0	· Subsidies to	
HE	31.5	providers on	
Student awards	16.5	participation basis	60.0
EC (ESF, etc.)	1.5	· Income support	
	‾‾‾‾	to trainees	19.0
	100		100
2. Employers: £18billion (55%)			
Large private firms	50.9		
Small firms	9.3		
Armed forces	10.9		
Public employers			
(central govt, LAS,			
nat. industries)	28.9		
	100		
3. Individuals: £8billion (24%)			
Total: £33billion (100%)			

Source: TA (1989).

135

expenditure. The majority of FE funding relates to fields of general further and adult education which only partly overlap with training provision. Over this the TECs/LECs have little or no control.

The TECs and LECs, therefore, have control over less than 10% of national training expenditure, split between YT, ET and WRFE. This alone gives them limited leverage in the market place. But that leverage is further reduced by two additional factors. First, has been the credibility of the training programmes themselves. Severe criticisms have been directed at the content and appropriateness of the inherited programmes of both YT and ET. Although improved from earlier models of the Youth Opportunities Programme (YOP) and Youth Training Scheme (YTS), there are still many problems. This has led to criticisms, from employers that their output of trainees is often inadequate, and from outside commentators that the educational content and quality of provision has frequently been poor.[3] TECs and LECs have started to tackle some of these problems, as we outline later in this chapter. But the starting point has not been good since the "brand recognition" of the government programmes of YT and ET has often been associated with a perception of poor quality – exactly the converse of the quality "branding" of "world class standards" that the government and TECs and LECs have been trying to create.

The second limitation on the YT and ET programmes has struck at the heart of the TEC and LEC agenda. Historically these training programmes have evolved to cope with training the unemployed. Yet the central purpose of the TECs and LECs has been to enhance the skills of the workforce presently *in employment*. The ambitious agenda for TECs and LECs, the business lead, and the focus on the senior and supposedly best business leaders, are all orientated to changing the employer culture of in-house decisions on training. These goals are not concerned with social programmes. But training the unemployed is predominantly a social programme: the unemployed are by definition those individuals in whom employers are not presently directly interested. Their training becomes a necessary issue for employers to confront only when a hiring decision takes place. Only at that point may a training programme be needed. Thus the dominance of YT and ET funding for TECs and LECs creates a very uncomfortable dilemma: that *TECs' and LECs' main financial resources derive from unemployment programmes for which they remain the main responsible agency in terms of contracting delivery, but the main mission and mechanisms which TECs and LECs were supposed to follow concern training in employment*. It is this dilemma which has caused a deep concern among TEC Directors that *TECs and LECs have major design faults*.

The wider context

Attempts to change Britain's training culture have to recognize each of the elements that contribute to its so-called low skills equilibrium. As a *system-*

wide problem, it is correct for the government White Papers[4] to be simultaneously concerned with the respective rôles of employers, individuals and government. But behind each of these elements lies a wide range of other agents and incentives. Hence, improving the national training culture is not simply a matter of changing the nature of the so-called "training market".

At the heart of stimulating change is the assessment of training requirements, how these are provided, what returns these yield, and to whom. Training is not something that can be simply "plugged in", either to the individual or the company. It involves the individual making a commitment and paying a cost (in lost time or deferred consumption), and the employer also making a commitment of paying a cost (either direct or in foregone output during the training period). The TEC/LEC structure does nothing directly to influence most of the main costs, incentives and commitments involved. It offers nothing (or at best very little) to employers for training the current workforce, and it offers nothing to employed individuals in terms of immediate incentives. Instead, TECs/LECs are chiefly a means for government to control its flow of funds to providers of training for the long-term unemployed or for young workforce entrants. They have little leverage on the negotiations between individuals and employers over the training received (or not), nor on the costs and returns to each party.

The absence of direct links to the key levers that affect both parties (individuals and employers) for people in employment is a fatal gap. Without it there is no leverage on either party; and there is no transmission mechanism. Instead TECs/LECs are left with only exhortation and the personal influence of directors as levers. And the government is left with only regulatory options such as improving the structure and transparency of qualifications (through NVQ), or regulating the nature of supply (through YT/ET and college funding). Given the system-wide diagnosis of the gap in Britain's training culture, the tools available to TECs and LECs are bound to be inadequate for the task.

Figure 7.2, which is a development of Figure 7.1, indicates some of the other main areas where leverage can be sought. At the heart of the bargaining process between individuals and employers in many countries is a strong structure of local organizations: employer bodies, on the one hand, such as the German Chambers of Commerce, that seek to link local and sectoral groups of employers into coherent systems of training commitment; and work-based employee organizations and trade unions, on the other hand, that seek to translate the relative productivity/training costs of employees into the wage structures and incentives available to the individual. Such organizations in Germany or Japan, for example, are a key part of the mechanism by which rewards and training are controlled as part of a negotiated pay-bargaining process. TECs and LECs were designed specifically to step away from host bodies (as used in the ill-fated LENs initiative) and to avoid corporatism (as used in the almost completely ineffective Local Area Manpower Boards (LAMBs)). But neither host bodies nor LAMBs are the models used in countries like Germany and Japan.

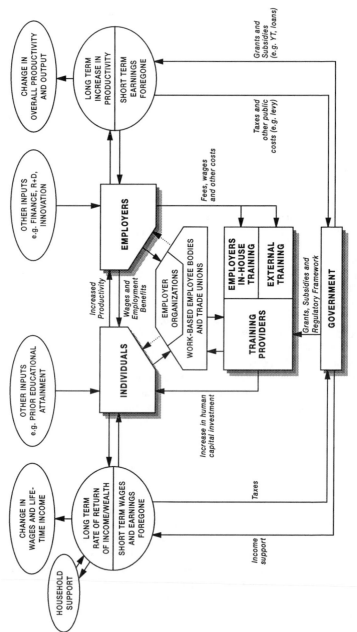

Figure 7.2 The wider context of decisions on training.

Rather, *representative* bodies, for employers and employees, are the *local* agents, *independent* of government, but closely linked to government (chiefly through employer bodies) as purchasers and *regulators* of training, both through financial contracts and through being given statutory powers of control over (i) accreditation and certification of company in-house and external training, (ii) assured sources of independent income, (iii) direct local legitimacy through a representational/membership structure, (iv) a regulatory structure of national trainee wages at fixed levels, applied to all employers and skills, backed up by (v) a strong guidance and careers counselling structure, and (vi) an entirely separate regulatory framework and concept for unemployed people. These elements are the foundations for the German and Japanese high skills equilibrium.[5]

Compared to these features, TECs are *not* independent (by virtue of their contract with government), have *no* strong regulatory powers (except over unemployment programmes), have *little* assurance or independence of income, have *little* local legitimacy (because Boards are self-appointing), have *no* regulatory relation to pay bargaining, and have a *weak* relation to careers counselling. They are, however, local and the programmes they administer have an emerging accreditation structure through NVQ.

The TECs and LECs look even more peripheral to enhancing Britain's skills requirements when the other wider elements shown in Figure 7.2 are examined. Behind the incentives to individuals to train lie the comparative returns to the effort entailed. As shown on the left-hand side of Figure 7.2 this concerns the appraisal that an individual makes, first, of short-term trade offs between present earnings in low skill jobs and forgoing earnings in the short term to acquire greater skills. The decision made is often highly influenced by the household support available, both by the income support that can be contributed and the peer/demonstration effect of parents and siblings. This often has a strong social differentiation: households with unskilled heads tend to have children that also have low skills.[6] There is also often a strong gender differentiation, with less pressure traditionally on young women to seek training "because they are only filling in time before they get married and give up work to have a family" (a feeling shared among many young women themselves, in their households, by many employers and by many of their prospective husbands!).

The lower the incentives to train and the lower the prior educational attainment of the trainee, the greater is the cost to the employer of increasing skills, and hence the higher are the barriers to achieving a high skill base or even perceiving its necessity. At the centre of this low-skill circle is the problem of incentives: that there have traditionally been relatively low levels of return to training. Recent LSE research, reported in Figure 7.3, demonstrates the strong, short-term benefits to individuals remaining unqualified and going straight into employment at age 16. Furthermore, the additional earnings derived from training remain zero or minor up to the age of about 23. For the comparison of

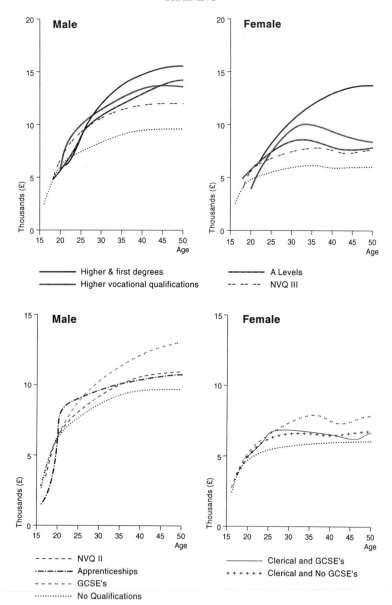

Figure 7.3 Lifetime earnings of individuals from various qualification routes based on 22,000 actual households in the General Household Survey (constant 1992 prices for full-time employees). *Source*: Bennett et al. (1992a, 1992b).

unqualified with vocational and intermediate training at levels equivalent to NVQ 1 and 2, the returns remain low even after 35. This means that an unqualified individual is perfectly rational at age 16 in going straight into a job without training. The individual gets a better return over a working lifetime from taking those wages, and either earning interest on them in a bank or in consumption, than by forgoing income and investing in training. Only for those people who make a much greater commitment to training, to attain a level NVQ 3 or GCSEs, are the returns so markedly greater that they are sufficient to provide a strong incentive to train rather than enter employment at 16. For the case of women the differences of earnings from the unqualified level are greater. But the only level of skilling that gives women comparable earnings to men is by taking higher education. This pattern suggests that the critical assumption in Becker's (1975) human capital theory breaks down in Britain: neither the returns to individuals nor to companies are at present strong enough to justify the investment in training for many skills.

The problem of incentives is no easier to tackle from the employer's point of view. On the right-hand side of Figure 7.2 stand the elements affecting the employer's incentives to train. Human capital investment is only one of a mix of options that the employer can bring to bear in order to increase/maintain profitability. Also available are changes in production technology, product innovation, marketing development, R&D, and managerial development. All of these may be more attractive, in terms of foreseeable returns at a given level of risk, than investments in skills. This may explain why in Britain there is the long-term pattern of a low level of relative wage flexibility with level of skill.[7] In order for an employer to prefer investing in enhancing existing workforce skills over other options, there must be a certainty that there will be a productivity gain. In many cases employers have seen alternative routes as more attractive or offering lower risks, particularly investment in plant and equipment to reduce labour inputs overall, or to *remove* some of the former traditional higher-skill jobs altogether. In a period of rapid technological change such as the 1990s these trade offs are becoming increasingly important to the employer.

A major element of the risk associated with skills investment from an employer's point of view is the unreliability of the long-term commitment by the employee to the firm making the investment. It is too easy for another firm to poach highly trained staff or for an employee to leave to seek career advancement. In a culture where only a few firms train to a high skills level, the incentives for business to invest in areas other than human resources is obvious. This is in marked contrast to German or Japanese labour markets where a national system covering all young people's training exists, and poaching is generally inconceivable, employers and employees make long-term if not lifetime commitments to each other, and the regulated structure of the labour market makes it difficult for either employer or employee to "break ranks".

The government can intervene in a number of ways to affect individual and employer incentives as shown in Figure 7.2. However, the powers so far available to TECs and LECs do not appear to be able to affect the main areas where a human capital investment is likely to produce a return for either individuals or firms:

- TECs and LECs de facto have had to focus, through TEED/Treasury controls, on the unemployed as opposed to the employed (despite having a mission statement suggesting the reverse).
- TECs and LECs seek to influence young workforce entrants through regulation of the supply of courses over which they have only marginal leverage (approximately 25% of FE college resources over which they have little influence) rather than through an "across the board" regulation of skills/ provision of all those in employment or training.
- TECs and LECs have no effect on employer or individual incentives, and little impact on costs, being frustrated at all times by a stronger return to the young person to go straight into work rather than to train – a set of returns that may be frustrating to the needs of each individual company and the economy, but which is supported and maintained by the collective decisions of employers, unions, individuals and government. To overcome these perverse incentives means attacking the politically sensitive question of reducing pay for young workforce trainees, and to ensure that no employment 16–19 can be undertaken without regulated and accredited training.
- TECs and LECs have no leverage over employers other than by exhortation. This means that they cannot directly limit or reduce the problem of free rider firms that do no training and they have to continue to support a system whereby firms will frequently prefer to invest in other assets (e.g. equipment) with perceived lower risks rather than the human skills of their workforce.
- One recent innovation, Training Credits, does give to TECs and LECs a method of influencing incentives to both individuals and providers by introducing a quasi-market. We assess Credits later in this chapter, where we again conclude that it is at best only a partial solution because its leverage affects only a small part of the training system, with the majority driven by other incentives.

Against this pessimistic evaluation we turn below to assess how far TECs and LECs have succeeded in overcoming these barriers.

National training targets

Among the ambitious targets set for TECs and LECs, the achievement of high quality national training standards for Britain is perhaps the most important. The question of pursuing quality in training can be broken down into two important areas: firstly, the fixing of standards of achievement and the setting of targets for more significant proportions of the population to attain higher skill levels; secondly, the monitoring of progress towards them. A number of measures relating to standards in training have been established in recent years and influence the training activities of TECs and LECs. These relate to both accreditation and targets.

National Vocational Qualifications (NVQs)

The National Council for Vocational Qualifications (NCVQ)[8] is outside the TEC/LEC system. NCVQ is responsible for overseeing a system of National Vocational Qualifications (NVQs), a set of national standards into which all forms of attainment and competence recognition are being integrated. Academic and vocational attainment alike are given a common evaluation. There are currently four levels of NVQ and there are plans to expand the levels to five to include degree-level and professional training.

The NCVQ does no examining itself but accredits the qualifications of other organizations. "Industry lead bodies" for each main industrial sector seek to ensure the input of business needs into this process. In addition, individuals can accumulate transferable "credits" towards the achievement of different NVQ Levels using the National Record of Vocational Achievement (NROVA). This credits the achievement of individuals, through either traditional full- or part-time courses or through the assessment of work-based competences. There are thus multiple and alternative pathways to reach the same target.

The development of NVQs has not proceeded without difficulties, however. Until mid-1991, the NCVQ used "conditional accreditation" virtually to rubber-stamp most existing qualifications as NVQs.[9] As a result, there was little control over quality or equivalence, particularly between craft and engineering skills, on the one hand, and clerical, catering or retail skills on the other hand. There were also doubts over the balance of many accredited courses: on the one hand the input of industry lead bodies has been criticised for producing too narrow curricula that neglect broader, basic educational requirements; on the other hand, industry lobbies have criticised the survival of too many academic elements in NVQs in preference to the need for core skills.[10] Since 1991, however, qualifications have progressively had to meet the NCVQ's criteria before they qualify for NVQ status. This should improve quality standards in the longer term. There has also been a new commitment to include in the curriculum blocks of time dedicated to developing broader understanding as well as job-specific skills, emphasizing core skills over traditional academic emphases.

Equivalence of NVQ to European standards needs also to be achieved. Discussions are well advanced in seeking EC equivalence, but there are major stumbling blocks to achieving true equivalence mainly deriving from (i) the complexity of the programmes, (ii) the lower British standards set in many areas, particularly clerical, catering and retail skills areas. For example, there are problems of using NVQ 1 or parts of NVQ 2 in a European standard since these would not even merit consideration in Germany.

The NVQ framework provides a major step forward by which TECs and LECs can have local flexibility in the types of courses they fund while ensuring that these courses count towards nationally recognized qualifications. NVQs also overcome one of the major problems with national YT – that there was no national target against which progress towards qualifications could be set.

National targets

In addition to the development of NVQs, an ambitious set of training targets has been agreed by the government and CBI to be achieved by the year 2000. The definition of national training targets was initially proposed by Norman Fowler in 1989. But his successor as Secretary of State for Employment, Michael Howard, initially stood back from any governmental commitment to targets, purportedly because he believed that they could not be met. Subsequently the national targets have been reasserted in a CBI (1991a) document "endorsed" by government and supported by most other key agents including TECs, the TUC, ABCC, and others. The agreed targets can be summarised as follows:

For young people:
–   By 1997 at least 80% of the 16–19 age group should gain NVQ level 2 (equivalent to 4 GCSE grades A–C) in their foundation year of education or training (normally by age 17). They will also have a *right* to structured training, work experience or education leading to NVQ level 3 (in 1990 45% of 16–19 year olds achieved NVQ level 2, and this increased to 55.1% in 1992);
–   By the year 2000 at least 50% of 16–19 year olds will gain NVQ level 3 or its equivalent (in 1990 30% of 16–18 year olds achieved NVQ level 3).

For employers:
–   By 1996 all employers should take part in training or developmental activities as the norm, with at least 50% of the employed workforce aiming for qualifications or modules leading to NVQ;
–   By the year 2000 50% of the employed workforce should be qualified at least at NVQ level 3 (in 1990 33% of the employed workforce had NVQ level 3 or its equivalent);
–   By 1996 at least 50% of medium and large companies (over 200 employees) should qualify as *Investors in People* (IIP) accredited by TECs/LECs (see below).

These have become termed the National Education and Training Targets (NETTs). They are very demanding. To help in development of the NETTs, the National Advisory Council for Education and Training Targets (NACETT) was established in March 1993. This has the purpose of monitoring the targets and stimulating their implementation. As discussed in Chapter 6, NACETT derives from the reorganization of the non-operational side of TEED and seeks to be an independent standards and quality-maintaining body.

The NETTs bear an uncanny resemblance to the three main targets of the

1981 New Training Initiative which were:
- Objective 1: to develop occupational training, including apprenticeship, in such a way as to enable people entering at different ages and with different educational attainments to acquire agreed standards of skill;
- Objective 2: to move towards a position where all young people under the age of 18 have the opportunity either to continue in full-time education or to enter training;
- Objective 3: to open up widespread opportunities for adults – whether employed or unemployed or returning to work – to acquire skills during the course of their working lives.

It must be asked therefore why so little has been achieved between the 1981 and 1992 setting of targets, and why there is any greater hope that they will now be achieved when most of the mechanisms to achieve these targets remain the same.

Significant doubts surround whether the NETTs can be achieved. First, for TECs and LECs there is the problem that they are *given* these targets, in a locally derived form as part of their negotiations with TEED (see below), but TECs are only one of many agents over most of which they have little or no influence. The NETTs for TECs and LECs, therefore, have been criticised by TEC/LEC chairs (e.g. 55) as "giving responsibility without the power or resources". A second problem has been that many NVQs will not be formally in place until 1994 or 1995 and arguments about equivalence and curriculum continue. Thus, early achievement of the goals is undermined by having only part of the system of accreditation and measurement in place. Third has been the difficulty of overcoming deficiencies in monitoring. The qualifications among the existing workforce require a major effort from employers and individuals to seek accreditation of prior learning or present training. There is little leverage to ensure this occurs, so that at present there are very imperfect mechanisms for gathering information on existing workforce NVQs or on how many people are working towards NVQs. Fourth, has been the question of whether the targets are too high to be achieved in the time available. The youth target for NVQ 2 requires an annual rate of increase of 5% per year. Fifth, there remain uncertainties about IIP as a system to lever change (see below).

One of the central dilemmas, however, is government's own commitment to the NETTs. The establishment of NACETT reflects more the difficulties of managing the evolution of TEED into a new rôle rather than developing a powerful new body that can integrate standards across the whole field of education and training. As we saw in Chapter 6, NACETT looks more like a continuation of the MSC methodology, of establishing an independent body under the DE, peripheral to the DFE, rather than instituting a system-wide change. Furthermore the endorsement by government of NETTs falls short of taking full responsibility. The government has felt, first, that the commitment to training is a shared one, not government's alone. For government to take the responsibility would be for the buck to be once again passed, "that training is someone else's problem". The government has thus sought to press the CBI and other employer bodies to deliver to the targets while accepting its responsibility to make sure government programmes are strongly focused on the NETTs. Second, the government has been influenced by the Treasury view that taking responsibility means guaranteeing more funding rather than stimulating alternative resources to come from employers and individuals.

Performance targets and ORF

Within the TEC/LEC system has been developed a more specific set of performance targets for training contracts which form an increasing proportion of funding. Output-Related Funding (ORF) is a somewhat controversial area of TEC and LEC training funding,[11] although it was not extended to LECs until 1992/93. In 1990/91, TECs were required to meet specified performance targets within programme areas accounting for 10% of their overall annual budget in order to release from TEED the relevant portion of their funds, the other 90% being guaranteed. In 1992/93 this ORF component was increased to 25%. In 1993/94 it ranges from 25 to 40%. The performance targets apply to TECs'/LECs' mainstream training programmes, and employ the achievement of NVQs, as well as successful employment placements, as measures of success. They are thus a strong lever on TECs and LECs to meet the NETTs. For example, one major condition for the payment to TECs and LECs of the ORF proportion of their annual funding for training depends upon a certain percentage of trainees achieving an NVQ at Level 2 on completion of their course.

Although specific goals in the form of ORF have been set for TECs and LECs by TEED, the TECs and LECs have also established training goals of their own. In one sense, this meets the generalised and rather abstract conception of flexibility expressed in TECs'/LECs' vision of their future activity. Most popular amongst such goals appear to be improving the quality of training, raising attainment levels, encouraging employers to carry out more training and increasing access to training.[12] In another sense, local targets allow TECs and LECs to pursue objectives which are not specified in contractual arrangements with TEED. Also, many TECs/LECs have introduced performance targets for their contracted providers over and *above* those required by TEED. One-third were doing this in 1991/92, and another 16% were planning to do so.[13] Nonetheless, one-half of TEC/LECs had no plans to exceed their formal ORF responsibilities. Many felt that to do so would not be feasible: in the words of one chief executive (TEC 37), "we have already been pushed too far too quickly anyway on ORF"

Monitoring, TSAS and NACETT

The monitoring of TECs' and LECs' training activity is a crucial part of the assessment of progress on NETTs. Traditionally TEED has conducted monitoring nationally and regionally through two principal mechanisms. One is desk-based, involving systematic gathering from TECs and LECs of detailed information documenting annual training proposals and targets and charting their achievement of stated objectives. The other is conducted through the MSC and Training Standards Advisory Service (TSAS), which operates from Moorfoot and the TEED Regional Offices. The TSAS is a carry-over from the central monitoring activities of the former MSC and TA and has a dual function. On the one hand, it makes monitoring visits to individual TECs and LECs in order to carry out direct assessments of their training programmes, checking delivery and assessing quality against the training proposals contained in the contract with TEED. On the other hand, it offers advice and support for individual TECs and LECs. Sometimes (in limited amounts) this is free, sometimes it is paid for by TECs/LECs on a consultancy fee basis. In this way the TSAS offers an inspection ser-vice that can be bought-in by individual TECs/LECs who wish to monitor their training providers, and as such competes with alternative consultants they might employ. At the end of 1991 half of all TECs and LECs had used TSAS at some time in this way.[14]

With the development of NACETT the rôle of TSAS and TEED monitoring has been put under new direction (see Chapter 6). Whether NACETT will be able to improve on past practice is open to considerable doubt. The problem that NACETT faces in monitoring is the poor system of recording in the MSC/TA Area Offices inherited by TECs and LECs. These poor systems are further thrown into question by confusion in the equivalence between qualifications before the NVQ system is fully established. For this reason the baseline of comparative information is poor. Surprisingly little information about this difficulty has become public. This is explained by the implications of such publicity for scrutiny by the National Audit Office. In addition, astute TECs and LECs have been able to use the poor quality of existing data to negotiate reduced baselines, hence allowing their targets for ORF to be more easily achieved. TECs and LECs have, therefore, had advantage in keeping confidential their own information on achievement of training targets.

The results of one TEC's own sampling is indicative of the national problem. This TEC (25) in the North West of Britain could not believe the baseline set for its levels of NVQs in YT and ET. As a result it commissioned a detailed survey following up all the participants in the former TA programmes. It found that rather than achieving a 100% level of NVQ 2 after a YT course that the TA statistics showed, the actual figure was 20%. For ET the figures were respectively 25% actual achievement instead of the TA's baseline statistic of 30% for any NVQ achievement. How could the TA statistics on the baseline be so dramatically incorrect? For the case of NVQs, the difficulty in MSC/TA procedures was that no record of prior achievement was made. Hence, when a participant recorded a NVQ at the end of their YT or ET course this was counted as a value-added irrespective of whether they had it before they started the course, or would have obtained it anyway! This accounted for almost all the upward bias in the statistics of qualifications achieved. It was also found that in many cases very low levels of responses were used (as low as 8) to extrapolate for all participants, and many respondents ticked the wrong boxes. For employment placements this TEC's investigation demonstrated that the main follow-up used by the MSC and TA was a telephone test, which was found to be grossly inaccurate. This led to most of the upward bias to the statistics of employment after YT or ET courses.

The lack of proper monitoring of the MSC/TA programmes is a national scandal on a major scale. There is no reason to believe that the sample survey by TEC (25) is untypical. It suggests not only that the government's YT programmes, in particular, added only a minuscule value in terms of qualifications or employability for the participants, but that the monitoring system was so badly run that it was capable of recording errors in magnitude of 1000%.

NACETT will be advantaged by the new monitoring systems that have been put in place by TECs and LECs, but the difficulties deriving from the previous structures demonstrate that the true baseline for YT and ET participants (compared to other parts of the population) is dramatically lower than anyone has been prepared publicly to admit, and that a formidable change in culture is required in the added value offered by YT and ET courses, and in the staff procedures used in TECs and LECs for monitoring their contracts.

Labour Market Information (LMI)

A major area of importance in monitoring training targets is the matching of provision to needs. The failure of the supply side of the British system to deliver training appropriate to needs is one of the principal and most sustained criticisms directed at it. As noted in Chapter 3, the potential accurately to assess employers' true skill requirements was identified by government as one of the major advantages of the employer lead on TEC/LEC Boards. However, a comprehensive local policy, truly responsive to a range of skill needs, cannot be drawn up using individual Board members' "soft" knowledge alone. The importance of the collection of comprehensive and reliable labour market information (LMI) has long been recognized as a goal vital to improving Britain's training record, yet success in achieving it has proved chronically elusive. With the birth of TECs and LECs, responsibility for collecting LMI was passed to them from TEED. The TECs and LECs had to assemble the LMI needed to inform their local training delivery so that it could serve local needs. Interesting conclusions can be drawn from investigation of the sources of LMI that TECs and LECs used to pursue this goal.

Under the previous local arrangements handled by the TA, the main skill-needs data was assembled by the Area Offices using the Computer-Aided Local Labour Market Information system (CALLMI). This was a computer database of local LMI based on "dipstick" visits to firms to assess future skill requirements. With the arrival of TECs and LECs, responsibility for CALLMI passed directly to TEED's Regional Offices. Nonetheless, the requirement for continued local data collection meant that TEC/LEC staff, most of whom had previously been Area Office employees, were still engaged in the data gathering rôle with the TECs/LECs but now contracted to TEED.

There has been a major doubt about the value to TECs and LECs of the LMI systems they inherited. In our surveys only one-fifth of TECs and LECs considered CALLMI statistics to be useful, and one-third considered them to be poor or very poor. In many offices the collection mechanism had fallen into disuse, particularly in Scotland, so that no data was collected at all! The dissatisfaction was greatest among former staff of the DE or TA: half the TECs/LECs with chief executives from outside the system indicated its LMI to be good or very good, more than three times as many as those from inside the system. Conversely, over one-quarter of TECs/LECs with chief executives from the TA or DE saw LMI as poor or very poor, compared with only a tenth of the outside appointees.[15] Conclusions are difficult to draw, but it could be argued that those with a better knowledge of the LMI systems were more aware of their serious limitations. More recent analysis suggests that now all TECs and LECs are aware of the deficiencies of earlier systems and are using new approaches to LMI: 90% are collecting more data than TEED contractually require, in 70% of cases using external contractors (Vaughan 1993).

The result of deficiencies in LMI has been the need for TECs and LECs to turn to other organizations for help. In England and Wales, local authorities were the most widely used external source, with 57% of TECs using their LMI services in 1991/92. The next most common source for TECs was collection of their own data, then use of Jobcentre statistics, and only CALLMI as a last resort. In Scotland, Jobcentres are the most important single source, with LECs' own collection and "soft" information as the next most important sources.[16] When all the different forms of self-collection used by TECs are combined, they form the main method of gathering LMI. Thus TECs and LECs have had to take a major responsibility for both the generation and interpretation of LMI, with little outside support. The consequence appears to be a rather ad hoc discontinuous local pattern of labour market intelligence, a fragmentation which may hinder the advancement of the national training strategy. Only in 1993 is NACETT beginning to tackle this need for more systematic approaches to LMI.

Contract negotiation

Contracts are the basis for most TEC/LEC training activity: no training is provided in-house. This maintains the pattern of the previous MSC and TA methodology aiming to create a "training market" whereby suppliers worked directly with resources provided by government. Latterly, in many cases, a training manager/managing agent was used as an intermediary to do the difficult work of matching course provision, employment placements, and the qualities of the individual trainees in order to match demand with the best form of provision.

However there was widespread scepticism about the value of the rôle of the managing agent which included perception that they were parasitic upon the training system, a large number of "BMW-driving" managing agents allegedly making excessive profit from their intermediary rôle without adding significant value to the quality of training. This point was made in numerous interviews with training contractors and is confirmed by the CAG reports of 1989 to 1992 (see Chapter 6). The TECs and LECs have been given the capacity to replace the rôle of managing agent, with the result that in most cases there are now direct contracts between the provider and the TEC or LEC.

Contracts carry the advantage that they make explicit what is required of a particular training course or package and for this reason must be seen as an advance on the approach prevalent for so long in the British system where the purchaser was also the provider. They also make explicit the relationship between cost and quality. However, they have raised a number of important issues for the training system. We focus below on costs, concentration, quality, length of contracts and difficulties of negotiation.

Cutting costs

The removal of an intermediary provides the potential to reduce costs. Considerable pressure on TECs/LECs to reduce costs has also been imposed by government. Lying behind this appears to be a TEED and Treasury conception that the system was providing too much scope for profit, and a political pressure to reduce the total level of expenditure on training by passing the responsibility to employers.

There is a major conflict over the level of profit that should be available to training providers. Private sector providers interviewed require a rate of return of 10–15%.[17] Local authority Further Education colleges are prepared to run programmes at a loss and with a subsidy "but there is clearly a limit to the level of subsidy we can continue to make" (local government chief executive 72). The financial pressures from the FE Funding Council are intensifying the effect of this limit. Chambers of Commerce are between the two extremes, being prepared to make only a small surplus in most cases (i.e. 5–7%), and in many cases being prepared to accept merely coverage of costs "because we feel a Chamber should be involved in training" (TEC area 95). But, like LEAs, they are not happy at giving a de facto subsidy and do not see training provision at a zero or negative return as a sustainable long-term proposition.

The pressure of TECs and LECs on costs has therefore probably now reached (by 1993) a limit beyond which further economies by the provider cannot be made. However, there are undoubtedly economies possible within the TEC or LEC's own management and staffing (see Chapter 11).

Concentrating provision

The driving down of unit costs has had the effect of removing many private sector trainers from the market for public-funded training, and increasing the need for achieving greater economies of scale of administration. This has stimulated the concentration of training among those few providers in any area that can offer a high level of throughput of trainees. The pressure for concentration has been further stimulated by TECs and LECs also seeking to economise on their administrative overheads. As a result the number of separate contracts they administer has dropped radically, probably by at least one-third in 1991/92. One Scottish LEC (9), which had already halved its *number* of contracts in 1991/ 92 was seeking to reduce them to about 15–20% of the 1989 number in the longer term. This contraction has had a large fallout effect on small providers, many of which were voluntary sector bodies. The result is that from 1992/93 onwards, in most TEC/LEC areas, there are only FE colleges, large Chambers of Commerce and a few large private providers/group training associations left in the field. The pattern of provision, widely expanded after the 1981 New Training Initiative, will therefore have returned largely to its former position.

Quality of provision

There is also a question as to how the quality of programmes has been affected by the drive to reduce costs. Many providers in colleges, as well as Chambers and the private sector, have complained that their higher quality programmes have been put in jeopardy in favour of cheaper and less effective ones. TECs and LECs have been monitored by TEED for the quality of their programmes. But this pressure has been coupled with that of driving down costs so that there has been a tendency for high cost–high quality programmes to be cut. Although low cost–high quality programmes have survived, there has been pressure towards a predominance of low cost–low quality programmes.

A further effect on quality has also been the way in which TECs/LECs have handled cuts in the overall training budget they have to administer. For many of the TECs, and all the LECs, that became operational close to the April 1991 date, very rapid decisions on what to cut had to be made. This caused many TECs to make indiscriminate across-the-board percentage cuts on all contracts irrespective of marginal costs or quality. Inevitably this penalized efficient programmes relative to overfunded ones. From the comments of other agents in a sample of 37 TECs and LECs 32% made percentage cuts and 68% made selective cuts in the commitment of their 1991/92 training budget. This was enough to remove many providers from the field, many of whom were of high quality. For the 1992/93 and 1993/94 years the longer time period available for negotiation has improved the situation a little.

Intrusive monitoring

All TECs and LECs are required as a matter of contract to monitor the finances of their training contractors, although not all use the same techniques. This has been supported by a computer accounting system (TFS – The Field System) which has been subject to substantial criticism by NAO and which few TECs have maintained after its transfer to them in 1993/94. The monitoring technique now preferred and promoted by TEED is called Financial Appraisal and Monitoring (FAM). This is a process commonly employed by many TECs and LECs. There is evidence of variation, however, in the detail that TECs/LECs require from their training contractors. Some demands have been highly intrusive. Interviews demonstrate that over 90% of training agents considered that TECs/LECs could legitimately request a business plan from contractors and determine their viability, but only 42% felt that requests for commercial information about unit costs and any surplus was appropriate (see Table 6.2). This must be correct as a commercial view: TECs and LECs should be concerned only with *outputs*, not with how outputs are met.

Short-term contracts

A major problem for TECs and LECs in the training field has been their 1 year contracts from TEED. Although negotiated as part of rolling 3 year corporate plans, TECs and LECs do not have the ability to make commitments to training providers through contracts longer than 1 year at a time. Even with the Treasury's agreement to guarantee a minimum level of 3 year funding levels for TECs and LECs since 1993/94, contracts with providers are still almost all for 1 year at a time as far as prices, specifications and volumes are concerned. In consequence TEC/LEC–provider relationships have been very tense and unstable, subject to sudden termination when funding cuts occur. Much of this problem derives from the uncertainties of the political process and Treasury PES-round discussions. The way in which the TECs and LECs have had to become enmeshed closely with PES has banished for ever the illusion that they are independent commercial entities. This has been exacerbated by a shift from pre- to postdelivery payment to providers, which has caused cash flow difficulties in many cases, and by clauses that allow TECs and LECs to terminate contracts early and at short notice.[18] A number of prominent voluntary organizations, notably the Apex trust and Rathbone Society, were seriously damaged by funding cuts and uncertainties in the early years of TEC/LEC operation. Many TECs and LECs have called for longer contracts so that valuable relationships with training contractors are not undermined.

Since 1992/93 an improved Operating Agreement has been used by TECs and LECs which has been further improved in 1993/94. This incorporates a response to some of the Bridge Group's (1991) criticisms of contracts. The Operating Agreement of the TECs and LECs with the Secretary of State is now "evergreen", in that it can continue until terminated by either party. But this improved arrangement has not been fully passed on to training providers. For example, almost all contracts in early 1993 were for 1 year and still allowed premature termination, usually within 28 days without explanation or fault; contracts still allow TECs and LECs to act unreasonably by imposing additional audits or certification requirements. In addition there is still an absence of reciprocity in contracts with regard to confidential information and intellectual property, with the TEC or LEC not obliged to safeguard these even though the supplier is. Not all TECs and LECs are acting as prompt payers, and there is no compensation provision to the supplier, even though a TEC or LEC can reclaim overpayment. Also contract variations by the TEC or LEC are still allowed unilaterally and arbitrarily without the need to renegotiate or revise prices.[19] What appears to have been achieved is improvement of the TEC/LEC relations to TEED, but an imperfect transmission of the TEED changes between the TEC or LEC and its contractors.

Negotiations

Apart from the external pressures on TECs and LECs, occasioned by the cuts in total budget, there has also been strong and continuing criticisms of the way their staff have conducted negotiations. The criticisms of staff in a sample of 20 TECs and LECs demonstrate that 96% of external agents rated their approach to be a major or minor problem in negotiations (see Table 4.3). All the staff negotiating directly with training providers in 1991/92, and almost all in 1992/93 and 1993/94, are from the former TA. The common criticisms of them are:

- Inability of staff to make decisions, always referring upwards and putting off the time when they would be held responsible;
- Insufficient grasp of the technical and commercial arguments of the provider's requirements;
- Insufficient grasp of the legal content of the contract that they were negotiating (the key elements of which are standardised TEED documents);
- Inadequate action agenda or ability to move ahead at the pace required by the provider, instead dominated by internal procedures and timetables;
- A tendency to continue to negotiate and seek changes in a contract, of a significant commercial nature, long after it had been signed: in some cases this has resulted in withdrawal of contracts previously signed and exchanged;
- Lack of authority of individual TEC staff, with too many tiers of referral, with TEED continually changing the rules and Treasury changing the budget.

These criticisms all result from the tension between the inherited public service culture of TEC/LEC junior and middle management and the commercial culture to which training providers are subject. This tension is also reflected in the relationship between the TEC/LEC Board and staff as mediated by the chief executive. Our evidence suggests that Boards frequently cannot understand what is going on, or are not informed sufficiently, to break the log jams and thus translate the commercial mission of TECs and LECs into a reality.

Assessment of contracting relationships

The development of the TEC/LEC relationship with contractors has been far from satisfactory. The example of one North of England training provider is informative and typical (TEC 63) of the general problem affecting training providers. This provider had 14 training staff and was the major provider for a significant part of the TEC area. The TEC itself is recognized in our analysis as one of the most innovative and has one of the most progressive chief executives who derives from the former TA/DE. The provider's experience, leading up to the new 1991/92 contracts, was as follows:

- 19 January 1991: provider informed that old system was to be scrapped with new TEC contract in place from 2 April. Notice period for redundancy of senior staff already passed on 2 January.
- March 1991: bridging contract agreed with TEC and detail of TEC's post-April budget awaited. This allowed some security of provider's staff. 2 March notice period for redundancy of junior staff passed.
- 2 April: cut of £30,000 to agreed bridging contract announced. New detailed terms of contract announced. After tough, and locally highly politicised discussion, cut reduced to £10,000.
- 14 May: final attempted forecast by TEC of its training income translated into final contract with provider but with further new detailed changes in content.
- September 1991: TEC forecast to underspend and not fill its places despite recession: seeks extra places from provider who was given 1 week to agree a new contract for these.

This cycle is typical, and was repeated in most TEC areas in 1992/93 and 1993/94. It demonstrates clearly (i) the inability of the TECs and LECs to act independently and flexibly to agree their training budgets, instead influenced by short-term changes in TEED and national budget priorities; (ii) the chasm of cultural difference between the commercial world of provision, which is subject to standard wage and redundancy conditions and the need at least to cover costs, with a civil service culture where commercial considerations play no rôle; (iii) the absence of delegated authority to many of those TEC/LEC staff who have to negotiate contracts, or the absence of ability to exercise it; and (iv) the need to resort to local political approaches rather than commercial considerations to match and to counter the public sector culture of the TEC/LEC.

Not all of the developments in TEC/LEC contracts have been bad. The cost pressures have removed some of the financial scandals as well as most of the poor suppliers from the system. But it has created major difficulties for important special need areas because of inflexible approaches to contract pricing, in which the voluntary sector was most prominent; it has created an atmosphere of continuous crisis management created by short-term contracts that has undermined TECs'/LECs' ability to innovate; and it has thrown doubt on the credibility of the government's commitment to training. But most important of all, the way in which contracts have been negotiated has completely undermined the mission statement of TECs and LECs that they are to be independent entities developing local programmes closely and flexibly related to the needs of business subject to a local business leadership strategy. If they are to fulfil this mission they must be given the freedom to negotiate stable, long-term contracts with their providers through a close relationship which focuses on developing *quality, cost-effective* training packages, analogous to the much-vaunted relationship that many large companies, such as Marks and Spencer, have with the suppliers of their products. But instead, at the moment, training funds have become a football of each PES-round, negotiated by a form of monopolistic civil service culture, driven by external TEED-defined targets, in an atmosphere of uncertainty and changing political priority.

Youth Training

The training of young people in the 16–19 age group has been long recognized as a major problem in Britain. The major restructuring of British manufacturing industry in the 1970s and 1980s saw a steep decline of the traditional apprenticeship and the rise of sectors requiring quite different types of training. This left a significant gap in the vocational training routes available to young people. Many commentators have drawn attention to evident problem areas. These include low educational staying-on rates compared to competitor nations, an inadequate and incoherent system of qualifications and accreditation, a lack of sufficient vocational alternatives to academic-oriented provision, and a public sector-driven system of provision (principally in the FE college sector) which was claimed to be both inflexible and poorly tuned to the needs of employers. The 16–19 question was brought into the public eye by high youth unemployment in the 1979–82 and 1990–92 recessions. Policy responses such as the Youth Opportunities Programme (YOP), Youth Training Scheme (YTS) and Youth Training (YT), however, have been criticized as more of a pragmatic response to unemployment than any real attempt to transform the training system for young people. By the late 1980s, in contrast, the demographic downturn in the number of 16–19s in the labour market was drawing attention to the dangers of a shortage of young people who were being drawn into well-paid unskilled work, to the long-term detriment of their skills and the growth potential of the economy as a whole. A consistent failure to create a single national system for the school-to-work transition was recognized in the White Paper announcements on TECs and LECs, whose rôle in tackling this area was given considerable weight in the original prospectus and White Papers. However, TECs and LECs have still been labouring within a framework which separates "education" (under the DFE) from "training" (under the DE). We examine here the consequences for training schemes, credits and the Careers Service.

YTS and YT

The emphasis on the youth training issue is reflected in the fact that the largest proportion of the budget of TECs and LECs is devoted to Youth Training (YT), the successor scheme to YTS and YOP. This alone accounts for 51% of TEC budgets and 13–14% of LEC budgets. YT is a programme offered to all 16- and 17-year-old school-leavers, and guarantees all applicants a placement on the scheme with an employer and a minimum of 13 weeks off-the-job training. The guarantee of a place and of an employer placement has been given large emphasis in government policy. It is a major part of what TECs and LECs are expected to deliver. Indeed, it has been argued by some commentators that the failure to get employers sufficiently involved in YT schemes was the primary motivation for the MSC to create TECs.

The importance accorded to YT by the government and TEED cannot be overemphasized. It was seen as the major way of influencing the long-term change in Britain's training culture. At the launch of YTS, for example, Geoffrey Holland, the then director of the MSC, termed it "the most significant development in education and training since the Education Act of 1944".[20] Yet the programme continued largely to fail as far as involving employers was concerned. They were either uninterested, or viewed it as largely a public sector unemployment initiative which, at best, they would participate in through a commitment to social responsibility, or at worst would view as a source of cheap labour.[21] As a result YTS and then YT continued to be dependent to a significant extent on a small number of large-scale *national* providers. Even in 1990/91, 28% of YT funds were allocated to national providers. This has now changed radically, with national providers receiving only 4% of YT funds in 1992/93.[22] The TECs and LECs, therefore, can be viewed as a continuation of MSC/TA attempts to widen the commitment by local and smaller employers.

The proportion of TEC/LEC budgets devoted to YT, covered by their Block 1 funding, was approximately £1 billion but fell to £0.8 billion in 1992/93. The structure of YT is fairly well defined, unlike successive adult training programmes which have varied considerably over time and are also subject to wider variation across TECs and LECs (see below). The training component of YT is undertaken by a number of providers, sometimes offered directly by employers in-house, often by private providers, and to a significant extent in local authority colleges. Nationally the FE colleges are the largest providers of YT off-the-job training, followed closely by the Chambers of Commerce. The TECs and LECs have potentially the greatest influence over the form of delivery of YT in the FE colleges, as a consequence of their additional supply-side rôle in influencing the WRFE budget as well as YT contracts. A major focus for TEC/LEC concerns has therefore been how the reform of college finance with the FEFC will develop. We examine this further below.

Credits

A major innovation in TEC/LEC provision for the 16–19 age group has been the introduction of Training Credits. The credit system was stimulated by the CBI and adopted by government.[23] It offers to every 16-year-old a voucher of a certain value which permits them to purchase education or training to approved standards of NVQs or its equivalent (at least at level NVQ 2). The value of the Credits ranges from approximately £500 to £5,000. They are paid through the TEC or LEC. Not only does this seek to produce flexibility and competition among training providers, but it also allows central government to modify YT supply. Such a strategy clearly fits snugly with the government's wider approach to public services. Credits were piloted in 11 TECs/LECs from April 1991, with extension to 9 further TECs/LECs in late 1991, and subsequent extensions since. It is intended to extend credits to the whole country by 1996. They were a prominent part of the government's 1991 Education White Paper proposals. All government's finance for YT will eventually be paid through credits, including a transfer of resources from the FE colleges for their elements of YT.

All pilot area bids for Credits were based on a locally-devised version of the scheme. TEED's choice of successful applicants in part sought to allow assessment of different approaches. Resources for the Credits programme derive from three components: (i) an additional funding of £12m in 1991/92 and £25m in 1992/93, (ii) a transfer from the FE colleges element of the local government Revenue Support Grant of £5m in 1991/92 and £15m in 1992/93, and (iii) a transfer of the YT Block 1 budget to Credits. The balance of these contributions has varied from TEC to TEC; whereas some TECs devoted only specific pilot funding to the scheme, others had transferred the whole of Block 1 funding to Credits by the 1992/93 financial year. In addition, all the pilot programmes received in-kind support from employers, which in some cases was expected to account for more than half the overall cost, but in practice has been rather disappointing.

Although broadly similar in coverage, the target age-groups for Credits varies between TECs and LECs, as does the period for which Credits are tenable. Although some Credits schemes aim specifically at 16–17-year-old school leavers, others are available up to the age of 19. Some schemes allow trainees to complete their programme over a 4 year period, others require that they do so over a shorter period. The type of training available also varies. In some cases only training in employment is permitted, in one case encouraged by the device of funding only part-time training. In other cases (e.g. Kent and Birmingham) the Credit programme is selective in terms of the skill level covered, or the sectors for which it is available, this being determined by reference to locally-identified skill shortages. In Bradford, Devon and Cornwall and Grampian the different skill needs are met by varying the value of Credits. One TEC offers Credits to all in the 16–17 age-group, including those remaining in full-time education, which is "purchased" by means of the Credit. In this TEC, selectivity between sectors is explicitly avoided, training being viewed as a matter of individual achievement, and not as a mechanism for tackling skill shortages.[24]

The Government is on record as making a commitment to offer credits to all young people as a *right*. This has occasioned extreme scepticism among many commentators in disbelief that the Treasury will, in fact, allow this expansion in public spending to occur.[25] The CBI (1993a) propose that the public sector costs can actually be reduced by transferring training from full-time education to part-time training with employment. The long-term policy has yet to be tested against government commitment or employer willingness to participate. Moreover, the concept of a *right* to credits is strongly tempered by the steering of provision and financial incentives to both young people and employers. For example, credits will only be *generally* available at a low level, but *selectively* available to different skill groups at different prices. It is an open question whether this approach can be sustained against vigorous lobbying from disadvantaged industry groups and special need sectors.

In all cases it has been recognized that credits have to be complemented by major enhancement of the advice available to young people. As a result, the Careers Service has been heavily involved in the Credits process, acting as the main source of information. These services have been frequently supplemented by extra TEC/LEC resources, and have increasingly focused on advising leavers prior to their finishing school. Usually careers advisers develop jointly with trainees some form of individual training plan, which can then be costed against the prices of the type of training involved. In a number of cases the value of Credits is banded according to the different skill levels involved. Commonly, the Credits are issued to young people by careers advisers as part of a training pack. The specific form which the credits take include vouchers, a "passport to work", and different notions of a "training account", in some cases accessed by means of a "credit card", "smart card" or "cheque book", whose "payments" can be redeemed by employers through the TEC. The purpose is generally to give the young trainees a sense of purchasing a marketable commodity, as well as developing their sense of ownership over their training programmes. In some cases extra funds are available for the subsequent pursuit of higher levels of NVQ achievement.

Although the early schemes described above were intended as pilots, it was announced in the 1991 Education White Paper that the Training Credits scheme would be extended to the whole TEC/LEC system by 1996 before any full evaluation of their success had been possible. This is surprising given problems in the early operation of the Credits system. The 1991 pilot starts produced a very low take-up amongst young people. The lowest was 18% in Grampian, but 5 out of the 11 pilots had take-ups under 50% (compared with a target of 65%). Only one TEC had a complete take-up (Northumberland) and the average take-up rate was 50%.[26] The Credits systems have rarely been meaningful to the trainee. The DE (1992d) evaluation concluded that "training has largely been arranged on their behalf, the credit being surrendered to the employer or training provider. This reduces the young person's rôle to little more than a possible recipient of courses defined by others". Some TEC employers found it difficult to see what benefit there was for them: "the scheme was devised at a time when the concern was a shortage of young people, not a surplus".[27] A report by NATFHE (1993: 8), the college lecturers' union, concluded that "far from establishing a new and efficient training market, most employers and young people in the pilot areas see credits as just an alternative funding route for what was already taking place under YT . . . young people . . . see the credit as money for the employer to buy training rather than themselves".

The question that has to be asked is why Credits are a better system for linking the government's fee, through TECs, to suppliers, than other systems. The rapid expansion of Credits only partly reflects enthusiasm on the part of TECs and LECs for the scheme. The rapid diffusion of a largely untried scheme more reflects political pressures, CBI support, and the recurrence of the MSC methodology of initiative-driven funding. This methodology has been widely criticised in the case of credits as stimulating a "flavour-of-the-month" approach rather than allowing proper assessment of the merits of the programmes. The continual creation by TEED of nationally-based initiatives, often rapidly thought up and poorly tuned to the local situation, seems at odds with the stated mission of TECs and LECs. However, it has suited the purposes of the CBI which has sought to encourage a Credits-based approach to 16–19 provision through TECs and LECs in opposition to the dominant culture of the FE college, used to a tradition of block grant funding. The success of Credits depends on how far the reforms of FE finance under the FEFC are consonant or dissonant with Credits. This is an issue which we address later in this chapter.

Careers Service

Linked to the issue of Credits, but also independent of it, is the rôle of information and advice. To make sensible choices, young people need not only financial incentives that steer them to areas of relative skill demand, they also need to make sound judgements of their own potential and capability based on information and advice. TECs and LECs have sought a variety of approaches to link credits and advice. For example, Northumberland and Hertfordshire TECs have attempted to improve schools-based careers libraries and advice, and many credit pilots have introduced free telephone helplines. Birmingham has developed 15 sector-Compacts to deliver advice and tailor Credits. Many Credits pilot TECs have enhanced the careers service and have developed individual Action Plans for trainees.

The Careers Service is at the centre of the problem of how best to provide information and advice. An enquiry set up by the DE in mid-1990 into the Careers Service resulted in radical proposals for reform including the channelling of its funds through the TECs/LECs. The DE has been responsible for only part of Careers Service funding and met a strong defence from the DFE to this proposal. The 1991 Education White Paper affirmed support for the existing LEA-based Careers Service, but called for improvement in its quality and closer relations to employers through TECs. It envisaged one of three possibilities: (i) LEAs and TECs working jointly on the Careers Service in partnership, (ii) legislation to open up the Careers Service to contracting out from LEAs, and (iii) being run by TECs.

Option (i) was adopted, reflecting the unresolved DE–DFE tension on this issue and in November 1991 the Employment Secretary set out plans for Employment Department funds to be based on *Careers Service Partnerships* between local authorities and TECs. Careers Service Partnerships require the Careers Service to bid for its DE funds but leaves its main DFE funding intact. The first pilots were set up in 1992/93. These provided £20,000–60,000 per TEC to help set up a joint structure; most TECs received pilot money. LEAs are affected very differently depending on their depth of organizational commitment to Careers Service development. However, there is a considerable evidence that the Partnerships are acting as "bolt-ons" to existing LEA Careers Service structures, rather than deeply imbuing the required changes in the range, approach to delivery, and quality of advice available to young people. As a result, the TECs/ LECs are developing their own initiatives related to Credits which will in some cases strengthen and in other cases by-pass the Careers Service. It also must be borne in mind that, in a number of areas, pressures from local management of schools (LMS) and opting-out are forcing LEAs to put their Careers Services on a trading basis with schools and their futures are by no means secure. It seems likely that in the longer term the Careers Service will be contracted out by government with TECs as a key part of the management structure. The CBI (1993a) would like to see its finance driven by Careers Guidance Credits. A step in this direction occurred in April 1994 with the setting up of "Pathfinder" bids from TECs to run careers services on their own.

Adult training

Adult training is an area of crucial importance in the development of TEC and LEC strategies for promoting investment in human resources in their localities. Indeed the goal of improving training of adults in employment was the main part of their mission statement in the White Paper and Prospectus. However, TECs and LECs have encountered considerable problems in developing this area. First, their budget gives virtually no resources to pursue this mission, except for LIF and "efficiency savings". Secondly, although mechanisms for the training of young people are relatively well developed, the notion that lifetime training of adults should be encouraged has not been well understood or its methods developed. As a result, TECs and LECs have not only had to establish workable methods of delivery, but to tackle the whole issue of convincing both individual adults and firms of the value of investing in training, updating individual workers' skills and developing flexible learning throughout working life. They have thus had to tackle the historical failure of British industry to regard training as central to its activities, and to promote a culture of training in work, the importance of which extensive government exhortation has hitherto failed to drive home. Furthermore, as noted above, they must do this in the face of a policy brief and funding regime which places the bulk of their activities in the realm of provision for youth and adult unemployed with few sources of influence on the incentives to employers or employees. There can be no question that in seeking to square this circle, TECs and LECs are facing a daunting if not impossible task.

Training in employment

One of the principal tools held to be at TECs'/LECs' disposal resides in their private sector leadership. The government notion was that the co-option of leading business people into management of the government's training budget would allow them to have an authority to persuade other employers of the importance of investing in training. In other words, national exhortation was replaced by local exhortation and "peer" pressure. But exhortation remained the favoured strategy. The past failures of this approach were attributed, implicitly, to the arguments being voiced by the wrong protagonists at the wrong level. This has been complemented by the Investors in People (IIP) scheme, which is being used by TECs and LECs to increase their powers of exhortation.

Investors in People (IIP)

IIP is intended to be a system of accreditation and quality assurance of employer-based training. It is acting as a *kitemark*. It is planned that TECs will use IIP as a leverage on employers so that their funds and Credits support trainees only in IIP accredited companies (CBI 1991b). Thus TECs and LECs can rely on IIP as the main mechanism to spread a training culture to the currently employed workforce. In mid-1993 IIP was set up as a national body under Sir Brian Wolfson as Chairman with a budget of £1.8m. The main objective is to steer employers' existing expenditure on training to meet the NETTs. It is hoped that using contract and supplier links the IIP targets can be spread from larger to small firms. It is also argued that the demographic downturn will affect the labour market so that companies seeking to recruit will have no choice but to meet IIP standards if they wish to be attractive to young people. In the face of renewed high unemployment, this latter expectation now appears optimistic.

IIP offers firms a tangible benefit of recognition for business's training policy. It involves the following elements:
- A business makes a public commitment at senior level to develop all employees to achieve business objectives using a written but flexible plan specifying how needs will be assessed and met; this will be communicated to employees showing how they can contribute to success, involving employee representatives and unions where appropriate;
- The business regularly reviews the training and development needs of its

employees through its business planning linked, where appropriate, to NVQ;
- The business develops a training commitment to employees throughout their career;
- The business evaluates its training investment at all levels against specific goals and targets in order to improve future effectiveness.

The IIP initiative is closely coupled with NVQ national targets and NETT. These two forces, combined with Training Credits and the business leadership of TECs/LECs all attempt to lever change. Also significant is the attempt to link IIP to the Management Charter Initiative (MCI) which seeks to enhance the quality and quantity of management development in British industry. Although this was set up independently, and indeed in advance of TECs and LECs, its local networks are in a number of cases hosted by them (see Chapter 9).

The development of IIP and MCI could stimulate many of the required system-wide changes in Britain's training culture. But the problem is that the leverage is not strong and they can be readily ignored.[28] First, many companies will continue to use their own systems which may have no formal equivalence to NVQ. Second, is the problem of IIP assessment itself. IIP is more concerned to demonstrate a commitment to a learning culture rather than introduce effective management of training. There is thus a confusion of purpose and capacity in IIP. Third, is the problem of take-up. The ability of TECs to exert strong pressures through the use of public money for trainees, Training Credits and NVQs, depends on skill shortages and youth recruitment. The result has been a very slow effective take-up of IIP. Only 50 companies were accredited between the launch of IIP in November 1990 and May 1992.[29] By July 1993, 2060 companies were commited and 202 recognized.[30] But many of these had applied for IIP only on part of their operations, or for part of the IIP standard. The quoted statistics have been misleading. The future still relies mostly on goodwill and exhortation: not a guaranteed recipe for success given the systems failure we have noted.

Fourth, is the absence of a well-developed route for trainer-training within companies. Although possible within NVQ, MCI, and IIP, none of these are specifically designed for the purpose of enhancing the quality of training managers and supervisors in the workplace. They have been largely outside NVQ, and somewhat neglected by MCI. Although crucial to IIP, supervisor training has not yet found a strong place within its system or within NETT. This gap is possible to fill, but needs a deeper and better-financed approach.

Finally, there is the question of consistency in standards. Although a national standard sought for IIP should be capable of uniform application, each TEC has gone its own way. Attempts to bring TECs together in integrated labour markets, such as London, have largely failed. The result is a variable system in its application and as far as can be determined in its quality. For example, it is not credible that the charges made by TECs for IIP assessment vary by as much as £150 to £400 per day.[31] TECs simply cannot be doing the same things if such extreme price variation applies. This has undermined the credibility of IIP as a "gold standard", suggesting that it is open to a variety of interpretations which TECs may take in order to satisfy the need for a rapid take-up to meet ORF targets. Some improvement in the generality of approach has occurred since mid-1993 with the re-establishment of IIP as a national body independent of TEED, but the lack of independence of the assessments is still an Achilles heel of the whole system.

Despite vigorous defence of IIP, not least by some leading companies such as Allen Sheppard's Grand Met,[32] IIP still offers too little to most companies. It is unrealistically burdensome to many, it is seen as an irrelevant "large company line management concept" by many small firms, and it largely preaches to the converted where it has been taken up. In the words of one London TEC chief executive (93) "IIP could make TECs the laughing stock of the business community".

Supervisor training: the forgotten dimension

IIP focuses on the transmission of a training culture within a firm. But largely neglected in this process has been the rôle of the supervisor. This is the individual foreman at a shop floor, or middle manager level in the management hierarchy. Traditionally there have been few qualifications available to this group. Many companies have sought to fill this gap by graduate-only or graduate-preference recruitment. But arguably these are the least appropriately qualified of all possible recruits, although they are likely to have a higher level of academic competence.[33] More recently the MCI, BTEC and BIM have developed courses recognized at NVQ levels 4 and 5.

The importance of the supervisor is only recently becoming properly recognized. Reports by the NEDC (1991b) and CBI (1992) drew attention to the difficulties faced in developing supervisor skills:

- Supervisor training is often sporadic and unrelated to the technical skills of the work environment.
- Wage differentials between supervisors and semi-skilled or unskilled workers are too small to constitute an incentive to training. Differentials are about one half of those in Germany or France (see Table 7.2 and compare Figure 7.3).
- Supervisors are undervalued by senior management and lack status, responsibility and authority;
- Britain's supervisors spend a greater proportion of their time organising the work unit, "fire fighting" and checking quality controls than German counterparts who play a stronger rôle in training and planning new developments (NEDC 1991b).

There is, in general, no comparison to Germany's Meister in the rôle of Britain's supervisors.

These differences have crucial consequences for attempts to develop Britain's training culture. First, the commitment of senior managers to TEC and LEC Boards will mean nothing if they do not strengthen the supervisor's rôle in their own and other companies. Second, IIP becomes impossible to achieve without related changes in supervisor renumeration and status: something the whole IIP agenda has largely neglected. Third, since supervisors either do a lot of the training in small firms, or supervise it in large firms, their own personal skills needs should be built strongly into the system of development. This involves both training of the existing workforce and YT/ET trainees who are normally under the charge of supervisors for the work-based part of their programmes. The supervisor is, therefore, the crucial "glue" and transmission mechanism that holds the answer to developing training in the workplace.

Employment Training (ET and TFW)

The tools through which the TECs and LECs seek to influence employers give them little direct powers or scope to introduce change in training the adult workforce. As a consequence their main adult training activity has been with the delivery of a national adult *unemployment* programme, Employment Training (ET) and Training for Work (TFW). Like YT, ET was inherited from the TA, with its structure and regulations already established. Aimed solely at the long-term unemployed, to qualify for an ET place candidates had to have been out of work for at least 6 months. They then become entitled to join the scheme while remaining in receipt of unemployment benefit. The scheme has raised considerable criticism since its inception in 1988. Many TEC/LEC interviewees echoed the negative evaluations of the scheme – described, for example, as "out and away the weakest programme we've inherited" (TEC 76). Reasons include its inflexibilities, such as the restriction to long-term unemployed entrants, the fixed duration of courses, and the low proportion of off-the-job training components. Many calls have been voiced for a relaxation of such rigidities and greater scope for local discretion in devising the most suitable form of the programme. It was also perceived widely that the very name "ET" was associated with a stigma of palliative responses to mass unemployment, a perception undermining any claim that might be made for its status as a high quality training programme. Of non-TEC/LEC actors interviewed, nearly all respondents felt that ET should be changed, 69% indicating that it should undergo major change. Since April 1993 TFW has taken over from ET. The developments which have taken place within the programme are considered below.

ET and special needs

A significant area for ET coverage by TECs/LECs in the adult training sphere is provision for disadvantaged and special needs groups. This activity is prominent in TEED policy, and all TECs and LECs are expected to make this area of provision a key component of their Corporate Plans. Given this, it is not surprising that the majority of TECs and LECs draw attention to their special needs

Table 7.2 Earnings differentials by skill level in Britain compared to France and Germany.

Skill level	Britain	France	Germany
Unskilled	100	100	100
Semi-skilled	113	124	115
Skilled craftsmen	126	154	121
Section foremen	139	171	169
Technicians	140	179	169

Source: Steedman et al. (1991).

training effort, especially as many express on their own account a particular concern that the needs of the disadvantaged be properly, and locally, catered for. Not surprisingly, an overwhelming majority of 90% of the TECs'/LECs' chief executives interviewed indicated that they were making, or planning to make, significant special training provision for disadvantaged groups.

Within the special needs sector, non-TEC/LEC agents interviewed judged that greatest emphasis for ET provision should be given first to the long-term unemployed (by 48% of respondents), followed by ethnic minorities (38%) and returners to the labour force (35%). These were the only categories to be mentioned significantly. Provision for the disabled was considered a priority by only 1 in 10. The inclusion of returners to the labour force, usually characterised as "women returners", was reflected in the frequently expressed intention of TECs and LECs interviewed to make provision for this group, a concern advanced widely prior to the onset of the recent recession, when labour supply appeared to be tightening.

This suggests some confusion in thinking about the composition of a group labelled as "disadvantaged", which would more properly be applied to those with learning difficulties or who are subject to systematic barriers to access to training or employment. It is certainly more in these groups that an incompatibility has been identified between the method of assessing TEC/LEC training performance (achievement of NVQs) and the importance of providing for the disadvantaged. The raw ORF criteria actually provide a disincentive to TECs and LECs to take on disadvantaged trainees: other trainees are more likely to deliver the performance achievements TECs require.[34] This might not be a serious threat at a time of budgetary expansion, but with a succession of cuts in the ET budget, concern has been expressed about TECs'/LECs' scope for manoeuvre in maintaining an adequate level of provision. Thus many of the elements of TEED methodology encourage local TECs and LECs to "cream off" the easiest to train, even though our surveys indicate a reluctance by TECs/LECs to screen in this way. In an attempt to counter this danger, targets for trainees with disabilities or from ethnic minorities were included by TEED in the annual TEC/LEC bonus scheme. In addition, financial incentives for TECs and LECs to train people with literacy or numeracy difficulties were introduced to the ORF criteria from April 1992. Since April 1993, TFW has given main emphasis to those unemployed for over 12 months or with disabilities, thus restricting the possibilities of creaming.

Conflict between targets

The discussion of the adult unemployment programmes illustrates the conflict between the TEED methodology of initiative-driven central targets with the concept of giving TECs and LECs the flexibility to approach special needs groups with programmes defined by locally relevant criteria. There is also a conflict for TECs and LECs between such social needs approaches and the main mission of TECs to improve training in employment. Although many TECs/LECs interviewed indicated that provision for disadvantaged groups was a central and highly prioritised area of their activity, a significant number made it clear that they did not regard social provision for "the sad, the mad and the bad" (as chief executive 26 put it) as the responsibility of a competitive commercial company. Another chief executive (88) whose TEC was not active in this area claimed that, while he recognized its importance, there was little that could be done effectively for disadvantaged groups within the existing funding regime. He felt that ORF discouraged TECs from acting, claiming that "our hands are tied", and that action could follow only from either increased or more flexible funding being made available. Of TEC and LEC chief executives interviewed, 10% indicated that they were neither making nor planning to make special training provision for disadvantaged groups. This is surprising if the intention of TEED is that provision should be universal. Furthermore, the possibility that many TECs were doing less than they might claim in this area was raised by one respondent who stated that in this sphere his TEC (43) had "been pretty ruthless – we do just enough to avoid major criticisms". When, as at the time of the interview, the TEC came under attack he would "go and pat a few more wheelchairs on the head – make a gesture", but the TEC's business was really about funding higher-level skills. A leaked document from Somerset TEC, reported in *Training Tomorrow* (May 1992: 11), is quoted as saying that the Special Needs Sub-Group is "a posting box into which anything labelled special needs can be dropped or forgotten about . . . Somerset TEC recognises no obligations in areas of homelessness . . . migration or rehabilitation of ex-offenders".

To overcome the many defects in adult training, particularly ET, the TECs have recommended its replacement by an "adult credit" entitlement. This could be available after 13 weeks of unemployment and should be more closely linked to labour market need than individual preferences with closer integration to the Employment Service (TEC WG 1992). Although this proposal may help to overcome the problems of ET, it does nothing to attack the question of how the goals of training of adults in employment are to be met, which still rely almost exclusively on IIP. Thus a continuing dilemma is faced by TECs and LECs in the adult field.

Assessment of change

Since TECs and LECs became operational and responsibility for training began to pass into their hands, a number of changes have taken place in the running of the system. Principally, these can be divided into system-wide changes in the way training is funded, and changes within the programme areas themselves. We discuss in turn national providers and the adaptation of programmes.

National providers

The purpose of TECs was to create a flexibility of training to *local* labour market needs. This has cut across two pre-existing national institutional frameworks. The first was the system of Industrial Training Boards (ITBs) and Industrial Training Organizations (ITOs). As a result of this potential conflict, the White Paper (DE 1988) recommended the abolition of ITBs. The ITBs had covered 15.5m employees, or 62% of the workforce in 1969. The number of ITBs reduced from 27 in 1969 to seven in the early 1980s. Most became ITOs. They became unpopular with government, and many were widely regarded as moribund, largely because they became merely another training provider after they lost their right to a training levy in 1981.[35] However, two ITBs survived (EITB and CITB) as well as many ITOs. The CBI (1989a: 9) pointed out that the "overwhelming majority" of members in the construction industry and the construction sector of the engineering industry wanted their ITBs and ITOs to continue. The two remaining ITBs and the ITOs have managed to negotiate directly with individual TECs, and with the TNPU (see below) and account for about one-half of the national provider training places. The other half is accounted for by large multi-site companies.

The second pre-existing national system was the TA Large Contractors Unit and the Large Companies Unit (LCUs), for YT and ET, respectively. These units provided a means by which companies and ITOs could negotiate contracts for their trainees at a national level without negotiating with individual TA Area Offices. The two LCUs were initially replaced by the TECs and National Providers Unit (TNPU). This was then superseded by the National Managing Agency (NMA, see below) to cover contracts for 1993/94 onwards.

The *TNPU* was intended to fulfil a similar function to the two LCUs, with the crucial difference that TECs had the *choice* of using it. Hence, it was envisaged that TECs might hold some contracts with national providers directly and others through the TNPU. However, in practice it was clear by 1991 that the TNPU had become little more than a "post-box" for contracts. The TNPU offered contracts with national providers to each TEC which were then executed directly with the TECs. This imposed a large administrative burden on national providers. At the start of 1991 the situation was exacerbated by the fact that many TECs were still in the process of deciding whether to use national providers at all when the point of time was passed at which providers had to issue statutory redundancy

167

warnings to their staff. Many were talking openly of the destruction of a national training infrastructure for the sake of local flexibility. In the event many large national providers have withdrawn from YT, e.g. B&Q, and Dixons.

TECs and LECs have not equally shared the view that the TNPU arrangements are of mutual benefit, and in many cases have chosen to contract locally. Their concerns include a feeling that TNPU arrangements for local areas are often based on poor information, which in some cases in the past had led to a funding shortfall for TEC/LEC provision and unfilled places. TNPU schemes do offer a higher level of employed-status trainees (80% compared to 40% for the rest of YT), but have a lower level of filling contracted places (75% compared to 90% for the rest of YT) and for achieving NVQs (50% compared to 98%). It was apparent from interview comments that use of the TNPU was in general not highly valued. Arguments presented against its use included: resentment of the loss of direct management which undermined local flexibility; that TNPU was overcentralised; and that much national provision was of poor quality. Many TEC/LEC officers saw no requirement for a TNPU brokerage rôle except at the margins where there existed a proliferation of small contracts. It was in these cases that they were happy to use TNPU as a "post-box".

Many of the TECs and LECs who did made use of TNPU were nonetheless negative about it, seeing it as perhaps a necessary but not particularly welcome collaborator. In examining reasons for staying within the system, one chief executive (TEC 49) noted the serious staffing implications of pulling out altogether, given the extra workload involved in administering these contracts locally. Other TECs and LECs note that the costs of TNPU contracts are much cheaper in management time because they come virtually ready made. Estimates suggest that in 1992 TNPU contracts were one-third to one-half of the management unit cost of local contracts.[36] Hence for those TECs finding it difficult to obtain local contractors, "TNPU proved a godsend" (TEC chief executive 75). Hence, despite evidence of a perceived widespread dissatisfaction with TNPU, in 1991 two-thirds of TECs were either still using or were planning to use TNPU for at least some services, with only a third not doing so, suggesting a rôle for some form of national contracting mechanism. Use of the TNPU was much more widespread in England and Wales where only 5 TECs chose not to use it than in Scotland, where only 10% of LECs initially contracted with TNPU and the service was withdrawn in Scotland soon after the launch of SE and HIE.

The National Managing Agency (NMA) took over responsibility from TNPU from 1993/94 onwards. Its establishment sought to recognize the dilemma of maintaining a national system of training contracts in the face of the priority for local delivery through TECs and LECs. The TNPU saw major declines in the national provider contracts, from £280 in 1990/91 to £28m in 1992/93. As shown in Table 7.3, TNPU came to concentrate almost exclusively on YT.

The NMA has been established as a partnership outside government. It is a company limited by guarantee with 12 directors – four from TECs and LECs,

Table 7.3 TNPU contracts with national providers 1990/91–1992/93.

	1990/91	1991/92	1992/93
No. of providers contracting with TNPU	180	137	110[3]
No. of TECs contracting with TNPU	82[1]	77	77
YT value (£million)	170	39	27
ET value (£million)	110	0.6	0.6
Total value (£million)	280[2]	40	28[4]
TNPU, YT and ET as percentage of national total	20	5	3

Source: DE, 1992b. *Notes*: [1]All TECs inherited national provider programmes in this year. [2]This year includes £28million subsequently transferred to Scotland and £17million transferred to the five non-contracting TECs in 1991/92. [3]Compared to 1991/92 16 withdrew from government training, 5 contracted locally and 6 no longer took trainees. [4]Contracted output figure which compares to £27million of actual payment in 1991/92 because of unfilled places.

four from national providers, and four independents including the chief executive. It is funded by a system of fees which derive from a "margin" of percentage price "mark-up" negotiated for its contracts between TECs/LECs and national providers. It is envisaged that this margin would be lower for higher volume contracts.[37] It was hoped that some companies that had dropped out of YT would express fresh interest in contracts under this new system.[38] For 1993/94, however, the NMA did little better than maintaining the level of contracts of the TNPU. The market-driven approach to the funding of the NMA reflects a level of frustration by ministers about the high management costs of TNPU and the desire that this cost should be borne by the large firms that benefit from training.

The NMA has an uncertain future. Its acceptance in Scotland is equivocal since its rôle conflicts with the leadership by SE and HIE, and its potential value is much higher to the national providers than to the TECs and LECs from which it must contract. It seems likely that as time progresses the value of these contracts will diminish as more and more TECs concentrate on local provision systems.

Adaptation of adult programmes

Adaptation within TEC/LEC programme areas has initially principally concerned the ET scheme. Quite new systems and innovations for training have been introduced by some TECs and LECs. It was noted earlier that the inflexibilities and perceived weaknesses of ET had led to many calls for a relaxation of its rigidities and an increase in scope for local discretion in devising the most suitable form of the programme. Although the transfer of ET to TECs and LECs did not involve a radical devolution of control over the programme's basic rules, it did provide an opportunity for some degree of innovation to be introduced. In particular, funding negotiations with the DE, after a cut in ET budgets in the Chancellor's 1990 Autumn Statement, led to increased flexibilities in 1991/92, and these were further increased in 1992/93.

The extent to which TECs and LECs have sought to alter the form of their ET programmes can be assessed from TEC/LEC interviews of whether they had introduced already, or were planning to introduce, innovations into it in their area. In 1991/92 nearly half of the TECs/LECs' ET programmes were broadly unchanged from the form that had been inherited from the TA. Just over a quarter were introducing significant variations, and a further quarter were planning major reform of the programme. Innovation appears to be part of a learning process. The age of the TEC/LEC is an important factor in determining the level of innovation in ET. The highest concentration of TECs who had carried out significant changes were those that had been operational for a year, whereas those that had only just become operational (which included all the Scottish LECs in the 1991/92 year) had left ET programmes broadly unchanged. An additional factor influencing innovation is TEC/LEC size. A respondent in one of the smallest TECs in the country noted that its small population (even though it had a high long-term unemployment rate) led to a small ET cohort, as a result of which marginal flexibilities in funding were negligible in absolute terms, once government guarantees had been met (TEC 52).

The type of innovations being introduced to ET vary widely, both in scope and in the degree to which they challenge centrally-determined principles. The programme was originally intended for unemployed persons who had been seeking work for over 6 months, and who would be full-time trainees on the programme. A small number of TECs are tackling the problem of providing incentives to employers to participate by using their ET budget to subsidize training in employment. Others have made employed status a condition for trainees receiving funding ("seeking to take training out of the ghetto of unemployment", TEC 72). Although technically prohibited, some TECs and LECs have been able to use this approach, through efficiency savings and satisfying ET targets on the rest of their small budget.

The expansion in scope of adult training from the limited brief of ET to the funding of adult training in the broadest sense appears to be the ambition of a number of TECs and LECs. Several have reintroduced courses resembling former TOPS provision (adult training schemes abandoned in the mid-1980s), and in a number of cases courses were being offered to trainees who were not yet unemployed. One TEC respondent stressed the status of the *recently* unemployed as "perishable goods" in the sense that prolonged unemployment would be damaging to their readiness for work or career prospects. This and other TECs and LECs therefore felt it more important to offer the short-term unemployed opportunities for training as early as possible, and in many cases in preference to the long-term unemployed.

Problems over the name "ET" were noted earlier, and a very common innovation was for this to be dropped and replaced by an alternative label which was free of the stigma attached to national schemes motivated by unemployment. Other innovations include the following: (i) shorter (or longer) courses, more tailored to skill needs and replacing fixed-length RESTART programmes; (ii) better counselling and referral services, sometimes including intensive induction programmes assessing need and appropriate provision, and reducing the number of stages in the referral process; (iii) developing a tiered system within the programme, in some cases involving progression from one to the next, with different types of provision at each tier; (iv) greater selectivity and emphasis on the quality of training, and seeking to attract committed trainees rather than "bullying the unemployed onto the scheme" (TEC 49); (v) greater levels of customized training; particularly identifying priority areas linked to identified skill needs, these in some cases escaping the cuts applied to the programme as a whole; (vi) using differential funding for different types of training, rather than a standard price; and (vii) the adoption of an "entitlement" approach to adult training, in contrast to the strict eligibility rules employed formerly by the TA.

Other innovations

Looking beyond the immediate scope of the ET programme, TECs and LECs have also introduced other innovations in their training activity. Examples of the innovations being introduced include training "health checks", which offer a basic assessment of the state of a firm's development and training needs, sometimes linked to developing a strategy for reaching the IIP standard. One TEC had devised the notion of a "Traineeship" – involving a training action plan drawn up with the Careers Service, to provide a more coherent programme for the 16–19 age range. Another offers the extension of YT to a third year to trainees who achieve high standards, and who are given the opportunity to reach a higher-level NVQ. This might be accompanied by incentives to employers whose YT trainees continue post-programme training in employment to reach NVQ Level 3. Voucher schemes for adult trainees are being planned in some cases, as a parallel to the Training Credits available to younger people. A number of TECs/LECs are developing strategies to attract labour market returners. In some cases this amounts to a major initiative: one TEC has developed a scheme called "Freshstart", which seeks to remove barriers inhibiting returners from resuming training or work, including childcare provision and flexible hours/weeks (TEC 31). A number of TECs/LECs have introduced redundancy schemes through which they seek to tackle, in an anticipatory way, the needs of redundant workers in advance of their unemployment. In some cases this includes seeking financial subsidy for the programme from next-destination employers who benefit from any retraining effort, as well as from the firm responsible for the redundancy. Other identified innovations include: more flexible forms of Business Growth Training (BGT); One Stop Shops (OSS) for training advice; styling training funding as a "bursary" rather than as a programme, to escape the stigma attached to government schemes with a poor public profile; and the provision of open learning training packages.

In order to make objective assessment of the extent to which TECs and LECs were innovating in training overall, 62 TECs and LECs have been systematically graded in this book with respect to their level of innovation in YT and ET. Only just over half had instituted innovations in 1991/92, a small number were planning innovations, and more than a third had no innovation plans at all. Of the innovators, more than one-third can be graded as "high levels of innovation", the rest being innovators at a "low to medium" level. There is a possible influence on innovation of the former origin of the TEC/LEC chief executive. The TECs and LECs with a high level of innovation are twice as likely to be headed by chief executives from the former TA or DE as those from outside the system. This confirms our earlier observations that in the early phases there was a considerable benefit for chief executives who understood the system and were able and anxious to develop changes from which they were previously held back. There is mounting evidence, however, that the early innovators are some of the only innovators. On the one hand, the national funding cuts and pressures to meet national performance targets have severely restricted the scope for initiative. On the other hand, TECs and LECs have increasingly moved away from considering innovation in YT and ET unemployment programmes as a major objective at all. They have instead been more anxious to develop the other elements of their remit, particularly training in employment and its necessary link to enterprise. In our assessment these areas of innovation have given those TEC staff who originated from outside the system considerable edge over former TA/DE staff who have continued to be more concerned with training innovation in the inherited ET and YT programmes.

Identifying the gaps

The recent evolution of training in Britain in which the TECs and LECs play a key part has gone a long way to putting in place a system-wide development. In a very real sense the foundations of a quality system have been laid. But, although a major leap forward has occurred, the question must be asked of how far this system can achieve the objectives it seeks.

In our analysis we conclude that the scope for TECs and LECs to change their inherited system has been modest. We identify the following problems that have to be overcome:

- *Stability*: The public funding structure for training is still effectively dominated by the Treasury PES-round and not by the needs of the market. The debate in the autumn of 1993 about reallocation of YT funds to the DFE colleges has reminded everyone in TECs of their dependence on government fiat. This has led to short-termism, expressed by 1 year contracts, and the details of training standards, which are still highly subject to detailed intervention by TEED rather than relying on the national system of standards of NVQ to guide local decisions.
- *No weapons to fulfil mission*: The TECs and LECs have been given few effec-

tive weapons to allow them to have any chance of succeeding in their defined mission of raising the skills of the workforce already in employment. They cannot access the negotiations between employer and employee, they cannot influence the incentives to either party, and they have no legitimacy to act widely with businesses in their areas because of their independence of hosts and absence of a representational base.

- *A renewed unemployment mission*: The 1990–92 recession has refocused minds and distorted both the public debate and the TECs' and LECs' own agendas. TECs and LECs were conceived in relatively prosperous times, but born during a recession. Despite evidence that companies' training budgets were holding up better than they had in the recession of the early 1980s, TECs and LECs have found it difficult to find enough work placements for YT trainees[39] or to allow Compact job guarantees to be met. With no levers on training in employment, and in an adverse economic climate, it is natural for TECs and LECs to focus on the area where they do have resources and discretion, but their Board, mission and constitution do not always fit them well for the task.
- *Flexibility*: TECs have not had the independence of TEED they would like. Senior TEED spokesmen have criticized the TECs because "they have not properly described what they want". But the gap is chiefly one of culture. A commercial concern looks to its outcomes and satisfaction of objectives (typically the profit "bottom line"), it concerns itself with minutiae of the process only where necessary. The TEED interventionist methodology, however, is dominated by a process-driven assessment and audit through Treasury or TEED's FAM. The CBI (1989b: 13) pointed out, at the outset, that senior business leaders "do not see themselves acting as rubber stamps for the delivery of existing programmes"; TECs should have "both extensive scope to adapt national programmes to meet local needs and sizeable discretionary budgets". The low level of virement between programmes and the provision of only 1.5% of the TEC budget available in its discretionary Local Initiatives Fund (LIF) all undermine the top business leaders on TEC Boards and prevent each TEC developing its mission. It can be argued that the LIF needs to be at least 10% of the total grant and virement 100% to allow sufficient management flexibility. This discretion has not been granted to TECs and LECs.
- *Employment training*: A particular source of irritation to many TECs and LECs is the inability to make the major changes that this programme needs. A relaxation is required of the requirements (i) that trainees recruited to funded adult training be unemployed, and (ii) that subsidies to employers to take on adult unemployed trainees as employees are prohibited.
- *16–19 Credits and the Careers Service*: There have been important reforms in the development of both of these areas. But there is a continuing conflict between the concept of entitlement for all 16–19-year-olds and the Treasury's view that, if employers want their staff to be qualified, then they

should pay for them. The concept of entitlement also opens up the wider question of the organization of 16–19 provision. Training credits sit uncomfortably with the way in which education is developing the main funding arrangements for 16–19-year-olds. Furthermore, there remains the problem of linking vocational development post-16 to a better information service for young people. The reform of the Careers Service and school-based careers guidance is still a political football; Careers Service Partnerships are a compromise between DE and DFE, not a solution; the full implementation of a national Record of Vocational Achievement (NROVA) is still in its infancy; and the development in schools of vocational education, business links and work experience hangs in the balance pending the evolution of the national curriculum (as discussed in Chapter 8). Section 24 of the Education Reform Act can be used as a strong lever to make NVQs and business involvement a common currency. But there has to be considerable doubt that this will be fully achieved.

– *Diffusion of training culture*: There is a major problem in developing training down the size spectrum to smaller and medium-sized businesses. The leverage of the IIP kitemark appears irrelevant to most SMEs and is unlikely to persuade many firms, unless labour supply is very tight which it will not be for some years to come. We argue in later chapters that there is a gap between thinking on training and thinking on enterprise development. The absence of a link between the needs of training, on the one hand, and the needs of business support in a wider sense, through the stages of foundation, development and growth, on the other, is a key gap in the case of smaller firms. Training needs to be driven by businesses' needs, not the reverse. Without a proper mechanism of transmission of demand from small businesses, TECs and LECs remain handicapped:

– *Supervisor training*: Although all the developments of TECs and LECs will stimulate the development of training management within firms, supervisory training has at present no proper organizational base within the institutional network and it is not fully built into the system of NVQs. For example, there is no equivalent of the German *Meister*. Although there are some outstanding examples of the implementation of MCI in large companies, even the most fervent supporters of MCI recognize that it is not an adequate system for transmitting the stimulus required for trainer training. It is aimed at a different set of problems. Moreover almost all the TECs' products of IIP, MCI, NVQ and APL have a relevance to the organization of larger firms that is not present in SMEs.

– *Public servant culture*: Although the contract of TECs and LECs with government has significantly improved since 1992/93, many of the main benefits of this have yet to reach training providers. TEC and LEC training managers have far to go in developing the business skills required to turn TECs and LECs into effective bodies.

TECs and LECs have struggled hard with their tasks through NVQ; the foundations of a strong training system have now been established that could allow Britain at last to achieve a world class standard in training – a goal that has eluded the country since at least the 1870s. However, it is essential to identify the problems that remain to be overcome. We develop our arguments about solutions in Chapter 12. Britain must learn to emulate the German or Japanese practice of continuing to develop systems rather than throw them away with each change in minister or new government. But to succeed, the strategy that has been developed over recent years needs a more formal structure of implementation. Relying on voluntarism alone seems a risky strategy where sustained developments are required for a period of at least 10 or 15 years before the attitudes of employers, employees, trainers, educationalists and parents have developed sufficiently to assure a self-sustaining momentum.

Chapter 8
Education

Shifting the diagnosis up and down the age spectrum

Education is one of the key resources on which individuals draw in order to respond to the demands of the world of work. On the quality of this response depends the quality of the economy. Education, as distinct from training, is not one of the primary functions of TECs and LECs. Nevertheless, education is the crucial base on which training is built. The 1980s demonstrated forcefully that tackling training problems, although important, could contribute to only part of the solution to Britain's skills problem. Schools, colleges and higher education also had to be a target for change. Indeed many of the problems inherent in meeting training targets rely to a significant extent on educational prerequisites. For example, the 1980s saw many employers struggling with YT programmes or their own in-house training increasingly having to provide basic prerequisite skills of *functional* literacy and numeracy before they could begin technical skills training. In 1993 a survey showed that over 20% of employers were encountering problems arising from employees' lack of reading or writing ability.[1]

In the light of these issues it was natural, therefore, that the debate about human resources should move towards schools and that TECs and LECs would be given a rôle. In addition, as TECs and LECs have matured, they have also begun to realize the importance of the educational base, and within that the significance of primary as well as secondary education. Moreover, the structure of further and higher education has also been increasingly understood as a constraint on younger people's patterns of choice so that it has been natural that Further Education (FE) colleges, as well as the universities and former polytechnics, should also become the focus for reforms.

In this chapter we assess the development of TECs and LECs in the fields of education. Their budget has approximately 2% allocated to education in England and Wales, and less than 1% in Scotland. Of this, the major part is for Work-Related Further Education (WRFE), £10.5m, nearly half of the total. WRFE is not a TEC responsibility in Scotland. There is also the TEC/LEC funding of part-time training through YT and Credits, which we have discussed in Chapter 7. Excluding the rôle of Credits, the TEC and LEC rôle in education is restricted.

As a result, the staff and resources they can devote are small, usually only 2–3 staff per TEC or LEC for the whole education field. Hence most of their objectives must be achieved through influencing other agents. In this chapter we assess developments through the following points:
- Developing national targets;
- Demarcating the field;
- Compacts;
- Education–Business Partnerships (EBPs);
- Challenges post-16;
- The rôle of higher education.

Developing national targets

We have already summarized in Chapter 2 the long-term difficulties that the British economy has experienced and the crucial rôle played by an educational system as both cause and effect of economic decline. The problem for the British economy created by a poor educational base for most of the population was recognized as early as the 1870s. But only in the 1980s has a wide range of initiatives sought to tackle specific problems. These derived from both the former DES and DE. But the late 1980s and 1990s have seen a more systematic approach to enhancing the educational system. This derives from two key developments: the development of a national curriculum, and the development of wider national education and training targets (NETTs).

National curriculum

The national curriculum derives from the implementation of the Education Reform Act (ERA) in 1988. It is based on three "core" subjects of Mathematics, Science and English (and Welsh in Wales) and "foundation" subjects at ages 5–14. At ages 11–14 the foundation subjects increase in number with the introduction of a modern foreign language. From 14–16 the core subjects continue, but the mix of foundation subjects varies and a further range of technical and vocational subjects are to be introduced. However, the technical and vocational studies have stood outside the national curriculum regulations and their rôle is still unclear. Indeed, technology, once one of "the shining new jewels of the national curriculum crown", is now being "singled out for urgent reform".[2]

These developments place a major emphasis on the "irreducible dimensions" of educational inputs and are linked to a system of assessment for pupils and teachers to identify what has been taught and the level of attainment on each of a very detailed range of targets. The national curriculum is not intended to be the whole curriculum, so that teachers will be free to vary the range of materials beyond the specific targets, and particularly will have freedom over the way they are taught.[3] However, the demands of the prescribed subjects and targets radically curtail teacher freedom in these areas.

The curtailment of teacher and school autonomy over the curriculum has been a key objective of the reforms. This autonomy has been seen as a major constraint on raising educational standards by those outside the profession. The roots of this autonomy reach back to the 1950s and 1960s. As we saw in Chapter 2 "the golden age of teacher autonomy"[4] gave the chance for an "ideology of teacher professionalism"[5] to take hold. This ideology assisted in the creation of a so-called "secret garden" of the curriculum. At worst this led to "anti-vocationalism" which opposed business involvement in schooling, and at best it reinforced an artificial separation of general education and vocational education and training.[6] The 1990s will see a system for local delivery of national attainment targets introduced which represents a fundamental break with the past.[7]

National Education and Training Targets (NETTs)

Paralleling the development of the national curriculum has been the development of a wider set of targets that cross the traditional education–vocational divide. In discussion of training, in Chapter 7, we have already outlined the structure of the NETTs, endorsed by government in response to pressures by CBI, TUC and other external bodies. These targets also impact on education.

The NETTs are measured in a "currency" of NVQs. For example, the targets at level NVQ 2 are equivalent to 4 GCSEs at grade A, B or C.[8] The target set has been to raise the proportion from 45% to 80% of young people aged 16–18 achieving this level by the year 2000. Many will achieve these at age 16 on completion of the national curriculum through GCSE. But it will be sought to encourage others to stay on to achieve this level, often through a further 1 or 2 years of full-time study. Others will achieve the equivalent through YT or other part-time courses while training on-the-job.

At level NVQ 3 the academic equivalent is 2 "A"-Levels (or 3 Scottish Highers). The target is to raise the proportion of the population achieving this level from 30% in 1990 to 50% by 2000.

In addition to the targets for 16–18-year-olds at GCSE and "A"-Level are a range of further targets: (i) for raising the qualifications for the presently employed workforce (50% at NVQ 3 by the year 2000), to be sought primarily through Accreditation for Prior Learning (APL), and (ii) for developing the training commitment by companies (50% of the 12,000 firms with 200 employees or more should be Investors in People – IIP, see Chapter 7).

In April 1993 a National Advisory Council for Education and Training Targets (NACETT), as well as an equivalent body for Scotland (SACETT) were established. These seek to draw together the activities of the DE, DFE and indeed DTI in the fields of education and training. This development offers an important step forward in co-ordinating different government departmental policies. From a TEC/LEC perspective, however, these bodies do little to facilitate their development of interactions with government. We appraise NACETT further in Chapters 6 and 11.

The rôle of TECs and LECs

The TECs and LECs are given, with others, responsibility for the achievement of the targets for YT, APL and IIP. To achieve these targets TECs and LECs need to develop deep and widespread links with a large number of companies. This is proving difficult, not least, as we have seen in Chapter 7, because the IIP product is difficult to sell and many companies perceive that they have no reason to buy it. The main TEC/LEC rôle in national targets is, therefore, difficult, as yet, to achieve. But they also have a rôle in providing support to the educational process through helping school–business links to develop through Compacts, the Partnership Initiative EBPs and through Careership Partnerships. We discuss these later in this chapter where we also find TECs and LECs struggling to develop a significant input.

The difficulties for the development of the TEC/LEC rôle in education stem from two key sources: first, the absence of an effective link with business on a broad and deep basis (we discuss this further in relation to enterprise activity in Chapter 9); and second, the lack of a close enough relation between business's needs and the mainstream education process. We discuss these further below.

Demarcating the field

One of the key educational objectives of TECs and LECs is to overcome the gaps that exist between schools and business. As James Callaghan and OECD pointed out in 1976, the failure of the educational professional was at least equally matched by the unwillingness of employers to take any direct interest in education or to develop major responsibility for vocational training. However, the culture and organization of LEAs has been a formidable barrier to overcome. Even educationalists recognise a culture of departmentalism, top-down direction, and multi-tiered LEA officer functions.[9] These features have made education inaccessible to business and other "outsiders" and have isolated business from education's wider objectives in both economy and society.

The gap between education and business is all the more startling when those educational areas in which business most commonly states its priorities are analyzed. Most studies of these objectives emphasise:[10]

- Acceptance of quality standards on the part of all involved;
- Punctuality;
- Teamwork;
- Persistence;
- Ability to plan and solve problems;
- Maturity;
- Readiness to learn.

In the words of Chris Marsden, Director of BP's Educational Relations Unit:[11]
"The emerging partnership between education and business is about Total Qual-

ity. It is about increasing the quality of performance of both education and business and the contribution each can make to the other. . . . A business is driven hard by its bottom line . . . education, on the other hand, has apparently never had the importance of its bottom line similarly questioned by the public."

Indeed it has never been clear what the bottom line of education actually is. But to the extent that education should be about basic standards of numeracy and literacy, almost all of what business is seeking from education is in line with mainstream educational objectives. Two things need to be made clear: first, raising general educational standards is an issue which has been highlighted by economic imperatives but is *not* an issue which centres only on business needs. Second, reorienting the curriculum so that it is more attuned to business is necessary, but does not just entail the teaching of specific vocational skills. It is also part of a "system" shift which focuses on moving the curriculum away from more abstract knowledge towards issues in the "real world".

A problem with government thinking in this area during the 1980s and 1990s is that it has failed fully to come to terms with the tension between those in the Conservative party who link educational standards to a "traditional" academic curriculum and those who wish to see the needs of business applied to education. For the former group the emphasis on the academic, as evidenced through its defence of the existing "A"-Level system, promotes a narrow system in which "vocational" subjects fail to achieve high status and hence become confined to the less able. For the latter group, the emphasis is on raising skill levels for business across the board, and on breaking down the difference in status between the academic and vocational curriculum which we have identified as a key aspect of Britain's system failure in education. Failure to resolve this dilemma accounts for much of the confusion in thinking in the detail of education policy over the past decade, notwithstanding the overall clear thrust towards a national curriculum and target setting.

As a result of this tension, the development of the rôle of TECs and LECs in the field of education has not surprisingly been problematic. Their rôle, although important, is clearly not central. The bulk of the financial leverage on education comes from the DFE, despite a series of new policies in the 1980s which eroded the extent of DFE domination in favour of the DE. Clearly, therefore, the strength of TECs/LECs' strategic capabilities in developing a rôle with education cannot be derived from direct powers.

But in addition to these practical limitations, another difficulty that the TECs and LECs have had to overcome is a serious deficiency in their understanding and experience of the operation of the education system. As noted in Chapter 4, over 90% of TEC/LEC staff were derived from the local offices of the TA. Most of the staff of the former TA, many of whom remain in TECs, were administrators of training schemes, whose expertise was in contracting for, monitoring and accounting for places on national training programmes, and gathering and processing labour market data.

The difficulties that have ensued were mirrored in the earlier experience of the MSC, the forerunner of the TA for whom most TA staff previously worked. When the MSC was allocated responsibilities for a significant portion of WRFE spending in 1985, a widely recognized problem was that its local staff had little or no experience in the new area for which they had become responsible. The development of a working relationship between local civil servants and LEA staff over the ensuing period was marked by a recognition that much reliance had to be placed on educational administrators. Similarly, the TA's other major areas of responsibilities in education, the Compacts and Technical and the Vocational Education Initiative (TVEI), were handled not by TA Area Offices but by Regional and Head Office staff. In consequence, the educational expertise located within TA Area Offices at the advent of TECs and LECs remained very limited, and even those local officers engaged in WRFE work were few in number and largely segregated from the Offices' mainstream activities.[12] In Scotland, the former SDA/HIDB had been without an education brief of any kind. The legacy inherited by TECs and LECs, therefore, afforded them little base of expertise from which to develop educational policies.

As a result of the demarcation of the education field which emerged in the late 1980s the DE has had responsibility for specific work-related aspects and the DFE has retained the control of core education programmes and the curriculum. In practice, this has given TECs and LECs a rôle in the following programmes:

In schools – managing the contracts for links between business and education through Compacts and the Partnership Initiative; a rôle with Teacher Placement Organisers (TPOs); a partnership rôle in Careership Partnerships to link employers and the Careers Service; offering help in finding school business governors;

In colleges – contracting directly for YT, ET and related programmes; allocating 25% of the WRFE budget (within which they were given 15% discretion in 1992/92); an important consultative rôle in the regional FE Funding Councils; offering help in finding college business governors;

In Higher Education – contracting directly for Higher Technology National Training (HTNT); links for research; partnerships to stimulate improved staying on 16–19 and into HE.

But despite these significant rôles, TECs and LECs have been excluded from direct relations to the classroom process. A strong interdepartmental rivalry resulted from the successes of DE following the 1984 White Paper *Training for Jobs*. The DE gained control over the allocation to LEAs and colleges of 16% of the Education Block Grant for WRFE funds, subsequently introduced WRFE plans for colleges in 1986, and introduced TVEI which allowed direct links with schools. Later, from 1988, Compacts began to develop, followed in 1991 by EBPs and the extension of Compacts to all LEAs. The then DES strongly resisted the expansion of these DE products into its domain and was "affronted" by losing part of its education budget for WRFE. Ironically, it was the DES, however, which successfully defended this element of WRFE expenditure when the Treasury wanted it cut in the Autumn 1991 PES round for the 1992/93 financial year.

Understanding the limited impact of TECs and LECs on education also has to be put into the context of the other great changes and uncertainty in education at the time TECs and LECs began their life. On the one hand, this offered TECs/LECs the potential to mould the direction of these changes. On the other hand, however, it also meant that, from the point of view of education, TECs/LECs were simply "just another initiative" that cluttered an already crowded domain. To the teacher in the classroom, and to most heads and officers, the debates about TEC/LEC rôles has seemed remote indeed.

The major changes in the education system derive from the 1988 Education Reform Act, and further Acts in 1991 and 1992. These have involved:

- Major changes to the relations between agents involved in the management of education at all levels of the service; between LEAs and central government, between LEAs and schools, between schools and teachers, and between teachers, schools and central government.[13] Most significantly, the LEA is gradually being written out of the equation altogether. Increasing numbers of schools are becoming grant-maintained, sixth-form and FE colleges have been removed from LEA control, and schools now manage their own budgets through local management of schools (LMS) legislation. Increasingly, LEAs are moving to the position of being a provider of services to schools with no guarantee that schools will wish to purchase what they have to offer; they may wither away altogether. Schools, for their part, are being encouraged to specialize and to compete for pupils, to become more diverse in terms of organization and curriculum within the new national framework of the curriculum and national target standards.
- Major changes to the curriculum and modes of assessment through the introduction of the national curriculum which is seeking to bring about (i) greater uniformity between schools, and (ii) the establishment of an assured minimum quality standard of knowledge and skills base of the pupils at each stage and of the quality of the teachers/schools providing it.

The field in which TECs and LECs have been given a remit for action is somewhat tangential to these major changes. It also suffers from being characterized by fragmentation and diversity. As a result, the main long-term service that they can provide has become school–business links. During the 1980s these were left largely to schools with little co-ordination either in schools or at LEA level, although the development of Compacts and locally-led EBPs began to bring some coherence to the field from about 1988 onwards. However, many business links, work experience activities, vocational inputs, technology and organizational structures to work with business have remained either peripheral or have acted as "bolt-ons" to mainstream education. There is little evidence of integration between the two:

- In *organization*, there are incompatibilities between, on the one hand, the

182

market-oriented approach of the Education Reform Act and independence of grant-maintained schools, and on the other hand, the LEA-level partnerships of Compacts, the Partnership Initiative and TECs/LECs. The resolution of these tensions is even more uncertain given current debates about the structure of local government as a whole. Moreover, with schools increasingly "buying-in" the services they need, including advice and support on links to business, important questions are raised about TEC/LEC activity in such a "free market". In particular, with tightening budgets, and in the absence of incentives to maintain them, the survival of school–industry links may come to depend more and more on the priorities of individual school management teams and governing bodies, a situation which has not proved conducive to effective and long-term links in the past.

– In the *curriculum*, the links between TVEI and the national curriculum are still to be fully determined, as is the precise rôle of the cross-curricular theme, economic and industrial awareness.

Given these factors, the rôle of TECs and LECs is likely to remain tightly constrained as far as education 5–16 is concerned. We examine below the main developments that have occurred.

Compacts

Compacts existed prior to TECs and LECs. Launched by the government in 1988, Compacts are agreements between education and business to raise attainment through the incentive of guaranteed jobs. There are joint signatories to these agreements at local level: the LEAs and a local business organization. Usually the local business organization was a Chamber of Commerce.[14] Where no satisfactory business organization existed, local companies had to be created to run Compacts. Since 1991/92 TECs and LECs have taken over all Compacts. Compacts were funded by central government and grants were available initially only in Urban Programme Areas (UPAs). Since late 1991 Compacts were made available to all LEAs, although their purpose outside of UPAs has never been completely clear.

The experience of developing Compacts has offered four important lessons for TEC/LEC development. First, it has put a major emphasis on the rôle of targets, close monitoring, and direct pupil–school–business relationships. Targets have been most important in focusing minds and giving all parties (pupils, teachers, parents, headteachers and businesses) clear aims with clearly identified rewards. This has in turn facilitated a process of much closer monitoring. Direct relationships between pupils and businesses have fostered a reward concept. The reward used – of a job guarantee – was thought to be the most appropriate to the areas in which Compacts were developed, the inner city UPAs with high unemployment levels.

Second, Compacts have been important as a means of setting targets relevant to education, contributing centrally to its development, but largely peripheral to the classroom process. The targets of attendance, punctuality and attainment that were sought are all of direct relevance to employers, provide obvious benefit to the pupils and teachers, but influence incentives rather than process. They left the teachers and schools free to develop teaching in their own way. Hence, although there have been tensions, Compacts have generally proved popular in schools.

Third, Compacts, like TVEI, have been path-breaking for government in forging direct links between businesses and schools rather than with LEAs. Compacts have thus reinforced the pressures to make direct links with the providers (teachers and schools) and to side-step the bureaucracies of the LEAs. This has occurred because although the LEA had to take responsibility for administering the education side of Compacts the management was kept "slim" and separate from the main bureaucracy. Compact directors had considerable discretion and could, in the main, respond quickly to events. This side-stepping was stimulated by the learning achieved in the Boston Compact where delivery of targets was initially prevented by an ineffective transmission through the education bureaucracy (the school Board) to the schools.[15] Compacts have thus been an important stage in learning about *means of developing effective transmission mechanisms* to stimulate change.

Fourth, Compacts were an important step in the development of thinking about TECs and LECs. Some of the senior TA staff responsible for Compact became the early core staff in the design of TECs.[16] Like LENs, Compacts sought to work with a local employer body that could manage its side of the delivery of targets: in this case a process of links with schools and the job guarantee. Compacts had to have a business body or group as signatory to the contract. Failure to achieve this resulted in the TA turning down a Compact bid (as occurred in Dundee) or seeking a new mechanism locally through the foundation of a local business group as a new company to administer the contract (as occurred in Newham). In practice a wide variety of Compact signatories emerged, with most being Chambers of Commerce. This led to a patchy structure of often uneven quality. What Compacts taught senior DE staff was that a more assured and nation-wide pattern of business leadership was required; that a contract could be developed with new groups of local business leaders through formation of new local companies, and that the stimulus of resources, and targets of a job to be done, was sufficient to entrain many local business leaders.

As TECs and LECs developed, most took *de facto* control of the contract themselves; *de jure* TEED made them do this as part of the rearrangement of their contracts to give more power to TECs/LECs, but in some areas the Compact have remained de facto with an outside body. By mid-1991 42% of TECs and LECs had assumed formal responsibility for Compacts, and by April 1992 all were in this formal position. The result of this change has been to produce a better integration of the TEC/LEC Board and Compact business group, usually through a subgroup of the Board with additional business members. But it has cut across existing local business groups in areas where these are strong. In this sense TECs and LECs have used Compacts to reinforce direct *provision* rather than using subcontracting and *enabling*. They have thus often reduced rather than enhanced local business leadership and transmission mechanisms to firms. Taking control themselves, the TECs/LECs have had to rely to a greater extent on their own capacity to make wide links in the business community (which has typically been poor) and have had to rely to a greater extent on the LEAs than their own staff (who in this field are usually small in number and inexperienced). As a result TECs and LECs have not always been able to manage Compacts as effectively as under the former management arrangements and there has been much reinvention of the wheel.[17]

Education–business partnerships

Formally-constituted Education–Business Partnerships (EBPs), like Compacts, pre-date TECs. These began to appear through the activities of LEAs and businesses in the late 1980s alongside the development of Compacts. They were stimulated by autonomous local action or by the development of initiatives from Business in the Community (BiTC), particularly through some major company secondment schemes. They were conceived as wider partnerships, embracing a range of activities different from Compacts, but still targeted at specific agreed objectives.

Thus EBPs are much more "bottom-up" in origin than Compacts. They have also had a wider set of targets, often extremely diverse. They initially tended to be LEA-led but with a major input from a business organization or company secondee. In many cases they have become a means better to co-ordinate and develop link activities and work experience. But most importantly, they have become the source of experience to expand the concept of organized business–education links beyond UPAs into a diverse range of schools and LEAs which in *most* cases patently do not suffer from the normally identified educational "problems". These areas, often rural, small town or suburban communities often have high staying-on rates, high attendance, high examination attainment, and high levels of entry to higher education.

The rôle of TECs and LECs with EBPs primarily derives from the Partnerships Initiative announced in early 1991. This initially allocated modest sums over a maximum 2 year period to assist in the establishment of one EBP per TEC area. In the first year there was up to £50,000, and in the second year up to £25,000, on top of an initial £10,000 available as development funding. In late 1992 it was announced that EBP funding would be continued for 2 further years.

The chief impact of the Partnership Initiative has been to shift the funding responsibility of many local initiatives towards the TEC. IMS (1993) found that 23% of all EBPs were part of the TEC and 16% were joint TEC/LEA managed. As a result the TECs have become the main co-funder of EBPs. In 1992/93 59% of EBPs were TEC co-financed with the DE, whereas only 22% of EBPs received financial support from LEAs, 29% from the private sector and 11% from other public sources. The Partnership Initiative is therefore the main funder of most EBPs and the TECs are the only other source of finance in most cases. The initiative appears to stand or fall on the back of DE money of one form or another.

Using their new responsibility for EBPs the TECs and LECs have had significant problems of managing these education initiatives. Before the Partnership Initiative some areas had one or more Compact, an autonomous EBP and other link arrangements. Each may have had different targets, different methods of monitoring and different management and Boards. In some cases they relied on the TEC's and LEC's own business leaders and substructure, in other cases they drew from other local business bodies or the LEA's management resources. In some cases the partnership was deep and genuine, e.g. in Cheshire, Salford or Newham; in other cases it was superficial or in the very early stages of development. There was thus considerable confusion: first, created by government through a conflict between Partnerships Initiative EBPs and Compact extension; second, created by mixed messages about targets and objectives coming from government, autonomous EBPs and over 20 link organizations each with their own often diverse aims for business–education links; third, by conflict between the DFE and DE over the depth, form, targets and monitoring of links; fourth, between national curriculum developments affecting the mainstream of education and the EBP process which has been left largely as a "bolt-on"; fifth, between the ambitious objectives for links and the paltry resources being made available in most cases; and sixth, by confusion among TECs and LECs about the rôle they are supposed to play.

Given the variety of EBPs, it is not surprising that the experience of TECs and LECs has been very varied. Also, the low level of educational expertise amongst TEC/LEC staff, noted earlier, led to many late starters in the EBP development process. In 1990, 67% of TECs and 100% of LECs thought that an EBP did not exist in their area prior to their own involvement,[18] despite survey evidence that all LEAs had at least some EBP activity in place at that time.[19] Interviews in 1991 indicated that the mistaken impression amongst some TEC and LEC staff seems to have been that their intervention in education–business links marked the first significant development of this kind in their area. Hence the knowledge by TECs/LECs of previous efforts of education staff and businesses in developing links was extremely limited. This error is repeated in the IMS (1993: 1) study which claims that "only half of the areas now covered by Employment Department supported partnerships had some form of partnership structure prior to the [EBP] initiative".

Detailed surveys show that TEC/LEC officers were more aware of EBPs where they were most strongly developed. In England and Wales, recognition of the prior existence of EBPs in relation to the CBI survey levels in ascending order of strength at 2/2–3, 3, and 3–4 and above, was made by 43%, 58% and 67% respectively of those areas' TECs. In Scotland, where in 1991 6 LECs had EBPs at level 3, and 1 at level 4, a perceived total absence of EBPs on the part of LECs prior to their existence confirms the generally poor awareness by their staff of prior educational developments.

Looking beyond the early stages, TECs and LECs appear to be now expanding EBPs. The most common approach has been to build on existing LEA arrangements (in the case of 53% of TECs and 21% of LECs),[20] with a much smaller number building on Compact arrangements or starting EBPs from scratch.

Since the 1993/94 year *Strategic Fora* have been developed. These have been led by TEED's Educational Division and passed to TECs to take the lead if no-one else does. The objective is to create a mechanism for dialogue "above the TEC; the TEC Board is not well equipped and does not have the right kind of interests to act as the vehicle for the forum",[21] although the TEC is clearly seen as "a first among equals". The TECs interest is levered by PRF. Bonus points (see Chapter 6) are awarded to a TEC which sets up a strategic forum with (i) a clear statement of aims, (ii) a plan for each component to meet aims, and (iii) responsibility to move towards locally-defined versions of NETTs. The fora have been one way for education–business links to move beyond specific TEED programme initiatives. They also seek to be more bottom-up in developing a strategy from the operational managers rather than transplanting it from TEED to TEC Board level and from there to local agents. It is a step in the right direction, and is beginning to improve the climate of local co-operation in many areas. But strategic fora do not directly tackle the problem of enhancing the classroom priorities for economic needs; rather they provide a mechanism to manage links better. Fundamental change to the curriculum is still awaited.

The most popular areas of activity for TECs and LECs in their education links is the development of Records of Achievement (ROAs), development of individual action plans and teacher placements (see Figure 8.1). The next most popular areas are fund-raising, work experience provision and classroom curriculum projects. In Scotland, LECs involvement in EBPs seems to have been more limited and more focused. In Scotland, teacher placements and business secondees to education were the most popular link activities.

The priorities set by TECs/LECs for EBPs are important, given the complexity and variety of views about EBPs. In order to explore the goals of TECs and LECs, a range of possible priorities are rated by TECs and LECs and other agents in Table 8.1. For TECs and LECs as a whole, the most highly rated priorities relate to the education side of partnerships. Raising students awareness of business, improving students' attitudes to work and developing teacher attitudes are the three most prominent goals. Curriculum matters are a slightly lower priority, as are priorities relating to specific skill areas. The inclusion of a job guarantee and the raising of new finance are significantly lower priorities. In terms of emphasis between different pupil age-groups, virtually all TECs and LECs place

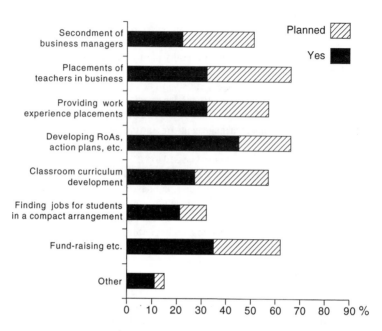

Figure 8.1 Main activities being developed or planned by TECs and LECs in the field of education–business links ($N = 62$; all topics prompted, multiple responses allowed).

a priority at the secondary level (97%), with FE (80%) coming ahead of primary (67%). There are noticeable differences between perceptions in England and Scotland, notably over level of emphasis: whereas TECs prioritize secondary over FE (98% against 79%), for LECs the situation is the reverse, with a 92% priority for FE and 84% for secondary. Also, the Scottish emphasis on primary is, at 25%, well below that accorded in England and Wales (70%).

The perceptions of other agents on EBP goals is surprisingly similar to that of TECs/LECs. Again, almost all targets attract a high level of support. Contrasts with the TEC/LEC opinions are restricted to the pre-eminence of promoting functional skills (90% rating), and an even lower emphasis upon raising new finance (43%). The other notable finding from the other agents is that business leaders place a lower priority on almost every area than either business organizations or local authority observers, with the exception of raising business's awareness of students. This is somewhat in contrast with the TEC/LEC higher emphasis upon raising students' awareness of business, to which business leaders give only a 67% rating.

The conclusion to be drawn from appraisal of the early experiences of TECs and LECs links with schools and colleges is that many earlier lessons have yet to

Table 8.1 EBP objectives: respondents rating each objective in 62 TEC/LEC areas. The figures are scores for a rating of priority in four categories which are then weighted: high priority = 3; medium priority = 2; low priority = 1, not important = 0. Maximum score will be 100 if all of sample rate that objective a high priority (all topics prompted).

	TECS England & Wales	LECs Scotland	All TECS & LECS	All other agents	Business leaders	Business organiza- tions	LAS
Job guarantee	60.0	63.5	62.2	68.8	80.6	66.7	41.7
Improving literacy	77.0	71.4	77.6	71.0	80.6	66.7	58.3
Improving functional skills	78.8	84.1	80.4	90.3	91.7	95.6	66.7
Improving social and life skills	80.0	60.3	79.5	77.4	86.1	71.1	75.0
Improving recruitability to work	90.2	100.0	91.5	83.9	86.1	86.7	66.7
Improving student attitudes to work	93.2	79.4	92.2	86.0	91.7	84.4	75.0
Raising students' awareness of business	96.2	92.1	96.0	87.1	94.4	86.7	66.7
Integrating business needs into the curriculum	84.1	91.5	85.0	86.0	88.9	86.7	75.0
Developing teacher attitudes	91.7	92.1	92.2	87.1	94.4	84.4	75.0
Raising business awareness of students	87.7	84.1	88.0	88.2	86.1	88.9	91.7
Curriculum development	80.7	71.4	80.7	82.8	83.3	84.4	75.0
Raising new finance	56.3	61.1	59.2	43.0	41.7	44.4	41.7
Other	90.5	41.7	83.3	41.9	41.7	40.0	50.0
Emphasis							
: primary	69.9	25.4	66.7	67.7	77.8	57.8	75.0
: secondary	98.4	84.0	96.5	95.7	100.0	97.8	75.0
: FE	79.2	92.1	80.3	91.4	91.7	93.3	83.3

be fully digested.[22] The IMS (1993) study showed the main priorities to be on increasing links and providing coherence. Although they found 71% of all EBPs having performance indicators, there was little common ground between them. Our results show that EBPs are still often a broad and widely-focused activity with most targets not fully monitored. They have tended to become a catch-all for links between education and business, with education agents usually playing the key rôle. Most respondents are therefore concerned with general attitudes and motivation, which are as much a part of the general education process as they are about specific link activities. This is reinforced by the emphasis on the need for curriculum development. The survey of TEC/LEC priorities for EBPs reinforces our general conclusion about the need to integrate the essential features of EBPs into the classroom process; and that this mainly concerns general educational attitudes and curriculum relevance to enterprise and entrepreneurialism.[23] In this sense the debate returns to the national level and to the definition of the national curriculum, with the TECs/LECs remaining rather remote from the major decision making which rests in the DFE. In May 1993 John Patten, the Secretary of State for Education, announced his intention to extend GNVQ to 14-year-olds opening up work experience to become part of the 14–16 curriculum for some pupils.[24] The 1993 Education White Paper also seeks to develop core skills further in this area. But none of these changes yet address the problem of full curriculum integration of business link activity.

Challenges post-16

Many of the issues affecting the 16–19 age-group have already been covered in Chapter 7 from the point of view of training. However, for this age-group the structure of training and education, and the incentives to follow one route or the other, are intimately interrelated.

In Chapter 2 we noted the low level of staying-on in education and training in Britain by the 16–19 age group. As a result of these international comparisons, education and training provision in the 16–19 age group has been an area of extensive debate in recent years. Central to this has been the issue of the balance between provision of different types of skill acquisition – on the one hand job-specific training, on the other hand core skills – and the development of a system of accreditation that can reflect the needs of all types of provision. This has led to attempts to integrate the whole of the education and training effort into a single coherent framework of accreditation and achievement. We address these issues here through each element.

Qualifications: the key problem

A major impediment to reform and improvement facing those who seek to transform provision for the 16–19 age-group has been the system of qualifications. For young people at 16 a major impediment traditionally had been a system of "O"-Levels and CSEs designed for, at most, the top 60% of the ability range. Until the advent of GCSE, the system left at least 40% of people following courses that led to no recognizable final target. This was a design failure. As a result, in the words of Correlli Barnett,[25] education played a major rôle in developing a culture of "habituated" failure among Britain's school leavers. Reflecting this, Handy (1985: 133) termed the educational system "disabling".

Apart from the stigmatizing and demotivating effects of the British system on pupils at age 16, the examination system has had a second consequence for businesses. Reliance on the traditional modes of assessment and certification have meant that businesses traditionally used "O"-Levels and CSE results as an initial method of "screening" applicants. Many surveys show that businesses use examination attainment as a crude index of basic skills as well as of other attributes such as attendance and work discipline.[26] However, the use of examination results for screening often leads to inappropriate decisions because the system of examination assessment is so poorly tuned to employers' needs. The problem has been that, until recently, there has been no means of crediting other capabilities. Although the development of the GCSE has improved the situation over the former "O"-Level examinations, it is with the introduction of ROAs linked to the national curriculum, and vocational qualifications based on NVQ and GNVQ, that these major systemic problems are beginning to be overcome.

A further consequence of the examination system has been its effect on staying-on rates. Education after the age of 16 has been largely the preserve of those destined for higher education. In the words of Sir Peter Swinnerton-Dyer, former chief executive of the Universities Funding Council: "it is designed almost exclusively for those going on to the next stage."[27] Age 16 has been seen as an inflexible end-point for most pupils, with little opportunity for slow-learners to stay on and thus reach a specific basic level of school-leaver attainment. Although the Scottish system is more flexible, in England and Wales particularly, those destined for vocational qualifications have either gone straight into work or have had to enter further education (FE) or tertiary colleges. But the route into FE is far from automatic or obvious. The multiplicity of qualifications has traditionally been far from satisfactory, with considerable variation in the type, quality and appropriateness of FE courses available in different areas because of the discretionary nature of local authority responsibilities and expenditure and the high degree of autonomy of college principals and teachers. This has led to an unco-ordinated and system-wide gap which is only now beginning to be closed.

Two prominent developments have emerged to challenge this history. Firstly, the National Council for Vocational Qualifications (NCVQ) has sought to systematize the vast number of post-16 qualifications into a coherent framework with so far four, and ultimately five, levels of achievement into which each separate qualification may be integrated. We have discussed this briefly in Chapter 7. Secondly, the dominant rôle of "A"-Levels as the guiding format for achievement at 16–19 has been challenged, with a series of proposals for it to be matched by the development of a series of vocational qualifications of equal status. This is leading to the development of a new structure of accreditation, in which academic and vocational options are given equal weight. The option that is being followed through the introduction of the General National Vocational Qualification (GNVQ) is in fact very close to the French *baccalaureate professionelle*.[28] This has been developed since 1991 by a Conservative government reluctant to abandon "A"-Levels. The development of GNVQ is being pursued through the development of core skills assessment and accreditation.

Core skills

The development of a GNVQ as an alternative and equivalent to "A"-Levels has evolved through a series of consultations held by the National Curriculum Council (NCC) and promoted in the 1993 Education White Paper. The NCC (1990) identified six *core skills* that should be part of the post-16 courses of both academic and vocational tracks:
- Communication;
- Problem solving;
- Personal skills;
- Numeracy;
- Information technology;
- Modern language competence.

Of these, the first three were identified by both NCC and NCVQ as the "fundamental" core skills. The NCC also identified three "themes" to be viewed as contexts in which core skills can be used to develop breadth and balance:
- Social and economic understanding;
- Scientific and technological understanding;
- Aesthetic and creative understanding.

By including such features in both academic and vocational courses, core skills provide a mechanism to help the transfer of individuals between each, and also reinforce the requirement of achieving a parity of esteem. This is particularly important to enhance the status of the vocational route. It will also help to stimulate greater incentives for pupils to follow vocational, and mixed vocational–academic, routes in the 14–16 age group. TEED, through TECs and LECs, have also been seeking to promote the use of ROAs linked to the core skills concept. The relation between ROAs and core skills has also been recognized by the transfer of the administration of student ROAs to NCVQ, who in turn are seeking to align their National Record and the TEED ROAs.[29] The objective of having a single Record for school, college and adult education is long overdue.

Despite the benefits of these developments there are, as yet, a number of problems to be overcome. The key issue relates to detailed implementation of a standard that will accord genuine equivalence between the academic and vocational routes. For each core skill four levels of "performance statement" are to be given (corresponding to the NVQ levels). But definition of the core skills themselves, and the levels within each, is highly problematic. Piloting work by the London EBP in the fields of "A"-Level, Business and Finance, Design, Construction and Catering, for example, has been rapid in some courses but very slow in others.[30] Developments within "A"-Levels as well as vocational courses have also been fraught with difficulties. Educationalists have argued that these skills are already effectively taught, but not explicitly labelled or assessed as such.[31] More fundamentally, it is questionable whether core skills really satisfy employers' needs beyond the most basic levels. They aim more to bring educational targets for employer needs up to a minimum rather than develop a proper vocationalism.[32] In addition, SEAC has argued that core skills cannot be developed in isolation of the substance or context in which they are applied. The conclusion is, therefore, that at present there is no systematic application of a core skills structure, few schools or colleges explicitly assess and manage them, and there is no consensus yet on performance or equivalence of standards.

GNVQs were successfully piloted in a number of schools and colleges in 1992/93 and are being taken up more widely. Whatever the final form of development of core skills in GNVQ, the rôle of TECs and LECs remains unclear. On the one hand TECs/LECs appear to be chiefly concerned with the products of Compacts and EBPs. On the other hand, the mission of TECs and LECs to shape employer involvement in education needs, an emphasis on core skills and the developments of GNVQ. There appears little mechanism to bring these areas together. The new NACETT leaves the dilemma still hanging in limbo between the DFE and DE (see Chapter 6).

Employers' attitudes to the curriculum post-16 have been important to the development of the core skills initiative. Not only has this become one of the CBI flagships for education policy,[33] but it is a key part of the 1993 Education White Paper. However, it is not as yet clear how, or whether, TECs and LECs can become meaningfully related to core skill requirements. The most likely rôle is through WRFE rather than EBPs or Compacts and the curriculum. But this is also beset by doubts, as we assess below.

Work-related further education

Work-Related Further Education (WRFE) refers to the training courses offered by the FE colleges as a part of nationally-funded education provision. Although colleges have always possessed a significant independence over curriculum and course structure, until April 1993 formal responsibility for the system had rested with local government officials. WRFE until then was mainly funded through the Education Block Grant paid by central government to local education authorities. Additional funding was derived from the course fees charged to individuals and employers, an area which expanded through the 1980s and early 1990s as more flexible full-cost and short-course provision was expanded. It had come to represent 10–25% of many college budgets by 1992. Prior to these developments, courses delivered by LEA colleges had been heavily criticized by private sector commentators for being outmoded, inflexible and frequently inappropriate to current business requirements. The problem was put down essentially to the system being provider-driven by the educational establishment.

Since April 1993 the responsibility for Further Education has been transferred to the FE Funding Council (FEFC). This allocates the majority of funds to

EDUCATION

colleges, but the TECs are fully responsible for all part-time funding for YT through Credits. TECs were accorded a direct rôle in WRFE from April 1992 (different arrangements apply in Scotland). Previously handled by the TA, the TEC responsibility derives from the earlier transfer of former local authority Education Block Grant money to the then MSC in 1985. This transfer from the DES to the DE sought to enhance the responsiveness of the FE system to the training requirements of employers. The original rationale had been to achieve more sophisticated labour market awareness with greater emphasis upon the requirements of industry, even though, as we have seen, the quality of DE–LMI is widely regarded as poor.

The handing on of the WRFE responsibility to TECs was a logical development of the employer lead on TEC Boards who, it was believed, would be better positioned to identify the demands for skills that should appropriately guide provision. The TEC-controlled proportion of the WRFE budget, although small, is significant at 25% of the total, and was perceived as a lever over the whole of provision. The system employed by the TA was designed to be replicated in TECs' approach. This required transmission of money to the LEAs, and in turn to colleges, being dependent upon the agreement of a WRFE plan drawn up by the LEA/college. The content of this plan was negotiated, and funded, once TECs were satisfied the plan met the objectives employers required. This characterized the 1991/92 and 1992/93 budgets. For 1992/93 TECs/LECs were given discretion over reallocation of 15% of their part of the WRFE budget.

Interview evidence suggests that, in the early stages in 1991/92, TECs did little to act on their responsibilities in this area, for four reasons: first, they gave a higher priority to the much larger programme areas such as ET and YT in their early operational phases; second, the WRFE plans for 1991/92 were almost entirely inherited by TECs – for most areas the negotiation was completed by the TA prior to TECs' assumption of the responsibility; third, WRFE plans are judged by many TECs in any case to be ineffective mechanisms to lever change; fourth, the reform of FE funding led to uncertainty as to the relation that would develop between TECs/LECs and the FEFC and whether TECs would continue to be involved in WRFE at all.

The difficulty for TECs has been that they are responsible for an element of FE which has itself been ill-defined. An important distinction emerged in the 1980s between work-related and non-work-related provision. The portion of former Block Grant money originally transferred from LEAs, and now held by TECs, is wholly concerned with the work-related areas. But any distinction betw-een courses or students is bound to be over-simplistic, as a series of inconclus-ive attempts to draw systematic definitions have demonstrated. The TECs were initially drawn into a funding quagmire in which the curriculum areas they wished to support were not easily separable from the rest. This returned the debate to defining core skills and has undoubtedly inhibited the development by TECs of proactive strategies for effective links with the colleges.

Table 8.2 Preferred level of discretion by TECs over FE funds (England and Wales only; $N = 54$) (66% response: mailed survey in mid-1992).

Preferred level of control of WRFE funds %	Proportion of TECs preferring level of control %
0	2
15	11
40	32
40–99	7
100	48

Since 1993/94, the issue has been clarified through the focus of TEC funding on Credits. From 1993/94 the FEFC has become the prime agent for funding colleges with which the TECs play a joint rôle. The newly independent colleges are overseen by regional councils of the FEFC.

Most TECs want to play a more important rôle in FE provision. They recognise this as the crucial link in the youth sector between education and the world of work. For example, in a survey of TECs in mid-1992 the average preferred figure for the discretionary control of FE college budgets was 66%, with nearly one-half of TECs (48%) wishing to be granted 100% control over FE allocation (see Table 8.2). Similarly, TECs wanted a more substantial control over the allocation of funds between and within colleges. Although most TECs had sought no reallocation between colleges in 1992/93 (61%), 62% planned reallocation for 1993/94.[34]

The level of control sought by TECs, the clash of the WRFE methodology with the allocation methods being developed by FEFC, and the dissonance of this with the Training Credit scheme for YT places, creates major dilemmas for the future. The FEFC has been working with a mixture of a Block Grant funding and a demand element. Moving cautiously in 1993/94 it paid £750 for each full-time student enrolled through the demand element. For the future it has examined a variety of funding options (FEFC 1992). It is to use allocations that meet bids from colleges using a tariff/price setting mechanism for each programme. It has been persuaded to follow this route rather than Credits mainly because Credits do not allow it to control demand or differentiate between full-cost and lower-cost students. It has also been strongly influenced by the HEFC success in reducing unit costs through a similar mechanism and has not believed that Credits will allow full control of costs. Whatever the merits of this decision for FE funding its effect has been to continue the confusion between Credits and full-time student funding, and has separated TEC funding allocation methods from the majority of FE college finance. This has the unfortunate consequence of confusing the students, undermining the status of the Credits, undervaluing TEC-funded courses and leaving TECs largely marginalized from the main incentives driving the FE system.

The rôle of higher education

The direct rôle of TECs and LECs in HE is limited. But they are increasingly recognizing the importance of developing collaborative arrangements as a means of developing the TEC/LEC mission. This provides an opportunity to work with local HE institutions that have important rôles in the animation of local development (particularly in the case of the former polytechnics) as well as being important influences on the choices of young people in the 16–19 age range. We assess below how these HE–TEC/LEC relations are developing within formal programmes as well as more informal agreements.

High Technology National Training

The only significant funding programme that involves HE in most TEC/LEC areas is High Technology National Training (HTNT). The aim of HTNT is to meet national skill shortages for highly qualified people which cannot be resolved locally. This is achieved through partnerships with HE to provide courses for HNC skills and above, e.g. emphasizing advanced manufacturing technology, IT, engineering, electronics, construction, export marketing, management and tourism. By 1992, around 400 courses of 3–12 months' duration were offered nation-wide, each of which must include a period of placement with an employer. HTNT is part of ET and therefore designed for unemployed people. It has some of the general weaknesses of that programme (see Chapter 7).

The annual finance of HTNT ranges from approximately £100,000 to £250,000 per TEC or LEC area. Where a local HE institution is available, this is naturally the provider. Where there is no HE institution a FE college is normally used although private training providers are also employed; FE is also a provider in some areas where HE institutions exist, as a result of difficulties of developing appropriate HE provision. Despite the direct contracting for HTNT, the funds are relatively small and the scope for TEC/LEC discretion is slight. Hence HTNT has not been a crucial issue for either side. This, combined with the ET background, has ensured that HTNT is primarily a specific and contracting relationship with HE, which does not usually infuse any management changes. It is not, therefore, a primary partnership mechanism for TECs and LECs.

Wider links with higher education

Some of the more progressive TECs and LECs have begun to recognize the potential for wider links with HE institutions. In 1991/92 the majority of both TECs and LECs had contact with HE institutions. In England and Wales, 43% had extensive contact with HE bodies, and another 41% had non-extensive contact.[35] Two further TECs planned such contact, and only 11% had no contact planned in the future. In Scotland, the figures are similar, with 46% of LECs having extensive contact, 31% having non-extensive contact, with 15% neither having nor planning any contact. The pattern has changed little in 1992/93. Some of these links are being pursued by TECs and LECs by using TEED development projects (see Chapter 6).

The nature of TEC/LEC – HE contacts varies enormously. They tend to fall into three groups. First, there is a major potential for links based on the R&D capacity of HE institutions. On the one hand, many TECs and LECs are using the capacity of HE acting as consultants to their own work. On the other hand, TECs/LECs can work with HE to develop innovation and R&D schemes with both small and large companies. In an early survey, LECs claimed to be developing R&D strategy in only 29% of areas, and in TEC areas the level was higher at 42%. However, detailed interview research in 60% of TECs and LECs revealed very little activity beyond HTNT. Detailed analysis of claimed R&D initiatives has found most related to internal TEC/LEC programmes for YT and ET, and not related to industrial R&D at all.[36] There is undoubtedly a much greater rôle for TECs and LECs to develop in this field, but it is likely to have to be based on strong partnership relations with the other key agents: such as the DTI R&D programme and Regional Technology Centres; the EC programmes such as SPRINT; consultants and Chambers of Commerce, as well as HE institutions. Few TECs or LECs have embarked down this road. Problems affect both sides of the relationship. A number of commentators (not in TECs or LECs) referred to their local universities as the most underused resource in their local economy. This particularly applies to London, but affects all British universities who have sought a national rather than a local rôle and make a major contribution to Britain's perverse policy syndrome.[37] The former polytechnics get more favourable comment from the same local interviewees, though they are also believed to have underused assets. From the TEC/LEC side, as we shall see in Chapter 9, the gaps in development derive closely from the weaknesses of TEC/LEC strategy in the enterprise field.

A second field of contacts of HE and TECs is through TEED's Enterprise in Higher Education (EHE) and the DFE PICKUP initiatives.[38] These were launched in 1987. By 1991 EHE schemes existed in about 50 HE institutions; PICKUP continued after 1992 through a more collaborative approach and lost most of its DFE funding. EHE seeks to foster in students the personal and enterprise skills sought by employers. It is supposed to apply to whole institutions. The skills sought are flexibility, creativity, communication, and practical experience through group-based and project-based learning. Up to £1m is available to an institution over a 5 year period, but most contracts are for far less.

Despite its aims and methods there is little evidence to suggest that either EHE or PICKUP have fundamentally changed any institution receiving it. In the main, EHE/PICKUP funds have gone to institutions or courses already involved in this mode of teaching, who have then made their activities more explicit. This applies particularly to former polytechnics and more technologically-based universities. For the mass of the system the funds are too small to act as other than bolt-ons, similar to EBPs in schools. Deeper curriculum change requires the direct relations to employer needs to influence the mainstream development of HE.

This has stimulated a third change: a shift towards a more market-based system of finance of HE based on a shift towards loans for student maintenance, and financial allocations to institutions based on student numbers. The objective is to bring demand for, and supply of, HE courses more closely into line, and to change the shape of demand towards courses with a more direct relevance to the world of work – either in their vocational substance, or in the vocational relevance of the skills developed through substantive areas. All of the sources of leverage are national and not local. Hence they are beyond the direct TEC/LEC local capacity. However, TECs and LECs can play a rôle by working with HE, FE and schools to influence the choices of young people.

The need to influence choices of young people is a key plank of the 1991 and 1993 Education White Papers. In Chapter 7 we have already argued for the need to structure the incentives and relations between demand and supply in the labour market in order to enhance the acquisition of training skills. The same mechanisms and requirements affect education. The rôle of NVQs, Credits and the Careers Service are again important. But to affect radically entry to HE, a more complex set of interrelations needs to be addressed to raise the level of pupil aspirations.

This has led to a focus on routes to increase *access* into HE. The resulting policies relate to both the demand and supply sides, but the supply-side changes required are the most significant. The *supply side* is being changed by increasing the fee base for HE funding, e.g. by raising the average undergraduate fee element by approximately 3 times and differentiating between courses. This will provide incentives for HE to recruit. In addition a wider set of entry qualifications and qualification routes are being developed. These focus on Credit Accumulation and Transfer (CAT), Accreditation of Prior Learning (APL), and a more general set of examination routes in addition to "A"-Levels, i.e. particularly NVQ and GNVQ and their interchangeability with "A"-Levels. These changes fit the demands for wider routes for access made by a wide range of commentators.[39]

On the *demand side* much research shows that demand for HE places considerably exceeds supply. But beyond the traditional pool of applicants to HE are a wide range of individuals who find it difficult to enter HE. They frequently have socio-economic or ethnic "disadvantages" compared to traditional students. These can be overcome by a number of options: advice and counselling, specially designed "access" courses, mentoring and a number of other methods. Employers can give crucial support in most of these areas[40] and TECs/LECs can be means of organizing that support. Employers rarely have the time and capacity to organize these links themselves[41] (though there are notable exceptions among large companies such as the Wellcome Foundation, BP, Whitbread). Hence TECs and

LECs can perform an organizational rôle similar to that performed by Compact managers with schools. So far, however, such developments are at a very early stage in almost all TECs and LECs.

Making further progress

We have examined in this chapter how TECs and LECs have been developing their rôle in education. This rôle commands a relatively low level of resources and influence. Hence the educational capacity of TECs and LECs is limited. That capacity is further limited by the relatively restrictive nature of the initiative-based finance that they receive, and by the much greater power and resources exercised through the DFE and FEFC. In the future, the influence of TECs and LECs is further thrown into question by two factors. First is the progressive replacement of LEA rôles by direct DFE-school links which is projected by the government to cover 50% of schools by 1995. If this proves realistic, such change will severely stretch TEC/LEC resources, merely in terms of capacity to maintain local liaison, particularly at primary school level, and it will tend to sideline them. New ways may have to be found of working with autonomous "groups" of schools.

A second factor potentially marginalizing TECs and LECs is the emergence of the FEFC since 1993. The regional elements of this Council are becoming the powerful arbiters of FE funds with direct links to colleges. The rôle of TECs through LEA-based WRFE Plans having been eliminated, a new rôle and experience must be built with each college. Given the lack of TEC/LEC staff experience in this field, their small numbers and resources, and the much more significant control of FE funds at the FEFC level, it is questionable whether TECs and LECs will be able to play a significant rôle in colleges' strategic decisions at all. Rather, the TECs and LECs will be restricted to their rôle as YT/ET purchasers.

In the light of these developments we conclude that there are major difficulties if TECs and LECs are to play a significant rôle in education. The main gaps are as follows. First, the general quality of education is still the prime target for policy change. The major developments required to achieve this relate to schooling teaching methods, syllabi, school objectives, management and finance; they do not necessarily require a direct business involvement. The Education Reform Act tackles many of these basic needs, although it will be many years before the changes initiated reach their final form. But it remains clear that the rôle of TECs/ LECs is at the margin of the key educational reform process.

Second, however, effective links between business and schools still require radically to be enhanced: too much effort, as we have analyzed, is devoted to relatively loose and diffuse targets, which are treated as "bolt-ons" to main school practice. The major gap that still exists is the absence of proper attention to business needs in the curriculum across all disciplines, and at all levels. This gap is still left unfilled by the new national curriculum. Some significant steps have been made, but there remains a significant divide between the national curriculum, driven by the DFE, and the links to workplace needs driven by the DE and the wider needs of business. This is evidenced particularly by the absence of work-based and enterprise-related projects in the national curriculum and the demise of much TVEI/TVEE experience as central funds for this initiative run out. The announcement in May 1993 of a possible opening up of the national curriculum to a GNVQ approach to work experience for 14–16-year-olds is the first significant step in the direction we have assessed as essential to positive developments. If work experience can be fully and properly integrated into the curriculum a major step forward will have been made, but the rôle of TECs and LECs in this process remains unclear.

Third, too many separate education initiatives with different link objectives and management arrangements crowd the TEC/LEC agenda. This is government's contribution to the "patchwork" of initiatives in the field of education. SCIP, TVEI, Compacts, the Partnership Initiative EBPs, TEC/LEC-based partnership initiatives and strategic fora all exist, often separate from each other, and are also too separate from mainstream education, from the core management of the Careers Service, and from initiatives beyond education in the fields of enterprise and training.

Fourth, TECs and LECs possess few, if any, tools to tackle most of the key elements of national targets in the field of education with which they are concerned. The rôle of TECs and LECs in APL and IIP is remote to education, their leverage on established companies is small, and their ability to influence schools and colleges is weak and appears to be diminishing. Most of the tools to fulfil the TEC/LEC mission in the field of education lie in the hands of other agents – chiefly schools, colleges and businesses themselves. As an intermediary to bring these agents together TECs/LECs seem unlikely to have major impact.

Fifth, the links with HE are at present meagre and tenuous, though often cordial. A closer relationship needs to be developed, but much depends either on national policy on HE funding, or on TECs and LECs developing more effective links in the enterprise field so that R&D and innovations strategies can be enhanced (see Chapter 9).

Sixth, there is the conflict in funding methodology between TEC finance based on Credits and FEFC finance of colleges. These treat similar students and similar courses in entirely different ways merely because they are full- or part-time. There is no rational basis for these differences. Instead they derive from the clash of the CBI desire to allow individuals and employers to steer courses, supported by the DE, with the FEFC approach of letting colleges plan and respond to demand, supported by the DFE. Rationalizing this conflict will require further pressure to erode the interests of the educational producers. It will clearly take considerable time before further reform of college finances receives a government commitment that allows full integration between the two funding systems. To

MAKING FURTHER PROGRESS

help overcome these difficulties the NTTF (1992b) and CBI (1993a) have called for interdepartmental reform by merging the interests of the DE and DFE. The debated shift of YT funding from TECs to FE colleges would improve integration, but is resisted by TECs and the CBI. Indeed, at the July 1993 TECs conference, Bill Stubbs claimed that Credits may no longer be necessary given the evidence of NETTs. Developments are still awaited.

To overcome these criticisms a NTTF (1992b) report recommended increased co-operation between the DFE and DE within a general post-16 structure, the establishment of a National Education Initiative Fund and a strengthening of the links of TECs and LECs to the FEFC. It put a heavy emphasis on the potential rôle of TECs and LECs as sources of influence on education through finance, individual relationships on TEC/LEC Boards, networking, information provision and raising the demands for skills through IIP. Our assessment in this chapter confirms the need for greater co-operation between the DFE and DE, but suggests that almost all of the NTTF recommendations for enhancing the rôle of TECs and LECs will prove ineffective. In the event the establishment of NACETT/SACETT has been the the only response so far by government to the NTTF proposals. We turn in Chapters 11 and 12 to more fundamental issues of reform.

Chapter 9

Enterprise

One of many agents

"Enterprise" concerns a wide field of activities within which TECs and LECs are one local player among many. Their special remit has been to help small firms to become established and grow, and to stimulate developments within established firms that will benefit the local economy as a whole. But the enterprise field is very large, and contains many other agents. It has been further complicated by the TECs having a dual responsibility to both the DTI and DE since 1993/94.

The TECs and LECs have a significant budget for enterprise. On average they have between £3 and £7m to spend, representing 16% of their budget in England and Wales, and 27% of the budget of SE LECs but rising to 66% in HIE LECs. Enterprise thus ranks second after training in TECs, but is the largest field in the LECs. The largest part of the programme money in this budget derives from the former Enterprise Allowance Scheme (EAS), Small Firms Service (SFS) and Business Growth Training (BGT). But LECs also gain considerable funds for promoting inward investment, business premises, environmental improvement, information services and company development finance/working capital provision. TECs and LECs have considerable freedom to change these programmes, although they are obliged to focus on small firms and the self-employed for at least part of their enterprise activities.

The centrality of enterprise to the vision which underlies TECs and LECs is apparent in their names. That the term *enterprise* should be used suggests its importance and emphasizes the intention that their long-term rôle be as stimulators of entrepreneurial activity in their local economies in the widest sense. In the words of Brian Wolfson, Chairman of the NTTF, "The E in the TEC programme, the Enterprise E, was meant to throw down an individual challenge on what the local vision should be. It was meant to open a window on the thoughts of the people running the TEC to say 'Alright, what do you want to do about Liverpool, about Hull?'; 'What are you going to do to relate to the real visionary challenges of your community'".[1] Wolfson noted that "the T and C in TECs was self-evident; the E was to attract and excite the right people to come on board". A number of the TEC and LEC actors we interviewed stated that they were trying to "put the *enterprise* back" into the TEC or LEC, implying that the initial pattern of development was not as they had envisaged. The gap in the development of practice was already recognized in Geoffrey Holland's comments at the July 1991 TECs conference, who stated that there was a "need to bring into focus . . . enterprise". Such a view suggests that there was a gap between the founding vision and the funding realities faced in the early years. It also points to a belief at the centre in the importance of improving this area of TEC and LEC activity.

We analyze the development of TECs and LECs in the complex field of enterprise over the following dimensions:

- The confused mission;
- Enterprise activities of TECs and LECs;
- Providers, purchasers or facilitators?
- Working as partners?
- European perspectives;
- Filling the real enterprise gaps;
- One Stop Shops (Business Link);
- The need to think further.

The confused mission

The responsibility of TECs and LECs for enterprise was confused from the outset. The 1988 White Paper gave only short mention of enterprise, and this in an ambiguous form under the heading *Training Through Life* (paras 6.17–6.23). In the White Paper the main focus was on pre-existing programmes such as small firm training and counselling, the DTI Enterprise Initiative and the PICKUP initiative of HE and FE colleges. The key plank of subsequent development proved to be the statement that TECs would "oversee the provision of the Employment Department's counselling and training for small firms . . . they will also be the Government's link with local enterprise agencies [and seek] to ensure that provision is coordinated to maximise its effectiveness and to make access as easy as possible" (DE 1988: para 6.22).

By the time of issue of the TEC Operating Manual (1989: para 1.2) enterprise had become the second listed point of remit to "expand opportunities for local people to start their own business and to progress through training to new careers and greater prosperity". The key pre-existing programmes listed were Business Growth Training (BGT), Small Firms Counselling Service (SFS) and the Enterprise Allowance Scheme (EAS) (para 1.9). But the line of ambiguity was already evident since there was an expectation that "in addition to its programme delivery responsibilities, a TEC will play an important rôle in developing information and advisory services" . . . "new and expanding firms need information on the full array of business services available at each point in their growth cycle" (paras 1.10, 1.11).

The broad TEC mission was constrained by a funding reality that "the Training Agency will provide core funding for information services which are the TECs responsibility (TAPs, BGT, SFS, EAS, ET)" but "a TEC will be encouraged to develop plans to attract extra resources to contribute towards the costs of providing more comprehensive services for local needs . . . including the possibility of charging for services" (para 1.14). Later in the Draft Operating Manual each TEC is invited to "establish a membership . . . may raise subscriptions [and] . . . will be able to finance its marketing activities from the Local Initiative Fund and from programme expenditure" (paras 5.3, 5.4).

In Scotland, the LECs' remit was more specifically derivative from earlier programmes and expressed with less grandiose overtones: "stimulating and promoting enterprise growth in their areas through business development services, small business investment and enterprise programmes such as the Enterprise Allowance Scheme, Business Growth Training, Local Enterprise Grants for Urban Projects" (Industry Department Scotland 1989: 4). The Highlands and Islands remit, however reflected wider targets to "improve business support services as a means of reducing failure and of achieving greater growth of new and existing companies . . . [and to] develop businesses with growth potential through the establishment of a centre to provide an integrated service of entrepreneur training, and guidance on company formation and growth" (HIE 1991a: 12). Both the SE and HIE LECs also have significant additional responsibilities in the enterprise field compared to TECs.

The confusion of the TEC/LEC mission follows from these statements. First, the TEC focus was on a training-led approach to business development. This reflects their origins in the DE. It is not invalid in itself, it is merely unbalanced. Second, despite the broad mission, the strong focus was on the transfer of inherited programmes. This was what "core" finance was for. Many of these had attracted rather negative evaluations of their effectiveness, particularly the SFS and EAS, but also most elements of BGT.[2] Third, there was a commitment to contract to enterprise agencies as a named subcontractor. Fourth, there was a wide mission to develop services and thus to compete with existing providers. Fifth, although wider services had to be supported, if possible, by fees or subscriptions, marketing could be financed from LIF and programme expenditure, hence allowing a public subsidy to service delivery, leading potentially to unfair competition with existing providers. Sixth, TECs had to consider business membership schemes and thus potentially compete with other membership organizations (see Chapter 4).

The LECs have had these elements of confusion in equal measure to the TECs, but do have additional responsibilities to support their wider range of services. These also potentially competed with other local organizations (particularly local authorities) and the private sector. However, in Scotland the longer history of local public intervention meant that other agents such as Chambers were less developed than in England and Wales. As a result, although competition with other agents has still become a problem, the LECs have generally managed to avoid tensions through a stronger partnership at the design stage of initiatives.

By the time of the 1992 Employment White Paper (DE 1992e: 49–51) the TEC focus had become formally more constrained to "(i) encouraging enterprise among young people, (ii) encouraging self-employment, (iii) maintaining a favourable business environment, (iv) offering coherent support to small firms, and (v) helping develop a wider range of sources of finance for small businesses". But on the ground, this did not stop TECs claiming a wider rôle in business growth and development as key areas of TEC innovation as well as developing inward investment:

> there has been a great deal more innovation with many TECs not only offering information, advice and consultancy [which would be expected – sic] but also now there exists a widespread use of business reviews, health checks, group consultancy programmes . . . clubs, events and seminars . . . The picture on direct delivery versus subcontract arrangements is also pretty clear. TECs are involved directly in frontline activities providing information and business and advice . . . there is no evidence of widespread subcontracting (G10 1992b: 8–9).

The TECs and LECs in their early years have thus been vigorous developers of enterprise programmes, as a result of encouragement by government. We turn below to assessing these developments in detail.

Enterprise activities of TECs and LECs

The enterprise field covers a complex set of TEC/LEC subprogrammes. Although the total enterprise budget is large and has more flexibility than the training budget, each subprogramme is demanding with the result that the total resources available are fairly limited when compared to their range of objectives (particularly the objectives as originally conceived in the TECs' mission statement), although this has not held back the attempts by TECs and LECs to develop programmes.

The TECs have five main programmes for enterprise inherited from TEED. These are the main elements that are core funded. They are:

- Enterprise Allowance Schemes (EAS);
- Business Growth Training/Business Enterprise Training (BGT/BET) which itself covers various options and subprogrammes;
- Small Firms Service (SFS);
- Investors in People (IIP);
- Management Charter Initiative (MCI).

In addition activities in the fields of Accreditation of Prior Learning (APL), Open and Flexible Learning (OFL), High Technology National Training (HTNT) and some aspects of Employment Action (EA) are relevant. TECs have also developed a suite of new enterprise programmes for business courses, consultancy, health checks, employer networking, membership schemes, as well as working with the DTI enterprise initiative and other programmes. The additional activities are funded by LIF, surpluses and joint action with other agents.

The LECs have a somewhat wider remit. In addition to all the programmes administered by TECs, all LECs also cover the following fields (Industry Department Scotland 1990):

– Provision of business sites and premises;
– Environmental renewal/derelict land;
– Advice and information including inward investment;
– Business development finance for use as working capital, management buy-outs and other business development.

In addition, the HIE LECs have further enterprise capacity through community development grants, some of which impinge on the enterprise field.

Because of the dominance of core funding through inherited programmes, the development by TECs and LECs of enterprise activities has mainly followed the foci of the previous programmes. However, as time has progressed new initiatives have also been developed. The results of the 1991 LSE survey of TEC/LEC activities is shown in Table 9.1. This indicates that counselling and training for small firms was the most significant area of both TEC and LEC activity. The delivery of advice to firms, in the form of providing local business counsellors, was the most common enterprise activity of all, conducted by 93% of TECs and LECs. The focus on counselling and the provision of business training (91% of TECs and LECs) reflects the specific brief of TECs and LECs and the inheritance of BGT and EAS. Similarly high levels of activity for the provision of specific advice to small firms (87%) and business start-ups (84%) confirm the significance of this sector as a proportion of enterprise effort.

The other prominent area was youth enterprise. Involvement with the Prince's Youth Business Trust (PYBT) was indicated by 76% of TECs and LECs, and 70% were involved with Young Enterprise. In addition to this, the provision of specific advice to youth business was identified by 74% of respondents. The reasons for this high interest in youth business can be attributed to TECs' and LECs' early focus both upon existing programme areas and use of enterprise agencies: the youth-dominated EAS and the existing structures for PYBT and Young Enterprise provided an area where action could be enjoined without major innovation and existing contractors could be used. The common provision of specific advice on government and other schemes (78%) further confirms the significance of the nationally-defined areas of responsibility.

One of the most commonly indicated activities was the provision of labour market information to businesses offered by 80% of TECs and LECs, although as an area with a broader relevance this reflects a concern not prompted by enterprise considerations alone. Other enterprise activities commonly underway are:

Table 9.1 Enterprise activities of TECs and LECs: percentage of TECs/LECs undertaking or planning activities in each field (multiple responses allowed, all topics prompted).

Activity	Undertaking activity	Planned activity	Undertaking plus planned
Provision of local business counsellors	92.6	3.7	96.3
Provision of business training	90.7	3.7	94.4
Specific advice: small firms	87.0	7.4	94.4
Specific advice: start-ups	83.6	9.1	92.7
Labour market information	80.0	16.4	96.4
Specific advice; government & other schemes	78.2	9.1	87.3
Involvement with Princes Youth Business Trust	75.5	5.7	81.1
Specific advice: youth business	74.1	7.4	81.5
Involvement with Young Enterprise	69.8	5.7	75.5
Specific advice: export information	69.1	10.9	80.0
Access to non-local business counsellors	66.7	5.6	72.2
Economic surveys	65.5	14.5	80.0
Specific advice: management structures	63.6	9.1	72.7
Specific advice: personnel policies	63.6	9.1	72.7
Specific advice:financial planning & taxation	63.6	9.1	72.7
Specific assistance: dentification of opportunities	60.0	10.9	70.9
Specific advice: access to venture capital	54.5	25.5	80.0
Specific advice: stock control procedures	52.7	10.9	63.6
Specific advice: payroll operations	52.7	9.1	61.8
Services to rural areas	51.9	7.4	59.3
Market consultancy service	50.9	20.0	70.9
Exhibitions	50.9	18.2	69.1
Training providers directory	50.0	31.5	81.5
Specific assistance: advertising/accessing markets	49.1	16.4	65.5
Specific assistance: design	49.1	3.6	52.7
Tourism projects	47.3	16.4	63.6
Competitions	45.5	20.0	65.5
Run clubs/support centres	42.6	25.9	68.5
Provision of premises	42.6	14.8	57.4
Involvement with LIVEWIRE	39.6	7.5	47.2
Managed workspace	37.0	18.5	55.6
Specific assistance: distribution & franchising	37.0	5.6	42.6
Group marketing activities	36.4	21.8	58.2
Work experience	35.7	9.5	45.2
Computerised database of enterprise info.	35.2	29.6	64.8
Outreach service	35.2	25.9	61.1
Business directory	35.2	20.4	55.6
Grants	29.2	8.3	37.5
Information about new product requirements	27.8	16.7	44.4
Operation of a loan/grant fund	27.8	11.1	38.9
Loans	27.1	2.1	29.2

Database of small firms	26.4	26.4	52.8
Encouraging large firms to open R&D facilities	26.4	15.1	41.5
Secondments	25.5	17.6	43.1
Non-executive director scheme	25.5	9.1	34.5
Expansion of DTI Enterprise Initiative	25.0	32.7	57.7
Soft loans/deferral methods	23.9	6.5	30.4
Other personnel-based	17.0	0.0	17.0
Other – general	14.6	4.9	19.5
Other grants/loans	9.3	0.0	9.3

Source: LSE survey (mid-1991: *N* ranges from 48 to 55).

Table 9.2 Comparison of enterprise activities of TECs and LECs: percentage of TEC or LEC undertaking activity, rank by differences between TECs and LECs (multiple responses allowed, all topics prompted).

Activity	TECS	LECS	England & Wales sample	Scotland sample	Difference
Loans	2.8	100.0	36	12	97.2
Grants	5.6	100.0	36	12	94.4
Operation of a loan/grant fund	7.1	100.0	42	12	92.9
Soft loans/deferral methods	2.9	90.9	35	11	88.1
Provision of premise	27.9	100.0	43	11	72.1
Tourism projects	32.6	100.0	43	12	67.4
Specific assistance: design	34.9	100.0	43	12	65.1
Specific assistance: advertising/accessing markets	37.2	91.7	43	12	54.5
Specific assistance: identification of opportunities	48.8	100.0	43	12	51.2
Specific advice: payroll operations	41.9	91.7	43	12	49.8
Specific assistance: distribution & franchising	26.2	75.0	42	12	48.8
Specific advice: access to venture capital	44.2	91.7	43	12	47.5
Other grants/loans	0.0	44.4	34	9	44.4
Market consultancy service	41.9	83.3	43	12	41.5
Encouraging large firms to open R&D facilities	18.6	60.0	43	10	41.4
Computerised database of enterprise information	26.2	66.7	42	12	40.5
Training providers directory	58.1	18.2	43	11	40.0
Specific advice: stock control procedures	60.5	100.0	43	12	39.5
Information about new product requirements	19.0	58.3	42	12	39.3
Specific advice: export information	44.2	83.3	43	12	39.1

Specific advice:					
management structure	55.8	91.7	43	12	35.9
Outreach service	27.9	63.6	43	11	35.7
Managed workspace	30.2	63.6	43	11	33.4
Specific advice: youth business	66.7	100.0	42	12	33.3
Group marketing facilities	30.2	58.3	43	12	28.1
Specific advice: government					
and other schemes	72.1	100.0	43	12	27.9
Labour market information	86.0	58.3	43	12	27.7
Services to rural areas	46.5	72.7	43	11	26.2
Specific advice: personnel policies	58.1	83.3	43	12	25.2
Specific advice:					
financial planning and taxation	58.1	83.3	43	12	25.2
Specific advice: start-ups	79.1	100.0	43	12	20.9
Access to non-local					
business counsellors	62.8	81.8	43	11	19.0
Work experience	37.8	20.0	37	5	17.8
Specific advice: small firms	83.3	100.0	42	12	16.7
Competitions	41.9	58.3	43	12	16.5
Other-general	12.1	25.0	33	8	12.9
Provision of business training	88.4	100.0	43	11	11.6
Other personnel-based	15.4	25.0	39	8	9.6
Provision of local					
business counsellors	90.5	100.0	42	12	9.5
Exhibitions	48.8	58.3	43	12	9.5
Involvement with Young Enterprise	71.4	63.6	42	11	7.8
Expansion of DTI					
Enterprise Initiative	23.8	30.0	42	10	6.2
Involvement with LIVEWIRE	40.5	36.4	42	11	4.1
Run clubs/support centres	41.9	45.5	43	11	3.6
Involvement with					
Princes Youth Business Trust	76.2	72.7	42	11	3.5
Economic surveys	65.1	66.7	43	12	1.6
Business directory	34.9	36.4	43	11	1.5
Database of small firms	26.2	27.3	42	11	1.1
Secondments	25.6	25.0	43	8	0.6
Non-executive director scheme	25.6	25.0	43	12	0.6

Source: LSE survey (mid-1991).

the provision of export information (69%); providing access to non-local business counsellors (67%); carrying out economic surveys (66%); specific advice over management structures, personnel policies and financial planning and taxation (all 64%); assistance with the identification of marketing opportunities (60%); specific advice over access to venture capital (55%); payroll operations and stock control procedures (both 53%); services to rural areas (52%); the provision of a market consultancy service (51%); and the organization of exhibitions (51%).

When consideration is made of the activities which were planned by TECs and LECs, few significant differences in the ranking of most common activities emerge. The training-related activities concerning labour market information (LMI) (90% of TECs and LECs offered or planned this) and the provision of a training providers directory (82%) show the most striking proposed increase. Other activities which appeared set to become significantly more common are: the running of business clubs and support centres (current or planned in 69% of TECs/LECs), and competitions (66%); computerized database of enterprise information (65%); tourism projects (64%); outreach services (61%); the provision of group marketing facilities (58%); expansion of the DTI Enterprise Initiative (58%); the provision of premises (57%) and managed workspace (56%); and the creation of business directories (56%) or local data bases of small firms (53%).

Not surprisingly, given their different responsibilities, the LSE survey demonstrates significant differences between levels of enterprise activity between TECs and LECs. This derives particularly from the LECs' physical and economic development brief, inherited from the HIDB and SDA, which goes significantly beyond the TECs' responsibilities. Table 9.2 illustrates the key contrasts. Scotland has a much higher level of enterprise activity overall. Of the 50 enterprise activities identified 19 were being provided in over 90% of LECs, with 14 being provided by all of them. In England and Wales, by contrast, only one activity, the provision of local business counsellors, was offered by more than 90% of TECs. The most striking area of difference was in the provision of grants and loans for enterprise activity. Whereas all LECs operated a grant and loan fund, only 7% of TECs claimed to do so, this being an activity beyond their public funding remit. Similarly, all LECs were involved in the provision of business premises, as compared to only 28% of TECs. Tourism projects, again conducted by all LECs, were underway in only a third of TECs. Although all the various aspects of specific marketing assistance (over design, identification of opportunities, advertising and accessing markets, distribution and franchizing) were offered by at least 75% of LECs, fewer than half of the TECs offered any of these. The number of activities that are more developed in TECs than LECs is very small. However, one striking finding concerns the two activities related to training: the provision of LMI, and provision of a training providers' directory. Whereas these activities featured very prominently in England and Wales, they were much less common in Scotland: 86% of TECs but only 58% of LECs were providing LMI, whereas 50% of TECs but only 18% of LECs offered a training providers' directory.

The continuation of these trends in TEC/LEC activity is borne out by the G10 survey in mid-1992. This showed that TECs had chiefly a small and micro-business focus dominated by the former EAS, half of which goes in income allowances to individuals. Little innovation or change in this area was recorded because the main delivery was through contracts to the pre-existing enterprise agencies, a commitment that derives from the 1988 White Paper. Beyond the inherited programmes, however, the G10 survey identified new services to support business growth and development as the key areas of innovation. As a result of this survey G10 (1992a, 1992b) quotes TECs as having 1,800–2,500 staff working on enterprise "many performing the function of "front line" advice and diagnosis to companies". The TECs had dealt with 238,000 companies, mainly through subcontractors. But "we can be certain that more than 100,000 SMEs are being dealt with directly". "This is a major success area for TECs in the SME field . . . it does illustrate the power of local bodies in accessing large volumes of SMEs . . . TECs have a great strength in this area" (G10 1992b: 7).

All these comments echo and reinforce the findings of the detailed survey shown in Tables 9.1 and 9.2: first, TECs are primarily focused on small, start-up and micro-businesses; second, the programme inheritance is very influential, particularly of EAS and BGT; third, the rôle of enterprise agencies that has dominated contractor relations has led to a low level of innovation in core programmes; fourth, as a result, innovation has focused on a very wide and diffuse field – as wide and diffuse as the initial mission statements. From the G10 survey we can also infer a fifth conclusion: a very low level of value-added by TECs in the enterprise field. The figure of 100,000 SMEs in contact with TECs is actually *less* than the number in contact with the enterprise agencies pre-TECs. This was estimated to be 250,000 counselling sessions in 1988 (BiTC 1989). As a contact system with 1,800–2,500 staff this statistic also raises a sixth question about value for money. Over the 1991 year ABCC Chambers of Commerce covering only part of the country and with a staff of 2,500 handled 580,000 enquiries. None of these statistics exactly compare like with like. But the comparisons each raise questions about value-added and value for money offered by TECs and LECs which we evaluate further in Chapter 11. In general, the conclusion must be that despite many new activities and roughly £180m of expenditure and 2,000 staff, on the G10 evidence, no more penetration of the market had been developed by TECs beyond that which they inherited from enterprise agencies.

Providers, purchasers or facilitators?

A key part of the original TEC/LEC mission was for them to act as "catalysts" and stimulators of local economic change. Subsequent to their launch, however, a clearer distinction has emerged in relation to how TECs/LECs should play this rôle. The distinction is between TECs as (i) direct providers, (ii) purchasers and (iii) facilitators through grants and other support. This distinction arises as an issue in each area of activity, but it is particularly sensitive in the field of enterprise first, because there are private and quasi-private sector providers who already exist so that insensitive TEC provision has a danger of crowding

Table 9.3 Mode of provision of TEC/LEC enterprise services: (i) direct TEC/LEC provision, (ii) contracted, (iii) facilitator/partner and other (single responses only, all topics prompted).

Activity	Direct provision	Contracted	Facilitation and other	Sample
Computerised database of enterprise information	90.9	6.1	3.0	33
Competitions	88.6	8.6	2.9	35
Labour market information	88.2	3.9	7.8	51
Outreach service	87.1	9.7	3.2	31
Training providers directory	86.0	4.7	9.3	43
Services to rural areas	82.1	7.1	10.7	28
Database of small firms	81.5	3.7	14.8	27
Other grants/loans	80.0	0.0	20.0	10
Tourism projects	78.8	12.1	9.1	33
Work experience	77.8	11.1	11.1	18
Business directory	76.7	3.3	20.0	30
Expansion of DTI Enterprise Initiative	76.7	13.3	10.0	30
Economic surveys	76.2	14.3	9.5	42
Exhibitions	75.7	13.5	10.8	37
Involvement with LIVEWIRE	73.9	0.0	26.1	23
Encouraging large firms to open R&D facilities	73.7	10.5	15.8	19
Grants	72.2	11.1	16.7	18
Information about new product requirements	71.4	19.0	9.5	21
Loans	71.4	14.3	14.3	14
Involvement with Young Enterprise	71.1	23.7	5.3	38
Group marketing facilities	70.0	3.3	26.7	30
Provision of business training	70.0	6.0	24.0	50
Secondments	70.0	15.0	15.0	20
Market consultancy service	65.8	10.5	23.7	38
Run clubs/support centres	65.1	16.3	18.6	43
Provision of local business counsellors	64.7	5.9	29.4	51
Specific advice: government and other schemes	63.8	2.1	34.0	47
Operation of a loan/grant fund	63.2	15.8	21.1	19
Soft loans/deferral methods	62.5	25.0	12.5	16
Specific advice: management structure	58.5	9.8	31.7	41
Involvement with Princes Youth Business Trust	57.5	30.0	12.5	40
Specific advice: start-ups	56.0	10.0	34.0	50
Specific advice: small firms	56.0	4.0	40.0	50
Specific advice: youth business	53.5	18.6	27.9	43

Non-executive director scheme	52.9	23.5	23.5	17
Specific advice: personnel policies	52.5	15.0	32.5	40
Specific advice: access to venture capital	50.0	14.3	35.7	42
Specific assistance: identification of opportunities	48.7	30.8	20.5	39
Specific advice: financial planning and taxation	48.7	5.1	46.2	39
Specific advice: stock control procedures	48.6	8.6	42.9	35
Specific advice: payroll operations	47.1	8.8	44.1	34
Provision of premises	45.2	41.9	12.9	31
Access to non-local business counsellors	44.7	26.3	28.9	38
Specific assistance: distribution & franchising	43.5	30.4	26.1	23
Managed workspace	43.3	36.7	20.0	30
Specific advice: export information	42.9	23.8	33.3	42
Specific assistance: advertising/accessing markets	40.0	31.4	28.6	35
Specific assistance: design	31.0	44.8	24.1	29
Other-general	100.0	0.0	0.0	8
Other personnel-based	81.8	0.0	18.2	11

Source: LSE survey (mid-1991).

out private with public activity thus reducing the level of competition in the economy; second, because the enterprise field has a wider range of other agents than training or education, many of which are at least as significant as the TECs and LECs themselves. The development of TEC/LEC enterprise activities thus has to be sensitive to the fact that they are being developed in an already confused and crowded market.

Despite these issues, the evidence of the LSE survey demonstrates that TECs/ LECs have largely sought to be direct providers of enterprise services, or certainly claim to be direct providers. This is a contrast to their rôle in training where provision is assigned via contracts. As shown in Table 9.3, in 39 of the 50 categories included in the survey, 50% or more of TECs and LECs claim to be direct providers of the enterprise service in question, and in 25 fields of activity 66% or more TECs/LECs claim to be providers. These included some of the main areas offered by the private sector and Chambers of Commerce (e.g. advice, counselling, consultancy, business training, product information, data bases, etc.). In contrast, specific advice and assistance activities are more commonly provided by indirect or subcontracted relations.

Table 9.3 demonstrates three features. First, there is the dominance, again, of the inherited programmes of EAS, BGT and the SFS. Second, many TECs/LECs are either not fully aware of, or do not wish to use, the range of alternative agents available and hence have sought to provide services de novo, even when they are already locally available. Third, there is a wide breadth of the field of TEC/LEC activities: a large number of TECs and LECs, in most cases 50–70% of the sample, is involved in almost all enterprise activities (either already or planned). This diffusion of effort on a base of fairly limited resources suggests that a major aim should be for TECs and LECs in the future to focus their provision in the fields where they can best fill gaps rather than duplicate. This diffusion of focus is a phenomenon characteristic of TEC and LEC enterprise activities. In the other TEC/LEC fields of activity the governmental programmes have focused TEC/LEC developments. With enterprise, there is a demonstrable lack of clarity as to the main goals and hence an understandable lack of focus in the resulting TEC/LEC activities. This is to some extent being overcome as a result of the lead given by the One Stop Shop initiative (see below).

Where the TECs and LECs have been most frequently prepared to contract services this has usually been for EAS and counselling services, and has usually been through enterprise agencies. Extensive contracts now exist between TECs/LECs and enterprise agencies. Table 9.4 shows that in 1992 60% of all TECs and LECs were contracting with enterprise agencies, and a further 21% were also core funding them. The proportion using enterprise agencies or trusts is higher in TECs (89.5%) than in LECs (12.5% in HIE and 83.3% in SE). The proportion of core funding is highest in SE LECs (41%), has reduced to 19.3% in TECs, and does not occur in HIE LECs where the enterprise trusts have traditionally been much less developed. Generally the support to enterprise agencies has stayed stable in TECs over the period 1991–1992, contracting increasing from 88% to 89% of TECs. In Scotland the level of contracting to enterprise trusts has increased by more: from 50% to 55% of LECs from 1991 to 1992. This probably reflects the late development of contracts in Scotland in the 1991/92 year that made it difficult to conclude contracts with enterprise trusts.

Table 9.4 Relation of TECs and LECs to enterprise agencies/trusts in mid 1991 and mid 1992. Percentage of responding TECs/LECs using agencies.

Use of enterprise agencies	England & Wales TECs		Scotland LECs			Total	
			total	SE	HIE		
	1991	1992	1991	1992	1992	1991	1992
Not using	12.1	10.5	50.0	16.7	87.5	23.4	19.5
Contracting for some programmes (EAS, BGT, etc.)	51.5	70.2	14.3	41.6	12.5	40.4	59.7
Core funding or giving premises as well as contracts	36.4	19.3	35.7	41.7	0	36.2	20.8
Sample size	33	57	14	12	8	47	77

Source: 1991 LSE face-to-face survey; 1992 mail survey: Bennett et al. (1993b).

The 1992 pattern in Table 9.4 is likely to prove stable in the future unless the overall funding regime changes. There is also evidenced that the enterprise agency contracting structure is being further strengthened by the One Stop Shop (OSS) initiative (see below).

The higher provision of core funding in central and southern Scotland would appear to reflect the wider brief of the SE LECs. In the Highlands and Islands the same objectives are pursued without the assistance of enterprise trusts, since they do not generally exist. This is in part a reflection of the dominant rôle of the former HIDB that made the development of enterprise trusts unnecessary. The lower provision of core funding in England and Wales may suggest a lesser commitment to long-term support amongst TECs uncertain of their future funding circumstances. It also reflects a stronger tendency, in general, in England and Wales for TECs both to provide services themselves, or to seek to control developments through contractor–supplier relations based on contracts with clear performance targets. In the SE area of Scotland a longer-term approach has generally been developed based on partnerships that seek to enhance a self-sustaining local capacity.

Working as partners?

It is important for TECs and LECs to be working with other agents in the enterprise field. Although there has been a strong tendency for TECs/LECs to become direct providers (as shown in Table 9.3) they have also begun to work with other agents. Table 9.5 examines the assessments by TEC/LEC chief executives of the key development agents for enterprise programmes in their areas. The dominance of enterprise agencies (enterprise trusts in Scotland) in this perception is very clear. These were identified as key agents in 91% of TECs and 54% of LECs. Local authorities (45% of TECs and LECs) and Chambers of Commerce (32%) are the only other major agents identified, with Chambers regarded as significantly more

Table 9.5 The views of TEC/LEC chief executives on the main local agents for the development of enterprise programmes ($N = 56$; multiple responses allowed). Percentage of cases where chief executive identified a body as a key local enterprise agent.

Main local agents	England & Wales TECs %	Scotland LECs %	Total %
Enterprise agencies/trusts	90.7	53.8	82.1
Chambers	37.2	15.4	32.1
LEN	0	0	0
Other business body	2.3	0	1.8
Banks	20.9	0	16.1
Local authorities	46.5	38.5	44.6
Universities	7.0	7.7	7.1
FE colleges	9.3	0	7.1
Other	55.8	46.2	53.6

important in TEC areas (37%) than in LECs (15%), reflecting the relative strengths of the local Chambers. Of other agents, a wide variety of specialist bodies was identified. Banks, FE colleges and universities all play an important rôle in some places whereas no TEC or LEC identified a LEN as a key player.

The views of TEC/LEC chief executives on which are the leading local enterprise bodies contrasts to some extent with other agents, except for the emphasis on enterprise agencies and trusts. A survey of non-TEC local agents and TEC Directors assessed the rôle played by different enterprise bodies in a sample of 16 TEC/LEC areas (Table 9.6). Enterprise agencies are again identified as the most important agents in most areas, but even more strongly by other agents than by TECs and LECs. Local authorities and Chambers of Commerce were identified with more prominence by other agents than by TECs and LECs; interestingly Chambers were picked most strongly by TEC/LEC Board members and Chairs, and local authorities were picked most strongly by Chambers and other business organizations. The banks and FE colleges were not seen as key agents by any other agent interviewed, despite, respectively, 25% and 6% of TECs/LECs seeing these agents as important. LENs, which no TEC/LEC saw as important, were identified by 8% of all other agents as important, with a stronger identification among TEC Chairs/Board members and local authorities. This reflects their importance in the formation of some TEC/LEC Boards which drew heavily from LENs.[3]

The contrasts in these perceptions are indicative of TECs and LECs being driven by funding priorities. The enterprise agencies have become obvious

Table 9.6 The views of other agents, compared with TECs/LECs, on the main agents for development of enterprise in a sample of 16 TEC/LEC areas (multiple responses allowed).

	Subsample of TEC chief executives	All other agents	TEC Chairs/ Board	Business organiza- tions	LAs
Enterprise agencies	75.0	80.8	81.8	80.0	81.0
Chambers	62.5	51.9	63.6	60.0	33.3
LEN	0	7.7	18.2	0	9.5
Other business body	0	7.7	9.0	5.0	4.8
Banks	25.0	0	0	0	0
Local authorities	50.0	69.2	54.5	70.0	28.6
Universities	12.5	3.8	0	5.0	0
FE colleges	6.3	0	0	0	0
Other	56.3	44.2	45.5	35.0	23.8
TEC/LEC	-	34.6	18.2	50.0	9.5
Sample size	16	52	11	20	21

Note: [1] This is an average for a subsample of 16 areas derived from Table 9.5 and differing from that table mainly for the case of Chambers and enterprise agencies.

216

targets for TEC/LEC contracts for inherited enterprise programmes, which many had previously contracted for in any case; particularly EAS and BGT Option 3. The Chambers, local authorities and FE colleges are identified as important by TECs/LECs, probably because they are generally the main training providers in an area (trainers are also an important part of the "other" category). LENs are not perceived by the TEC as important because they have no programmatic funding and are "part of the past" as far as TEED is concerned (see Bennett et al. (1990b) for summaries of views on LENs *vis-à-vis* TECs).

In contrast other local agents have a stronger perception of the traditional key local players in enterprise programmes. They therefore tend to emphasize the long-term agents such as Chambers, local authorities and enterprise agencies, as well as remembering the previous LEN initiative that attempted to bind local agents together. Indeed many TEC Board members and Chairs emerged to prominence through the LEN. The other agents, therefore, tend to have longer memories and a broader grasp of the key players than TEC/LEC chief executives.

The sense in which TEC/LEC perception is distorted by funding programmes, rather than taking a more detached and longer-term view, is reinforced in Table 9.7. This compares the assessment by TEC/LEC chief executives of the strengths of local Chambers and enterprise agencies against objective assessment of their local strengths derived from other data. The analysis of the strengths of local agents is taken further in Chapter 10 where the method of measuring local strengths is described. The TECs/LECs assess enterprise agents as key agents in 50% of areas where they are small or virtually non-existent, and in 66.7% of areas where they are weak. In the case of Chambers these are identified as key agents in 16.7% of areas where they are virtually non-existent, and in 36.4% of areas where they are weak. Nor do TECs/LECs in all cases correctly see enterprise agencies and Chambers as the key agents where they are in fact strongest.

The lack of match between TEC/LEC perceptions and objective data may reflect imperfections in the data in some cases. But the differences are too great to result from these imperfections alone. The differences suggest instead the influence of three other factors: (i) poor understanding by the TECs and LECs of the enterprise system: this was clearly evident in conversations with many TEC/ LEC staff, many of whom did not get their minds fully engaged with their enter-

Table 9.7 The view of TEC/LEC chief executives in 16 case study areas on the relative strengths of local Chambers and enterprise agencies compared to objective data on the strengths of these agents (details of these definitions are given in Chapter 10). Percentage of cases where chief executive identified a body as a key local agent.

TEC/LECs views on:	Objective strengths of agents			
	Little/nothing	Weak	Medium	Strong
Chamber a key player	16.7	36.4	23.5	60.0
Enterprise agency a key player	50.0	66.7	81.0	75.0

prise strategy until the launch of the OSS initiative in December 1992; (ii) external dependence on TEED-defined programmes and finance; (iii) a "macho" sense that existing local agents did not matter, TECs/LECs could go it alone.

These factors have ebbed and flowed with time. The pervasive influence of the One Stop Shop initiative and its prospectus, with no non-conforming bids, confirms the effect of the externally-driven agenda in the enterprise field: in this case by DTI as well as TEED. The "macho" sense has declined somewhat over time, but the high level of continued direct provision by TECs and LECs (Table 9.3) and tone of the report on the G10 (1992b) survey suggests that there is still a long way to go before wider local partnerships will develop.

A further way of assessing how far a partnership rôle has been developing is to compare TEC/LEC activity with how other agents see the main goals that need to be fulfilled in the local economy. The results of this assessment suggest that other agents prefer to see TECs and LECs primarily as catalysts or facilitators of cohesion locally. Their view of what the TEC/LEC enterprise goals should be is very clear. As shown in Table 9.8, over three-quarters of respondents felt that the chief goal should be to facilitate greater integration or to improve the coherence of enterprise provision.

Beyond the aim of integration, all other goals are more diffuse. Whereas 34% of agents felt that TECs/LECs should focus on SMEs, 8% felt that key local firms should be the focus. The next most commonly sought goals were stimulation of an enterprise culture and acting as a major lobby, neither of which readily lead to direct programme outputs. The key findings from this analysis are, therefore, that TECs/LECs are seen by other agents as needing to have a primary goal of stimulating coherence in enterprise provision. That in most fields of activity they have become direct providers (see Table 9.2), demonstrates that early development of TECs/LECs has frustrated the goals supported by other agents.

Table 9.8 The principle enterprise goals that TECs/LECs should follow in the view of other local agents. Percentage of agents in the 20 case study areas, open responses ($N = 38$; multiple responses allowed).

Goals	%
Increase integration/coherence	76.3
Focus on SMEs	34.2
Encourage self-employment/enterprise culture	21.1
Act as a major enterprise lobby	15.8
Encourage inward investment	10.5
Provide information/directory	7.9
Focus on key local firms	7.9
Stimulate innovation, R&D	5.3
Focus on counselling and start-up after care	2.6
Other	23.7

This frustration is evident from the response by non-TEC agents to evaluation of TECs'/LECs' actual enterprise strategy (Table 9.9). Although many respondents (42%) felt that TECs and LECs had become key agents, or participants, in the enterprise field, 30% of respondents felt that TEC/LEC enterprise strategies were at best "poor", and 12.5% believe the TEC/LEC to be positively harmful. This strong negative view is reinforced by the fact that a further 25% of respondents were at present neutral about TECs/LECs, or felt it was too early to judge. These results show that over one-half of respondents have at best a neutral view about existing TEC/LEC enterprise activity. There is thus a long way to go before TECs and LECs can build the local trust and add the local value that they were intended to do.

Part of the negative response to TECs and LECs is focused on the inherited programmes. The response of other agents shows that in nearly equal measure (approx. 30% each) the key criticisms of these programmes were the lack of selection, low quality and separation of these programmes from broader enterprise strategies (see Table 9.10). Only a few respondents felt there was an issue of resources (7.1%).

This led other agents to suggest that the main goals TECs and LECs should develop for the inherited enterprise programmes (Table 9.11) should be to improve integration and coherence (47%), develop a one stop capacity (24%; this was before the announcement of the One Stop Shop initiative by Michael

Table 9.9 The evaluation of TEC/LEC enterprise policy by other agents. Percentage of agents responses in 20 case study areas ($N = 40$; multiple responses not allowed).

TEC/LEC enterprise policy	%
TEC/LEC is key enterprise animater	15.0
TEC/LEC is linking well to other agents	27.5
TEC/LEC neither key animator nor inactive	20.0
TEC/LEC enterprise policy is poor or inactive	17.5
TEC/LEC is in conflict or positively harmful	12.5
Too early to judge	5.0
Other	2.5

Table 9.10 The deficiencies associated with the TEC/LEC policy with inherited programmes of EAS, SFS and BGT/BET. Percentage of agents' open responses in 20 case study areas ($N = 41$; multiple responses not allowed).

Deficiencies	%
Insufficiently selective of clients	32.1
Quality must be raised	28.6
Should be part of a broader strategy	28.6
Price too low	7.1
Other	3.6

Table 9.11 The goals that other agents believe TECs/LECs should develop for the inherited programmes of EAS, SFS and BGT/BET. Percentage of agents' responses in 20 case study areas ($N = 45$; multiple responses allowed).

Goals	%
Develop integration/coherence	46.7
Make no major changes	26.7
Develop a one-stop capacity	24.4
Major reform required: programmes inadequate	22.2
Link to SMEs programmes beyond start-up	20.0
Develop aftercare	2.2
Other	8.9

Heseltine in July 1992), institute major programme reforms (22%) and link to SMEs beyond the start-up category (20%). However 27% of respondents felt that TECs and LECs should make no major changes to programmes but should develop them as they are, jointly with other agents.

European perspectives

An important aspect of enterprise activities is preparation for the Single European Market (SEM) introduced in January 1993. The SEM is perhaps the single most important long-term challenge to business. It is useful therefore to com-

Table 9.12 Involvement of TECs and LECs in European enterprise activities directly or as a joint provider (percentage of TECs/LECs in sample).

Activity	England & Wales TECs		Scotland LECs		Total	
	Direct provider	Joint	Direct provider	Joint	Direct provider	Joint
Joint ventures in EC	0	10.6	0	21.0	0	13.1
Promotion of language skills	21.3	17.0	14.3	7.1	19.7	14.7
Provision of information centre	0	10.6	7.1	7.1	1.6	9.8
Provision of European business centre	0	12.7	0	7.1	0	11.5
Trade missions & visits	2.1	4.2	0	14.3	1.6	6.6
Appointment of 1992 coordinator	10.6	4.2	7.1	0	9.8	3.3
EC seminars & conferences	14.9	17.0	35.7	21.4	19.7	18.0
European business directory	2.1	0	0	0	1.6	0
Pursuing EC grants	2.1	6.4	7.1	7.1	3.3	6.6
Other	17.0	14.9	14.3	7.1	16.4	13.1
Sample size	47		14		61	

EUROPEAN PERSPECTIVES

pare the activities of TECs and LECs with that of other agents to see how far they
have focused on the longer term as opposed to inherited programme activities.

Table 9.12 assesses TEC/LEC direct and joint provision of activities related
to the SEM. The most notable finding is that more than 60% of TECs and LECs
have no specific European activity at all, and in all but 3 areas more than 85%
failed to act as a direct or joint provider of any European initiatives, however
small that might be. Although this minimal activity can be attributed to TECs'
and LECs' more immediate concerns with establishing primary programme areas in their early days, it nonetheless suggests a slow start to what many of the
respondents in TECs and LECs acknowledged to be a vitally important field.

The most common TEC/LEC European enterprise activity related to the spreading of European awareness by means of seminars and conferences. In Scotland,
36% of LECs conducted these, compared with 15% of TECs. The most common
activity in TECs was the promotion of language skills, for example through YT
or ET provision (21% of TECs gave direct provision). The percentage of LECs
promoting language skills was lower, only 14% directly providing these.

Compared to other agents, TECs and LECs have been much less active in all
fields related to the SEM, except the promotion of language skills. Table 9.13
shows that, in a controlled sample of 20 TEC/LEC areas, other local agents were
normally two or three times more active than TECs and LECs. The TECs and
LECs in this subsample are generally more active in European enterprise than
the main sample (compare Tables 9.12 and 9.13). The most common activities
were services and conferences, joint ventures, promotion of language skills,
information centres and missions/visits. Chambers and business organizations

Table 9.13 Involvement of other agents in European enterprise activities compared to
TECs and LECs in a sub-sample of 20 TEC/LEC areas (percentage of responses of each
agent; multiple answers allowed).

Activity	TEC/LEC subsample	All other agents	Business organizations	LA
Joint ventures in EC	20.0	48.6	57.9	38.9
Promotion of language skills	60.0	51.4	47.4	55.6
Provision of information centre	20.0	45.9	52.6	38.9
Provision of European business centre	15.0	32.4	36.8	27.8
Trade missions & visits	25.0	45.9	47.4	44.4
Appointment of 1992 coordinator	20.0	35.1	42.1	27.8
EC seminars & conferences	45.0	56.8	63.2	50.0
European business directory	5.0	13.5	10.5	16.7
Pursuing EC grants	15.0	29.7	10.5	50.0
Other	45.0	40.5	36.8	44.4
Sample size	20	37	19	18

221

were generally more active than local authorities, but both were considerably more active than TECs/LECs.

This analysis shows TECs and LECs as slow to develop a European context for their enterprise activity, either directly or jointly, and it is clear that in the 20 sample areas other agents are in many cases developing important initiatives. It would thus be desirable if TECs/LECs were more involved in this activity as a partner. More worrying is the feature that the main form of TEC/LEC direct provision, language skills and conferences/seminars, are also major areas of other agents' provision. Since these areas are also ones with a significant capacity for raising fees, the survey results indicate that where TECs and LECs have been most active on Europe, they are often doing this competitively rather than jointly.

The assessment of the European issue again reinforces the view that TEC/LEC enterprise policy is driven by inherited programmes, with new initiatives more usually developed directly and competitively rather than jointly and sensitively.

One Stop Shops (Business Link)

The One Stop Shop (OSS) initiative was announced by Michael Heseltine, President of the Board of Trade, in July 1992. A prospectus was published in December 1992 for the first local implementation from April 1993 after a bidding process. The term Business Link was coined as a marketing brand in mid 1993 (DTI 1993) In the first round for 1993/94 there were 58 bids, of which 20 were shortlisted and 15 accepted. In addition a London bid was converted into a development project to build a pan-London model. The chief objectives of One Stop Shops are:[4]

- To bring integration and *coherence* between the main suppliers of enterprise services, particularly TECs, Chambers and enterprise agencies;
- To achieve this by *partnerships* with these agents;
- To improve the overall *professionalism* and *quality* standards to the best in Europe: this is often equated with those in Germany;
- To have a *physical presence* – an office/shop with maximum co-location of partners;
- To develop, over time, a network for the whole country;
- To use fairly modest amounts of DTI resources, approximately £200,000 per One Stop Shop, depending on size of area;
- Moving to self-sufficiency as rapidly as possible;
- Bidding and contracting by TECs, in partnership with other agents.

Mr Heseltine recognized that the key problem of the enterprise field was to bring coherence between agents: "We still have a long way to go. Firms are still faced with a welter of advice and information of variable quality from a confusing maze of local agencies whose services often appear to be in competition with each other".[5] He also saw that one of the key problems was to sort out the rôle of the TEC. Heseltine saw no doubt that the TEC was "the `enabler', coordinating the network to achieve the greatest added value and to create coherent services".[6] He further saw the problem as not lack of money: "There is already a minimum of £40m each year being spent by TECs on business advice, information and counselling alone. This represents roughly £0.5m per TEC, plenty I would have thought to lever a major uplift in the quality of current support activity".[7]

One of the most crucial of Mr Heseltine's leads was, however, to press TECs not to fill gaps in present local support systems by their own provision, but to build a self-sustaining base in the local community:

> I should make it clear that if a Chamber, TEC or enterprise agency is weak in any particular area, this should not be an argument for turning our backs on it or to develop duplicate products or services from an alternative source. Rather it is a strong argument for taking decisive action to build the capacity of that particular organization and with it the capacity of the network as a whole.[8]

This view came to dominate decisions on the DTI award of One Stop Shop resources.

However, analysis of the bids and allocation of awarded resources shown in Table 9.14 demonstrates that it was not generally the areas with weakest levels of development of other agents that were successful in the DTI competition. The final allocation of DTI OSSs money went in only 37% of cases to areas with

Table 9.14 Analysis of success of the 58 bids for DTI OSS funds in January 1993 in relation to the existing strengths of Chambers of Commerce and enterprise agencies. Source of Chamber and enterprise agency strengths, as in Tables 5.2, 5.3, 10.2.

	Chambers of Commerce			London	Total
	Strong	Weak but enterprise agencies strong	Weak and enterprise agencies also weak		
Bids:					
No.	25	10	17	6	58
% of total bids	43	17	29	10	100
DTI allocation:					
No.	10	2	3	1	16
% of successful bids	62.5	12.5	19	6	100
Success ratio:					
(allocation as % of bids in area)	40	20	18	17	28

Note: DTI allocation is defined as the 6 bids which were brought on quickly as pilots plus the 9 bids requiring more detailed negotiation as at April 1993. London is separated from the other columns where the DTI allocation includes only the Central London bid.

weaker agents (London included). The success rate of bids in these areas was also half that in the areas where Chambers were strong. It is not clear, then, that the OSS allocations followed Heseltine's launch statement that "we will be looking for a . . . *greater market penetration* achieved through real partnership with other local organizations".[9] The strongest areas may have been able to put up the strongest bids, but penetration is already highest in these areas.

In areas where bids were not successful or were not made, Mr Heseltine wants to see OSSs develop anyway. By this means, a national network is to be developed. There had been the hope of more funds for subsequent DTI rounds, but it is now clear that the main development is intended to be self-funded so that areas that do not receive DTI funds will go ahead on their own using their own resources. From whichever origin, each OSS will have to be accredited by DTI to meet specified standards.

It is unclear at the time of writing how effective this accreditation will be, how far it will force TECs to make their own initiatives conform to the DTI standards, and hence how far the OSSs will be able to exert effective leverage on TECs to develop partnership across the whole country. The main method so far developed to give TECs incentives to work in partnership has been a set of sanctions against TEC OSSs that are not true partnerships. Such developments will be excluded from the benefits of the national brand name and promotion; will not be eligible for training, IT and other network developments; will not receive DTI accreditations; will not receive contracts for delivery of DTI and other government services; and as a last resort will suffer cuts in the DTI-funded enterprise budget.[10] For this leverage to be effective will require the partnership model to be asserted and evaluated against a close scrutiny of how each area is actually developing local coherence.

In Scotland the developments of OSSs among LECs has followed a different route. Bids have not been competitive. Instead SE and HIE have been asked to identify which of the LECs have best developed a local coherent enterprise structure. These have then been used as a set of best practice models to launch SO guidance, jointly with SE and HIE, on the model for enterprise targets to be sought by LECs. In this process Grampian in the SE area, and Inverness in the HIE area have been used as offering leading models. Having developed the model, the launch of the first two of Scotland's OSSs in November 1993 (Glasgow and Aberdeen) has then allowed the initiative to be franchized to a variety of local agents.

This approach has allowed significant advantages to be gained over the approach in England. First, the whole system for SE is being developed together, rather than piecemeal. Second, a general model with local variability has been developed from the start through consultation with the key players, rather than letting a repetitive learning process evolve in each area. Third, this allows more rapid development of a common identity and agreed common standards to be sought. Fourth, much less senior management time has been used, compared to the DTI/TEED approach which "continues to use up endless amounts of senior management time in getting small increments in funds" (in the words of one senior Scottish commentator).

In Scotland the SO has been able to use SE and HIE as effective intermediaries in the development of local solutions. There has also been a contrast with England since Chambers are not usually credible alternatives to LECs and have been happier to look for a satisfactory basis for co-operation and contracting. Also in Scotland the SO has acted as a single co-ordinating body. There have not been two departments, DTI and DE, acting as rival champions, respectively, of Chambers and TECs. In contrast, in England a senior Scottish spokesman sees OSSs as essentially "having to be a healing device" between TECs and Chambers, and between DTI and DE.

Despite differences in origin and style, the objectives of OSSs in LECs and TECs have been essentially the same and the new services developed very similar. In this sense they have constituted a national model. They have sought to provide a new service, "business advisers", while offering a gateway to access the full range of other local business services available: "It will be essential that customers can access from each [OSS] centre a full range of local and remote services. . . . For services delivered by local partners, it will be important to maximise the extent to which these are co-located in a single set of premises" (DTI 1992: 8). The conceptualization of how the services might be organized is shown in Table 9.15. The business advisers act to maintain contact with companies and offer the main source of information and advice, while counselling, consultancy, skills, awareness and other activities and facilities are subject to referrals.

It is early days to assess the development of the OSSs initiative. But already three difficulties are becoming evident. First, the model for the new services to be developed by the OSSs has severe questions over whether it fits the needs of the market and can be sustained once DTI support is withdrawn. The OSS Prospectus defines the core new service as:

> business advisers, organised on account manager principles . . . independent and on the side of the customer, and they will need to work proactively to develop a long-term relationship with a portfolio of local business, focused particularly on small companies with growth potential . . . Their objective will be to put together a package of services tailored to the needs of each customer.[11]

Beyond this, OSSs will provide a "single point of access", a "gateway" in Mr Heseltine's phase,[12] "to the widest possible range of support services required by a business".[13]

The difficulty of the business adviser model is that it is very expensive per unit output – almost all work has to be one-to-one on business sites. It is therefore, not a model capable of wide diffusion across many businesses. Even if only a small proportion of employers nationally were covered, there is a formidable challenge. There are about 90,000 businesses nationally in the size range

Table 9.15 Services to be provided (i) in OSSs, focused on business advisers as well as information and advice, (ii) through OSSs by referrals, networking and co-location with other partners (* indicates that a service is desirable, but not essential).

Information and advice:
Provide high quality information and advice on:

Grants and support schemes	Business start-up
Exporting	Technology and innovation
Finance	Training
Late payment	Marketing
VAT, tax and Uniform Business Rates	Design
Licensing requirements	Product sourcing
Legislation	Environmental issues
(Health & Safety, Planning, etc.)	(including BS7750)
Standards (including	* Application of IT
BS5750/BS7850 and TQM)	* Property
BSI services	* Patents, trademarks and copyright
SEM information	* Education/Business Partnerships
(including new legislation)	

Account management:
Personal Business Advisers who maintain regular contact with a portfolio of companies and construct an integrated package of services to meet their needs

Counselling/consultancy
Provide *access* to:

Diagnostic/health check services	IIP
Start-up counselling	Other subsidised TEC consultancy
General business counselling	schemes
Survival counselling	Commercial consultancy
	Enterprise initiative consultancy

Business skills and awareness
Provides *access* to:

Business skills seminars	Business start-up schemes
(including business planning, quality,	Other relevant TEC activities
marketing, purchasing, etc.)	* Management Charter initiative
Managing in the 1990s	

Other services/activities:

* DTI clinics	* Small firms clubs
* Design Council services	* Professional clinics
* Customer/supplier events	

Facilities:

Information Centre	* Training resources
Counselling rooms	* Meeting/training rooms
Hot lines to external expertise	* Companies House (on-line ordering)
Data bases	

Source: derived from DTI (1992), Prospectus, Annex 2.

20–200, or 230,000 in the size range 11–200 employees.[14] Analysis of the counselling and visits run by existing Chambers of Commerce and enterprise agencies suggest that sessions range from 2 to 8 hours and that an annual staffing ratio of one member of staff per 200 hours is the most efficient normal load, because of other administrative commitments, travel time, etc. This means that providing one session per year to 90,000–230,000 firms requires 330–770 business advisers, if each session were 4 hours long. A more realistic assumption, based on past practice,[15] is that each business requires 5 sessions per year with, say, 2 of 1 hour each and 3 of 4 hours each. This requires 14 hours per year per business for which 1,050–2,680 business advisers are required. This would mean between 10 and 26 advisers per TEC or LEC if all were at average size. This demand is large and clearly beyond the budget set aside for OSSs. However, the estimate of working hours used derives from enterprise agencies and Chambers. If the working hours and employment conditions of DTI-supported Regional Technology Centres, which are in some ways analogous to business advisers, are used then between 3,750 and 9,600 advisers will be needed to provide an effective service. Apart from the funding gap for this demand, there are probably not enough people with the relevant skills.[16]

If TEC staff are used for estimating needs, counselling and administration, estimates provided in Chapter 11 suggest that an efficiency ratio of at best, only one-third that in Chambers or enterprise agencies will be available (Table 11.1, row 3). Hence to the extent that OSSs are run within a public administrative culture the number of counsellors rises by a ratio of about three times that in enterprise agencies and Chambers.

No enterprise agency or Chamber has been able to sustain a full adviser/counsellor service without subsidy, either from sponsors, government grants or from other sources of income. Usually the ratio of subsidy required is 60–70% of costs.[17] Hence, not only is the OSS emphasis on business advisers very demanding on resources, these resources cannot usually generate a self-sustaining fee income beyond 30–40% of their costs. The OSS Prospectus (17) is ambiguous on income strategy. It expects established businesses "to contribute to the costs of services, especially those with high unit costs" (which must include business advisers) but "subsidised services should not undermine commercial services". It is clear that business advisers cannot survive without subsidy and that, since so much of their rôle does interface with private sector advisers, it is unlikely that this subsidy will not undermine the market. The adviser model bears all the hallmarks of being thought up by civil servants, in part as a continuity, or exit strategy, for DTI from the enterprise initiative and Regional Technology Centres. It was not market tested and does not appear, on the evidence available, to be sustainable by the market in the long term.

The second difficulty of the OSSs has been the steerage of the system. OSSs have not been allocated DTI funds predominantly in areas where other enterprise agents are weak. This would have been the best use of public funds: to fill gaps in the market and to act as catalyst or enabler to improving local systems. But the enterprise policies of those TECs that are outside the OSSs initiative are left under a cloud of uncertainty. Will they follow the partnership approach pressed on OSS; or will the TEC's enterprise strategies remain hopelessly broad, ill-focused and seeking to act as providers rather than enablers, as we have shown in the earlier parts of this chapter. Michael Heseltine's objective was to focus the TECs' minds. He stated at the TECs 1992 conference that "All too often turf battles continue – about TEC membership schemes, overlapping services and the like. I tell you frankly; we can no longer afford to continue to waste our collective energy on this unhelpful debate. I see TECs very much as *enablers* rather than direct *deliverers* of . . . services".[18] To ensure that this happens will require vigilance by DTI and other players. The 1993/94 TECs strategy statement, the first joint DE–DTI strategy, goes some way to meeting this aim. But a shift from TECs attempting to deliver, to enabling the delivery of, enterprise services will require tight partnership targets to be set, with detailed programme guidance to be specified on the services to be operated, levered by a high proportion of ORF or other controls on the TEC budget.

This debate leads us to identifying a third area of difficulty. This is how the model of TEC relationships with other agents will evolve in the future for the cases in which the local agents are very strong. The OSS allocations appear in some cases to be filling a gap where other agents are weak and TECs relatively strong. But they do not offer as clear a guide for a way forward where the other agents are strong. The Heseltine vision is to see the TECs as purchasing from other agents. This is fine in purely financial terms. But it draws us back to the central dilemma in the TEC mission: why on earth should a strong and viable local entity, such as a Chamber, get involved with the tortuous contractual process and contentious local leadership of a TEC. The OSS promotes a model for the strong/weak relations (i.e. strong TEC/weak other agent) but not for a strong/strong relation (where the TEC is just another player in a complex scene). This suggests that a different model is required which accepts the weaknesses of TECs and allows their mergers with the strong agents in an area. Although envisaged in the Heseltine brief, and being examined by 2 or 3 TECs and Chambers, there is as yet no model of Chamber–TEC merger which satisfies both agents and government. Indeed all of the England and Wales OSS bids are very thin in their detail of partnership. One leading Scottish spokesman felt they were all "pretty weak". We assess the requirements for merger in Chapter 12.

Our concluding assessment on OSSs is that they have been a useful initiative. For the first time they have focused TEC and LEC strategy in the enterprise field. Previously, as our analysis demonstrates, TECs and LECs have drifted into a system of direct delivery to all-purpose, ill-focused targets. OSSs have in England and Wales offered a major "healing device" between TECs and Chambers of Commerce. And they have provided a useful mechanism for DE and DTI to work together in defining targets for the TECs and their ORF from 1993/94 onwards. Our critical evaluation is aimed at demonstrating both the pitfalls that lie in the way of a course that deviates from the Heseltine strategy and the longer-term thinking that is still required to address the relationships between TECs/LECs and other enterprise agents. That there will be many forces seeking to steer the strategy away from these longer-term questions is evidenced in the pressure that the Chambers and other enterprise agents have had to continue to exert on Mr Heseltine, the TECs, TEED and DTI civil servants, in order to ensure that the progress on OSSs has closely followed the partnership objective. There have been complaints by other agents that meetings of TEED Implementation Groups have been held without partners and that the initiative has taken on a TEC-led and civil service-led agenda. The fact that many of the DTI civil servants in the small firms division, involved in drafting the OSS Prospectus, have been transferred from TEED demonstrates the difficulty of reversing the momentum of the civil service-led, training-led agenda driven by direct supply and subsidy developed by the former MSC.

Similarly the TECs themselves are only reluctantly taking up Heseltine's concepts of a partnership-based enterprise mission. One TEC chief executive (77) of a leading OSS pilot summed up the TEC attitudes of mid-1993: "We will take the DTI money if there are no strings attached, or if the strings fit to our plans, but not if the DTI push us in a different direction to the one we want to go. We don't need the One Stop Shop money, we have enough surpluses and EC grants". As a result of this viewpoint the TECs with pilot OSSs have been negotiating hard with DTI: "they need us more than we need them: the DTI cannot afford to have any one of its lead pilots refuse to go forward" (TEC chief executives 77 and 31). The structure of the OSSs bidding process has made it clear that the TECs have been given too strong a hand in negotiations compared to their partners. Having TECs as the contracting body has most frequently tended to undermine, rather than reinforce, partnership. We turn in Chapter 12 to how a more progressive purchasing relationship could be established.

Filling the real enterprise gaps

The analysis given above of the TEC/LEC enterprise mission and the development of their actual activities in 1991 and 1992 allows only a very mixed evaluation. The initial mission was very ambitious, like the rest of the TECs agenda, but has had limited potential in practice because of both a lack of realistic vision and significant restrictions on funds and the form of inherited programmes. Where innovation has occurred, it has often been through direct provision at the expense of existing agents, rather than partnership with them. The rôle of direct provision in the enterprise field seems odd when there are many other agents only too willing and quite capable of providing services on a contractual basis, and when TECs and LECs are quite used to subcontracting their training programmes. As a result little value seems to have been added to main programmes beyond that which was already offered by enterprise agents, consultants and other providers. The development of membership, although seeking to legitimize TECs and LECs and increase market penetration, has added a further competitive dimension to the already crowded local domain of enterprise activities. Of course there are exceptions to these conclusions where, in some TEC/LEC areas, genuine joint development and significant programme improvement has occurred. But generally the assessment of enterprise development must be that, until the OSSs, only a little of new value had yet been developed. Why has this rather unhappy situation arisen?

The primary difficulties faced by TECs and LECs in enterprise development have been that their programmes have evolved from earlier government initiatives. No fundamental assessment of what was needed in the enterprise market was made for the launch of TECs and LECs. We make such an assessment in Chapter 12, in order to evaluate where TEC/LEC programmes should develop in the future. We conclude this chapter by highlighting the key areas of deficiency that need to be overcome.

The need to think further

First, is the question of overcoming existing programme fragmentation. The TECs inherited a suite of programmes concerned with stimulating self-employment, helping start-up companies, providing consultancy and advice to smaller firms, information services through the SFS, management and supervisor development through IIP and MCI. Each of these programmes was largely disconnected from each other in the past and had their origin in separate initiatives from different sections of TEED. Indeed EAS and SFS had their origins in DTI and the other programmes originated in DE. The TECs, therefore, inherited a suite of programmes, rather than a system of enterprise support, often with different objectives and targets.

Although some of the inherited programmes sought to serve well-identified segments of the market, others were less clearly targeted, the need for others was not always clear, and other market segments may not have been covered at all. A first priority for TECs and LECs should, therefore, have been integration and restructuring of their own existing programmes into a more coherent structure of priorities. While there is evidence that this has occurred in many TECs and LECs, the general conclusion from our surveys must be that (i) they are still dominated by existing programmes, in part as a result of the separate programme targets set by TEED, in part as a result of deficiencies in staff vision, (ii) most programmes are still delivered by the same providers, although reduced in numbers, with little integration or effective referral between agents, and (iii) most TEC/LEC enterprise strategies have become wide and unrealistically ambitious, resulting in conflict and competition with the private sector and existing agents, rather than enhancing broader strategy or value-added.

Second is the issue of programme quality. The programmes have been mostly inherited and have been largely maintained. Most programmes, because of their derivation from the DE, have a focus on self-employment or unemployment rather than business development. This has resulted in a focus on the very small businesses; single-person or a few employees. Recently, IIP and MCI have had primarily initially to be focused on very large firms. There is thus something of a gap in programmes between the micro-business (up to, say, 5 employees) and large business of over 200 employees. Also, where services are provided they have tended to focus on *income support* (e.g. EAS) or are relatively *passive* (e.g. information services in response to enquiries) rather than being active. Where programmes have been more active, such as IIP and MCI they have been *difficult to sell* because resources have been slender and the main appeal to a business has been that the programme "will do you good".

Thirdly, an important distinction must be made between the performance of TECs and Scottish LECs. Although the inherited programmes from TEED had a similarly chequered history in Scotland, the LECs have been advantaged by a wider remit, larger resources, and a longer experience inherited from the SDA and HIDB. This has allowed them to play a much more effective rôle in their areas. Having responsibility for provision of sites and premises, business development advice and working capital has allowed the LECs to position themselves with established as well as start-up businesses. They have also had much more to offer inward investors as a package. Clearly LECs are advantaged by their wider responsibilities and resources. However, the contrast of LECs with TECs also highlights the crucial strategic defects of the latter. Whereas the LECs have often started from a strategy of business development led by the needs of business in their area, the TECs have been given a training-led theory and products to sell that are designed by someone else. Thus, rather than filling the gap for established businesses of intermediate size, they have in almost all cases chosen to stay within the concepts designed by TEED based on training health checks, and IIP.

Fourthly, there has been considerable confusion among TECs and LECs over the branding of their programmes. With their new-found independence, particularly in the field of enterprise, most TECs and LECs have sought to distance themselves from the titles of their awkward programme inheritance and have adopted new labels and more vigorous marketing of their products. Unfortunately this has seldom been accompanied by significant redesign of the programmes themselves. This has led to the frequent criticism that the TECs have been mostly concerned with "hype" rather than developing quality. Ironically this has been the result almost equally of civil service inertia to facilitate programme change, and business-led Boards that have been encouraged to believe that marketing can sell any product, however poor: "It is certainly all about marketing, and we have been told effectively by the Department [of Employment] that if Ratners was able to succeed by selling rubbish to its customers because that is what they wanted so can we. I don't accept that, but that is effectively what I believe we have been told to do" (TEC Chair 93).

The unfortunate outcome of this emphasis on marketing and re-branding has frequently added confusion to the already confused enterprise field. One example is the term STEP used among the 9 London TECs: STEP is the South Thames Enterprise Programme; STEP is part of LADDER of enterprise programmes in AZTEC; STEP is part of two Shell plc programmes for the homeless (CENTEC) and for graduate trainees (LETEC). STEP is just one example of this confusion; many similar TEC/LEC enterprise programmes also differ in name, and many similarly named programmes differ in the detail of what they provide at what cost. Few TECs have been concerned about this confusion. They have been responding as administrators with a marketing "bolt-on", not as facilitators of products related to customer demands.

The fifth and most significant area of deficiency of the TECs and LECs concerns working with others. As we have seen, many early TECs took a rather "macho" approach, in the words of one TEED senior commentator, and believed that they could do everything themselves. This is a strong contrast to their use of contractors in the training field. They have been encouraged in this outlook by TEED. The TEC launch and Prospectus did not mention other agents in a committed or thought-through way. Agents such as Chambers of Commerce, LENs, local authorities or enterprise agencies were to be met with, and led by, TECs and LECs; the fuller conceptualization was not thought through of what local partnership and new capacity building should mean. In many ways the government may have been deceived by its own rhetoric into believing that TECs could take a lead everywhere. But later cuts in funding, the lack of staff expertise, the equivocal reception of TECs and LECs by business, and the need to use other agents to make realistic developments in the enterprise field has subsequently led to the need for a more realistic approach. This follows the experience of some TECs "on the ground", the accord developed between the Chambers, TECs and enterprise agencies at Sunningdale in September 1991 and the subsequent 1993 development of OSSs.

Most TECs and LECs, even since 1993, are in the early stages of developing enterprise programmes. They have developed contracting relationships with many enterprise agencies and some specialist business centres, e.g. for ethnic and women's issues. They have sought to work with Chambers, local authorities and other agents mainly through discussions and mutual exchange of information. But links to the main agents in which potential overlaps of services, and hence where economies can be sought, have been limited. This applies particularly to the local authorities, main Chambers of Commerce, and to some other national agents. Where links do exist, they often rely on the former EAS and SFS. The use of SFS staff and methodology has probably had the effect of holding back thinking on wider, as well as local, links that could be developed. For the future, major developments of enterprise programmes are required. The new focus of DTI thinking on OSSs should encourage TECs and LECs to move forward. But what is still lacking is a system of enterprise support, nationally-driven, locally-tailored. The activities of TECs and LECs often tend so far to have made the attainment of such a system more difficult and remote. We turn in Chapter 12 to how progress might be made.

Chapter 10
Economic and Community Development

Agents for local development

TECs and LECs were given the vision of becoming key agents for change in local communities: "to serve as a forum for local leaders . . . to contribute to the regeneration of the community they serve . . . to be a catalyst for change within their community . . . to be able to influence and lever other agents . . . to forge local partnerships".[1] The wider development of local capacity in their local communities was therefore a key part of the initial vision. Yet TECs and LECs were planted into an already crowded domain where, particularly in England and Wales, confusion, fragmentation, overlaps and competition were rife. In Scotland the LECs inherited a different starting point where a greater local coherence of central government initiatives existed as a result of the development of the former SDA and HIDB, although in many cases these initiatives were resented by local government.

The key problem which TECs and LECs have faced is that economic development is not a rôle which government has full authority to give away. Many other agents, and not least the private sector as a whole, are the economic development forces of a local community. TECs and LECs were therefore given a vision by government, but could not be given the full power to match the vision. As a result, the government's view became confused between the vision and the reality and the TEC/LEC rôle in community development has become more a part of government's attempt to co-ordinate its own programmes locally: to act as a national system of agencies that would focus local activity by central government into a stable local structure. In the words of the TECs Prospectus (1989: 4):

> The boundaries that fragment training, vocational education and enterprise must be tackled. . . . Working in close partnership with business, all relevant government departments and the education services, the TEC will focus its investment to serve the broader aims of community revitalization and the best possible coordination of policies and programmes.

This vision of local focus for central government activities is clearly an important and useful development. But the wider vision was flawed. Nevertheless the

234

importance of economic development to TECs and LECs has been reaffirmed by a NTTF Report (1993) which led the July 1993 TECs conference to call for the TECs rôle in this area to be developed and targeted. Like enterprise, economic development has been seen as one of the important areas necessary to TECs to get the private sector Directors interested. In 1993 Brian Wolfson noted that it had to be included "to attract and excite the right people to come on Board". With TECs established, Wolfson felt the key objective was "to edit down the alphabet soup in the field of enterprise and economic development into a few important synergistic initiatives".[2]

The position differs significantly between TECs and Scottish LECs. Unlike the LECs, the TECs have no formal responsibility for environmental services, or physical economic development. They have to rely on the LIF, "efficiency savings" or new funds gained from other agents including the EC. As a result the community and economic development expenditure of TECs amounts to only a small percentage of their total budget.

The Scottish LECs, in contrast, have major responsibility for the physical regeneration programmes which they inherited from the SDA and HIDB. The Scottish Development Agency (SDA) covered the whole of Scotland, and an important strand of its activities involved improving the environment. Its activities in this area included rehabilitation of land, the provision and improvement of industrial property, land reclamation and integrated projects with a physical dimension.[3] The Highlands and Islands Development Board (HIDB) had statutory powers to offer grants and loans, to acquire and dispose of land, and to erect buildings and provide services, in addition to a community development rôle. These responsibilities have been taken over by the LECs and are reflected in their budgets, which have specific provision for environment and, in the case of Highlands and Islands LECs, also for community development.

As a result, environmental and community development accounts for approximately 19.6% of total SE LEC expenditure, but only 2.4% of HIE LECs budgets. On top of this they have the same resources available to the TECs, from LIF, "efficiency savings" or funds gained from other agents and the EC. This allows them to spend up to an average of £7.5m in SE on environmental projects and £0.5m in HIE areas on environmental and £80,000 on community development (1992/93 year). The smaller sums available in HIE LECs reflects the greater control of the budget retained at the centre.

In this chapter we assess how the TECs and LECs have developed their very different approaches to local community development. We discuss in turn:
– Interpreting the vision;
– Defining working goals;
– Understanding local problems;
– Developing new projects;
– The example of Scotland's greater LEC powers;
– Scotland's HIE community development programme.

Interpreting the vision

The TECs and LECs have been given a difficult task to interpret the broad vision of their launch, as agents of change in local communities, into a meaningful reality that can achieve anything at a local level. TECs and LECs have been dropped into a locally crowded and confused arena.

In England and Wales this fragmentation has been recognized by central government in its Action for Cities programme and Urban Regeneration Agency. These have sought to co-ordinate the activities of the Whitehall Departments of Environment, Employment, Trade and Industry, Education, and the Home Office, in areas related to inner cities (Urban Programme Areas – UPAs). It is recognized that the results of such co-ordination are incomplete, and in any case do not do much to cover areas outside of the UPAs. An Audit Commission report (1989: 1, 16) found that the result has been for the local leadership to be severely undermined by "a *patchwork* quilt of complexity and idiosyncrasy. [Government programmes] . . . baffle local authorities and businesses alike . . . it is hard to escape the conclusion that at the level of the individual city there can be programme overkill with a strategic vacuum" (1989: 32). The relative

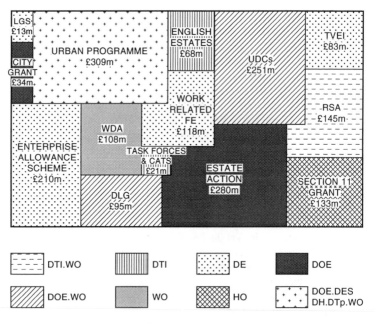

Figure 10.1 The "patchwork quilt" of governmental programmes that seek to assist urban economic development. Size of square is proportional to magnitude of expenditure in 1988–89. *Source*: After Audit Commission (1989: exhibit 2).

impact of the different departmental programmes within this patchwork is shown in Figure 10.1.

As we have seen in Chapter 5, in England and Wales, the fragmentation of government's initiatives is often matched by fragmentation among other agents and institutions. Part of this phenomenon derives from the impact of governmentally-separated initiatives. Some government departments favour one institution, other departments favour others. For example, TECs are the creation of the DE; schools and colleges are the preserve of the DFE; mainstream enterprise programmes are the preserve of the DTI; inner city regeneration is mainly the responsibility of the DOE. The establishment of departmental "ownership" and vertical lines of accountability is a strong influence on the agencies that deliver government programmes or collaborate with government.

In Scotland the agents concerned with the development of local communities have proceeded differently. The SO has acted as a means to co-ordinate government departments. As a result, the capacity of LECs to work coherently at a local level far exceeds that of TECs. The greater economic development rôle of LECs is also to be expected from their considerably greater range of responsibilities, larger budget, and the tradition inherited from the former SDA and HIDB.

The wide range of bodies which influence local community and economic development include central government, local government and non-government bodies of different kinds. The principal agencies active in the same fields as TECs and LECs are:

- SO/WO/WDA;
- Local authorities;
- Chambers of Commerce or trade;
- Enterprise agencies (enterprise trusts for Scotland) (ENTAs);
- CBI regions;
- Trade unions;
- Private firms;
- Colleges;
- Universities;
- UDC;
- Task force/City action teams (CATs);
- Rural Development Commission;
- Port, airport and other transport authorities;
- Voluntary organizations;
- Key individual businesses and other local leaders.

The TECs and LECs must forge relationships with these agencies if they are to develop their local leadership brief. Their relationships with other agents will vary from place to place, as a consequence of the style of the significant differences in the pre-existing local networks into which TECs and LECs have been introduced. In some areas, typically metropolitan centres, there are strong local agents which have already developed strong local networks prior to the introduction of TECs and LECs. In other areas there is a complex and weak development of local agents. These contrasts have presented TECs and LECs with different types of challenge in different areas.

In localities where existing institutional capacity was weak, TECs/LECs have had the easiest opportunity to add value and pull actors together. They have been able to develop a leadership rôle much as the government originally intended. Such localities were likely to respond to TEC/LEC initiative of this kind more readily than others. For example, many metropolitan districts had a fairly thin existing capacity, e.g. Barnsley or Oldham. These have presented an opportunity for TEC leadership to galvanize agents into a new local partnership. Similarly, in many shire counties there is a high degree of fragmentation between areas. But the opportunity for the TEC to effect change is much more limited. One chief executive (TEC 88) described the prevailing culture as distinctly "non-clubable and hostile to being 'led' by the TEC". We examine these contrasts further below.

Defining working goals

For TECs and LECs to make a contribution to local community development requires them to fit their mission statement to the needs of the economy and into an appropriate relation, preferably through an agreement, with the other key local agents. The goals of TECs and LECs fall into three broad groups:

(i) Visionary goals embedded in the mission for the TEC/LEC initiative, the nationally-defined "stars to steer by" which inform their purpose and underlying rationale;

(ii) Programme-orientated goals which relate to specific objectives that are associated with the responsibilities they inherited from their predecessors;

(iii) Goals emerging from the planning required to go beyond programme targets in order to achieve the national vision. These frequently include locally-specific goals prompted by the situational circumstances of the TEC or LEC. It is in this third area that the unique strength of the TEC/LEC system was envisaged. As a direct consequence of the high calibre and experience of local TEC/LEC Board members, it was hoped that a new *local* entrepreneurial flair and inspirational leadership would be offered by TECs and LECs. This would allow them to tackle, through *local* solutions, the problems encountered in the fields of training, enterprise support and local economic and institutional development.

TEC and LEC Corporate Plans are the main place in which the visionary goals are translated into specific policies. Heading all of the Corporate Plans is a mission statement which summarises the TECs'/LECs' vision in a single sentence. Typically, this will state its aims in terms such as:

To develop the economy and prosperity of this growing region by the optimization of its human resources, through the development of high standards of education and training and the encouragement of enterprise (Norfolk and Waveney).

Others use rather more upbeat mission statements, such as Calderdale and Kirklees "Economic excellence by investment in people", or London East "by the year 2000 the East side of London should be as prosperous as the West". Sections of TEC/LEC Corporate Plans tend to list the standard strategic objectives in a fairly uniform way, based on the national strategic guidance, and the most prominently stated are:

- To promote greater investment in and achievement of higher volumes and qualities of training to make local firms more competitive and profitable, raising skill and qualification levels;
- To encourage the development and improve the survival rate of new and existing business;
- To change local attitudes to priorities in training, enterprise, education and economic development;
- To promote education–business links;
- To improve sources of local labour market and other business information;
- To promote the needs of disadvantaged groups.

Less frequent but still common additions include promoting the success of the TEC/LEC amongst the local community, and the generation of new income. In most cases, the stated strategic objectives are phrased in very general terms which are not tied to specific, local, measurable outcomes. In only a small number of cases is there evidence of strategic corporate objectives being closely linked to *locally* specified targets derived from existing local agents. As a consequence, nearly all TECs and LECs have closely followed the national guidance on the areas to be covered in the corporate goals and the outcomes defined by TEED, SE or HIE for measuring their achievement. The result has been a very top-down definition of mission, goals and assessment of outcomes. The consequence has been that, however visionary and entrepreneurial their Board, the detailed working out of the TEC/LEC goals that the Board approves at its meetings has been undertaken by staff (up to and frequently including the chief executive) more accustomed to following the lead of the centre in defining local policy. This point is illustrated by the response of one seconded chief executive who, when asked to comment on his TEC's strategy for WRFE, replied that "we're not sure what we're doing until we get some guidance down" (TEC 16).

As a result of these constraints, goals and especially actions that relate to local vision and entrepreneurial response to the local area's needs appear to have had little opportunity to develop. An analysis of local goals is shown in Figure 10.2. This presents the broad categories of goals that chief executives specified as particularly significant locally or as particularly important beyond their specific contract. Figure 10.2 demonstrates the dominance in local perceptions of the main programme fields of training, enterprise and education–business links. Beyond these there is a broad spread of goals, in decreasing order of

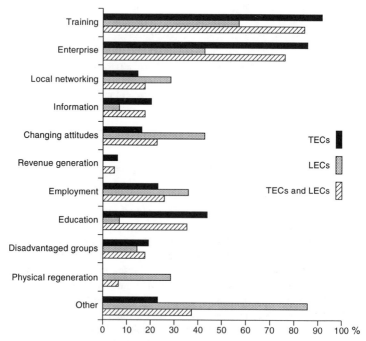

Figure 10.2 Main goals specified by TEC/LEC chief executives as their primary concerns. *Source*: LSE survey in 62 TECs and LECs.

importance: changing local attitudes, developing employment, improving information, provision to disadvantaged groups and, at a very minor level, physical redevelopment and raising new revenue.

The "other" category is quite large and ranges across a number of objectives such as promotion of internationalization, improving sector diversity, merging training and business development, improving careers guidance and boosting tourism. The identification of these goals seems to reflect a much stronger concern with the prime contractual programme areas than special local circumstances.

There is a strong contrast between TECs and LECs. Figure 10.2 shows that many more TECs (92%) than LECs (57%) stressed training goals, and enterprise goals (85% of TECs compared to only 43% of LECs). However many more LECs (43%) than TECs (17%) mentioned the goal of changing local attitudes. Education goals were much more common for TECs (44%) than LECs (only 7%), and twice as many LECs (28%) as TECs (14%) were concerned with local networking. Scotland also stands out in the area of physical development, where no TECs have major goals for development. LECs also have a much wider range of goals in the "other" category suggesting that they are more locally flexible than TECs.

These differences reflect the contrasting contractual briefs north and south of the border, although this does not account for all of the variation. Although LECs' greater concern with physical regeneration is to be expected from their additional powers compared to TECs , other discrepancies illustrate some important differences in the institutional cultures that LECs and TECs inherited. In England and Wales, TECs derived from the TA system emphasizing training programmes and a "paymaster" style of operation in which contract arrangements mostly take the place of partnership decisions. In Scotland, the TA component inherited by LECs was much smaller and less influential than that derived from the SDA and HIDB which had a wider range of activities, staff expertise, and experience of partnership. LECs greater concern with goals of building local partnerships, and their lesser concern than TECs with detailed training objectives and changes to local attitudes confirm the rather wider approach and partnership bases in Scotland.

The way in which TECs and LECs have become positioned in the local economy can be judged from the views of other agents about what their goals *should* be. These are shown in Figure 10.3. There is a strong contrast both between other agents and TECs/LECs and between the other agents themselves. For all agents "other" goals are the dominant category. For the main categories of objectives, training gets a much lower emphasis among many agents than among TECs and LECs. Even among business leaders training is seen as a primary objective by only 50% of those surveyed. Since most of the business leaders surveyed were TEC and LEC Chairs or Board members, this is all the more surprising. Physical and environmental strategies are the most important category after the "other" category for business organizations and local government. These results are similar to those of the 1993 *Financial Times* survey of TEC Board members (10 May). Thus the mission given to TECs and LECs appears to reflect more the objectives of its parent department, the DE and TEED, than the needs assessed on the ground.

More detailed contrasts can be assessed by disaggregating the detail of the goals. There are some notable differences of emphasis in this detail: for example, improving access to training was a goal for 24% of TECs/LECs (but only 2% of other actors), the promotion of education–business links (mentioned by 29% of TECs/LECs, 2% of other actors), and provision for disadvantaged groups (mentioned by 25% of TECs/LECs, but by no other actors). An interesting difference in emphasis occurs in the case of the goal of improving the quality of business support, which was mentioned by 25% of TECs/LECs and 13% of local authorities, but by no business organizations or business leaders. This appears to provide some evidence in support of the idea that TECs and LECs have been

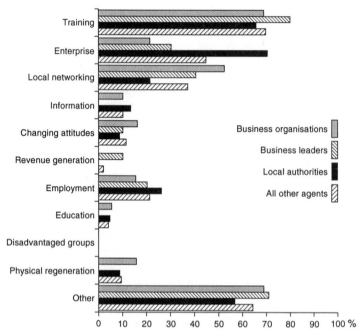

Figure 10.3 Main goals that TECs and LECs should be pursuing in the views of other local agents: proportions of respondents. *Source*: LSE survey of 20 TECs and LECs.

seeking to improve business support whereas those in business or potentially using the TEC feel that current provision is adequate. Goals which were more frequently identified by other actors include improving local linkages, in which twice as many business organizations as TECs and LECs stressed this goal, only local authorities mentioning it less often.

The analysis of goals strongly suggests that TECs and LECs are primarily driven by their programme areas and their nationally-determined briefs in training, enterprise and education. To a lesser extent, TEC/LEC goals also emphasize improving information and provision for disadvantaged groups. These findings broadly agree with the only other systematic analysis of TEC goals by Barnes (1992). Using Corporate Plans of 18 of the earliest TECs Barnes demonstrates that although there was local flexibility, much of this was in the general framing of mission rather than tailoring of programmes. Our results also show that the LECs generally fit closer to the perception of goals of other agents than do TECs. The LECs also have a different emphasis, with training secondary to broader economic development. Other agents generally have a view of TECs and LECs that is closer to their original mission – of improving linkage and networking, particularly between fragmented central government initiatives. Other agents also identify, but with considerable variety, a wide range of gap filling rôles that TECs/LECs could adopt at local level. The nature of these gaps, and the way in which they should be filled, draws us to assessing the capacity of TECs and LECs to understand local problems, discussed below.

Understanding local problems

The mission of TECs and LECs to be key agents for change in local economies requires them to be able correctly to identify the local problems in order to develop appropriate policy. The evidence about the extent to which they have been able to do this suggests that, so far, this capacity for TECs , in contrast to LECs, is very limited. A major difficulty that they have experienced has been that most of the detailed work required by TECs and LECs to identify local problems and solutions is conducted not by their Boards but by their staff, with the chief executive playing a pivotal rôle in assessing and pursuing strategy. Given that the background of many TEC chief executives and almost all staff was as civil service lower and middle managers with narrowly focused experience of specific TA programme areas, it is not surprising that they did not possess the skills for accurate local understanding that a truly effective TEC or LEC strategy requires. As a consequence, there has been a general scepticism over whether TECs are suitably equipped to make the required range of judgements necessary to develop a coherent analysis of the local economy and develop a proper policy. We assess below the identified priorities of the TECs and LECs, the representativeness of their views, their accuracy, and their local leadership.

Identification of local priorities

The advantages and disadvantages of TEC/LEC areas, as identified by their chief executives, are shown in Figure 10.4. This shows that the main advantages identified by TECs and LECs relate to the business base, transport and communications, employment and labour issues and environmental factors. A large range of other advantages are widely spread across a varied group of TECs and LECs. The advantages of TEC/LEC areas are largely mirrored by the fields in which disadvantages are experienced. The business base, transport and communications, community service, local business networks/organizations and environment issues are most significant.

Clearly TECs and LECs identify many issues as offering them both advantages and disadvantages depending on the challenges they have to address. The significance of their perceptions, therefore, is not in the specifics of each area, but in the overall ranking of the perception of problems. On the one hand, the

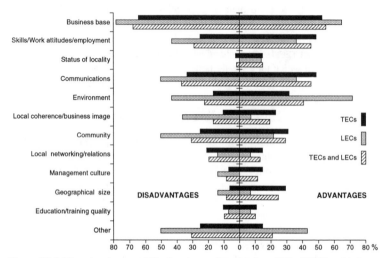

Figure 10.4 The advantages and disadvantages of TEC/LEC areas identified by chief executives: proportions of respondents. *Source*: LSE survey of 60 TECs and LECs.

quality of the business base, work attitudes and labour relations are all fields in which TECs and LECs can play a rôle, although many aspects relate more to macroeconomic and national, rather than local, policy arenas. On the other hand, issues such as the local environment, transport and communications are far beyond TECs capacity, although LECs play a major rôle in this area. The conclusion from these results, therefore, has to be that TECs do not have a major capacity to solve many of the key local problems they identify. LECs do have a capacity in the crucial fields of environment and (to a limited extent) transport and communications. In both cases, however, it is clear that there are two *design gaps*: (i) between the mission and needs at local level, and (ii) between the responsibilities and the resources that TECs and LECs possess.

Representativeness of TEC/LEC views

The perception of local advantages and disadvantages by TECs and LECs can be compared with the views of other agents. The results of this assessment are shown in Figure 10.5. Examination of the categories of local characteristics for *advantages* shows major differences in the emphasis on the local environment. Two-thirds of all other agents compared with only 45% of all TECs and LECs identified this as an advantage of their locality (with business organizations 58%, local authorities 76% and business leaders 80%). Other differences are those concerning perceived advantages of international status (20% of other agents against 5% of TECs and LECs) and regional status, recognized by 24% of

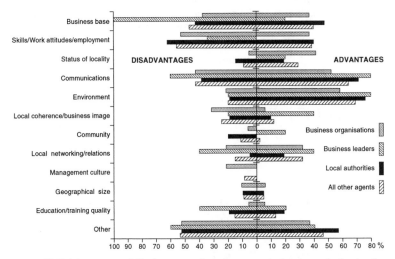

Figure 10.5 Advantages and disadvantages of TEC/LEC areas in the views of other local agents: proportions of respondents. *Source*: LSE survey of 20 TECs and LECs.

other agents against 15% of local TECs and LECs. Differences between other agents and TEC/LEC views over local *disadvantages* are fewer. The major contrast is that 20% of TECs/LECs perceive local attitudes to training as a major problem compared with only 5% of business organizations, no local authorities or business leaders.

Accuracy of TEC/LEC views

The accuracy of TECs'/LECs' appraisal of their area can also be compared with objective data measuring local characteristics. For the key issues of unemployment, skill shortages and the enterprise base, Table 10.1 gives comparisons with the objective data for TEC/LEC areas reported in Chapter 5. For *disadvantages*, 47–67% of respondents correctly match the problems of high unemployment, enterprise culture, and skill shortages with indicators of these given by objective data. But the results are very poor for matching to the base of small firms. For *advantages* there is a lower level of correct matching, with low levels of unemployment problems being the most correctly perceived and the base of small firms the least correctly perceived.

These assessments confirm that the TECs and LECs have the clearest grasp of the unemployment and training situation. This is to be expected given the origins of their staff from the former TA and the dominance of their funding by its former programmes. The rather unclear response with respect to enterprise culture and highly incorrect view about small firms reflects, in part, the diffi-

245

ECONOMIC AND COMMUNITY DEVELOPMENT

Table 10.1 Comparison of TEC/LEC assessment of local advantages and disadvantages compared to objective data on unemployment rates, long term unemployment (LTU) rates and the proportion of small and medium sized enterprises (SMEs) in the local economy.

Advantage/disadvantage compared to objective data	Correctly matched %	Incorrectly matched %	Mid-range neither correct nor incorrect %	Sample size (no. of TECs and LECs)
Disadvantages:				
High unemployment vs. unemployment rates	60.0	–	40.0	15
High unemployment vs. LTU rates	46.7	–	53.3	15
Skill shortages vs. unemployment rates	40.0	5.0	55.0	20
SMEs base vs. proportion of SMEs	16.7	–	83.3	6
Enterprise culture vs. proportion of SMEs	66.7	33.3	–	3
Advantages:				
Low unemployment vs. unemployment rates	62.5	–	37.5	8
Low unemployment vs. LTU rates	37.5	–	62.5	8
SMEs base vs. proportion of SMEs	20.0	–	80.0	5
Enterprise culture vs. proportion of SMEs	–	–	100.0	3

culty of the TECs and LECs in finding an appropriate rôle beyond their inherited programmes of the EAS scheme and BGT. But the more confused understanding of local problems with respect to small firms also reflects a deeper confusion of purpose. A large number of TEC and LEC commentators mention the high or low proportions of small businesses in their area, but relatively few identify this specifically as a strength or weakness, and even fewer correctly perceive the reality of local small firm proportions. In fact all areas have a very large number of small firms: nationally 64% of firms have under 10 employees and 99% under 50 employees. Figure 5.11 shows that the variation between TECs and LECs is very small except for 6 or 8 areas.

As example of the misconception is Teesside, an area which has been dominated by a few very large employers (chiefly ICI and BSC). This has led many commentators to conclude that the small firms' base locally is small. Yet it ranks only 38 out of 104 in the country among TEC/LEC areas for dominance by

246

firms with over 200 employees; i.e. it is close to the centre of the distribution. Similarly with respect to firms with less than 20 employees it ranks as the 17th lowest out of 104 areas, but its difference from the middle of the distribution is insignificant: as shown in Figure 5.11, it is not one of the extreme cases. The extreme cases of areas with a low proportion of SMEs are, in fact, in London and Derbyshire yet these areas are not as widely perceived as having a "small firms' problem". The identification of the small firms' issue in Teesside and similar areas such as Lanark or Rotherham, therefore, appears more as a concern about the industrial restructuring of a few major companies, rather than a genuine gap in the local small firms' base.

These findings further support the view that national programme priorities rather than local circumstances are dominating TECs'/LECs' thinking. As a result locally-defined goals related to local strengths and weaknesses are much less important to TEC and LEC strategies than their founding vision required.

Priorities for developing local leadership

A further comparison of TEC/LEC identification of problems can be made against the strengths of local agents. One of the key missions of TECs is to bring greater leadership and focus to local actions. In areas with pre-existing strong local leadership this has been less urgent and TECs/LECs have had to develop partnership relations. In areas of weaker existing leadership, however, TECs and LECs should have identified as key priorities leadership, improving coherence or enhancing local networks. Table 10.2 compares TEC/LEC identification of priorities against these features.

Taking first those areas in which TECs/LECs recognized *disadvantages* deriving from pre-existing local leadership, Table 10.2 shows that there is a relation between the TEC/LEC perception of need for greater coherence with areas in which there is only weak or medium capacity among the other main agents of Chambers, enterprise agencies and local authority EDUs. Similarly the weaknesses of local business organizations, in general, are identified as a problem to be overcome in areas where these agencies are weakest, but the situation is less clear.

For the case in which *advantages* are seen by TECs/LECs existing in local coherence and networks the results are more confused. In general the areas with the strongest Chambers and enterprise agencies are not places where greater coherence and quality of local organizations is identified by TECs and LECs. In the case of local authority EDUs, the strength of the EDU is not related to the TEC view of local coherence. Similarly, local coherence is not seen as a problem in over 40% of the areas which have weak or very weak enterprise agencies and Chambers. These results, in general, suggest a low level of accuracy of the views of TEC/LEC commentators at the most senior staff levels.

These survey results in relation to other local agents can be compared with the more general analysis of TEC aspirations shown in Table 10.3 undertaken by NTTF (1992a; see also SQW 1992). From this it is clear that a minority of TECs

Table 10.2 Comparison of TEC/LEC assessment of local advantages and disadvantages compared to objective data on the local strengths of enterprise agencies, Chambers of Commerce and local authority EDUs: percentage of 62 responding TEC/LEC chief executives identifying a local disadvantage/advantage that matches objective data.

Advantages/disadvantages compared to strengths of local agents	Strength of local agency				No. of TECs and LECs identifying this issue
	Strong	Medium	Weak	Very weak	
Disadvantages:					
Coherence vs. quality of enterprise agencies	0	30.0	70.0	0	10
Coherence vs. quality of Chambers of Commerce	30.0	50.0	0	20.0	10
Coherence vs. quality of LA EDU	20.0	50.0	30.0	N/A	10
Good local business organisations vs. quality of enterprise agencies	0	0	80.0	20.0	5
Good local business organisations vs. quality of Chambers of Commerce	0	0	0	100	5
Good local business organisations vs. quality of LA EDU	40	20.0	40.0	N/A	5
Advantages:					
Coherence vs. quality of enterprise agencies	16.7	16.7	41.7	25.0	12
Coherence vs. quality of Chambers of Commerce	16.7	8.3	58.3	16.7	12
Coherence vs. quality of LA EDU	16.7	58.3	25.0	N/A	12
Good local business organisations vs. quality of enterprise agencies	33.3	33.3	33.3	0	3
Good local business organisations vs. quality of Chambers of Commerce	33.3	67.0	0	0	3
Good local business organisations vs. quality of LA EDU	66.7	33.3	0	N/A	3

Source: LSE surveys (1989 and 1990): measures of strength from Bennett (1991), Bennett & McCoshan (1993), Sellgren (1987, 1989).

see themselves as now able to take the main leadership, and nearly three-quarters see the development of strategy as a joint process. However, Table 10.3 also shows 61% of TECs aspiring to create and manage partnerships or networks, to run development programmes, or co-ordinate services. Given their powers, resources and local legitimacy, this is an unrealistically high proportion given the number of other leaders in most areas.

Table 10.3 Aspirations of TEC roles and functions in local economic development: responses by responding TECs in 1992.

Function	Take a lead	Participate with others in lead	Lend support	Not get involved
Direction/leadership:				
– prepare local strategy	26	66	8	0
– create and manage	61	34	5	0
partnership/networks	46	41	13	0
– run development programmes	45	51	4	0
Information for economic development:				
– research	28	66	6	0
– monitor	36	56	8	0
– lobby	37	50	13	0
Activities:				
– deliver services	38	44	14	4
– quality control systems	38	44	14	4
– promote services	37	56	7	0
– secure funding	36	50	11	3

Source: NTTF (1992a: Figure 5).

When it comes to providing information on developing economic activities, about one-third of TECs have aspirations to take the lead. This may also be unrealistically high. The NTTF study (1992a, Figure 6) also showed TECs having a high level of desire to get involved in almost all enterprise and economic development services, either now or later. The lowest proportion of TECs aspiring to develop involvement in any activity was 80% for support for technology infrastructure. The realistic contribution of TECs to most of these fields to date can be argued to be minimal. The level of aspiration of TECs seems, therefore, unrealistically high.

Developing new projects

The assessment of goals and leadership can only be undertaken at the most general level. To gain a better understanding of detail requires analysis of specific projects. In this section we assess how far TECs and LECs are meeting the objective of providing a strategic lead to local initiatives through local projects. In a sample of 20 areas TECs and LECs identified their most important new project initiatives. The other key local agents were also asked to identify which projects they considered to be most important to the local economy. Each initiative is analyzed to determine who is critical at each stage of a project: initiation, development, management and finance.

The TEC/LEC view

For *initiation* TECs and LECs are most commonly the initiators of the projects they identified; 69% of all projects in which they are involved are self-initiated. Only 14% of projects identified by TECs/LECs are initiated by other agents, the remainder being joint initiatives. For the *development* of projects, TECs and LECs most commonly work independently (53% of cases). For the *management* of projects, a clear majority of TECs/LECs also manage their projects independently, this being true of 60%, with only 5% being managed wholly outside the TEC/LEC. For *finance*, almost the same proportion of projects are funded jointly (51%) as by the TEC/LEC alone (49%).

This structure of TEC/LEC projects shows a dominance of locally-independent activity, working with other agents chiefly for finance and development of the initiative, but retaining initiation and management most commonly at the TEC/LEC. On the positive side it can be argued that this approach could indicate that TECs and LECs are filling gaps that other agents have left. For such gaps a new initiating agent with the capacity to co-finance is often a critical lever for change. Undoubtedly TECs and LECs are performing this useful rôle in many cases. But on the negative side there is considerable evidence to suggest that the majority of the initiatives reflect more the inheritance of MSC/TA methodology for bright ideas to be developed of a short-term nature with little sensitivity to local needs. This is particularly evidenced by the large proportion of TEC/LEC projects identified which relate to TEED NDPs (see Chapter 3).

The view of other local agents

The dilemma inherent in change initiated by TECs and LECs is evident from analysis of the projects identified by other agents as being the most important in their localities. The major local projects rarely involved the TEC or LEC. In only 3% of cases are such projects *initiated* by TECs/LECs, with 94% being initiated entirely by other agents. TECs and LECs are responsible for the *development* of such projects in only 1% of cases, and are jointly involved in only a further 9%. Similarly low levels of TEC/LEC involvement are apparent for the *management* of these projects, which they are solely responsible for only 1%, and jointly involved with only 10% of cases. In the case of *finance* there is a higher TEC/LEC input, but nonetheless 62% of the projects that other agents considered most important are funded entirely without TEC/LEC support, and only 2% are funded by them wholly. Of the 36% of those projects funded jointly, the TEC/LEC input is typically low: in 58% of cases it is less than 10% of the total cost. Thus, although the average expenditure of TECs and LECs on their own projects is 72% of the total cost, for projects indicated by other agents the TEC/LEC average contribution is only 9%.

The views of other agents on local projects makes it clear that the projects in which TECs and LECs are engaged are small, and are not those that are consid-

DEVELOPING NEW PROJECTS

Table 10.4 Proportion of key projects developed by 62 TECs and LECs compared with those identified as most important in the local economy by other agents.

TEC/LEC projects		Projects identified by other agents	
Type of project	%	Type of project	%
Enterprise support	11.6	Major private sector developments	17.3
ET/YT innovations	9.8	Physical redevelopment	15.8
Integrated development	7.1	Co-ordintaion body/partnership	11.5
(physical and training)		Integrated development	10.1
Other training	6.3	(physical and training)	
LTU/redundancy, etc	5.4	Tourism/heritage (non-hotel)	5.8
Credits	3.6	Enterprise support	4.3
EBPS	3.6	EBPS	3.6
Consultancy/"health checks"	3.6	International promotion	3.6
Modularized/customized training	3.6	LTU/redundancy	1.4
Physical development	3.6	Hotel/tourism	1.4
HE links	3.6	HE links	0.7
Special needs	2.7	ET/YT innovations	0.7
Adult careers service	2.7	Modularized/customized training	0.7
Hotel/tourism	2.7	European (not EC funding)	0.7
European (not EC funding)	2.7	Multiple objectives – not specified	15.8
Membership/subs. scheme	2.7	Other	6.5
Enterprise training awards	1.8		
Management education	1.8		
Environmental	1.8		
Women returners	0.9		
PRF	0.9		
Sector training initiative	0.9		
Childcare	0.9		
Multiple objectives	4.5		
Other	11.6		

ered to be the most important to the economic development of their localities. This is further emphasized by examination of the types of projects each agent identifies as important. Table 10.4 shows that the types of local project vary widely. Table 10.4 shows that among TEC and LEC projects, there is a wide spread of foci with no individual category featuring heavily except initiatives relating to enterprise support and innovations in ET and YT. This reinforces all our earlier comments that the TECs and LECs have, not surprisingly, mainly sought development of their main programme areas. When all the categories of project which embrace some form of training activity are aggregated, it emerges that training as a whole accounts for 30% of all projects launched by TECs and LECs. The more visionary goals feature much less prominently. Projects integrating a number of economic development activities, for example, although the third most prominent category of initiative, were being carried out by only

7% of TECs/LECs, and only 4% had physical redevelopment initiatives, all but one of which are in Scotland, where LECs have a more clearly defined physical regeneration brief. Further survey analysis of the projects developed in 77 TECs and LECs in the 1992/93 year confirm the same broad emphases.[4]

Contrasts with other agents

The initiatives identified by other agents as important in their localities contrast quite markedly in type with those being pursued by TECs and LECs. In particular, an emphasis upon physical redevelopment and private sector initiatives is the key concern. Only 1% of other agents identified any form of training initiative as being a key local project, and only 4% identified specific enterprise support projects. The most prominently mentioned categories are major private sector initiatives and physical redevelopment projects, which account for one-third of all projects. Although the promotion of local co-ordination or partnership bodies (cited by 12%) and integrated, multi-purpose projects (cited by 10%), are identified by other agents as crucial, and although a key part of their mission, only 7% of TECs/LECs are developing them.

The relative positioning of the TECs and LECs is well summed-up in the response by other agents to the question of whether TECs and LECs are a major local initiative compared to those they had identified. After prompting 36% said they were, 30% said they were not, and 34% did not know or were waiting to see. Follow-up interviews in 1992/93 suggest that the proportion of doubters has markedly increased.

Size and impact

Projects identified by TECs and LECs on the one hand, and other agents on the other, contrasted not only according to type, but also by budget. In general, the most important local projects identified by other agents tended to be of much higher cost than those undertaken by TECs/LECs. The contrast between the projects of TECs and LECs and other local initiatives is shown in Table 10.5: 70% of the significant projects in the sampled areas had no TEC and 48% had no LEC involvement at all. A further 20% had a TEC/LEC financial contribution of less than 11%. TEC initiatives finance at least 90% of their expenditure in 65% of cases, although LECs finance over 50% of project expenditure in only 27% of cases. The impression given is, therefore, of TECs predominantly "doing their own thing" while other agents develop most of the major initiatives in their area. LECs play a much more significant rôle in local projects. They are the main financier for 20% of the significant projects identified in their areas compared to only 5.5% majority finance by TECs for significant projects.

These contrasts are even more evident when comparing the budgets of projects. As shown in Table 10.6 the total annual expenditure on TEC projects fell mostly under £500,000 (80% of cases), with 52% costing less than £100,000. Only

Table 10.5 Proportion of TEC/LEC finance for TEC/LEC initiatives and initiatives identified by other agents in 20 case study areas.

% of finance from TEC/LEC	% of finance for projects identified by TECs/LECs			% of finance by TECs/LECs of significant projects identified by other agents		
	All	TECs	LECs	All	TECs	LECs
0	4.4	5.3	–	64.1	70.1	48.0
1–10	8.8	7.0	18.2	19.6	23.9	8.0
11–20	5.9	5.3	9.1	4.3	–	16.0
21–30	2.9	–	18.2	1.1	–	4.0
31–40	2.9	1.8	9.1	1.1	–	4.0
41–50	10.3	8.8	18.2	2.2	3.0	-
51–70	-	–	–	2.2	1.5	4.0
71–80	2.9	1.8	9.1	3.3	-	12.0
81–90	4.4	5.3	–	–	-	–
91–100	57.4	64.9	18.2	–	1.5	4.0
Sample size	68	57	11	92	67	25

Table 10.6 Size of projects by TECs/LECs compared to other significant initiatives in the area in 20 case study areas.

Size of project finance	TEC/LEC initiatives %			Other significant initiatives in area %
	All	TECs	LECs	
Less than £100,000	43.5	51.9	13.3	8.8
£100,000 – £500,000	24.6	27.8	13.3	8.8
£500,000 – £1million	4.3	5.6	-	5.5
Over £1million	27.3	14.8	73.3	76.9
% recurrent funded	65.6	69.6	53.3	71.4
% one-off funded	34.4	30.4	46.7	28.6
Sample size	69	54	15	91

14% of TEC projects had an annual budget of greater than £1m and all of these involved developments of YT and ET programmes. In contrast, more than three-quarters (77%) of projects identified by other agents exceeded £1m annually, with only 18% falling below £500,000. There is a strong contrast of this low level of financial involvement by TECs with that in LECs where 73% of all initiatives involve over £1m of expenditure and only 13% are less than £100,000. Expenditure on projects identified by other agents was slightly more likely to be recurrent rather than a one-off cost (in 71% of cases) than amongst TEC-identified projects (66% of cases). But in LECs there is a much stronger pattern of one-off funding than in TECs or other projects.

Table 10.7 Size of administrative staff and employment expected to be generated in TEC/LEC projects compared to other significant initiatives in the area in 20 case study areas.

	TEC/LEC initiatives %			Other significant initiatives in area %
	All	TECS	LECS	
Staff size:				
0–5	72.7	73.9	66.7	38.2
6–10	7.3	8.7	–	9.2
11–100	20.0	17.4	33.0	23.7
over 100	0.0	–	–	28.9
Sample size	54	46	9	76
Expected employment:				
0–5	53.1	69.6	11.1	17.0
6–10	6.3	–	22.2	2.3
11–100	12.5	8.7	22.2	5.7
over 100	28.1	21.7	44.4	75.0
Sample size	32	23	9	74

Further differences emerge in the staffing devoted to each set of projects, and their expected employment impacts. As shown in Table 10.7 the overwhelming majority (73%) of TEC/LEC projects involved no more than 5 staff, with only 20% employing more than 10, and none employing more than 100 staff. The contrast between TECs and LECs is less strong in staffing levels than in other features, but LECs still employ nearly twice as many staff (33%) in large-scale projects with staff over 10 as TECs (17%). In contrast to TECs and LECs, nearly one-third (29%) of projects identified by other agents employed over 100 staff, with a majority (53%) employing more than 10. In terms of employment expected to be generated by these projects, those identified by other actors typically displayed much higher expectations. Three-quarters of projects were expected to generate over 100 jobs, compared with only 22% in TEC projects and 44% in LECs. Most TEC projects (70%) were expected to generate no jobs or no more than 5 jobs, whereas in LECs only 11% of projects expected to generate less than 5 jobs. The other initiatives in each area are therefore generally the major job creators, even in the case of LECs.

Projects as partnerships

The structure of the key local projects can be analyzed in greater detail at each stage of project implementation. Tables 10.8 and 10.9 summarize the initiation, development, management and finance of the projects identified by other agents.

Often multiple agents are involved. In terms of project *initiation*, for exam-

Table 10.8 Number of agents involved in each of the main stages of project implementation. Analysis of all key projects identified by all local agents in a sample of 20 TEC and LEC areas.

No. of agents involved	Initiation	Development	Management	Finance
%	%	%	%	
1	46.8	38.0	51.0	37.1
2	25.7	26.9	19.0	28.6
3	22.0	21.3	18.0	21.0
4	2.8	8.3	6.0	13.3
5	–	2.8	3.0	–
6	–	–	–	–
7	2.8	2.8	3.0	–

Table 10.9 Proportional importance of the 15 main agents identified as involved as the main agents or partners in local projects. Analysis of all key projects identified by all local agents in a sample of 20 TEC and LEC areas.

Initiation	%	Development	%	Management	%	Finance	%
Local govt	22.0	Private firms	24.9	Private firms	24.0	Private firms	26.2
Private firms	18.4	Local govt	20.6	Local govt	17.8	Local govt	21.5
Govt depts	9.9	Chambers	7.1	LENS	9.8	Govt depts	9.3
SDA/HIDB	6.7	Govt depts	6.7	Chambers	8.0	TEC/LEC	7.6
UDC	6.7	TEC/LEC	6.3	Govt depts	6.7	LENS	7.2
Chambers	6.3	LENS	5.5	TEC/LEC	6.2	UDC	5.1
LENS	5.8	ENTAS	5.1	UDC	5.8	Chambers	5.1
TEC/LEC	4.5	SDA/HIDB	5.1	SDA/HIDB	5.3	SDA/HIDB	4.2
ENTAS	4.5	UDC	5.1	ENTAS	5.3	LA EDU	3.4
LA EDU	2.2	Other	3.2	Other	3.6	ENTAS	2.1
Individuals	2.2	LA EDU	2.4	LA EDU	1.8	Port authorities	2.1
Other	2.2	LEA	2.0	Individuals	1.8	Other	2.1
Port authorities	2.2	Port authorities	1.6	Port authorities	1.8	WDA	1.3
LA chief exec	1.8	LA chief exec	1.2	LA	1.3	LEA	1.3
LEA	1.8	WDA	1.2	Reg. CBI	0.4	LA chief exec	0.4

ple, although just under half (47%) are initiated by a single agency, 27% were initiated by two agents and 20% by three, with a further 4% being initiated by four or more agents. The most frequent initiators are local authorities (28% of cases), with private firms being the next most significant at 18%. Behind these come government departments at 10% and UDCs at 7%, with SDA/HIDB involved in initiating 34% of Scottish projects.

In terms of project *development*, just over one-third of projects are developed by a single agency, with more than a quarter being developed by two and a little over a fifth by three bodies, the other 14% being developed by four or more agents. Local authorities and private firms are by far the most frequent developers of projects, local authorities doing this in 26% of cases, private firms in 25%. The next most frequently mentioned agents are Chambers of Commerce (only 7%), and SDA/HIDB (30% of Scottish projects). Similar patterns emerge for the *management* of projects, where private firms are mentioned in 24% of cases and local authorities in 21%. For the *financing* of projects, local authorities fund projects in 27% of cases and private firms in 26%. Government departments, TEC/LECs, UDCs, Chambers and in Scotland SDA/HIDB are also significant for 4–9% of cases. Although project management is conducted by a single agency in most cases, financing is more typically joint, with 63% of initiatives being funded by two or more agencies.

The clear picture that emerges from this analysis is that although a wide range of economic development initiatives is being developed locally, TECs in particular have been largely isolated or insignificant in most of them. Their own projects are much more restricted in terms of partnership, budget and scope. Whereas the most important local initiatives tend to be in areas such as physical redevelopment and major private sector projects, TECs and LECs have generally concerned themselves with smaller-scale projects, often conducted without partners, directly related to their mainstream programme areas of training provision and enterprise support. TEC and LEC projects have, compared to other local projects, lower budgets, employ fewer staff and offer lesser prospects of new employment as an outcome of their operation. The analysis therefore suggests that TECs have not become the key agents for change of local economies that they were intended to be. LECs, in contrast, are becoming key agents in their areas to a much greater extent, but they too are not the dominant agent of change in many cases. They also have had to work in partnership with other central and local agents.

The example of Scotland's greater LEC powers

As time has progressed TECs have looked to LECs as a possible model for their development, particularly with a view to acquiring greater environmental powers. The NTTF (1993) report examined this as one of a number of options, but significant change has not occurred and remains unlikely.

Wider focus

The differing powers of TECs and LECs do lead to some major contrasts in emphasis in economic development. To assess contrasts in their focus a survey of TECs and LECs shown in Table 10.10 indicates the initiatives being pursued beyond what was specifically required of them by TEED, SE or HIE.

The analysis shows that TECs are developing many fewer initiatives than LECs. Table 10.10 also shows that TEC initiatives mainly relate to social widening of access to training and associated training improvements. Amongst TECs

Table 10.10 Initiatives pursued by TECs and LECs in 1992/93: percentage of respondent TECs and LECs having an initiative in each area (all topics prompted, except "other")($N =$ 76).

	England & Wales TECS	SE LECs	HIE LECs	Total	Total ranking
Objective of initiative:					
Women	73.2	75.0	62.5	72.4	1
EC grants	60.7	91.7	75.0	67.1	2
HE links	58.9	83.3	75.0	64.5	3
Language skills	66.1	66.7	37.5	63.2	4
Hotel/tourism	46.4	91.7	87.5	57.9	5
Minorities	64.3	50.0	12.5	56.6	6
EC-based information	41.1	83.3	75.0	51.3	7
Unemployed	4.6	58.3	37.5	46.1	8
Redundancy assistance	44.6	33.3	12.5	39.5	9
Integrated projects	25.0	83.3	75.0	39.5	10
Euro-business centre	28.6	75.0	25.0	35.5	11
Sites/premises	16.1	83.3	87.5	34.2	12
Environmental improvement	14.3	91.7	87.5	34.2	13
Physical redevelopment	7.1	91.7	37.5	23.7	14
Housing/unemployment	12.5	58.3	25.0	21.1	15
Trade missions	17.9	33.3	25.0	21.1	16
Other	32.1	33.3	12.5	30.3	17

Source: LSE survey (Bennett et al., 1993b).

the most common initiatives are directed towards women (73%), which is followed by the promotion of language skills (66%), initiatives for minorities (64%) and the pursuit of EC grants (61%). Initiatives to promote links to HE, at 59%, was the only other listed initiative being undertaken by more than half of TECs.

Few TECs have broad-based economic development foci for initiatives. Among TECs, the initiatives of physical redevelopment found only 7% support and environmental improvement found 14%. Both are among the least common TEC foci, but are most common in Scotland, reflecting the differences in the TEC/LEC briefs.

LECs, in contrast to TECs, are primarily focused on initiatives to improve the physical environment for business, develop sites and promote hotels and tourism. Popular initiatives in the SE LECs included most prominently hotel/tourism initiatives, physical redevelopment, environmental improvement and the pursuit of EC grants, all pursued by 92% of SE LECs. Also popular in the SE area are the promotion of HE links, the acquisition of sites/premises, integrated developments (such as physical/training/jobs initiatives) and the provision of information relating to the EC, all of which are being pursued by 83% of SE LECs.

257

Even for initiatives in training LECs are generally as active, or more active, than TECs. Initiatives for women, though only the ninth most common SE LEC initiative, at 75% are still more common than among TECs, for which it was the most common initiative. Similarly initiatives for minorities finds 50% of SE LECs active, not many fewer than TECs (64%). The most popular initiatives in the Highlands and Islands LECs were hotel/tourism initiatives, environmental improvement and the acquisition of sites and premises, all pursued by 88% of HIE LECs. The promotion of HE links, integrated developments, the pursuit of EC grants and the provision of EC-based information also proved popular, all being pursued by 75% of HIE LECs. However, no other form of initiative was being pursued by more than 38% of HIE LECs.

Enterprise- and partnership-led

In addition to these contrasts there seems to be a wider conception of partner-ship in Scotland than England and Wales. This conception embraces the idea of *integration* and owes a lot to the earlier work of the SDA and HIDB. Both the LECs themselves and other agents acknowledged the importance of SDA staff to the SE LECs. They seem to be regarded as "less bureaucratic" and more "entre-preneurial". This appears to be a function of their larger autonomy from the civil service culture and their origin in many cases in the private sector. They have brought a vigour to the SE LECs which is not generally found to the same degree amongst TA staff. One commentator asserted that the SDA staff act as "a catalyst of style"; it was the mix of TA/SDA which was "the chief catalyst" for LEC effectiveness. In addition there is a cultural difference between Scotland, and England and Wales, in terms of a "carefully nurtured and deeply-rooted consensus approach"[5] to economic development north of the border.

The SDA/HIDB input and the powers of LECs in the field of physical develop-ment leads to differences in their local projects (Tables 10.5–10.8) compared to TECs. In Scotland in SE LECs:

- LEC projects are bigger: 73% of LEC projects exceed £1m compared to only 15% of TEC projects, 52% of TEC projects are less than £100,000 compared to 13% of LEC projects;
- LEC projects embrace a wider range of agents, and tend to be more based on partnership than exclusive TEC-led and TEC-developed ones: 75% of TEC projects are self-initiated compared to only 35% of LEC projects, 58% of TEC projects are self-developed compared to only 32% of LEC projects, 64% of TEC projects are self-managed compared to only 43% of LEC projects, 56% of TEC projects are self-financed compared to only 12% of LEC projects;
- LEC projects are more likely to be integrative across a number of policy fields.

The physical development powers of LECs tend to lead to a completely different definition of "the problem", of who should be involved and how it should be tackled. By contrast, in England and Wales a limited, TEED-based conception of the potential of local initiatives often amounts to no more than minor adjustments to programmes. Indeed, it is apparent that for some TEC chief executives little thinking has yet gone into what constitutes a significant initiative.

The difference in emphasis of LECs and TECs is not just a result of differing powers. It is very clear in interviews that LEC staff have an entirely different capacity and perception of their rôle. Local economic development is the key part of their objectives with training taking a place related to economic development needs. This reflects the SDA industry-led focus as opposed to the DE/TEED training-led approach to development. Their different approach has led LECs to work closely with specific companies to develop initiatives focused on what gaps business identifies and then to fill them. In contrast, TECs have designed surveys of business needs and skills gaps and then sought to tailor programmes to meet them in a diffuse, generic and untargeted way. LECs have thus built their programmes to the specific sectoral needs of groups of companies, "TECs have been led by products largely designed by someone else in TEED".[6]

As a result of these differences TECs will not be able readily to follow the lead set by LECs without change in staff, departmental parentage and a shift away from their overemphasis on a training-led mission as a means to achieve economic development goals. The NTTF report (1992a) confirmed that there was a "need to change the internal culture of the other TEC staff to make them more market-orientated rather than programme-focused". In LECs, for example, over half of former TA staff had been replaced by early 1993 by staff with specific skills and recent private sector experience. In TECs in late 1993 this process had still hardly begun.

Distinctive issues for Scotland

Despite its advantages in LEC development, Scotland faces other problems compared to England and Wales:

- There is a lack of strong local agents in many areas. In Argyll, for example, there have been "millions of committees" but none of them has lasted long.
- Accessibility is a general problem, e.g. it is a 3 day round trip for officers from the Argyll and Islands LEC to get from their headquarters in Lochgilphead to Tiree.
- These two problems combine to make the work of some LECs very difficult. As one LEC (10) commentator noted of her area: "the whole place is a challenge"; their overall goal was "to survive the next three years".
- HIE LECs are clearly not all going to be as significant in their local economies as originally envisaged by their mission statement. This is because of their greater levels of geographical dispersion, smaller size, and the retention by HIE of significant powers at the centre, even after the reallocation of staff to LECs in 1992/93. Given the immense practical problems of getting a LEC to work in the Highlands and Islands, a high level of decentralization is less possible but, as a result, HIE LECs will remain different entities to those in the SE area.

259

The general conclusion from this assessment is that Scotland's LECs certainly gain from their greater powers. They do have a much stronger economic development focus. But as much of this derives from their SDA/HIDB staff and inheritance as it does from their greater powers. The analysis of this chapter suggests that it is much more a gap of vision and staff skills than it is formal powers that demarks TECs from LECs.

Scotland's HIE community development programme

In the HIE LECs there is an additional range of programme responsibilities for "community development". This needs specific discussion. The community development responsibility is not part of the remit of SE LECs or TECs. It reflects the development of programmes by the former HIDB. The main objective has been to stabilize population in already sparsely populated rural areas. Specific projects have included community enterprise, assistance to Gaelic speakers, recreation, the arts and amenity provision. Community Action Grants were the main instrument of HIDB policy.

The HIDB created a body called the Association of Community Enterprises (ACE–HI), through which it offered advice and finance in support of the existing community enterprise network, and sought to promote self-help solutions to community problems. The principal examples of this are the community co-operatives established on a number of the smaller islands, where the economic base is too minimal to support conventional enterprise. All residents become shareholders and elect a committee, which combine funds from ACE–HI with self-generated revenue for general community use.

The community development budget now given to HIE LECs continues this work. HIE's strategy statement notes that "social, as well as economic, development will be essential for the fulfilment of the overall aim. It will be achieved largely at the local level by enabling communities to nurture their own distinctive identities".[7] Specific priorities remain similar, and include the greater integration of social, community and cultural development with economic development, innovative projects, development of the Gaelic language and improvements in community social life. Activities which are funded vary widely, ranging from funding community co-operatives to support for the arts. One HIE LEC chief executive highlighted the upgrading of village halls, helping small clubs and supporting community events as the main uses of his very small (£40,000) annual budget, although the part-funding of a Regional Council officer charged with identifying appropriate recipients of Community Action Grants was also covered by this.

Table 10.11 shows the main activities of the Community Action Grants. They are concentrated in community, leisure and cultural activities, with specific facilities being a major aspect of support. The emphasis of initiatives has remained unchanged between 1991/92 and 1992/93. The coverage is also very

Table 10.11 Community development activities among HIE LECs in 1992/93 ($N = 5$) compared to the previous LSE survey of 1991/92 ($N = 6$).

Social/community development activities	No. times cited 1991–92	No. times cited 1992–93
Sports/leisure	5	3
Arts/cultural	2	1
Community hall	2	1
Village development	1	1
Scouts	2	0
Gaelic language	0	1
"Facilities" (unspecified)	1	1
"Equipment" (unspecified)	1	1
CAG (unspecified)	1	1
Other unspecified initiatives	1	3

Source: LSE surveys (Bennett et al., 1993b). *Note*: Each LEC was asked to specify up to 3 activities for each year.

close to that of the previous HIDB. The HIE LECs have, therefore, preserved a strong continuity of their community support from the HIDB experience.

In terms of budget, social and community projects form only a very small component of the HIE LECs' overall brief. The funding pattern follows a small-scale, low cost, high volume approach. The average annual budget in 1992/93 was around £50,000, only 2.4% of the average total LEC budget. Despite this, community funding is regarded as an important activity, "very deeply rooted in the HIDB culture". The LEC chief executive (38) who made this comment claimed the principal objective of cultural support was "to maintain self-confidence, which has crucial economic consequences".

Assessment

This chapter has assessed the emerging rôle of TECs and LECs in economic and community development. The LECs have emerged in general as strong local economic development agents, working closely with companies, and generally adding significant value and leverage to local activities. They have not always been able to achieve their development without tension with other agents, particularly local authorities. LECs have also had to struggle with some difficult problems of accessibility in the more remote mountain and rural areas. But generally their development has been a success. The Hughes and SO vision to link SDA/HIDB and TA functions has created a significant enhancement and targeting of training programmes.

The TECs in comparison appear to be floundering in the field of economic and community development. Their mission called for leadership but gave little real power or resources. Government in fact had little power to give in this field: the strategic guidance until the NTTF (1993) report was unclear. Even since 1993 the concept of partnership that has emerged still calls for TEC leadership in a field where other agents have more power, resources and better developed capacity. But above all, TECs have had thinly developed staff skills to fulfil the economic development mission.

A major constraint lies in the tight funding regime within which TECs and LECs have to operate. Only a small proportion of their overall budget is available for the development of local strategic projects since it must come largely through efficiency savings or the LIF. Thus the scope for direct financial intervention through initiatives is limited. The strong emphasis upon funding YT and ET provision, coupled with the effect of the majority of TEC staff coming from the former TA, seem to have deflected the wider vision through becoming dominated by a constant concern with the detail of day-to-day programme delivery. This deflection from mission targets is being continually reinforced by detailed accounting and audit monitoring by the Treasury and TEED. Moreover, the whole concept of local initiatives has been degraded by the TEED continuation of the MSC/TA methodology of inventing initiatives in Moorfoot that each TEC/LEC can then bid for. This reinforces the top-down methodology of the whole TEC/ LEC design (see Chapter 6). Furthermore, the size of TEED support for initiatives developed locally is small: typically most National Development Projects have been £10,000–£25,000. In addition, the basis of funding allocation, which is strongly related to local levels of unemployment, effectively penalises those TECs and LECs which are successful in stimulating economic growth and employment. The TEC Challenge concept in 1993 has done nothing to change this situation.

Thus, at present, central government has offered TECs encouragement, but no effective mechanisms, for pursuing an effective economic strategy. Government in fact has no power to do otherwise: economic development is not a function which it can give away. TEC directors were persuaded to join the Boards by the promise that they would have the opportunity to use their local experience and vision to pursue wide-ranging and imaginative projects that could harness local energies in a way that uncoordinated initiatives never could. Instead they find themselves in a position where their hands are largely tied and they are unable to put into effect the visionary goals they devise, beyond small-scale, low-impact projects which appear minor when compared to the genuinely significant projects ongoing in their areas. Although successful intervention and partnership generation does not always depend upon large financial inputs, the low grade significance accorded by other key local agents to TEC/LEC activity would appear to leave them far short of their original vision.

The evidence presented in this chapter confirms TECs struggling to make a mark in a difficult field with unrealistic goals and inadequate guidance from TEED. In this struggle most projects and initiatives that the TECs have developed are minor, create few jobs, and would not stand the scrutiny of private sector criteria for value added. This public sector inefficiency is addressed further in Chapters 11 and 12. For the future it is clear that TECs have an important rôle to play, but only as partners in a much wider process. Their partnership development has, in general, been slow compared to Scotland's LECs. A recent AMA[8] report found that there was significant room to improve working relations between TECs and local authorities in almost all areas. We turn in Chapters 11 and 12 to how the partnership rôle could become part of a wider local empowerment.

Chapter 11
Fulfilling the Mission

A bridge too short

The TECs and LECs are a very adventurous experiment. As we have seen, they have delivered some major gains to the organization of government's training and enterprise policy. But their structure is imperfect and they face the central and continuing dilemma that their practical design has not allowed their mission to be fulfilled. They have not been given the power that government promised. Frustration and disillusionment are beginning to develop. A rescue is required.

Our central argument in this book is that the key TEC/LEC mission was to empower business through the development of a strong business-led local agency. In this chapter we assess the areas of development of TECs and LECs that must be confronted if this mission is to be fully realized. We argue that the present structure of TECs and LECs cannot be seen as the end point, but only as the start of a reform process. In this chapter we highlight the weaknesses of the TEC/LEC design. In Chapter 12 we outline where we feel developments should take place.

In the discussion below we cover four aspects where we feel developments are required:
- Deficiencies of structure;
- Redesigning geography, rethinking size;
- Gaps in programmes;
- Restructuring government-TEC/LEC relations.

Only by tackling these problems squarely will Britain achieve the world class standard of excellence that we argue at the outset of this book is the over-whelming requirement for its economic growth.

Deficiencies of structure

The key problem in the TEC/LEC system is one of structure. The design of the system does not match the mission originally laid out, nor the requirements for excellence and empowerment we have identified. This can be justified if the present design of TECs and LECs is seen as a step on the path of a long-term reform. But if further radical change does not occur we believe that a "failure of design" will result in a "design to fail". We assess these issues of design failure through each of its key aspects of unclear mission; inadequate empowerment; conflict in local leadership; personnel to deliver; ability of the Board to lead; cost inefficiency; and uncertain budget.

Unclear mission

The central objective of TECs and LECs was to increase the investment in training by firms for their current workforce. It is for this purpose that the employer lead on TEC Boards is so crucial. But it is the conflict of this mission statement – which was what attracted and enthused business leaders – with the reality of TECs/LECs that has caused so much tension. There are six key dilemmas:

- The vast majority of the budget of TECs/LECs concerns the unemployed, not employed people; therefore TECs/LECs have little influence over the areas the Boards thought they were empowered to develop.
- Because major public funds are involved, a strong monitoring and audit trail for public accountability exists; this conflicts with the mission statement to give maximum independence to TECs and LECs; and it creates severe difficulties for the accounting format for many training providers.
- Because the programmes are public ones, it is essential that they have sensitivity to special needs groups; Boards have not always been comfortable with these pressures.
- Because the finance is public, its level is determined both by a political process and by bargaining between central departments and the Treasury; TECs and LECs have found themselves dependent on ministerial competence in playing this game, as well as suffering the uncertainty and instability of all publicly-funded agents.
- Because TECs are still primarily the creatures of one government department, the DE, they have been treated "edgily" by other departments, particularly the DFE and DTI. This is true despite the development of the joint DE–DTI strategy documents since 1993/94 and reflects the persistent differences of style and culture of the different departments. The TECs have not therefore possessed the broad range of tools promised by the Employment Secretary of State that would allow them to fulfil their mission to facilitate the broad "economic development" of their communities. It was indeed a fallacy for government to believe that it owned the "economic development" field so that it could be given away to TECs.
- The constitutional structure of TECs initially left major power with TEED, particularly over training contracts and unit prices. This power has not yet been eroded. Despite the 1993 changes there is still an air of uncertainty, a continuing intrusion of central rules, and a trammelling of local flexibility. In the words of one LEC Chair (9) "there have been too many changes by those bloody people from Sheffield and this has left us no time for anything else".

The dilemma for TECs/LECs is well summed up in the words of one senior DE commentator – "the TECs and LECs will gain the flexibility they require by lobbying and exerting their considerable power". This is the language of public sector debate and civil service patronage. It is not the language of local empowerment, corporate independence and a business approach led by objectives rather than process.

Inadequate empowerment

The rhetoric of the TEC/LEC launches and the back-up process of national media advertising and meetings across the country raised false expectations of the level of independence that would be available. The key mission brief was summed up in the 1988 White Paper: "employers must assume active leadership . . . planning and management of enterprise and training need to shift from the public to the private sector".[1]

This is echoed by Cay Stratton, who drafted many of the TEC/LEC launch materials. She argued that "if a locally based system is to succeed [it] . . . must be free to mobilise and deploy resources in the way they judge best solve their problems"; the "starting point must not be to fit TECs into well-established Training Agency patterns. Rather, it must begin from a position that empowers".[2]

These visions have appeared to be born of a benign sense of unreality. Given the rules designed by Treasury and TEED, given the number of other agents involved at local level, and given the power and entrenched interests of other highly relevant central departments, there was no way in which TECs and to a lesser extent LECs could immediately become the powerful agents for change that they were conceived to be. We would argue that the key gaps are:

- Absence of a proper relation with other local business-led bodies, particularly Chambers of Commerce, that covered similar territories and were involved in similar functions.
- Absence of any significant leverage over firms, particularly small firms, through divorce of the training process from the structure of employer–employee relations (e.g. through any regulatory controls of training or of training wages, such as are available to German Chambers of Commerce).
- Inadequate conceptualization and gaps in the leverage of all programmes (such as IIP and MCI) aimed at stimulating management development and supervisory training. These are products designed from outside business, there is no equivalent to the German Meister.
- Absence of any centrally co-ordinated proper relation with local authority economic development, either through a partnership or contracted/control process; no detailed consultations with local authority associations have occurred.
- Absence of significant involvement in the education budget related to the world of work. TECs and LECs were allowed control of Compact, EBPs and

except in Scotland some WRFE funds, but have been withheld from any meaningful relation to classroom processes in schools and FE (e.g. through TVEI, curriculum development, or stronger controls of FE funds).

- Absence of effective links, in the early stages, with DTI programmes for enterprise development such as the enterprise initiative, active exporting, technology transfer, etc, where TECs come into conflict with Chambers of Commerce, DTI offices, European Information Centres, Regional Technology Transfer Centres, etc. This problem has been partly overcome by One Stop Shops (OSSs).
- A complete gap between the broader economic development rôle and expenditure of TECs and their mission, although a major environmental and physical development responsibility is available to LECs. Hence TECs in many areas are "just another local initiative" together with UPAs, UDCs, Task Forces, City Action Teams (CATs), Rural Development Commission, WDA/DBRW, etc.
- Major constraints on the flexibility of their budgets.

As a result, the conception of TECs being "a catalyst for change" will never be possible to attain without major enhancements. LECs, in contrast, are undoubtedly major agents of change, but also suffer some of the same gaps in leverage and empowerment.

Conflict in local leadership

The TECs and LECs were deliberately designed to be independent of any existing local agents who could have acted as "host". The senior DE/TEED civil servants did not like the way in which the former Local Employer Network (LEN) programme[3] had developed in which Chambers of Commerce acted as the main host to an initiative to improve links between FE college provision and employer skill requirements. There was a sense in which LENs had been subject to capture by the host who redirected the programme to its own objectives. The decision to make TECs/LECs free standing was also informed by the US PICs experience in which the PICs that were independent companies with independent Directors were perceived to be some of the most effective. The influence of the independently-based SDA and HIDB experience in Scotland was also important for the way in which the Scottish debate evolved, somewhat separately, as an attempt to develop an independently-led structure (as advocated by Bill Hughes in 1988).

The problem of not using existing local bases has been crucial particularly to TECs, but also to LECs:

- The links with local community agents had to be built from scratch, unless key individuals can be recruited or co-opted on to the Board or into action groups; but even when recruited they cannot guarantee delivery by their companies or agencies.
- The networks of links with employers required to fulfil the mission has been dependent on other organizations which have membership lists or data bases

(particularly Chambers of Commerce, Chambers of Trade, enterprise agencies, local authorities and Compacts). Building independent bases has proved costly, duplicates existing effort and often wastes public resources.
- The incursion of a public sector body into a domain populated by private sector and existing public–private bodies has opened TECs and LECs to the criticism that they are "crowding out" the private sector and offering unfair competition.[4] Combined with the tendency of many TECs and LECs to develop initiatives that reinvent the wheel locally, there has been a strong tendency for TECs and LECs to "break many eggshells" in local communities. Generally the more "macho" the TEC/LEC, the more this has occurred.
- Being free standing, there has been a severe danger that TECs are seen as "just another initiative". This is not a significant problem in Scotland because LECs are key co-ordinators of most local elements of SO activity. They also inherited a base of HIDB and SDA experience. In England and Wales, however, TECs arrived just after the expansion of UDCs, CATs and TFs, the development of Compacts, and at about the same time as Enterprise and Education Advisors, Education–Business Partnerships (EBPs) and other initiatives. In the local community, many viewed the TECs with a sense of awe and/or horror that here was another central government invention, "made in Sheffield", much bigger than most previous ones, which would trample the local turf, turn a few sods, and then be likely to be abolished just like most previous MSC initiatives, only to be replaced by some similar short-lived Moorfoot brainchild.
- The TECs and LECs have the capacity to kill other initiatives and, rather than adding value, can reduce the level of business involvement in the local community. This is particularly true of finance where the emergence of TEC/LEC funding has encouraged donors to withdraw from enterprise agencies, has thrown into jeopardy the subscriptions and membership of Chambers of Commerce, and has sometimes undermined the commitment of businesses to voluntary bodies and school links.

Against the background of these problems, it is not surprising that many local agents have viewed TECs and LECs with considerable caution; still do not believe the assurances of permanence and long-term commitment; and worry that the employer lead will erode the employer base necessary to sustain the Chamber, Compact or other local partnership activity. As a result, they have tended to treat the TECs/LECs either defensively or have sought to "capture" them in order to assure a permanence for those local activities that were precious to the local community. In the words of Brian Coldwell, a key business leader in Teesside and subsequently deputy Chair of its TEC, "Care must be taken not to 'throw the baby out with the bathwater' and to make best use of local existing expertise" the local community "can be likened to a 'crate of initiatives', clearly marked 'fragile' and 'handle with care'".[5] Or in the words of a Yorkshire TEC business Director (32) the best thing to do with the TEC was "to set them up, put them in a kennel and keep them there, making sure that they are muzzled and do not bite".

Personnel to deliver

The TECs and LECs were given a large staff complement at the outset: an average of 50 in England and Wales and Southern Scotland and 10–11 in the Highlands and Islands. In this way they became in most areas the largest central government local economic development initiative. But the ability of these staff to deliver was questioned at the outset and these doubts have been borne out in many cases by experience. The gaps that have emerged are:

– A problem of commitment by individuals who were on a 3 year secondment and looked to TEED and later the Employment Service for their long-term careers.

– An inherited structure of multi-tiered job grades (6 or 7 levels in most cases) accompanied by insufficient devolution of responsibilities and budget which has resulted in a lack of experience of staff in taking the responsibility and exercising discretion. Only one or two TECs had radically reformed these structures by mid-1993[6] (see Chapter 4); where significant reforms have taken place reductions of staff of at least 40% have been possible and flatter structures of higher-level, skilled personnel have been developed.

– An inherited work culture that involved extensive, often inappropriate, use of flexi-time so that core staff could not be reliably found at the office over the same part of any day – resulting in managerial breakdown and very slow processing of work. In addition there were extensive "Spanish work practices" that in some cases amounted to public scandals. For example, the Chair of one of the most progressive of the Scottish LECs (9) found that under the TA "there was no flexi-time register, no sick leave register, the staff had no systematic contractual arrangements and there had been a long-term practice of staff making regular monthly trips to Edinburgh and Glasgow for 'relaxation training': trips which counted towards flexi-time leave entitlement and seemed to be mostly spent shopping".

– A lack of commercial sense or ability among most former TA staff which restricted their competence and speed in their contract negotiations with providers. Most TECs/LECs now negotiate these directly rather than through training managing agents, but many staff are judged to be "just not up to it" (see Chapters 4 and 7).

– A lack of experience of staff in new areas of responsibility, particularly in enterprise, education and general economic development. The lack of experience has tended to result in mistakes being made, wasted resources, extensive "reinvention of the wheel" and a very modest capacity to innovate or create significant local initiatives (see Chapter 10). LECs, in contrast, had much more inherited experience, of a generally high quality, from the former SDA and HIDB.

Although these problems can be overcome by training and managerial development within TECs and LECs, the staff and management have often been slow to grasp the need for change. *The secondment contract and transfer of staff from the civil service has been a fundamental impediment to personnel development.* Secondment was resisted from the outset by CBI/ABCC and business groups. This battle was fought and lost with DE. Although secondment is due to be phased out by 1996, this will be too late for TECs and LECs to have grasped the early initiative. It is also far from clear that government will actually honour its commitment to take back all secondees in 1996. Even if they do, TECs and LECs will already have been judged politically to have succeeded or failed by 1996 – a full 6 years after their foundation. Without a more rapid recruitment of staff with business experience and skills we would argue that they cannot hope to succeed.

Ability of the Board to lead and manage

The Directors on the Boards of the TECs and LECs are part time "volunteers" who, on average, commit between 1 and 4 days a month.[7] They are crucially limited by their available time, knowledge and the rôle played by the TEC/LEC staff. The key gaps are:

- The gap between the TEC/LEC Articles of Association empowering the Board "to manage" and the Operating Agreements that limit control of staff, finance and programmes (see Chapter 4).
- A domination by large firms and manufacturing firms, as opposed to small firms, and growing businesses.
- A gap in knowledge by most of the senior business leaders on Boards of the real problems experienced by trainers, small firms, education providers and other agents.
- A control of briefing by TEC staff of the Board. This gives the chief executive, in particular, much more substantial control of the TEC/LEC than would be the case in a private company and far more than is implied in the mission statement. One commentator likened this to an hour-glass with the chief executive at the centre: see Figure 11.1. This has meant that a chief executive can strangle the Board's capacity to manage. A TEC chief executive (8) likened his rôle to that of briefing local government counsellors – a far cry indeed from government's intention! The problem has arisen because, on the one hand, the Board members are often not experienced at taking a view across the field that TECs cover and do not have time; on the other hand, not enough responsibility is devolved to staff, or they are unable satisfactorily to exercise it. The chief executive is thus a crucial power broker; as a result much of the effectiveness of the TEC/LEC depends on his/her personal effectiveness.
- There is a strong possibility of "capture" leaving the Board de facto powerless. The former civil servants have exerted a strong influence to maintain

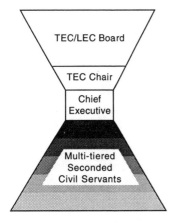

Figure 11.1 TEC/LEC Boards and their relation to their chief executive and staff following the analogy of an hour-glass (interview comment of TEC business Director in TEC: 63).

inherited work practices: they are not likely to change unless given major guidance and incentives. This is less true of the Scottish LECs which have benefited from a large proportion of former SDA/HIDB staff who had recent private sector experience and had not been subject to the MSC culture. The rôle of chief executive is also crucial to staff capture and his/her allegiances can be very important. For example, many chief executives from the former TA see their career development still very closely related to their former patrons in TEED/DE. In Scottish LECs the allegiances to the former SDA/HIDB are often an important part of the relation of the LEC to SE/HIE. Chief executives or other staff who derive from other backgrounds can also sometimes be part of capture through allegiances owed to their former employers: this appears to be particularly true of former local authority staff from the same area.

Each of these gaps creates a dilemma for the TEC Board members and chair. With lack of time, and gaps in detailed knowledge, they have often been powerless to intervene to influence strategy. As a result they have found themselves caught in awkward positions: of being pummelled by various interests outside the TEC/LEC (particularly training providers, local authorities and Chambers) but without an effective capacity to respond, and often have little sense of whether the external criticisms of the TEC/LEC are realistic or not. Directors have thus found themselves increasingly in a position of responsibility without real power. This, and their sense of the over-burgeoning regulations and red tape from TEED, has been a major factor in Board disillusionment and resignation (see Chapter 4). These problems cannot be overcome without a major change in the relations with TEED, modifications of the Operating Agreement, and the development of at least a funded part-time Chair.

Cost-inefficiency

The inheritance of civil service staff, public sector management structures, public accountability and a part-time Board of Directors who can rarely exert strong control over the internal management of TECs and LECs has meant that most existing management practices have survived from the MSC Area Offices. This has resulted in significant cost-inefficiencies in how resources are combined to produce programmes. This has thus undermined the capacity of the TECs and LECs to perform as commercial organizations.

An estimate of comparative efficiency is possible through comparing those TECs which have radically reformed their staff, management and delivery structures with those that have not. Only two or three TECs had made radical changes by April 1993, at the end of the first 3 years of TEC funding. A detailed comparison of one of these with an "unreformed" TEC demonstrates that fixed costs were on average 18% higher, variable costs were 7% higher, all overhead management costs (fixed and variable) were 15% higher, and the variable costs of managing the three main training programmes of YT, ET and Employment Action (EA) were 111% higher.[8] These cost savings chiefly derive from a 13% cut in staff, or an enhancement of the staff skills to produce a flatter management structure. For an average TEC budget of £20m, these differences in efficiency represent approximately £3m. Across the whole system of TECs in 1992/93 these efficiency losses would amount to a public sector deadweight burden of about £250m.

A second way of estimating comparative efficiency is to compare TEC unit costs with those in the private sector. There are few comparable private sector activities to those of TECs, but it is possible to compare costs with Chambers of Commerce and enterprise agencies in the fields of employer networks/membership schemes, enterprise courses and consultancy, EBP/compact management, WRFE liaison and central management (personnel, finance and local liaison). In these fields TECs appear to be approximately between 4 and 800% more costly per unit of output (see Table 11.1). Although comparisons cannot be precise, the consistency of the pattern suggests an alarming cost-inefficiency of TECs. It is probably safe to estimate the *average* extra costs of TECs to be at least 70% higher using the central management costs as a guide. Detailed analysis of these inefficiencies shows that they derive from higher staff/output ratios, higher staff costs per staff member and, in the case of enterprise courses and consultancy, low volumes below a viable minimum size. It is unclear that a defence against the charge of inefficiency can be mounted by claiming that higher quality is applied in TECs. It should also be noted that the estimates in Table 11.1 derive from TECs' estimated staffing ratios where anticipated improvements in efficiency have been implemented. Table 11.1 therefore presents estimates of current TEC *best* practice, not the average current patterns, which are even poorer.

Table 11.1 Unit costs per unit of volume in TECs and Chambers of Commerce and Industry (CCIs) and enterprise agencies for selected services.

	TEC costs/volume £	CCI costs/volume £	TEC to CCI ratio of costs
Membership/employer networking (per firm contacted/member)	24	23	1.04
Enterprise courses (per participant day)	538	66/102[2]	8.15/5.27[2]
Enterprise consultancy (per company session)	427	107/153[2]	3.99/2.78[2]
EBP/Compact (per EBP/Compact)	37	30	1.23
WRFE liaison (per education authority)	44	20	2.20
Central management[1] (per total staff fte)	8735	5107	1.71

Sources: TEC costs from confidential assessment of two TECs by Bennett (1993f) based on foreseeable efficiency gains possible; CCI costs from Bennett (1993e). *Notes*: [1] covers finance, personnel, chief executive office and central management. [2] second figure is for enterprise agency costs.

The higher costs of TECs, and by implication the comparable programme areas in LECs, results from a variety of factors which it is impossible to discriminate between in terms of relative costs. These factors are:
- Inherited staff, personnel structure, salary levels and working practices.
- Large administrative burden to satisfy relations with TEED/G10.
- Excessively detailed public accounting systems, and duplicated accounting needs for DE and DTI.
- Administrative burden of liaison with other local agents (often based on committee-driven approaches, particularly in education).

The combined effect of these factors is a cost/output ratio often 3 to 4 times higher than the private sector fields where comparison can be made, and 70% higher in central management costs. These costs are on top of the scope for at least a further 15% of efficiency economies if the potential from restructuring of staff were achieved in each TEC/LEC.

Uncertain budget

To achieve their goal of being significant new agents for change in their communities and on local firms, TECs and LECs have to exude a sense of confidence and reliability. This is necessary both to convince other agents of their permanence and to convince the Directors themselves that these are institutions worth dedicating their time to.

Unfortunately the budget of TECs and LECs has been continually modified and subject to steady contraction in each of the financial years until 1993/94. This uncertainty and contraction has been a critical factor in undermining the confidence of other agents in the TECs/LECs, particularly training providers, enterprise agencies and others contracted to TECs. Although in each year a proportion of the threatened cuts was subsequently restored, the overall uncertainty has forced TECs and LECs to stick to their core programmes and has made them wary because of fear of further budget changes. This has reduced the amount of staff time available for innovative schemes because they are busy coping with the problems caused by spending cutbacks. Budget certainty is one of the largest single factors that could restore confidence among the TECs and LECs, at the same time developing a greater distance for TECs from TEED. But, given that this is an in-built characteristic of the allocation of the public budget in the UK, the introduction of budgetary stability is difficult to achieve.

But uncertainty has perhaps been even more crucial in sapping the confidence and commitment of the Directors. They have often felt misled, cheated and in despair as to why they should have become involved in something that required so much time and effort only to have funding promises to them by the government reneged upon, and their attempts to resign in some cases leading to personal vilification or threats.[9] The disillusionment is confirmed by what we consider to be the high rate of turnover on TEC and LEC Boards as a result of "pressures of work", or those who are recorded as simply having "left" or been "replaced" (see Chapter 4).

TECs and LECs have fought, and gained only a minor victory, in seeking to replace 1-year budget settlements with 3 year contracts. To enhance long-term funding commitments would be a simple and most significant benefit to them.

Redesigning geography, rethinking size

The TECs and LECs are a local initiative. They are an attempt both to decentralize programme management to a local level and to empower local communities. For either management or empowerment to make sense, the area of geographical coverage must also make sense. In fact the local design has often been one of the most flawed aspects of the structure, with TEC/LEC geography satisfying the objectives of neither management efficiency nor local community empowerment. There are four main aspects: the establishment of so many small TECs which suffer diseconomies of scale; the poor development of management technology; lack of regional strategy; and the poor local fit of TECs. Each is assessed below.

Diseconomies of scale

Many TECs and LECs have been set up which do not reach a viable size to run at an economically efficient level. The original TEC Prospectus in England called for labour markets of at least 100,000 working populations, and a budget of £15–50m. The final pattern has been 9 TECs with working populations of less than 100,000, 55 with less than the average desired of 250,000, 41 with 1991/92 budgets of less than £15m, and 36 with less than £15m in 1992/93. In Scotland, the design criteria were different, and two LECs have budgets of less than £10m. The original design criteria have not always been met. No assessment was made of these design criteria by the MSC or TA in the set-up phase. Rather the Prospectus guidelines were drawn up largely with the number of TA Area Offices and existing budgets and staff in mind.[10] *No economic analysis of the size of a TEC required to assume a given level of management – and cost-efficiency – was undertaken. This was an amazing approach to follow.*

Subsequently, only one detailed assessment has been made of the question of TEC size in relation to budget.[11] This has constructed estimates of unit costs of managing different TEC programmes for different volumes of activity. This has then estimated fixed and variable costs and has led to the definition of a minimum viable size for any one programme area, and for the TEC as a whole. This study is based on detailed assessments of costs in two sample TECs. The study assumes that the present structure of staff and payrolls continues. The scope for efficiency gains was estimated only for "immediately foreseeable" benefits of restructuring likely to be achievable in a 1–2 year period. The estimates are detailed and cover 27 budget headings and 12 cost categories.

The chief implications that can be drawn from this assessment is that many TECs are below a minimum size for optimal cost-efficiency of management. The level of fixed costs for TEC management across its fields of activity, and the overheads related to management of training, are high (approximately £930,000 at 1992 prices). On to this must be added the management and marketing costs for a given volume of programmes. Estimating these at median volume levels, Figure 11.2 shows how fixed and variable costs at a given volume of TEC activity interrelate. This estimate suggests that the minimum management budget for a TEC is between £1.3m and £1.5m. This can be compared with the management fee (Block 5) actually allocated to TECs. In 1992/93 32 TECs had management fees below £1.3m, 10 had fees between £1.3m and £1.5m, and a further 3 had fees of £1.5m to £1.7m. Although the estimates of minimum viable size of management fixed costs shown in Figure 11.2 are accepted as only "ball-park" figures, they nevertheless suggest that 51% of TECs are trading close to or below the estimated optimal viable size for management cost-efficiency (of £1.3m to £1.5m). The whole viability of the TEC system is thus in question, with the consequence that many TECs cannot perform as effectively or cost-efficiently as they should. There are six possible outcomes:

- The management budget has to be supported by a large part of the programme budget, giving high unit costs and/or low volumes of programme output.
- Strategic development of programmes may be less because senior manage-

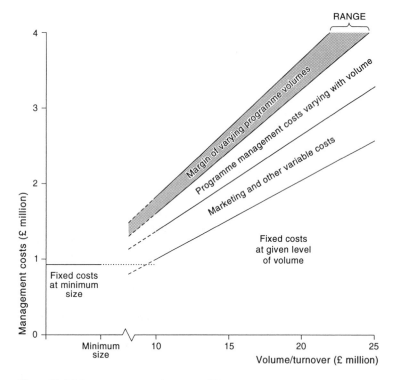

Figure 11.2 Management costs of a TEC at different levels of volume. *Source*: Bennett (1993d: Figure 4).

ment staff are insufficient in number, and tend to get bogged down in detail.
- Some areas are relatively neglected because of shortages in management time and resources.
- Initiatives that are developed are more likely to respond to external pressures, particularly from TEED, rather than local priorities. In the words of one commentator in one of the smallest TECs (96), "it is easy for the local voice to get drowned by the list of things TECs should be doing".
- The demands on staff are higher, with the consequence that higher skill-levels and salaries are required which, with a gap in TEC powers to sack ineffective staff, feeds directly to increased costs. Conversely, staff feel that the extra demands on them in a small TEC are inadequately recognized by TEED.
- There are indivisibilities which mean that small issues become big problems for small TECs. One small TEC (52) quotes the frequent difficulties of TEED's TFS data base system (see Chapter 7) as a major loss of their time. A small

loss of staff for a small TEC is a large part of their output, e.g. one member of staff spending a day linking software with a printer can represent 5% of the output of that TEC for the day.

All of these outcomes appear to be occurring to different extents in different TECs. But the dominant form of outcome in the smallest TECs appears to be the first in the above list. In the most extreme case, of AZTEC, all Block 5, LIF, surpluses and a substantial proportion of the programme budget is devoted to employing TEC staff. AZTEC's staff on average are each responsible for administering £184,000 of its budget, compared to an average of £300,000 for all TECs. This outcome, and indeed each of the possible outcomes listed above, should be most concerning to a reforming government since they suggest that (i) public money is being wasted by allowing small TECs to continue to exist, and (ii) the programmes to which government is directing funds are being eroded by maintenance of an expensive management structure that can be economically supported only by a larger-scale organization. The pressure on management resources also undermines the aim of empowering local leadership and reinforces the power of TEED. The chief executive of one small TEC (55) likened the management process to "trying simultaneously to keep a large number of plates spinning on sticks; I am always running from one urgent problem to another": the capacity to lead change at the local level is thus undermined.

The inescapable conclusion is that, given the structures within which they have actually to operate, many of the benefits originally envisaged to be available to very small TECs and LECs cannot be achieved. This suggests the need for amalgamation of most small TECs.

Poor development of management technology

The TECs and LECs have been developed with the supposition that a local base is important. To encourage local empowerment it is probably the case that the more local the focus the better. But management costs and efficiency dictate a fairly large local entity. The TECs seem to have fallen in between two possible geographical scenarios. In most cases they are too large and non-local to match localized business communities; where they are small and localized they cannot achieve satisfactory cost/output ratios. A different approach to management would have overcome this dilemma. This requires combining centralized management systems with local outreach.

We have already seen in Chapter 9, for the case of One Stop Shops (OSSs), that a combination of "hub and spoke" principles can resolve this dilemma. Few individuals or businesses visit their local TEC or LEC, Chamber or enterprise agency. The more that a TEC or LEC is an enabler the less is there a need for the TEC/LEC office to be a central focus for attention. This means that many resources can be drawn together in large centres which can then be accessed remotely (through telephone, fax or IT systems) or only for periodic negotiation and monitoring of supplier contracts. This conception drives TECs and LECs

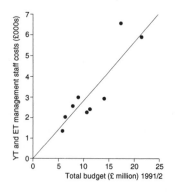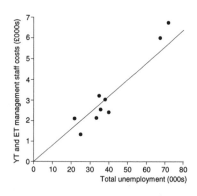

Figure 11.3 The approximately linear pattern of YT and ET management costs with different volumes of budget and unemployment numbers across 9 London TECs. *Source*: Bennett (1993d: Figure A2.1).

towards a small number of large offices with extensive "outreach" facilities.

In the larger areas the benefits of this type of development has already been recognized and implemented. For example in Humberside, Cumbria and London East a large network of local offices is being set up to which OSSs are being added. The local offices are small from a TEC staff and budget point of view – usually only 3–4 staff. But they may become quite large entities if co-located with other agents such as Chambers of Commerce, enterprise agencies or local authority economic development offices.

The selection of which aspects of TEC/LEC staff and systems can be decentralized in this way has generally emphasized the staff negotiating training contracts. As shown in Figure 11.3 management costs are essentially linear with volume in the cases of YT, ET and EA down to very small volumes, but this does not apply to most other TEC/LEC programmes. This means that the management of training budgets can be strongly decentralized within TEC/LEC areas. This has indeed provided the chief foundation for decentralization within HIE and has been attempted in some large TECs, e.g. London East.

Although decentralization is occurring within larger areas, the capacity to economize by combining management costs into larger units has not yet been sought. If the 42 smallest TECs with under £1.5m Block 5 budget were amalgamated with the resources of the larger remaining TECs, it is likely that almost all of their management budget could be saved. This would result in a saving of about £50m that could be put back into programmes.

Lack of a regional strategy

The technology issue is bound up with a larger question of how TECs should work together with each other to a greater extent. The LECs already achieve this through the operation of the networks of SE and HIE. In Scotland these networks allow a strategic view to be taken, economies of scale in a variety of joint activities are achieved, and a greater capacity for regional promotion is possible which is particularly valuable in increasing international awareness.

Although, since 1992/93, a restructuring has occurred in England to give a greater emphasis to the Regional Offices of TEED, as well as giving control of TECs to the WO, the TEC regions are still weak sources of co-ordination compared to SE and HIE. The importance of a regional framework for TECs has been recognized by the NTTF (1993). But the practice has been mostly focused on TEC contract negotiations with virtually no effort to develop TEC-wide strategies. In one of the most difficult cases, London, the NTTF LEG report (1989) had called for a strategic Board for the region. But all attempts to create any significant and well-founded body have been so far frustrated. It appears that TEED has been allowed to continue to impose the inherited MSC view of treating all local entities as competitive with each other, and government has been unwilling, as yet, to strengthen regional structures sufficiently to allow effective co-ordination. As a result the regional strategic development of England's TECs still flounders. The problems still be to be confronted are:

- The need for region-wide or national recognition of many TEC products (particularly in the enterprise field).
- Difficulties of transferability in some cases (e.g. use of training Credits across TEC boundaries).
- Loss of economies of scale in marketing and publicity that would reinforce rather than confuse the impact of product labelling.
- The loss of impact of general efforts to raise the profile of all products in all TEC areas (i) to improve on the inherited poor profiles, and (ii) to overcome the possibility that the negative experiences of products of one TEC adversely affect others.
- A sense of region-wide action, strategy and momentum that could be of particular benefit in international promotion.
- A capacity to understand and readily to compare experiences between TECs across a region or through G10.
- A prioritization of approaches to the EC, international companies and other agents, so that wasteful competition between local bodies is removed and targeted economic development can be achieved.

Poor local fit

The choice of TEC/LEC boundaries was heavily biased towards being co-terminous with Local Education Authorities (LEAs). This was relevant in a period where FE colleges, polytechnics and schools were all administered through LEAs. However, it has become a very peculiar base when colleges and polytechnics have already been fully transferred to national funding councils and where the government hopes that all schools will eventually become grant-maintained. At the same time, recommendations on the structure of local government may redefine many of the boundaries that proved relevant to TEC/LEC formation. Already the government's proposals for Wales will remove most of the main links with Welsh TEC boundaries. Although the review for England is still in progress, it is clear that a structure may emerge of counties and separate major towns, e.g. Derby and Derbyshire. The advantage for TECs and LECs from these reforms will be the introduction of unitary authorities, which will simplify many relationships.

The failure of the geography of TECs and LECs to fit with businesses' needs was obvious from the outset. Businesses define their local pattern of relationships either through product supply and trading networks or through the labour market of journey-to-work flows. As shown in Chapters 3 and 5, neither criterion proved easy to apply in order to define a sense of local business community. It was understandable, therefore, that the LEA boundaries became the dominant criterion for demarcation. LEAs, after all, administered the single largest training operation through the FE colleges, and TEC and LECs also have an education brief with school–business links and the Careers Service.

With the erosion of relevance of the LEAs, however, it now must be questioned whether a better basis for defining TEC/LEC boundaries should be sought. An emphasis on local business communities rather than LEAs would also have the advantage of returning closer to the mission of a business-led body linked to the needs of employees in employment. No systematic data are available to allow ready definition of local business communities. But the Chambers of Commerce have developed a national strategy for reorganization of their network of Chambers. This has considerable relevance to TECs and LECs. As we have argued in Chapters 5 and 9, the fit of TECs and LECs with business organizations rather than LEAs should be of prime concern if the TECs and LECs are to develop their mission of developing effective employer links and empowering business. As the NTTF (1993: 5) concluded "many TECs . . . have boundaries which make little sense in terms of economic development. They need to consider the relationships between their boundaries and those of their partners and seek changes to their own boundaries where it would be beneficial". But no mechanism, or encouragement from TEED exists to allow this to happen.

The Chambers of Commerce have developed their national strategy using two chief concepts: (i) local business geography, but like TECs and LECs taking co-terminacy where possible to local authority boundaries because of their leading rôle in representation of business interests where co-terminacy offers several important advantages, and (ii) the division of financial and staff resources across the country in a manner that achieves a critical mass that can deliver economies of scale for delivery of an effective, quality-accredited service in all areas. The outcome of this strategy is a system of core Chambers which will number about 45–50 when all are in place. This is almost exactly one-half of the number of TECs and LECs. It is suggestive of a way forward for reform of TEC/ LEC geography in which, like each of the arguments developed above, larger areas of geographical coverage of TECs and LECs are complemented by local points of outreach on a "hub and spoke" principle.

Hence, not only is there good reason for TECs to be redesigned on a larger scale from the point of view of economies of scale, cost-efficient management, and a stronger regional aspect. This also emphasises the rôle of business-led rather than public sector definitions of boundaries.

Gaps in programmes

The central chapters of this book have assessed separately the TEC and LEC developments in their main fields of training, education, enterprise and economic development. These assessments compound with the structural and management issues raised in this chapter so far. They also suggest that the TECs and LECs largely fail to meet their design objectives. We assess each in turn.

Training and education

In the fields of training and education, discussed in Chapters 7 and 8, the TECs and LECs are primarily agents for the disbursement of government funds for unemployed people. Of these funds a substantial proportion relates to income support from YT and ET which more properly is the preserve of the DSS through the Employment Service. The main influence that TECs and LECs therefore have is on the contract price of training for the unemployed. There is also leverage and influence over other areas of provision, for example through a rôle in FE. It has also been hoped that the framework of NVQ and IIP will enable TECs and LECs to stimulate more training by employers of their existing workforce.

Considerable improvements have been made in the scale of training being undertaken in Britain. But there is still a long way to go, primarily because the level of attainment of a high proportion of school-leavers is still very low: 45% of school-leavers do not achieve at least an intermediate qualification (equivalent to one "A"-Level) in Britain, compared to only 10% in France and Germany (see Table 2.2).

The difficulties for TECs and LECs in levering change lie in seven main areas. First, they have little or no real influence over the main incentives that encourage individuals or employers to train. This particularly affects relative wages and the rôle and status of supervisors. Second, they lack an effective transmission mechanism for their training concepts to businesses, both ET and IIP having little influence on most employers. Third, the training-led solution to the problems of the British economy is only part of the larger solution required: it is both product and cause of other areas of deficiency, most notably in company entrepreneurship and management development. Fourth, many of the main aspects of programme development for young people lie within the responsibility of the DFE and have not been amenable to significant influence by TECs and LECs. Fifth, the contract procedures used by TECs and LECs with training providers are tending to undermine quality training as frequently as they are enhancing it because of pressures of funding and concentration on too narrow a definition of skills. Sixth, the mechanism of Credits favoured by CBI and DE as a mechanism for empowering individual choices and inducing an improved relation of training supply to demand are largely peripheral to the main funding mechanism of FE colleges. The TECs and LECs are therefore left with a difficult local liaison with colleges which are driven by two different systems with different prices and objectives. Seventh, most of the education products over which TECs and LECs do have control (Compacts, EBPs) are minor aspects of the educational field, with little impact on central issues in the classroom and curriculum to which a greater employer link is required.

Despite the razzmatazz and controversy over TECs, therefore, they seem to have settled down as relatively minor entities primarily focusing on the needs of the unemployed with an important secondary focus on special needs groups within local communities. They do not appear to have the power, resources, nor remit, let alone the staff and management capacity, to be the fundamental change-agent that was sought at the outset. They appear, therefore, more as a new means for government to manage its unemployment commitments, and as a mechanism to reform the former MSC, than a means of shaking Britain from its low skills equilibrium.

The TECs and LECs may nevertheless be important agents for change in their chief sphere of WRFE and unemployment programmes. They *do* provide a mechanism to get on board the capacity of senior employer strategic management in making allocative decisions about programmes. They are certainly an improvement in this regard over the LAMBs, LENs and other former MSC products. The revolution in youth and adult training and 16–19 education they offer, then, is to reorientate an important part of the system of provision for the unemployed, unskilled or relatively low skilled. To bring this field of provision closer to the needs of employers must hold out the hope that the individual trainee will be better able to become employed as a result. Certainly the innovations by TECs and LECs in the fields of YT, ET and EA have been significant developments. And the level of positive employment outcomes following YT and ET has increased significantly with the advent of TECs and LECs.

These changes are significant achievements. But they offer positive benefits for only a small part of the launch mission of TECs and LECs. The gap of rhetoric and reality from the mission suggests that a pull-back to an emphasis on the central rôle that TECs and LECs can satisfy would help them, and others, to clarify their objectives. It would also lay open for more ready attack the yawning gap which still lies open to be filled in the two areas of (i) linking the development of existing workforce skills to the internal development of business's needs, and (ii) the development of incentives for training through systematic modification to the wages and status of workers at both 16–19, and subsequently, to relate pay to acquired relevant qualifications or accredited workplace skills.

Enterprise

In the case of enterprise, discussed in Chapter 9, TECs and to a lesser extent LECs are one of a number of agents seeking to stimulate business start-up and growth. As in the training field, TECs and LECs have managed to improve the quality and/or reduce the costs of many inherited programmes. Considerable progress has been made. But they have found this field of activity more difficult than training because they have to be facilitators and partners to a much greater extent. Working with other agents has been slower and more difficult.

Our discussion has identified seven main areas of deficiency. First, has been the absence of a proper market assessment of the gaps that TECs and LECs were supposed to fill. No market testing was made of what TECs and LECs were supposed to be doing to enhance business support. This deficiency has applied as much to One Stop Shops (OSSs) as to all the earlier initiatives. Second, the inherited programmes with which TECs and LECs began their work gave them a poor start. They were also targeted primarily on the self-employed and micro-business, rather than filling any market gaps that exist in established growth businesses. Third, there has been the quality of programmes. EAS, SFS and most of the BGT/BET programmes had generally poor reputations; TECs and LECs have only slowly been able to build a reputation for proper quality controls. Fourth, few TECs have chosen to follow the route of the SE LECs in getting close to businesses and defining their policy through business needs. TECs have almost uniformly chosen to address needs through diffuse survey research and consultancy, not partnership with firms. Fifth, there has been significant confusion of branding of programmes accompanied by an overburdening emphasis on marketing rather than enhancement of quality. Sixth, and most crucial, the TECs have been encouraged by TEED to go it alone rather than in partnership, with the consequence that money is wasted on duplicating services, other agents suffer unfair competition, and the market for local business services is further confused. Overall TECs appear to have added confusion to the enterprise field rather than being "catalysts for local strategy". Too often, even by mid-1993, most TECs still appear as just another agent trying to supply local services to business. Seventh, is the question of how the TEC/LEC policy on business services is to be defined. If the Board is to be business-led, how is it to relate to local businesses, how does it find a local legitimacy, and how can it seek to define market need?

For the future considerable hope may be raised that the OSSs will encourage TECs to play a more effective rôle. Certainly the change in emphasis of the strategic guidance to TECs for 1993/94 is important. An often difficult, but nonetheless important development has occurred with DTI and DE now both involved in "parentage" of the TECs. This is a step towards the interdepartmental co-ordination that the LECs benefit from through the SO. It is a major step forward. But the reactions to the OSSs by the pilot TECs demonstrates that the battle to bring TECs into partnership is far from won. A long-term sustainable solution is still awaited. A business support system comparable to the best in Europe is not going to be achieved by the DTI or Mr Heseltine having to play policeman to the continual deflection of priorities by TEED, and the TECs' former civil servants. The future of TECs, if they are to play a rôle that adds any value to the enterprise field, must lie in sustained partnerships tailored to demonstrable business needs. We turn in Chapter 12 to how this might be achieved.

Economic and community development

The necessity for TECs to work in partnership with other agents is even more pressing in the fields of economic and community development, discussed in Chapter 10, than in their other fields of activity. Although the LECs have been able to play a rôle as key agents of change in their local economies, the TECs are still floundering.

The advantages of the LECs, ranked in order of priority in our view, have been: a single office of government (the SO); removal of the incursions of the TEED methodology emphasizing short-termism and initiative-driven approaches; greater responsibility and resources in the environmental and business development fields; a history of previous experience inherited from SDA/HIDB; a staff more generally with the necessary skills to cope; and a pattern of local agents which is generally weaker, thus giving the LEC a more open field. The LECs have, as a result, generally become forces for programme integration at a local level. They have also been led to a greater extent by business needs. Certainly they have not achieved a completely satisfactory development, but they offer key lessons to how TECs might be developed to enhance their capacity. We turn to this in Chapter 12.

TECs, in contrast to LECs, appear generally to be floundering in the field of economic development. Despite the NTTF (1992a, 1993) reports and the development of a clearer and more realistic vision following the July 1993 TECs conference, the TECs remain as largely peripheral and confused agents in terms of their contribution to the broader development of their economies. Generally this is because they lack their own resources, have to obtain finance by bidding for EC and other programme funds which bring their own external emphases rather than a focus on local needs, and they have failed to develop a satisfactory relationship, in general, with the local authorities in their areas. There are clearly exceptions to these generalizations, and relationships with local authorities are now generally good.[12] But these improvements do not put TECs in an axial position: rather they emphasise that their rôle is mainly to bring along skills and training programmes to meet needs defined elsewhere.

It is clear from our analysis that the capacity, quality and realism of TEC approaches in the economic development field has a long way to go. But to make progress fundamental hurdles have to be overcome. Crucial among these are, first, how government departments, particularly the DoE, relate to TECs; second, improved coordination at the regional level; third, the development of much enhanced staff skills, capacity and management; and fourth, developing a proper business-led strategy where the TEC can be seen to be advocating genuine business needs rather than what civil servants think businesses need. This involves a fundamental change to enhance the Board's control and its relation to local businesses. Like the enterprise field, therefore, the development of a proper rôle for TECs and LECs in economic and community development draws us to their relations with local businesses, how their Boards are appointed, and how their policies are defined and implemented.

Restructuring government – TEC/LEC relations

The assessment of each of the preceding chapters has required the relationship between local developments and central government departmental priorities to be unravelled. Difficulties deriving from different central government departmental priorities are also key elements of the deficiencies of structure we outlined at the outset of this chapter. Here we move the debate to the broader level of the relations of TECs and LECs with government as a whole. We assess, in turn, TECs and LECs as exit route for government; as dumping ground; and as filling a structural gap.

Exit route

The government since 1979 has been seeking to remove the state from direct provision of a wide range of former public services and instead to stimulate market and voluntary provision. It has therefore been looking for exit routes. Masden Pirie and others have argued that privatization is only one of a number of methods for changing the boundary between the state and the market.[13] The TECs and LECs are part of that exit route for government for which a very special design has been chosen to bring a business lead to former MSC unemployment programmes. But was the intention to be purely a business lead, or a more clever device to kill the programmes altogether? Left-wing critics of TECs have argued that, in the field of training, the intention was to allow the dumping of the training programmes that had been developed, or at least to reduce their size and cost.[14] For example, a *Times Education Supplement* editorial (16 December 1988) claimed that handing a lead to employers on TECs was bound to lead to declines in programmes: "The truth is that in regard to training, it is free enterprise which has failed over many decades to deliver the goods. Why should we expect it not to do so now?"

It has certainly been declared Conservative policy since at least 1964 to see training as essentially the responsibility of employers.[15] In this sense transferring responsibility for YT and ET to business was indeed a desirable exit route. It was probably really believed by ministers in the launch phase in 1987–89 that the demographic downturn and continued rapid economic growth would be the twin pressures that would force a rapid change in employers' attitudes. If this occurred, then TECs and LECs could indeed be a satisfactory exit route for government to pass to employers the remaining government levers of training policy. However, the 1990–92 recession has dispelled any belief that this opportunity exists as a long-term strategy. As a result YT, successors to ET, and other community programmes such as "Training for Work", have re-emerged as central parts of government's immediate concern to manage the political consequences of unemployment. Unemployment has deflected the government of the early 1990s, just as it did in the early 1980s and the mid-1970s. The TECs and LECs have thus had to take on the old mantle of the MSC, with the same dilemma it had, of focusing on upgrading training with funds largely targeted on the unemployed for whom there was frequently no immediate market demand. If TECs and LECs were originally a desired exit route for government they have therefore had instead to be adjusted to the alternative demand that they are unemployment training lead bodies. This leads to the concept of TECs and LECs as dumping grounds.

Dumping ground

Before unemployment again became a problem, there was a tendency for TECs and LECs to be seen by ministers as an all-purpose agency that could be used for a wide variety of purposes. There are many positive aspects to this concept, as we shall argue below. However, there is accumulating concern that there are also negative aspects – that TECs and LECs could be used to off-load their more awkward demands: "you can take it that if the government has passed the job to TECs then it is very difficult or impossible to achieve, or there is little government priority to allocate it resources" (TEC chief executive 93).

This concern was particularly raised with the Out of School Childcare initiative. Although eventually launched with £45m to cover 3 years of resources from 1993/94, initially it appeared to be an unresourced initiative. It still appears that this is only partly "new" money so that this initiative also harks back to the MSC process of earmarking and initiative-driven resourcing.[16] Many TECs were also reluctant to become involved in another TEED initiative, EA. In those 10% of areas where TECs and LECs did not take up EA it has been directly administered by TEED regional offices. In the early years of Training Credits and Investors in People (IIPs) there was also similarly resistance from some TECs to become involved. Some Chairs felt that both these programmes were underresourced or ill-thought-through. One London TEC Chair (8) commented "my whole Board has wanted to oppose credits, but we have reluctantly come round to it", largely as a result of Credits becoming a declared national policy which is now to be fully-funded in each area.

But the greatest concern has surrounded programmes for the unemployed. As we saw in Chapter 10, unemployment is perceived as an important problem in many TEC/LEC areas. But a low proportion of TECs and LECs were actually focusing on unemployment as a major goal in their early years (1990–91), although the position changed with the deepening recession in 1992–93. This indicates the reluctance with which TEC and LEC Boards have been drawn back into addressing the unemployment problem, which is confirmed in the 1993 *Financial Times* survey of TEC Directors (10 May).[17] Many Directors have seen the recession as their greatest problem of all in trying to adhere to the original mission. Although recognizing that "something has to be done" by TECs and LECs, unemployment is not necessarily the problem that Directors signed up to solve. There is some evidence of resignation by Directors growing in 1992 and 1993 as a result of the shift back to the old MSC agendas, as shown in the 1993 *Financial Times* survey.

Filling a structural gap

The confusion over mission and the gaps in programmes identified earlier has led to an inevitable questioning of whether government itself is appropriately organized for dealing with TECs and LECs. Many of the problems experienced by the TECs and LECs are similar to those of the former MSC. The TECs suffer a fundamental problem of being the creature of one government department – the DE. This has set their mission to enhance Britain's training, but has had as its chief weapon unemployment programmes, most of which have probably done little or nothing to meet the chief training needs of employers. Over a crucial period the DE was also successful in winning for itself control of part of the education budget for TVEI, WRFE and latterly FE Training Credits. It has also had a collaborative rôle with the DES and then the DFE in other aspects of FE and the Careers Service. The DE was also successful in creating an in-road into the DTI budget by capturing from 1986 to 1992 the small firms programmes connected to business counselling (BGT/BET), enterprise allowances, and the Small Firms Service (SFS). The DE, largely through its executive agency of the MSC, has been a prodigious force for change. But many of the changes that have occurred have been largely superficial, some have been negative, and most have been short-lived. Often any benefits have died with the end of the funding initiative that created the changes. A wider reform of government's departmentalized approaches, therefore, seems urgent if TECs and LECs are to have a coherent rôle.

An example has been set by the 1993/94 Strategic Guidance. This is a joint statement by DE and DTI. But to be effective the guidance needs to go further to encompass at least the DFE and DOE as the other key related departments. But this co-ordination of strategy, although desirable, has two drawbacks. Firstly, it acts even more to give TECs top-down directives by reinforcing the guidance and ORF routes of TEC–government relations. Second, it leaves the Board as still powerless to define flexible local priorities through a general budget power. This has led to consideration of more fundamental reforms of government departments.

One scenario is to integrate the DE with the DFE. Another scenario is to absorb the youth programmes of the DE into the DFE, remove the adult unemployment programmes and Employment Service to the DSS, take the remaining enterprise programmes into the DTI, and absorb the statistical services related to measuring unemployment and employment into the CSO. These proposals have the political advantage of reducing youth unemployment, but they also have considerable merit in themselves. Elsewhere it has been argued on numerous occasions that the youth education and training systems can be successfully restructured only by bringing the organization of qualifications and finance of the system into one common framework.[18] This has also been introduced into the autumn 1993 proposal to transfer YT funds from TECs to FE colleges. Merger of the DFE and DE would ensure that young people were faced by a structure of financial and other incentives aligned to the nation's strategic goals rather than to a divergent set of ministerial objectives. The NETT and NACETT/SACETT systems recently established, and the pressures from the CBI[19], all point to the need for improvement in this direction. However, as shown in Chapters 7 and 8, Britain still has two divergent structures, one based on courses and student fees through the FEFC and HEFC, the other based on vouchers through training credits. Still, too, there is a divergence of routes, earnings potential, status and transferability of students involved in NVQ, GNVQ, BTEC or "A"-Levels. As a result Britain still lacks a pattern of incentives which young people and employers face in their decisions to invest in skills which actually encourage training: the "perverse policy syndrome" is still very dominant in this area.

Similarly, in the field of enterprise and local economic development, our analysis in Chapters 9 and 10 has demonstrated the divergence of DE, DTI and DOE objectives. Considerable progress has been made in drawing these departments together since the 1993/94 year, particularly through the OSSs initiative and in Scotland. TECs and LECs are also being used successfully as exit routes for TFs and UDCs in inner cities. But there is still a clash of objectives and styles between these departments. Until a cross-departmental structure is developed, local agents will labour between divergent incentives, and businesses and individuals will face divergent, conflicting and weak incentives in the choices they face in investing in skills and business development.

Conclusion

This chapter has addressed how TECs and LECs are failing to fulfil their mission. We have focused on the chief dimensions that should not be allowed to continue unreformed. The future must deliver a local agent truly in line with the original mission. The wide gap between rhetoric and reality must be bridged if

the mission is to be satisfied. We have demonstrated in this chapter how difficult this is. We have identified crucial *deficiencies in structure*:
- Unclear mission.
- Inadequate empowerment.
- Conflict in local leadership.
- Inadequate staff skills to deliver.
- Inadequate ability of the Board to fulfil its leadership rôle.
- Cost-inefficiency.
- Budget uncertainties.

We have also called for a *redesign of geography and a rethink of size* because of:
- Diseconomies of scale.
- Poor development of management technology.
- Lack of a regional strategy.
- Poor local fit.

We have reviewed how these difficulties interrelate through each of the key programmes of training and education, enterprise, and community and economic development. This has led us to the crucial conclusion that what was designed to be an "exit route for government" has been turned into a "dumping ground". To overcome these deficiencies needs further structural reforms. We turn in Chapter 12 to what we believe is required.

Chapter 12
The Search for Business Empowerment

World class targets

In this book we have given a detailed analysis of the TEC and LEC experiment. It is the first study of the full range and depth of all their main programmes, and it seeks to be definitive and objective. Clearly we have not been able to reflect all the fine detail of variation at the local level. However, our method of assessment at the various levels of detail – national, and local, as well as through a wide range of supplementary interviews – has allowed the richness of local experiences to be assessed within the overall strategy. Much of the assessment has itself required methodological innovation, which we discuss in detail elsewhere.[1]

We have analyzed TECs and LECs against the needs of the economy and the institutional problem of improving Britain's economic performance. To achieve better performance Britain certainly needs to look to each of its mainstream factors of production – human resources, management, capital and innovation, and the local development environment. But, we have argued, tackling each aspect as a separate problem may well not lead to enduring solutions. A *perverse policy syndrome* has affected the British economy to such a penetrating extent in the past that merely applying new resources or innovation in one area is likely to fail to achieve sustained change. This is because of internal barriers to change within the area to which resources are applied, because of barriers in other areas, and because of an institutional structure that can divert resources and innovation back into maintaining existing habituated practices.

The TECs and LECs have their origin in the systems of the former MSC. Nowhere more vividly than the MSC has there been both the recognition of the need to change and the creation of its own barriers to change. The MSC was both a product of, and a cause of, the perverse policy syndrome in the fields that it covered. Every time it launched a focus on the need to enhance the skills of Britain's workforce in employment, efforts were diverted into programmes for the unemployed. This was particularly true of the 1981 New Training Initiative. It has now affected the TECs and LECs. Every time the MSC tried to create a local management solution, its central structure and the aims of government held back the granting of meaningful local powers. This was true of the LAMBs, the LENs and to a lesser extent the local aspects of the ITBs and NSTOs. It is now affecting the TECs and LECs. The reforms of TEED following the Styles Report have so far been marginal: TEED, ministers and the Treasury still exert controls that reach from the top to the smallest sub-contractor level of each TEC and LEC. Virement and flexibility in many areas have been reduced, not increased, since TECs and LECs were created, and ORF has become a mechanism more firmly to trammel TECs and LECs to central targets than to empower local leadership.

These deficiencies do not allow the TECs and LECs to achieve the world class targets that was their mission. Recall the launch statement: "We need to pursue world class standards", "Not a quick fix solution or latest flavour of the month", "We look for visions, for strategy, for mobilization of the whole employer community".

What does being *world class* mean? It means doing as well as or better than the best, not merely doing better than before. It means tackling the most difficult areas for change. The most tenaciously defended barriers will often be the ones where change is most required. And it means giving out real power from the centre, because only from real power can real change occur. In this chapter we examine how the experience learned from the TECs and LECs can be used to indicate a way forward to more fundamental reforms to meet world class targets. We address in turn below:
- Leadership and empowerment;
- TECs and LECs as strategists, purchasers, facilitators and providers;
- Learning from Scotland;
- Organizational merger;
- Bringing TECs and LECs to the market.

Leadership and empowerment

The introduction of change into a system that is highly impermeable is never going to be easy. But central power and control will always be limited in its effectiveness by the limitations of the centre to form meaningful strategy and implement it. In Chapter 6 we argued that in the choice between the four generalised models of how TECs and LECs could relate to government, the government had actually chosen a *formal recruitment* model. In this model central bodies exert control down to the programme level and funds are earmarked, Boards are merely advisers and strategists on how funds are allocated. The rhetoric of the launch phase, however, suggested that an *informal recruitment* model was being implemented. This would have been truly empowering by giving autonomy to a new Board with a general budget power. There was thus a major gap between rhetoric and reality, as we have seen throughout our earlier discussion.

Some of the gaps that have emerged were anticipated, but it was expected that they would be overcome by TECs and LECs getting greater autonomy as time progressed. For example, Tony Cann, Chairman of ELTEC, stated in 1989 that "nearly all the funding is for the training of young people, which is important, but we believe that enormous savings can be made and applied to the very vital task to promote lifetime training".[2] But as time has progressed less, not more, power has been available to Directors and Boards. The powers given to Directors in the TEC/LEC Articles of Association have been increasingly limited, not increased, each year through modifications of the Operating Agreement. This had led to increasing concern that the whole initiative is doomed to failure through disillusionment. As forecast in 1989 by John Banham, then Director-General of the CBI: "I do think that there is a real risk that if the TECs simply wind up as reconstituted Area Manpower Boards . . . the chances of keeping most of the Directors in the room committed for more than about 50 seconds are very slight".[3]

The TEC and LEC mission was born of the concept that new leadership and empowerment would facilitate change. It was born of an informal recruitment model as a possible solution to Britain's perverse policy syndrome. The concept was closely underlain by management models promoted in *New Age Values Leadership* (see, e.g. Peters and Waterman 1982). The key parts of this theory are also foreshadowed in Selznick's classic studies of the 1940s and 1950s that we introduced in Chapter 6.[4] The rhetoric of these concepts was sold to government by the CBI, Charles Handy, Cay Stratton and others. The New Age leadership model can be summarised as follows:

- Leadership is about *achieving change*; change is necessary to satisfy accelerating technological demands and the assertion of the power of the customer over the producer.
- Leadership is exercised through satisfying all of the groups and individuals who *have a stake* in the success of the organization. The leader has a type of "trustee" relationship or stewardship with the "stakeholders".
- *Stewardship* requires leaders to disseminate the vision and educate the other stakeholders, encouraging and facilitating their development.
- The leaders's rôle is to create a *strategic vision* for the stakeholders which focuses on quality, unity and cohesion, that allows opportunities for independent action to be left to each stakeholder to act within the vision.

The rôle of the leader is summarised by Fairholm (1991) in terms of the structure shown in Figure 12.1. In this approach, leadership is fundamentally about change through the development of the capacity of the stakeholders. This uses the culture and technologies of excellence, through counselling and teaching, to encourage self-led productive managers and stakeholders who are results-oriented. The vision establishes the values that let stakeholders increase their capacities for self-direction.

The rôle of the leader is thus in developing values, enhancing participation, enhancing capacity and developing motivation. This has underpinned the devel-

Figure 12.1 The role of leadership in the change of organisations (redrawn after Fairholm 1990: Figure 5.1).

opment of a greater emphasis on decentralization of power and responsibility within businesses, to produce flatter management structures, and to require a higher level of skills to produce higher levels of job satisfaction and staff involvement in each field.

In the management of businesses this has been referred to as a "tight–loose" structure: tight in terms of visions, strategies and design, loose in terms of freedom of individuals to act and the development of their capacities to do so. One consequence is that of "proximate" management – most decisions should be put to the lowest level.[5] From this it is argued that total quality and excellence should develop, which in turn should assure greater orientation to customer demands. In simple terms the over-the-counter sale is led by a complete focus on the customer which is backed up by a similar focus through the production process and after-sales support. But the vision that works is one which values the people in the organization as well as the excellence of service delivery: the two go hand in hand.

The rooting of TECs and LECs in these ideas is reflected in the emphasis of the 1988 White Papers on leadership, change and setting a strategic vision. There was also the frequent use in 1988 and 1989 by Cay Stratton, Norman Fowler and David Main of the concepts of "empowerment" and "stakeholders". These concepts, so important in the launch phase, have since been less heard and have been subject to reinterpretation. The launch phase emphasis on vision, strategy, flexibility and empowerment of stakeholders was clearly at odds with the long-term thinking and interests of self-preservation of the MSC/TEED or, indeed, the real interests of ministers. That the orchestration of this phrasing should have come to a significant extent from outside of the traditional hierarchy of the civil service – through a special adviser Cay Stratton and through the political leadership – is indicative of the difficulties of implementing real change.

Meanwhile, back in the MSC, much of the design of TECs and LECs was fed by a different use of similar management concepts. Influential in this was Charles

Handy, who had been the key adviser to the MSC's *A Challenge to Complacency* study (1985).[6] Handy had developed a series of publications, on the *Future of Work* and the improvement of organizations. These suggested to MSC and CBI leaders the crucial rôle that could be played by local networks, stimulated by new leadership and specific tasking. The rôle of enhanced leadership fitted both the political agenda, to give the private sector greater power, and pressures from other organizations that suggested that local leadership teams could make significant impacts on local economies. Influential in the local leadership debate was the CBI's report *Initiatives beyond Charity* (1986b), and Business in the Community (BiTC) which, since about 1986, had been developing Business Leadership Teams and other concepts to bring the private sector into a leading partnership position in local economies.[7]

Handy's conceptualization of the rôle of leaders is not so much one of empowerment as of core strategists defining a complex tasking structure. In the field of developing local economies it is essentially a centralizing structure because it stresses the need to bring actors together to perform specified tasks, even though it emphasizes the need for new human resource skills and upgrading the rôles of decentralized decision units. Handy's concepts were also used to fit development more closely to standard management consultancy models with a bias towards tasking in the structure of vision – strategy – tasking – implementation.

The idea that leadership could be injected into local units was the prevalent idea of the 1980s. It found an apogee in BiTC's attempts to "parachute" leadership[8] into local economies through Leadership Teams in the late 1980s. Injection of leadership was important to TECs and LECs because it appeared to suggest an instant recipe for success. Hence the TEC launch emphasis on the importance of the "highest quality business leaders" and the "crucial role of the chief executive". That the then Director-General of the CBI, John Banham, had come through the McKinsey management consultancy is suggestive that the idea of decentralization through top-down leadership found a ready ear in the CBI as well as in the MSC. The CBI in any case has also found it difficult to move beyond its history of centralism linked to its previous corporatist rôle. As a result, in this top-down version of the leadership model, the vision-setting placed at the core of Figure 12.1 was led by the CBI and MSC (and then TEED), leadership was to be exercised by the TECs and LECs, who would then disseminate a culture of excellence through new management systems and retraining of existing staff. The concept of a central vision and targets has been further reinforced by the CBI–TEED emphasis on NETT and NACETT.

We believe that this use of the leadership model is bound to fail because it relies too strongly on exhortation rather than delivery mechanisms and because the only genuine stakeholders in TECs are the civil servants among the staff. The leadership and vision are divorced from a broad range of employers, who are represented in positions on Boards, but have few effective mechanisms to transmit their requirements to others in the local community. Without transmission mechanisms and incentives, no-one will change their behaviour. There is thus a fundamental gap of genuine empowerment, from Board level to staff level to community level in TECs and LECs.

In the words of Linbert Spencer in the 1989 launch phase: "Without a vision the people perish. But what is also true is that without the people, the vision is unattainable."[9] TECs and LECs, without proper empowerment, cannot succeed. We turn in the next section to how this situation might be retrieved.

TECs and LECs as strategists, purchasers, facilitators and providers

Four models of relations between TECs, LECs and local employers have developed in practice. Each has been an attempt to link central funding and goals with local delivery. Each is capable of achieving some results. None are truly empowering; and each has been undermined, until One Stop Shops (OSSs), by TECs' and LECs' tendency to follow their own model of direct provision in the field of enterprise.

Strategists

As strategists TECs and LECs have a major rôle in transmitting a national vision for change to a local community. This is their key objective. But a strategy that has no stakeholders to transmit to is like so many of the planning documents of the 1960s and 1970s: the strategy becomes a glossy booklet that sits on the shelf. Effective strategy therefore requires a transmission mechanism that makes people and other key agents hear, listen and respond. A strategic mission to stimulate change must have a means for actually executing change. A strategy must *offer tangible benefits and be derived from the demands of those who must implement it: a strategy must be owned by the stakeholders.*

As our analysis has demonstrated, for employers TECs and LECs offer few tangible benefits in their present form: the main programmes concern the unemployed, doubts surround the sustainability of the enterprise base, even in OSSs, and in the field of education the TEC/LEC strategy has become more distant from the central focus of DFE developments. The products that could offer direct benefits to employers, such as IIP and MCI, have questions over their relevance and quality, and have few resources or leverage to encourage employers to develop change mechanisms.

Some measure of the difficulties being faced can be gauged from the *Financial Times* surveys of TEC Directors which show that over 90% of Directors were still committed to YT and ET schemes as important or very important priorities for TECs (Table 12.1). But in 1992 the highest priority was for "in-company training generally", and in 1993 73% put economic development and

Table 12.1 Rating by the TEC Directors of priorities for training schemes and satisfaction with Investors in People initiative.

	Very important		Important		Not important	
	1992	1993	1992	1993	1992	1993
Priority for Government YT scheme	62	59	34	37	1	3
Priority for Government ET scheme*	39	–	52	–	8	–
Priority for in-company training generally*	80	–	19	–	1	–
	Top priority		Second priority		Third priority	
Priority for economic development including job creation	–	73	–	27	–	0
	Very satisfied		Satisfied		Not satisfied	
IIP progress	9	13	51	52	37	33

Source: Financial Times Surveys, 25 March 1992; 10 May 1993. *Note*: * no comparable data for 1993.

job creation as the top priority. In both these areas TECs have little impact. Similarly, as also shown in Table 12.1, although 60% of TEC Directors were satisfied with progress on IIP, 37% were dissatisfied in 1992. This changed to 65% satisfied in 1993. These results indicate an overwhelming commitment by Directors to the original TEC mission, but a significant questioning that one of the main instruments of policy, IIP, was satisfactory.

The development of strategies depends on Directors who, although able and well intentioned, can rarely know or articulate the demands of local businesses as a whole. Because the overwhelming majority of local businesses are rarely involved in its design they are unlikely to hear of the strategy itself or, if they hear, are unlikely to understand or be interested in its implementation. They have not been empowered by the TEC or LEC, at best they have received marketing materials; they do not own the TEC or its policies. The rôle of TECs and LECs as strategists therefore frequently fails at the design stage. They do not satisfy the requirements set out by Norman Fowler, Secretary of State, at the launch:[10]

"If we expect employers to take the reins locally, we must give them real powers to make decisions" – "We want people .. to influence their fellow employers" – "Everyone who has a stake in the community has a stake in the TEC" – "We look to the TEC for vision, for strategy, for mobilization of the whole community".

They also have not satisfied the requirements set out by Michael Heseltine, President of the Board of Trade, at the 1992 TECs Conference:[11] "Most remarkable of all was the [TEC] philosophy . . . first, the introduction of business leadership . . . [to] inject a clear sense of focus; secondly, the importance of *partnership*, with TECs encouraged to play a co-ordinating and *enabling role*;

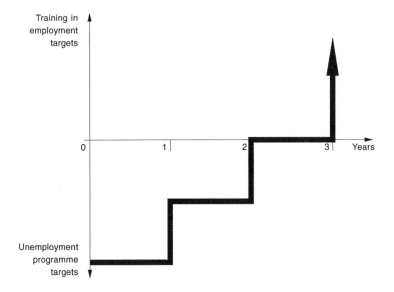

Figure 12.2 The shift in targets expected by one TEC Chair based on the developments he had been led to expect. *Source*: Interview comment by TEC Chair 95 (June 1991).

thirdly, and above all else, the emphasis on *action*". As recognized in Cay Stratton's[12] words: "Without real discretion, without the ability to make real choices about policies and programmes, we will stifle the ownership, energy and initiative of TECs before they get off the ground".

A very telling comparison can be made of the practice of TECs and the mission as it was understood by business leaders. One of the leading TEC Chairs (95) in the early phases drew a conception of the changes he believed he had been empowered to make as shown in Figure 12.2. It involves the systematic shift from unemployment to workforce training over a 3–4 year period. That was his conception, that was what he believed he had been given power to plan for, and that was what he got his Board to sign up to. As a nationally-known TEC figure this was also the mission he helped government to sell to other business leaders between 1988 and 1991. But it is not what TECs or LECs have been allowed to do with YT and ET programmes. In terms of changing targets little, if any, progress has been made from those specified in year zero in Figure 12.2.

Purchasers

As purchasers TECs and LECs have succeeded far better than as strategists. They can use government funds to purchase provision in line with their objectives. This is parallel to the strategies for Hospital Trusts, grant-maintained schools and FE colleges. A contract can be used to lever other bodies to provide training and enterprise programmes to TECs' and LECs' own requirements. Purchasing is a powerful tool for significant change, it can impose new standards and can change output/cost ratios. However, the extent of power to achieve change depends upon the importance of TEC/LEC funding sources to the contractors and the extent of alternative financial sources at lower management cost to the contractor. In the fields of YT and ET and the new Workstart programmes, TECs and LECs are dominant funders; they can make or break many providers; they have begun to exert considerable change on the former systems of provision in terms of both quality and content. In the fields of enterprise TECs are important sources of finance, but are one agent among many. LECs, in contrast, are often the key source of local enterprise finance. But both TECs and LECs have come to the enterprise field as late developers. Only with the OSSs has a clear strategy for enterprise developed which is now being implemented on the ground.

The development of OSSs illustrates the dilemma of the TEC and LEC mission. As we have seen in Chapter 9, before the OSS, there was only a weak central leadership of the enterprise vision. As a result the TECs and LECs tended to be rudderless, drifting into direct provision on a significant scale, at low levels of efficiency in terms of costs/output ratios, with an over-broad and ill-formed agenda, and frequently competing with and displacing, rather than complementing, other local agents or the market. The OSSs have provided the strategy previously lacking: but it is a *central* strategy. Similarly, central leadership and ORF targets have been necessary to achieve change in the training fields. But ORF is a central mechanism. Central guidance has been required because local strategies have not been business-led and concentrated on real business needs. Instead they commonly derived from the haphazard inheritance of former TEED programmes and from local strategies led by Directors with rarely a wide enough power or experience of government programmes to adapt them to market demand. No commercial organization seeks to spread itself over an ill-focused range of products and tries to compete with cost/output ratios which we have shown to be up to four times higher than competitors. Only a public sector programme could do this, but it is not clear why it should. Lack of proper empowerment of employers, therefore, explains the ineffectiveness of the TEC and LEC early enterprise policies, not a lack of centralization.

Facilitators

As facilitators, TECs and LECs have sought to use their influence either through their main sources of finance (i.e. by leverage), or by becoming involved in local planning processes with other agents as partners. Facilitating involves encouraging other agents to participate and undertake an activity. This should produce a multiplier effect by levering other resources or improving effectiveness. This contrasts with the rôle of a purchaser buying specific products. In Cay Stratton's view at the launch, the TEC and LEC "must use its resources to leverage new funds for community reinvestment, for programme innovation, for institutional change".[13] The capacity of TECs and LECs to lever change through their rôle as facilitator is obviously more limited than their rôle as purchaser. It depends on the extent of commitment to change by the other agents with which they are involved, and the extent of financial leverage. Clearly when financial leverage becomes significant, the rôle of facilitator comes close to that of purchaser. Where the leverage is low and the partner is distant from the vision for change, the likelihood of positive development has smallest potential. This is where the learning and educational rôle of the leader in the New Age Values model would come into play. But in the field of institutional links there have been few reasons why agents should attend the class in which TECs are the teachers.

The experience of TECs and LECs evidences these dilemmas. The most successful facilitation has been in targeted areas where the TEC/LEC rôle has been significant or where the change sought has been least dramatic. This has characterized many of the small firm and self-employment programmes developed with enterprise agencies. Facilitation has been least successful where TEC/LEC leverage is low and the external agent has been least amenable to change: for example, in the fields of education and employer involvement. The problem for TECs has been that in most of the areas which are most central to their missions they are relatively minor players or are one agent among many. For example, in the field of enterprise, facilitation should have a good chance of success because it is here where the TECs and LECs are important players who could work with the two or three other key agents (Chambers of Commerce, enterprise agencies and local authorities). But in this field their rôle as facilitator has been undermined by their drift into direct provision which has removed their scope for leverage; direct provision has also undermined their credibility both to ensure quality provision and as partners for change. Facilitation can work as a general model only when partners come to share a common vision and strategy. Thus the problem experienced in the facilitator rôle echoes the difficulty of forming a strategy that is founded on, and is owned by, the local business community.

Providers

Direct provision is probably the most dangerous of the traps which TECs and LECs have fallen into. Cay Stratton recognized at the outset that

> The TEC is not about direct programme delivery. Its success depends in many respects upon being distanced from delivery. If it is to be a catalyst for change, if it is to influence people and institutions beyond its immediate control, the TEC must be broadly perceived as an objective intermediary organization. It must be convenor, facilitator, broker, the builder of coalitions and networks".[14]

Stratton saw that direct delivery reduced the scope for the TEC and LEC to influence others. But she also saw direct delivery as a deflection from the vision to be a strategic body: "The TEC can achieve its ends only if it retains its position as . . . a strategic body, eschewing the temptation of dabbling in direct service delivery".[15] Direct provision, therefore, has been a critical trap for TECs and LECs to fall into. It is completely at odds with the public sector management reform that was intended, but should not come as a surprise since the TECs are staffed mainly by former civil servants with administrative rather than business skills. Since direct provision is also the mode of delivery most frequently adopted for the enterprise and IIP areas, the flaw is the more crucial. Enterprise programmes and IIP are the areas connecting the TEC/LEC to local employers. Direct provision compromises this vital connection as well as undermining its independence. Direct provision by TECs and LECs is also very difficult to market effectively. The early assessments of the market potential for OSSs have demonstrated that there is nothing more likely to put off employers than anything that looks like government or is linked with government[16] – which a TEC and a LEC are pre-eminently recognized to be.[17]

The critical gaps from which TEC and LECs suffer are, therefore, at the level of strategist and facilitator. The contractor relationship can generally be made to work well. Being a strategist or facilitator requires a link to employers and other agents on a wide scale, a mechanism to transmit change, and a means of framing strategy on the basis of a broad concept of demands. Since demands from employers are extremely diverse, and are often conflicting and competitive with each other, the framing of strategy cannot be as a simple *static plan*. It must instead be based on a *dynamic mechanism* or a *process* that responds to market demand. The idea of a Board of leaders overseeing a centrally-defined model of meeting national targets, therefore, looks ludicrous. It mirrors the Soviet 5-year planning model. Market demand can be satisfied only by a market system of supply. This leads us next to consider how TECs and LECs might be improved in a strategic sense. We first consider what lessons the more successful Scottish LECs offer, and then move to consideration of organizational merger, and the development of a model for bringing the strategy to market through a proper system of local empowerment.

Learning from Scotland

Scotland's LECs have already become considerably more successful local agents than TECs, as we have demonstrated in Chapters 9 and 10. They have achieved this through being more business-led in their strategy, by being a strong focus of local integration with other agents, and by moving away from a programmatic emphasis towards a strategic focus, staffed with personnel with higher levels of business skills. In making this considerable achievement the LECs have been advantaged, as we saw earlier, by having only one government department

Table 12.2 Contrast of the key characteristics of TECs and LECs (modified and developed from presentation by John Lord, Chief Executive of Ayrshire LEC, 21 April 1993).

TECS	LECS
· Contract with government	· Contract with SE/HIE
· Head office/subsidiary relationship	· Federal structure
· Several sponsoring departments	· Scottish Office
· Complex local delivery and links	· LECs lead locally
· Focus chiefly on training and enterprise	· Full range of economic development services
· Funds allocated by volume/performance	· Funds allocated monthly by strategic fit to needs
· Civil service-led, programme-focused	· Locally led with specific skills of staff "unpicking" programmes
· NAO audit trail to smallest subcontractor	· NAO audit trail stops at SE/HIE

to deal with, having SE and HIE as intermediary bodies, and by getting close to business needs through partnerships with targeted sets of companies.

The contrasts of the key characteristics of TECs and LECs are summarised in Table 12.2. As a result of these benefits the LEC has been able to become the major local business agent developing and focusing the lateral links in each locality. The contrast of this focal position with the confused rôle of TECs is illustrated in Figure 12.3.

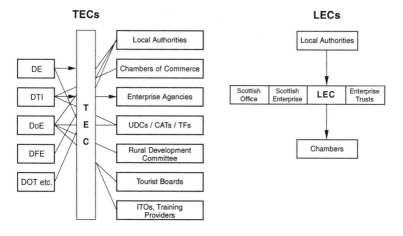

Figure 12.3 Contrast of the lateral links TECs have to make and the position of LECs as the key local linkage body. *Source*: Based on a presentation by John Lord, Chief Executive of Ayrshire LEC (21 April 1993).

The marked contrast in structure and relative success of LECs compared with TECs has led to the question being asked of whether TECs could become LECs. This became a focal debate between TECs, G10 and TEED in 1992, but now has little immediate chance of happening. The concept of a form of SE or HIE for English regions has not proved easy for ministers to handle, even though there is favour for enhancing the rôle of the regional offices of government departments. For the TECs, there have therefore remained many of the awkward relations of TECs with government that we have outlined in Chapter 6.

To allow TECs to reach the effectiveness of LECs first requires a government commitment to achieve integration; on the one hand, to bring departmental initiatives together, and on the other hand, to lever change by empowering the local level, which can be achieved only by giving up power at the centre. A second issue is departmental parentage: the need to shift TECs further from the single departmental parent of the DE. Learning from the lesson of the joint DTI/DE strategic guidance to TECs in 1993/94, the DFE and DOE should also be fully committed to TEC development in the future. Third is the credibility gap of TEC staff. Whereas Scottish LECs have replaced over half their former TA staff with personnel with specific skills and recent private sector experience, many TECs have yet to begin this process, on average over 85% of TEC staff were derived from the TA even in mid-1993, and most TECs have committed themselves to their staff until 1996. Fourth is a readiness by government to accept that TECs may have to become junior partners in some areas where other existing agents are strong and effective, e.g. in Birmingham, Manchester or Sheffield with strong local government and Chambers, or in the Thames Valley with strong Chambers. Fifth is the need to drive the whole system of debate closer to the customer – the individual trainee and the employer.

English region versions of SE and HIE would have the capacity to achieve many of these developments. Even for Scotland a greater power to SE and HIE has been urged.[18] In general, the regional level offers benefits of being an intermediary between TEED and TECs, offers strategic economies of scale, increases international promotability, and overcomes many of the issues of boundaries and geography. Although it has slipped from the agenda for reform in England, we feel that the regional issue must be readdressed.

In the case of the integrated economies of the conurbations, particularly London and Manchester, this is extremely urgent. These two conurbations are highly fragmented by local government – 33 London boroughs and 10 metropolitan districts, respectively. The TECs number 9 and 6, respectively. The fragmentation of agents is already extreme and no significant force exists to bind agents together. For TEED to treat all TECs as independent and competitive bodies in these areas further exacerbates the fragmentation.

But the regional issue is not the only way of developing an intermediary rôle between TECs and government. A body for England as a whole could have been developed which would have the same characteristics as SE or HIE. At the end of the day, the failure to develop such a model for England has not been because government did not want to allow it, but because TECs rejected any form of strong central body. They argued vigorously that each TEC must keep a direct line to ministers and that this was critical to the idea of the business lead. Senior DE spokespeople would argue that the direct line would survive the creation of an intermediary body, but its benefit they feel is in any case "largely an illusion: the TECs over-estimate its importance".

The TECs have lost out on significant benefits as a result. We would argue that the most significant elements of the Scottish model is that the intermediary:
- Largely eliminates the programmatic budget-line accounting: programmes do not appear in the parliamentary vote, therefore they are not in the specific Treasury scrutiny. This facilitates virement, prioritization and the move to develop a strategic overview.
- Stops the audit trail at the intermediary level, thus freeing LECs to develop their own accounting priorities, cultivating a relationship of trust with the centre and reinforcing local empowerment.
- In turn allows a broader budget power that need not be based on ORF with its implications for trammelling TECs line-by-line of the budgets and sub-budgets.

These gains are enormously significant. The TECs and government have rejected the concept of an SE for England too lightly. The Scottish LECs offer an important lesson for England on how to move towards a chance of achieving world class targets. Without reform, the structure of central–local relations will remain an impediment to TECs for the foreseeable future.

Organizational merger

A critical means for business empowerment is to develop TECs and LECs as membership organizations. Like other voluntary bodies, membership can then be developed into a representative system – through election, a governing council, and so on. This is one mechanism for linking individual businesses to a local strategic body that can develop a vision that is owned by business and that has a hope of being implemented by its business members.

We have assessed TEC/LEC membership schemes in Chapter 4, and further seen in Chapter 9 the conflict that they inevitably produce with the established business membership bodies at the local level, the Chambers of Commerce. Membership as a mechanism for enhancement of the TECs and LECs as bodies for local empowerment of businesses cannot therefore be developed without considering the relationships between TECs/LECs and Chambers. Chambers are the long-standing business membership bodies that are owned by, and are empowered to represent, local businesses. Recognizing this issue has led to the evolution of various plans to link the TECs/LECs and Chambers, leading up to full merger.

Merger of TECs/LECs and Chambers is constrained by the fundamental characteristics of each body. *Chambers* must preserve the key characteristics of (i) ownership by business, (ii) independence of government control, (iii) business service focus on information, international trade, representation, communication, networking and skills, and (iv) a focus for businesses' liaison with other agents.[19] *TECs and LECs* are subject to equally rigorous guidelines from government: (i) members of TEC Boards must be of chief executive status, one-third non-business members, size of about 15, (ii) they must show clear leadership skills and vision, (iii) there must be separation of training contracting and training delivery, (iv) there should be clear audit trails for government funding allowing external scrutiny of subcontractor accounts, (v) staff contract and employment conditions are set by TEED, (vi) there should be independence from local hosts, reflected in Secretary of State controls on TEC partnerships and subsidiary companies.[20]

Some of these different characteristics of TECs/LECs and Chambers are incompatible or difficult to align. However, as we have argued, leadership has nothing to do with large firms and SMEs have been shut out by the Board requirement. Others can more easily be brought together. Many are concerns raised by civil servants concerned to protect the rôle of TEED, rather than government policy.

In the most senior views of the DE it is the criteria for Board membership which are "the last thing to go". The most fundamental problem has been the desire for TECs/LECs to be independent of hosts. This derives from the experience of LAMBs and LENs and is very much part of history as interpreted by the MSC. It is the desire for this independence of hosts that ironically is the fundamental brake on empowerment: local employers and the community cannot be empowered if they do not own and hold responsibility. There is now evidence that the assertion of the need for independence is being played down through recognition that it is not the independence of leadership of the board that is so crucial, but independence of TEC/LEC contracting:[21] i.e. that TECs and LECs should be facilitators and purchasers rather than providers. The concerns over independence and enhancement of mission can be achieved through the contracts with TECs and LECs (via SE and HIE in Scotland) and using TECs and LECs as "enablers" as with tendering of work from local authorities. Franchizing is also a further mechanism that can be explored.[22] Hence, it is now clear that the initial concept of "untrammelled leadership" can be unpicked and reinterpreted as the need for clear accountability ("someone to get at if things go wrong"). This development of views allows a major step forward in the possible form of merger that can be envisaged.

The merger issue was initially raised at the 1991 Sunningdale meeting, but the pace has been set only since the 1993 emergence of OSSs. This has led G10, the ABCC and the enterprise agencies to become engaged in detailed discussions of how merger, and steps towards merger, might be developed. Two possible options for merging TECs and Chambers are now being used as a starting point[23] (see Figure 12.4):

OPTION A

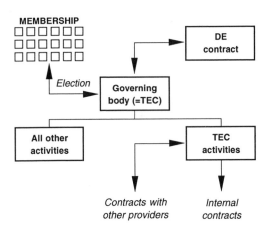

OPTION B

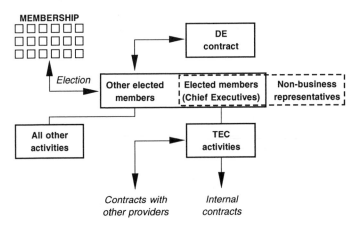

Figure 12.4 Two options for merger of TECs and Chambers (modified after Price Waterhouse 1992)

A new wholly-integrated organization: full merger: This has the *advantages* of integrating management and achieving economies of administration, enhanced critical mass of the whole, a simple structure to market and sell, removal of "turf" competition, making the TEC responsible to members and allowing a high level of devolution of services. The new body would lose the separate identity of each previous body, and would have to wrestle with restrictions on the Board to meet DE requirements, difficulties of linking non-business Board members fully into management to retain compatibility with business leadership, and no single group might have its eyes fixed clearly on the DE–TEC contract. The Board of the Chamber would also become a much smaller entity equal in size to the TEC Board (this can also be seen as an advantage);

A new organization with a separate TEC sub-committee: This has many of the advantages of the first option, although each is less strongly developed. The chief characteristics are the same, with the addition that the structure is more complex. The DE contract for the TECs also has to be made with the organization as a whole, which might dilute the TEC vision.

Merger has not been an easy issue to confront. Most mergers are usually de facto takeovers so that, between TECs and Chambers, there has been concern for who wins and who loses. We would argue that ultimately it does not matter who wins or loses provided that a strong business-led solution results that means that the local business community gains. But we would also argue that the merger of TECs and Chambers is potentially a win–win merger: Chambers gain greater resources and influence, enhanced links to government and national vision; TECs gain legitimacy, credibility, access to employers and a self-sustaining base. In the words of one of the leading TEC chief executives (6) in late 1992: "The key point is the fragility of TECs, which are becoming more fragile with time as Treasury controls increase and as initial momentum wanes. It is critical to link TECs with structures that have an independent life, credibility and local employer ownership".

Experience to date of attempts to develop mergers demonstrate that in most cases there are still some fundamental difficulties to be overcome. This particularly concerns the *objectives* of the merged organization, its *management* style, the *staff* terms and conditions, balancing *enabling and purchasing* (the TEC rôle) with *delivery of services* (the Chamber rôle). But, as we have argued throughout this book, empowerment means allowing local solutions to overcome these problems. The merger of the key Chamber objectives of *representing and servicing* can be fitted with the TECs' mission of *changing and influencing* local developments. To make progress requires local commitment, as well as national leadership from TEED, G10 and ABCC. We conclude that government must be prepared to allow mergers to develop. Government must be prepared to let go of TECs.

The path of development that appears to be occurring on the ground is one of a stage-wise process allowing a learning and experience to develop. A fundamental building block of development is co-location. Some examples are now evolving of de facto mergers. Leading cases are in South and East Cheshire, Barnsley and Doncaster, and with a wider remit involving the local authority in Northamptonshire. Since the launch of the OSSs initiative in 1993 many other local initiatives are developing. We argue that this local *learning process* is an important part of the way forward: we have to learn by *doing*. What is being sought is not easy and has no ready-made solutions, certainly not ready-made to suit the individuality of local circumstances. Government must be prepared to allow the true flexibility locally that lets these local solutions develop.

The merger of TECs/LECs and Chambers has the capacity to bring together Britain's two main concepts of business leadership. On the one hand, TECs and LECs have:
- A mission for *change*.
- Mechanisms of *leverage*.
- *High-level* business *leadership*.
- A partnership with government that embraces a *national vision*.
- Substantial government *financial backing* (although this also brings government interference).
- A *national network* covering the whole country.
- A *well-resourced* core staff and resources offering potential critical mass in each area.

On the other hand, Chambers of Commerce have:
- *Ownership* by businesses through membership, elections and governing councils/boards, what TEC Chair 60 called giving "legitimacy of access".
- A *representative* structure of local businesses.
- A capacity for *strategic vision*.
- A *self-sustaining and independent resource base* (though often small this is a crucial ingredient to ensure that money is properly valued and that the agent *acts like a business*).
- A *national network* (though patchy in some areas).
- A focus on *local services* bringing them into a position of seeking to fill gaps in the market.

The merger of the two concepts offers the opportunity to create a very powerful local vehicle for business development. It would empower the business stakeholders. Mergers are to be encouraged where they can be developed. In the words of the 1991 Sunningdale Concordat, the concept of TECs-plus-chambers-plus-enterprise agencies offers the potential to be equal to the best local service bodies in Europe (e.g. the *Handelskammern* in Germany).

But merger alone leaves two critical gaps. First, as long as membership is voluntary, penetration of the market will be weak. The best large-scale Chambers in Britain achieve a 20–30% membership of the businesses in their areas. There is no reason to believe that merger with TECs and LECs would increase this proportion more than marginally, although it would offer resources to help increase penetration in areas that do not presently achieve that level. Hence merger alone will not empower or allow access to the whole business community. Second, the mechanism of Chamber elections with governing Councils or Boards is an imperfect way of responding to the market need for local business services. It can suffer similar defects to that of election to local authority councils. It is not a market system at all, it finds difficulties in representing the full diversity of business needs, and it can become a means for a small group of people to exercise an ineffective control. The higher the proportion of businesses that are members, the more there are difficulties of making electoral systems work as representative systems to satisfy market demands. The experience of the Chambers in Britain and the much larger public-law Chambers in Europe evidences the danger of becoming driven by committees and not by response to the needs of the market.[24] Hence, to be effective, any merged organization has itself to *act like a business*. Membership is an important ingredient for empowerment of business, but it is not an effective mechanism alone for satisfying business's needs. We turn below to how ownership can be combined with satisfying business's needs in order to enhance the benefits of TEC/LECs mergers with Chambers.

Bringing TECs and LECs to market

Business' needs are defined by the competitive situation of each employer. A business looks to its profitability, long-term growth potential, change in demand for its products and returns to its factor inputs. It does not look to visions and missions defined by government, or anyone else but itself, unless they clearly offer a gain to the business in any of its main trading requirements. The redesign of local business agents such as TECs, LECs and Chambers must start from this premise. The starting point is business needs. Empowerment for employers is about meeting the needs of the market, not about the "turf" of different agencies, about which businesses know little and often care still less.

The rôle of intermediary agents like TECs, LECs and Chambers can only be justified, therefore, by the focus of their activities being on needs that would not be covered in any other way by the market. This leads us to understanding that the basis of policy development must be to enhance those areas where businesses acting individually cannot improve their performance. There are four chief areas where individual businesses can fail to enhance performance:

(i) Externalities to individual businesses – these are activities such as training and environmental concerns by which each individual business has incentives to opt out even though it is in their collective interest to act. This stimulates "free riding". (ii) Limits on the ability of businesses to perceive the key issues for their development, especially for small and medium-sized firms. To overcome this gap often needs pooling of resources, information, peer support and extensive management education. (iii) Long time periods for development, particularly of business R&D. This often requires start-up funds and long-term strategic commitment, where government can play a rôle. But the key requirement is for government to provide a sustained and supportive environment for innovation. (iv) Lack of information on what are business' needs. This requires a business information service tightly tailored to business needs.

These areas can each be tackled through developing local mergers of TECs and Chambers. This alone would establish a force to integrate agents into a shared vision and range of programmes that can deliver quality local business support services.

Service merger is the aim of OSSs, the ambitions of which have been widened in some agents' perceptions to cover economic development as well as business services. Service merger has the key advantages of overcoming overlaps and competition, filling gaps, enhancing the emphasis on quality, gains through common marketing, and linking the TEC and Chamber missions. Service merger also gives a primary emphasis to responding to businesses' needs.

The development of OSSs has stimulated a number of surveys to research where these market gaps lie.[25] These generally indicate that the potential market for a Chamber TEC OSS is:

- Greater market, client and legislative *information*.
- Client, consultant and advice *marriage-broking*.
- *Marketing advice*.
- *Management* and *supervisor training*.
- *Disputes processing* and prompt payment.

There is, in contrast, only a small market for training-led products such as YT and ET, or for the specific management training products of MCI and IIP. As we have shown, the criticisms of IIP centre on businesses wanting management and supervisor training to be closely tailored to their needs, not the reverse.

What is also clear from surveys and experience is that the main demand for services is at a basic level and the next level up. This reflects the demand for existing Chamber and enterprise agency services, and also European Chamber systems which provide at least 65% of advice, counselling and consulting services over the telephone or by correspondence/fax. Even beyond basic technical advice, the next level of consultation and technical information can still often be delivered over the phone or by correspondence/fax. Except for start-up advice and areas of new technology, the level of face-to-face contacts can be low. But to give this high-level advice by phone, or face-to-face, needs a high level of staff expertise. The *new* service focus of the OSSs could fit into this rôle. The Prospectus (DTI 1992: 7–8) calls for "business advisers, organized on account manager principles . . . [who will] develop a long-term relationship with a portfolio of businesses, focused particularly on small companies with growth potential". These advisers could play a key rôle at the centre of the market niche outlined above.

However, there are major difficulties for a merged TEC–chamber OSS going far down the service development route. Many business advisers already exist in the market, so that merged TEC–chamber OSSs must be clear what value they add. If the costs are to be free or low-cost, there must be care to prevent "crowding out" of the private sector and hence the removal of competition. There is also an important question of the tradeoff of Chamber subscriptions and fees. The link of business advisers to membership is therefore crucial to target services on expressed collective business needs that fit market gaps, rather than developing a body that displaces the market and reduces competition.

At the same time, services focused on market needs must be delivered by organizations with a critical mass sufficient to provide acceptably low unit costs to its members and to government. The total resources available for enterprise support will always be smaller than the potential demand. Basing the OSSs on TECs and small areas within TECs risks dividing resources into "penny parcels" between too many geographical outlets. The ABCC National Chamber Development Strategy has been one of the few to recognize the need for critical mass. It has costed the requirements of a quality staff and premises: approximately £1m to put a German quality standard of Chamber of Commerce in place. TECs also cost at least £1m to "put on the road" in terms of central management costs (see Chapter 11). Thus significant economies could be achieved from a TEC–chamber merger and this should reduce unit costs. But these economies will not be fully achieved in a network of 82 OSSs to cover each TEC in England and Wales. A major merger of TECs is required. The ABCC strategy suggests that the number of merged TEC–chamber hubs for Britain as a whole is realistically of the order of 40–50, based on the economics of delivery. This suggests the need to rationalize delivery of OSSs between groups of TECs rather than single TECs. This is particularly evident in London, the North West and West Midlands. In Scotland economies of scale have been gained through the division of rôles with SE and HIE.

The TEC–chamber merger route can, therefore, bring Chambers closer to market. OSSs provide a strategy for the development of these business services. Merged TECs and Chambers could allow these services to be developed within a strategic body combining the strengths of both systems and overcoming some of their crucial weaknesses. It brings the main business stakeholders into control of TECs and LECs. But is merger and service development enough? For the present these developments represent important steps forward to fill the four gaps in market provision identified earlier in this discussion (p. 308), the last three would be well on the way to being filled.

The critical gap that remains is the first: how to overcome the externality incentives to individual firms to opt out or not to participate. The government has so far set itself against public-law Chambers following the German model, although in his 1989 book Michael Heseltine mooted developments of this form. But with a government-funded agency such as a TEC merged with a business-led agency such as a Chamber, it becomes far more feasible to envisage a political solution. One element of this could be the development of business registration. The ABCC (1993) has launched a campaign for business registration as a means both to reduce red tape and to co-ordinate government's regulatory leverage on businesses. The Chambers are advocated as the local agent within OSSs to manage this register and to advise businesses on regulatory controls.

Business registration would also overcome a further difficulty. The DE have argued that the lack of compulsory membership in British Chambers is a brake on government's ability to let go of enterprise policy. Because Chambers only represent approximately 10% of all businesses, government has to be concerned with policy towards the rest. But this is a fallacious argument: if government is worried about the poor level of membership and genuinely desires to empower a local business body that can take on government's policy requirements, then it is in government's hands to help create a fully representative body through a registration scheme or other mechanism.

A registration system for all businesses would also have significant side-benefits of providing for the first time in Britain a reliable information base on the number, character and location of businesses – a most significant resource for business policy. But the main purpose would be to identify clients and to allow business liaison and government policies to be better developed. A second step could be the levy of a small fee for registration, which would then be available to the new local agent as a "subscription" for core services. This fee would have to be graduated by size of company, and could be zero for the self-employed and micro-businesses, or these could be exempt from registration altogether. These developments would give to the local agent a "property right" over local business representation to government, particularly for middle-sized businesses, that ensured business representation in local authority, education, vocational education, training, enterprise, planning and local environmental policy decisions. This right could then used to subcontract and manage a variety of services through contracts with the merged TEC–chambers. This approach would have many similarities to the key aspects of the Chambers of Commerce in Germany: it would provide quality "business self-administration". But it would build on Britain's special experiences and would be far more closely led by the market.

A further opportunity also exists to overcome many of the present tensions with local government. This is to develop an explicit rôle for the new local business agent over non-domestic rates. The defects of the uniform business rate system since 1990 have severely undermined the relevance of local government consultations with businesses. In an earlier study (Bennett and McCoshan 1993) we have already advocated using the non-domestic rates as a basis for funding merged TECs and Chambers. As a powerful independent local taxing body merged TECs and Chambers would have a natural and strong influence with local authorities. It would also replace the lost consultative rights resulting from the national setting of the Uniform Business Rate since 1990. Business would be for the first time in an equal position to lobby and bargain with local government. This would be the most significant step for empowering businesses locally. Significant resources would be available for businesses to work with local government for the economic development of their area. This power of local taxation of business by business is similar to that existing in Germany and Austria. In these countries it is a key part of the concept of "business self-administration".

Business self-administration through Chambers has offered to the German government a means to contract out a variety of business-related services, to hand over regulatory issues, to develop leverage on businesses, as well as offering a means directly to stimulate business innovation and economic growth. If the objective of encouraging business innovation is as central to Michael Heseltine's objectives as he implies in his new emphasis for the DTI,[26] then giving a merged TEC–chamber body control of the administration of registration would be a significant *necessary condition* to develop the concept of business self-administration in Britain. Granting of an autonomous revenue source through a power to levy on a part of the non-domestic rates would be the most effective *sufficient condition* for local self-administration which would guarantee the independence from government that is essential to empower. We recognize that this is a radical step. But it would be one of the most effective routes to bond a partnership between government and business which offered to government a body with which it could develop effective contracting and policy programmes with guaranteed ability to transmit them to most businesses.

Looking forwards

We have argued that one of the key elements of Britain's economic capacity that needs to be addressed is a form of "system failure" – a perverse policy syndrome where the networks of effective communication that connect the signals of demand and supply for business requirements break down. The needs of the economy have often been forgotten behind social and other policy. This breakdown can be ascribed, above all, to an absence of effective networks that allow the appropriate economic signals of the demands of economic producers to be received by suppliers. Each supply issue in an economy depends upon an institution, or group of institutions, to assure its delivery. A "systems failure" indicates that some or all of these institutions are performing imperfectly. TECs and LECs have sought to improve the performance of many of the most important of these institutions. But, we have argued, they themselves have become caught up in the same systems failures and are a further manifestation of the deep-seated influence of the perverse policy syndrome, through deflection of their economic mission away from a focus on the workforce to the social problem of targeting the unemployed.

The most crucial system failure to which TECs and LECs contribute is to repeat the traditional belief that a central mission can be parachuted to local leaders. Local empowerment has not been complete. The local leaders represent no-one, have no broad base of legitimacy, and no means of transmission of the message. We have argued in this chapter that empowerment can be won only by bringing TECs and LECs to market. That bringing a proper market emphasis to the mission sought for TECs and LECs can be achieved only by working with the concept of Chambers of Commerce and a membership/registration structure. But a true market base to stimulate change among employers and managers needs a radical change to both TECs/LECs and Chambers. The concepts of both have much to offer. Mergers are an important way of developing the model of a powerful local business body. But we see mergers of TECs and LECs with Chambers as only part of the solution to the needs of the market.

We argue that the only effective way to achieve the reforms required is to translate the "tight–loose" concept into a different structure altogether. The tightness should not be institutional and ORF budgetary straight-jackets deriving from one or several ministries and the Treasury. It should be through the regulatory environment which we advocate should be delegated by government to the merged TEC–chambers to administer. The looseness should not be the fine tuning of the ORF targets of government programmes. It should be a general financial power which we advocate is offered through the ability to levy from all or part of the non-domestic rates. Government cannot expect initiatives like TECs and LECs to work effectively if local business leaders do not own and cannot transmit their mission. To achieve meaningful change government has to empower "business self-administration". This is both a necessary and a sufficient condition for sustained economic growth.

The model we propose can move in steps as a learning process. It cannot be designed in all its detail for all areas from the centre. A framework for evolution, adaptation and learning should be developed. We identify the following action steps:

1. Allow the experience of OSSs to feed directly into progress towards local models for Chamber–TEC merger and the identification of business service needs.

2. Government must be prepared genuinely to let go of detailed controls so that businesses can genuinely run TECs and LECs. This means acting to overcome the key defects summarised in Chapter 11:

- Reaffirm the mission of business-led local development.
- Back up the mission by handing power to local groups through Chamber–TEC mergers.
- Lead the way nationally to merger solutions.
- Free the merged body to recruit and manage staff flexibly; end civil service secondments immediately; restructure staff and recruit business skills.
- Develop an election and membership framework for TEC Boards.
- Reduce the number of TECs and LECs by about one-half to make efficiency gains, applying these resources to the development of proper local outreach

services.

- Develop a proper strategic intermediary body similar to SE or HIE, not G10, for cooperation between merged TEC–chambers to mediate negotiations with government.

3. Develop a much wider framework of market-testing and experience with local business services, shifting from ORF targeting to market definitions of needs using enabling and franchizing, with a level of discretion over budgets at least equivalent to that in LECs.

4. Shift from government grants and contract funding to genuine "business self-administration" through business registration and the grant of a local taxing power on business through part of the non-domestic rates. This should then allow the removal of Treasury limitations and detailed audit trails in favour of business self-limiting its resource demands to fit its needs through its own collective decision making vehicle.

These are practical steps, the first three of which could be developed within 1 or 2 years. The fourth step is consequent upon the development of the first three, and could also follow quickly.

TECs have become a quango: a business-led body mainly doing government's job for the unemployed. They have given government a private sector lead to these programmes that was badly needed. Many significant improvements have been made that should not be underestimated. But far from fulfilling their mission of being world class, business-led entities supporting mainstream development of skills and enterprise, TECs are increasingly likely to drift into a second tier rôle as business leaders lose interest and staff with few business skills exert ever greater control. Business empowerment has become largely a sham. A rescue package is needed, and it is needed urgently. Scotland's LECs offer many of the concepts that a reform package requires. Driven to a much greater extent by the economic needs of business, exercising much greater flexibility of delivery, developing more appropriate staff recruitment and skills, and mediating government and civil service centralized mechanisms through SE and HIE, Scottish LECs have made many of the most important developments needed to become a truly effective local economic body. But TECs and LECs require further radical reform if they are to fulfil the mission Britain needs for a completely effective and high quality local business development body. We have outlined a draft agenda for these further reforms that would be truly empowering of business self-administration. Only by such radical reform will Britain make the genuine economic leap it requires for its economy to be able to overcome many of the most important gaps in economic growth and development which we have referred to as the perverse policy syndrome. We hope that our discussion has advanced that process of reform.

Appendix

Methodology

The information presented in this book is based to a large extent upon surveys and interview research conducted specifically for the analysis. The bulk of the material was gathered through original surveys conducted by the authors, the data from which have been combined with secondary sources including published national statistics to develop a comprehensive picture of the early development of TECs and LECs. The aims of the project were to establish in detail how the new TEC and LEC initiative was developing, and to evaluate its effectiveness. Most of the main surveys were conducted in 1990–92, but interviews with key individuals at national and local level have continued to mid-1993.

The major objectives of the surveys were:

- A requirement for both intensive and extensive data, both "hard" and "soft" information;
- Comprehensive coverage of all aspects of TECs' and LECs' operations;
- Information from TECs and LECs themselves about their aims and activities;
- Independent data about all TECs and LECs, and comment from other agents about their performance.

These requirements led to the methodology adopted. Its approach employed five distinct techniques, as follows:

(i) National coverage of statistical information objective indicators across all TECs and LECs;

(ii) Postal questionnaire surveys of all TECs and LECs;

(iii) A set of detailed face-to-face interviews were conducted with a majority sample of TECs and LECs;

(iv) In-depth case studies of a subsample of 20 TECs and LECs (supplemented by a specific sample of all 9 London TECs);

(v) Broad-ranging interviews with other national bodies and a wide spread of TEC/LEC Chairs and Board members.

The national coverage across all TECs and LECs concerned both the organizations themselves and their local areas. This was gathered from a range of sources, and in some cases involved reaggregation of raw figures where TEC/LEC geographical areas were not co-extensive with those for which data are published.

APPENDIX

These data included:
- Population (totals and density);
- Employment/unemployment (totals and rates);
- Local industrial mix;
- Number of businesses by different size groups;
- TEC/LEC staffing;
- TEC/LEC budgets.

Postal questionnaire surveys of all TECs and LECs sought a wide coverage of TECs and LECs at each stage in their development. The survey posed a small number of straightforward questions despatched on a single sheet to all TECs and LECs. The exercise was very successful, with follow-up response rates ranging from 70 to 100%. Three surveys covered 1990, 1991 and 1992 (Bennett et al. 1993b). Question areas included:
- TEC/LEC substructure;
- Links to local enterprise agency or trusts;
- Links to Chambers of Commerce;
- Physical development activities;
- R&D strategies;
- Development of education–business partnerships;
- WRFE;
- Membership schemes;
- Specific initiatives/projects.

Detailed face-to-face interviews with a majority sample of TECs and LECs. This followed detailed piloting and was undertaken by an intensive series of meetings with TEC and LEC officers (in almost all cases the chief executive) across the country during 1991, with some follow-ups in 1992 and 1993. A range of themes was examined which was both extensive and intensive in scope. The extensive coverage sought to represent all types of TEC and LEC by size, type (e.g. metropolitan/rural coverage) and by region. The visits covered 62 TECs and LECs in all, which represents 60% of the total, the proportions in Scotland and Wales being higher in order to capture sufficient diversity in these areas. The intensive survey was designed to explore issues in depth, and allowed flexibilities for free-ranging answers not always forced into preordained boxes. Much in-depth material was gathered about TECs' and LECs' plans and attitudes, as well as detailed data about programmes, staffing, budgets and so forth. The survey was extensively piloted to ensure the best format. It ran to 22 pages and covered 41 questions, some of which required short simple tick-box answers, others were prompts to an open-ended discussion.
The main areas of enquiry were:
- Perceptions of TEC/LEC actors about the circumstances and needs of their localities;
- Goals set by TECs/LECs;

- Networking with other local bodies;
- Strategies for the Single European Market;
- Involvement in BS5750, IIP, MCI;
- Role of board members;
- LMI;
- Links to training contractors;
- Small firms strategies;
- Performance-related funding;
- Monitoring of programmes;
- Provision for disadvantaged groups;
- Training credits;
- Programme innovations;
- Education–business links;
- WRFE;
- Links to higher education;
- Enterprise provision and strategies;
- Major local initiatives;
- European initiatives;
- Interfacing with other TECs/LECs;
- Staffing issues;
- Budget composition and external funding strategies.

This survey was followed up by an additional set of in-depth interviews conducted with all 9 London TEC Chairs, chief executives and main staff during 1992 as part of a research contract (Bennett 1993d).

In-depth case studies of a sub-sample of 20 TECs and LECs. This phase involved 55 in-depth interviews across the country, its coverage being more intensive. It focused on a subsample of TECs and LECs, representative of all major types by region, size, economic characteristics and so forth, and exposed each to a scrutiny that went beyond talking only to the TEC or LEC chief executive. In this survey the views were sought of representatives from local authorities, business organizations such as Chambers of Commerce, training providers, and people identified as "key business leaders", who it became apparent were significant in their TEC or LEC area by dint of their involvement at high levels in local business initiatives. The business leaders interviewed covered the TEC/LEC Chair or a Board member, who frequently offered a distinctively different perspective from that offered by TEC or LEC chief executives. From these varied sources the project sought to triangulate a more objective view on TECs and LECs with which to compare their self-evaluation.

The main areas of enquiry were:
- Perceptions of other actors about the circumstances and needs of their localities;
- Goals which should be set by local TEC/LEC;

- TEC/LEC training programmes and approach to contracts;
- TEC/LEC small firms strategies;
- PRF/OF;
- Number/quality of TEC/LEC staff;
- Education–business links;
- Provision for disadvantaged groups;
- TEC/LEC enterprise strategy and programmes;
- Environmental strategy (LEC areas);
- Major local initiatives;
- Strategies for the Single European Market;
- General comment on start-up of the TEC/LEC.
  Organizations covered included:
- Chambers of Commerce;
- Enterprise agencies/trusts;
- Key firms;
- Local authorities;
- LEAS;
- Other key organizations such as the local tourist board, Milk Marketing Board, etc.

Broad-based interviews: supplementing each stage was a large number of interviews with other commentators, national and local, who could offer valuable insights into the workings of the TEC and LEC system from a position of experience or inside knowledge. This included 23 TEC/LEC Chairs, 34 TEC/LEC business Directors and 27 TEC/LEC non-business Directors, as well as all the leading national agents and civil service departments. All interviews were undertaken by a small team of the 3 authors. To further ensure consistency there was a division of team roles.

To retain confidentiality all individuals quoted in the text are attributed to TEC/LEC area by an anonymous number code.

Notes

Chapter 1

1. One LEC is joint between SE and HIE: Badenoch and Strathspey.

Chapter 2

1. House of Lords (1990, 1991); CSO Annual Survey.
2. *Financial Times* (3 December 1990).
3. OECD.
4. Examples are Chandler (1989), Porter (1990), Prais (1987), Jones (1990), Carr (1990), Whipp and Clark (1986), Lorenz (1991), Singleton (1991), Campbell et al. (1989), Northcott et al. (1985), Hendry (1990), Oakley and Owen (1990), SI (1990), Steedman and Wagner (1987), Mackenzie (1991), Thurley and Wirdenius (1989), Lane (1989).
5. Freeman et al. (1991), Roussel et al. (1991).
6. CEST (1991), Financial Times "No chance of an even match" (18 June 1991); NEDC (1991a) and Wilkie (1991).
7. e.g. Layard and Nickell (1985), Minford (1983), Blanchflower et al. (1988), Metcalf (1988), Nickell et al. (1991).
8. Evidence for the domination of anti-industrial tradition is given by AST (1956), Thomas (1959), Stanworth and Giddens (1974), More (1980), Wiener (1981), Hampden-Turner (1984), Rubinstein (1986).
9. Quoted in *Times Educational Supplement* (22 October 1976).
10. Sarup (1982: 39).
11. See, e.g. Ainley & Corney (1990).
12. See, e.g. Finegold & Soskice (1988), Roderick & Stephens (1982), Esland (1990), Anderson (1992).
13. See Barnett (1986), Himmelfarb (1984), Greenleaf (1983a, 1983b; 1987); other sources are Thompson (1990), Barnett (1972), Middlemas (1990), Bennett (1990, 1993a); Rubenstein (1993).
14. In BiTC (1989).
15. See Lucie-Smith (1981).
16. Bennett (1982, 1993a).
17. Barnett (1986: 291).
18. Audit Commission (1990: 126).
19. Audit Commission (1990: 126); see also Audit Commission (1989), Bennett (1989,

1993b), JURUE (1981), Chandler & Lawless (1985), Lawless (1988).
20. Walker (1983a, 1983b); Gyford (1985).
21. See, e.g. Mawson & Miller (1986), Chandler & Lawless (1985), Audit Commission (1986, 1987).

Chapter 3

1. In BiTC (1989).
2. Stratton (1989: 71–72).
3. Stratton (1989: 74).
4. Industry Department Scotland (1988: 9).
5. In BiTC (1989).
6. In BiTC (1989).
7. Stratton (1989: 71).
8. In BiTC (1989).
9. In BiTC (1989).
10. In *ET News* (April 1989).
11. Stratton (1989: 72).
12. Main (1989: 71).
13. "The Hughes initiative that is revitalising Scotland", *CBI News* (October 1991: 26).
14. Quoted in *Glasgow Herald* (14 July 1989).
15. Interviews with leading former SDA staff, locally and centrally.
16. Local interviews (see also Bennett & McCoshan 1993: Ch. 14).
17. HIE (1989: 29).
18. Interviews with LEC Chair and Board member (LEC 15).
19. Quoted from LEC Director (15).
20. See HIE (1990, 1991a); Industry Department Scotland (1990); Scottish Enterprise (1990).
21. In BiTC (1989).

Chapter 4

1. This has led to the criticism that in some cases US PICs engage in "creaming" – selecting only those candidates for training who would get jobs anyway in order to ensure that federal placement targets are met (see Bennett, 1989, 1993c; Peck, 1990).
2. JTPA is the Job Training Partnership Act which in 1982 established the main funding programme for US PICs. This replaced the previous Comprehensive Employment Training Act (1978) which originally established PICs.
3. Main (1989: 70).
4. Interviews with senior DE and CBI staff.
5. These quotations are derived from interviews with chairmen of US PICs (see, e.g. Bennett 1989, 1993c; see also Stratton 1989, and in BiTC 1989).
6. *Financial Times* TEC surveys (25 March 1992; 10 May 1993).
7. Interview comments. The *Financial Times* survey (25 March 1992) showed 83% of private sector Directors attending all meetings compared to 88% of trade union representatives and 90% of public sector Directors.
8. Statistics derived from Robert Jackson, *PQ* (1 November 1990). By October 1990, 12

operational TECs had suffered resignations of 19 Board members. Eleven of these TECs were among the 21 to go operational in the first 4 months, only one resignation occurred among the 14 TECs going operational in the next 4 months. Because resignation is likely to occur only after a period of time sufficient to see the operations of the TEC, it is appropriate to calculate the turnover rate only from the first group of TECs. There were 182 private sector Board members in the first 21 operational TECs.

9. Recalculated from that quoted in Times Educational Supplement (13 March 1992), after consultation with TEED; 1993 data from TEED.
10. Analysis of SO data on Board membership of SE and HIE LECs.
11. Analysis of SO data.
12. Fairley (1992).
13. In House of Commons, Employment Committee, Minutes of Evidence (19 April 1989: 32).
14. Wicks et al. (1992).
15. We derive this both from our own interview assessments related to the extent of programme innovation (see later chapters) and from interview comments from senior DE officials who have privately acknowledged the problem.
16. Comment quoted is from TEC Director 79.

Chapter 5

1. Quotations from BITC (1989).
2. All statistics from DE (1992c).
3. This statistic is biased downward by the use of the Employment Census. If VAT records by size by area were available they would probably give a range for most areas of 40–50%, but the same close similarlity between areas would be evident.
4. See Bennett (1993d).
5. See Bennett et al. (1989a).
6. Bennett (1993d: para 59).
7. Bennett & McCoshan (1993: Chs 9–14).
8. Sources mainly from Bennett & McCoshan (1993).
9. TECs Prospectus (1989: 4).
10. Comments of TEC Chair (25) (1991).
11. Tony Banks, Chairman, North Nottinghamshire TEC (in BITC 1989).
12. TECs Prospectus (1989: 5).
13. TECs Prospectus (1989: 5).
14. TEC conference presentation (5 July 1991) quoted in TEC Report 1990–91 (DE 1990/91).

Chapter 6

1. See, e.g. Bartlett (1989).
2. Brown & Fairley (1990).
3. Jim Wright, Training Manager, Ferranti Defence Systems, Scotland and a Scottish CBI leader (quoted in Brown & Fairley 1989: 186).
4. Bill Spiers, Deputy General Secretary of the Scottish TUC (quoted in Brown & Fairley 1989: 203).

5. IPM conference 1992, quoted in Employment News (December 1992: 5).
6. Confidential interview comment.
7. See e.g. Kaufman (1971), Perry (1976), Mason (1988), Wicks (1990), Ainley & Corney (1990).
8. Jim Wright (in Brown & Fairley 1989: 212).
9. Quoted in Brown & Fairley (1989: 36).
10. Analysis of local decisions and central government overriding them is reported in Brown & Fairley (1989), Mason (1988) and Ainley & Corney (1990).
11. "A note from the Chairman"·, in MSC (1985) Annual Report.
12. See the analysis by Randall (1986).
13. Interview comments (TEC Chairs 56 and 95).
14. See Benn & Fairley (1986), Brown & Fairley (1989), Ainley & Corney (1990).
15. Confidential interview comment.
16. Brown & Fairley (1989).
17. See Brian Wolfson "NTTF's new programme of work for TECs and Training", *TEC Director* (July/August 1991: 6-7).
18. Both quoted from "Representing the views of the TEC movement – G10 and its rôle", *TEC Director* (October/November 1991: 15).
19. TEC Chair 7 in the northern region.
20. Quoted in *Financial Times* (18 February 1991).
21. Banham (1992: 7).
22. CLD (1992); this figure is disputed by TEED. Whatever the reality, a £46 million increase occurred for all London TECs in 1992/93. This was in part a recognition of the difficulties of the historical baseline, as well as adjustment to changing relative unemployment levels. It occurred at a time of level funding for TECs as a whole and hence represents a reallocation from elsewhere.
23. Quoted in CLES (1992).
24. Quoted in the *Financial Times* (19 August 1992).
25. Confidential comment by senior TEED officer.
26. See, e.g. *Financial Times* (25 January 1992) which reports the employment minister blocking a proposal by Norfolk and Waveney TEC.
27. Speech to TECs conference (November 1992), quoted in *Financial Times* (10 November 1992).
28. Quoted in the *Financial Times* (14 May 1992).

Chapter 7

1. The development of this approach derives especially from Becker (1975) and it assumes that training produces returns to both individuals and companies.
2. There have been criticisms of the estimates in the table (e.g. Ryan 1991; Finegold 1991), particularly concerning the level of employers spending on training. However they are the best available estimates and there are at least as many arguments to suggest that business's funding of training is underestimated as overestimated.
3. Finegold & Soskice (1988), Jones (1988), Cassels (1990), Main & Shelley (1990), Brown & Fairley (1989), Ainley & Corney (1990).
4. DE (1988, 1992), Industry Department Scotland (1988, 1989).
5. See, e.g. CBI (1993a), NEDO (1991), EC (1990), Soskice (1991), Bennett et al. (1992a,

1992b).
6. Willis & Rosen (1979), Halsey et al. (1980), Bennett et al. (1992), Greenhalgh & Stewart (1987).
7. See Layard & Nickell (1987).
8. Arrangements in Scotland follow similar principles through Scottish Vocational Educational Certificate (SCOTVEC) which oversees the Scottish Vocational Qualifications (SVQs): we use, in general, the English terms.
9. See HMI (1991).
10. See, e.g. CBI (1993a), Steedman et al. (1991), Green & Steedman (1993).
11. This is because it can lead to "creaming" and the exclusion of special needs groups.
12. LSE survey.
13. LSE survey.
14. LSE survey.
15. LSE surveys.
16. LSE surveys. The greater use of Jobcentres in Scotland and the North of England reflects their generally higher profile in the labour market in these areas. In London and the South East, where employment prior to the recent recession was more buoyant, it has been much rarer for employers to report vacancies to Jobcentres, preferring to recruit directly. As a result these Jobcentres have often been associated with a stigma of covering residual "unemployable" categories of the labour force.
17. LSE survey.
18. Bridge Group (1991), Financial Times (23 September 1991), Plummer (1991, 1993).
19. See Plummer (1993).
20. Quoted in *Times Higher Educational Supplement* (24 January 1986).
21. See, e.g. Bevan & Hutt (1985), Sako & Dore (1986), Roberts (1986).
22. DE (1992b) and national budget data by programme.
23. CBI (1989a).
24. LSE interviews, *Employment Gazette* (May 1991: 248–9), NATFHE (1993).
25. e.g. Corney (1991), Ashby (1991).
26. *Hansard, PQ* (20 January 1992).
27. SOLOTEC written evidence to House of Commons Employment Select Committee, 1991; quoted in NATFHE (1993: 21).
28. See, e.g. *Financial Times* comments (17 June, 22 July 1992).
29. *PQ* (11 May 1992).
30. *Employment Gazette* (June 1993): *Agenda* (July 1993: 9).
31. Survey by *Personnel Management* magazine, reported in *Financial Times* (6 October 1992).
32. See, e.g. letter from Allen Sheppard, *Financial Times* (29 July 1992).
33. See, e.g. Anderson (1992).
34. This finding from our interviews is reflected in other research; see, e.g. Payne (1990), Peck (1991), CLES (1990, 1992).
35. Interview comments from business leaders; see also Ainley & Corney (1990), Brown & Fairley (1989).
36. Estimates from confidential assessment of the unit costs in two TECs Bennett (1993f).
37. TNPP (1992).
38. *Financial Times* (9 February 1993).
39. One estimate of the gap in YT places required put this at 50,000 in early 1992: Unemployment Unit, reported in *Financial Times* (2 April 1992).

Chapter 8

1. Recent confirmations of the problem of functional literacy are ALBSU (1993), HMI (1990), NFER (1990).
2. Finegold, in Wellington (1993).
3. See, e.g. Bailey (1992), Clark (1992).
4. Lawton (1982, 1989).
5. Broadfoot (1980).
6. Rae (1989).
7. Barnes (1977), McCoshan (1990).
8. The details of targets are reviewed in CBI (1991a).
9. See, e.g. Bostok & Smith (1990) and comments by Daniel Silverstone, Deputy Director of Education in Hackney, quoted in *Times Educational Supplement* (29 March 1991); note earlier appraisals by Ball (1985) and Welton & Evans (1986).
10. E.g. IPM (1981, 1984), Cleverdon (1988), Warwick (1989, 1993), TVEL (1990).
11. In Blandford & Jamieson (1989: 55-6) and Marsden (1991).
12. Wicks (1990).
13. See MacLure (1988) for detailed discussion.
14. In 67% of cases in the first round of Compacts (Bennett & McCoshan 1993: Table 7.1).
15. See Rossano (1985), Stratton (1989), Bennett & McCoshan (1993: Ch. 7).
16. See Main (1989, 1990).
17. Interview comments from non-TEC agents.
18. See Bennett et al. (1993a).
19. See CBI and Bennett (1992).
20. LSE survey (1992).
21. Comment of senior TEED officer.
22. See more detailed discussion in Bennett & McCoshan (1993: Ch. 7), Bennett & CBI (1992).
23. An evaluation of methods for linking the curriculum to work experience and business needs is given by Miller (1993).
24. *Times Educational Supplement* (14 May 1993).
25. ESRC Newsletter (10 June 1991: 2); see also Barnett (1986).
26. Performance of participants on YT is also often used in this way (see Gleeson 1989; Finegold et al. 1990).
27. Quoted in *Times Higher Educational Supplement* (5 April 1991: 2).
28. Even though it is clear that the French vocational reform has not been able to develop a full equivalence with the academic baccalaureate.
29. NCVQ (1990).
30. See Morris (1991).
31. E.g. DES (1991), BTEC (1991).
32. See also the discussion of this tension by Watts (in Wellington 1993).
33. See CBI (1993a).
34. See Bennett et al. (1993a: Table 22).
35. LSE survey.
36. See Bennett et al. (1993a: Table 28).
37. See Anderson (1992) and Chapter 2 above.

38. See, e.g. DES (1989).
39. CBI (1989a, 1993a), RSA/IM (1989), IM (1989).
40. See, e.g. Fulton & Ellwood (1989), Smithers & Robinson (1989), UDACE (1989, 1990).
41. See, e.g. Graham (1989).

Chapter 9

1. From BiTC (1989).
2. See, e.g. PA (1986), Marshall et al. (1993).
3. See also Bennett et al. (1990b).
4. Forward to One Stop Shops Prospectus (DTI 1992: 1); see also Bartlett (1993).
5. DTI (1992) Prospectus, and *Hansard* (3 December 1992: cols 414–44).
6. Heseltine (1992a: 9).
7. Heseltine (1992b: 9).
8. Heseltine (1992b: 10).
9. Heseltine (1992a: 9 emphasis added).
10. DTI guidance to Regional Offices (May 1993).
11. DTI (1992: 8–9).
12. Heseltine (1992b).
13. DTI (1992: 14).
14. Size distribution of businesses from DE (1992c).
15. This estimate derives from existing practice in Chambers of Commerce (see Bennett 1993e) and enterprise agencies (see BiTC 1986, 1988, 1989; Bennett & McCoshan 1993: Ch. 6).
16. This estimate is derived from analysis of confidential data in one of the most highly regarded Regional Technology Centres (TEC area 47) which has a "user base" of 1,000 companies and a "membership" of 120 companies managed by a staff of 5 advisers. The user base suggests that a ratio of 200 companies per adviser is possible, whilst the membership base suggests that a ratio of 24 companies per adviser is required. Given the aim of business advisers to be "close" to companies, the latter is the more probable requirement. The estimate given uses the latter figure.
17. Bennett & McCoshan (1993: Table 6.8).
18. Heseltine (1992b: 13–14).

Chapter 10

1. Quotes from DE (1988: 1), TECs Prospectus (1989: 1, 4) and DE (1991: 27).
2. Speech at London and South East Region TECs seminar (21 April 1993).
3. See Moore & Booth (1984).
4. See Bennett et al. (1993b: Table 23).
5. Fairley (1992: 195).
6. Chief executive LEC 57. Confirmed by NTTF (1992a: 26).
7. HIE (1991).
8. Thomas (1993).

Chapter 11

1. DE (1988: 39); TECs Prospectus (1989: 4).
2. Stratton (1989: 72, 71).
3. See Bennett et al. (1990b).
4. *The Economist* (24 April 1993).
5. Coldwell (1989: 75–6).
6. E.g. ELTEC, CENTEC and Glasgow.
7. *Financial Times* TECs survey (1992, 1993).
8. These estimates all derive from a confidential assessment made with the co-operation of the financial directors of two TECs by Bennett (1993f).
9. Confidential interview comments (March/April 1992).
10. Interview comments of senior DE staff.
11. Bennett (1993d).
12. E.g. Thomas (1993) for the AMA.
13. See Pirie (1988), Bennett (1990, 1993a).
14. See Peck (1990, 1991), CLES (1992), Coffield (1991), Danson et al. (1992), Boddy (1992).
15. See, e.g. Brown & Fairley (1988), Ainley & Corney (1990).
16. DE and Kids Club Network (1993).
17. *Financial Times* (10 May 1993).
18. See, e.g. Barnett (1986), Ainley & Corney (1990), Bennett et al. (1992a, 1992b), Barr & Falkingham (1993), Cassels (1990), CBI (1991a, 1993a).
19. CBI (1991a, 1993a).

Chapter 12

1. See Appendix.
2. In BiTC (1989).
3. In BiTC (1989).
4. Selznick (1949, 1957); see also Peters (1987, 1990). The role of leadership was also drawn to attention in a series of studies in Ohio and Michigan in the 1950s and 1960s. These emphasized for businesses the role of initiative and incentive setting by their leaders (see Halpin & Winer 1957; Fleishman et al. 1955; Katz et al. 1950; Bowers & Seashore 1966; Lickert 1967). A good summary of historical developments is given in Bryman (1986).
5. See Bartlett (1989) drawing on experience of major corporate restructuring, e.g. at Standard and Chartered Bank.
6. MSC (1985), Handy (1985, 1989); Handy & Aitken (1986).
7. CBI (1988), BiTC (1990), Grayson (1990), Wade (1990), Business in the Cities and Bennett (1990).
8. A phrase used in interview comments by critics of BiTC in Sheffield, Teesside and other areas.
9. In BiTC (1989).
10. Quoted in *Employment and Training News* (April 1989: 2) and BiTC (1989).
11. Text of speech at 1992 TECs Conference (1992: 5, emphasis in original).
12. Stratton (1989: 73).

NOTES

13. In BiTC (1989).
14. In BiTC (1989).
15. In BiTC (1989).
16. Brantwood (1992).
17. See business surveys reported in Bennett & Wicks (1993), TVEL (1990), Gibb (1993) and interview comments.
18. Bachtler et al. (1993).
19. ABCC guidance and accreditation documents, see e.g. ABCC (1991, 1992).
20. TEC Operating Agreement, 1988 White Papers, and interviews with senior DE staff (1992/93).
21. Interviews with senior DE staff and Regional Director (1992/93).
22. See Towler (1993).
23. Price Waterhouse (1992), Bartlett (1993) and interviews of ongoing local developments.
24. See discussion in Bennett et al. (1993), which shows that the German Chamber response to market testing has been predominantly run through committees.
25. See, e.g. Bannock (1976, 1989), Curran & Blackburn (1992), Bennett & Wicks (1993).
26. See *Financial Times* (26 April 1993), "Heseltine's plan 'to help Britain win'".

Bibliography

ABCC 1991. *Effective business support: a UK strategy: phase two*. London: Association of British Chambers of Commerce.

ABCC 1992. *Minimum requirements for Chamber of Commerce services*. London: Association of British Chambers of Commerce.

ABCC 1993. *Business Registration Centres: the first step to easing the compliance burden and improving competitiveness*. London: Association of British Chambers of Commerce.

Ainley, P. & M. Corney 1990. *Training for the future – the rise and fall of the Manpower Services Commission*. London: Cassell.

ALBSU 1993. *The cost to industry: basic skills in the UK workforce*. London: Adult Literacy Basic Skills Unit.

Anderson, R. D. 1992. *Universities and elites in Britain since 1800*. London: Macmillan.

Ashby, P. 1991. Doing the Government a favour. *Training Tomorrow*, February, 5–7.

AST 1956. *Management succession*. London: Acton Society Trust.

Audit Commission 1986. *Reports and accounts, year ended 31 March 1986*. London: HMSO.

Audit Commission 1987. *The management of London's authorities: preventing the breakdown of services*. London: HMSO.

Audit Commission 1989. *Urban regeneration and economic development: the local government dimension*. London: HMSO.

Audit Commission 1990. *Urban regeneration and economic development: audit guide*. London: Audit Commission.

Bachtler, C., J. Downes & R. Yuill 1993. *The devolution of economic development: lessons from Germany*. Glasgow: Scottish Foundation for Economic Research.

Bailey, P. 1992. A case hardly won: Geography and the National Curriculum in English and Welsh Schools. *Geographical Journal* **158**, 65–74

Ball, C. 1985. The triple alliance: what went wrong, what can be done? *Oxford Review of Education*, **11**(3), 227–34.

Ball, R. J. 1989. The United Kingdom economy: miracle or mirage? *National Westminster Bank Quarterly Review*, February, 43–59.

Banham, J. 1992. Taking forward the skills revolution. *Policy Studies*, **13**(1), 5–12.

Bannock, G. 1976. *The smaller business in Britain and Germany*, Farnborough: Wilton House.

Bannock, G. 1989. *Governments and small business*. London: Paul Chapman.

BIBLIOGRAPHY

Barnes, A. 1977. Decision-making on the curriculum in Britain. In R. Glatter (ed.) Control of the Curriculum, *Studies in Education* **4**. Institute of Education, University of London.

Barnes, D. et al. 1987. A second report on the TVEI curriculum: courses for 14–16 year olds in twenty-six schools. *TVEI Evaluation Report* **5**. Sheffield: The Training Agency, Employment Department.

Barnes, G. 1992. *An examination of the formulation of policies by Training and Enterprise Councils*. Working paper 7. Warwick Business School.

Barnett, C. 1986. *The audit of war: the illusion and reality of Britain as a great nation*. London: Macmillan.

Barr, N. and J. Falkingham 1993. *Paying for learning*. BP-STICERD discussion paper. London School of Economics.

Bartlett, A. 1989. TECs – will they succeed? *Regional Studies* **24**, 77–9.

Bartlett, A. 1993. OSSs – extending the vision. *Inter-TEC News* (May).

Becker, G. 1975. *Human capital*. Chicago: University of Chicago Press.

Benn, C. and J. Fairley (eds) 1986. *Challenging the MSC on jobs, training and education*, London: Pluto.

Bennett, R. J. 1982. *Central grants to local governments*. Cambridge: Cambridge University Press.

Bennett, R. J. 1989. Business bids for a role in the Philadelphia story. *Times Educational Supplement* (2 June), A13.

Bennett, R. J. (ed.) 1990. *Decentralization, local government and markets: towards a post-welfare agenda?* Oxford: Oxford University Press.

Bennett, R. J. 1991. *Developing a national chamber network*. London: Association of British Chambers of Commerce.

Bennett, R. J. (ed.) 1993a. *Developments in decentralization to local governments and markets: contemporary experiences*. Tokyo: United Nations University Press.

Bennett, R. J. (ed.) 1993b. *Local government in the new Europe*. London: Pinter (Belhaven).

Bennett, R. J. 1993c. PICs, TECs and LECs: lessons to be learnt from the difference between the USA Private Industry Councils and Britain's Training and Enterprise Councils. *Journal of Education and Work*, forthcoming.

Bennett, R. J. 1993d. *London TECs: a programme for working together. Report commissioned by the TECs London strategy group and the nine London TEC chairs*. Research paper. Department of Geography, London School of Economics.

Bennett, R. J. 1993e. *Costs and organization of British Chamber of Commerce business services*. Research paper. Department of Geography, London School of Economics.

Bennett, R. J. 1993f. Are tecs cost-efficient? *Policy Studies*, forthcoming.

Bennett, R. J., Glennester, H. and Nevison, D. 1992a. *Learning should pay*. BP Education Services & London School of Economics.

Bennett, R. J., H. Glennester & D. Nevison 1992b. Investing in skill: to stay on or not to stay on?, *Oxford Review of Economic Policy* **8**(2), 130–45.

Bennett, R. J. & G. Krebs 1991. *Local economic development: public–private partnership initiatives in Britain and Germany*. London: Pinter (Belhaven).

Bennett, R. J. & G. Krebs 1993. Chambers of Commerce and the challenges of the single market. In *Chambers of Commerce in Britain and Germany and the single European Market*, Bennet et al. (1993a), Chap. 1. Anglo–German Foundation, London and Bonn.

Bennett, R. J., G. Krebs & H. Zimmermann (eds) 1990a. *Local economic development in Britain and Germany*. Anglo–German Foundation, London and Bonn.

Bennett, R. J., G. Krebs & H. Zimmermann 1993a. *Chambers of Commerce in Britain and Germany and the single European market*. Anglo–German Foundation, London.

Bennett, R. J. & A. McCoshan 1993. *Enterprise and human resource development: local capacity building*. London: Paul Chapman.

Bennett, R. J., A. McCoshan & J. Sellgren 1989. *TECs and VET: the practical requirements: organisation, geography and international comparison with the USA and Germany*. Research paper. Department of Geography, London School of Economics.

Bennett, R. J., A. McCoshan & J. Sellgren 1990b. *Local employer networks (LENs): their experience and lessons for TECs*. Research paper. Department of Geography, London School of Economics.

Bennett, R. J. & P. Wicks 1993. *Potential development of Chamber of Commerce business services: a survey*. Research paper. Department of Geography, London School of Economics.

Bennett, R. J., P. Wicks, P. & A. McCoshan 1993b. *TECs and LECs early development: the priorities of Training and Enterprise Councils and Local Enterprise Companies shown in surveys 1990–1992*. Research paper. Department of Geography, London School of Economics.

Bevan, S. & R. Hutt 1985. Company perspectives on the Youth Training Scheme. *Report* **104**. Institute of Manpower Studies, University of Sussex.

BiTC 1986. *Enterprise Agencies, Trusts and community action programmes*. London: Business in the Community.

BiTC 1988. *The future for enterprise agencies*. London: Business in the Community.

BiTC 1989. *Leadership in the Community*, transcript of the national "Business in the Cities" conference (London: 6 December 1989). An edited version of this is available in Business in the Cities & Bennett (1990).

BiTC 1990. *A local enterprise agency accreditation charter*. London: Business in the Community.

BiTC 1991. *Quality in business support*. London: Business in the Community.

Blandford, D. & A. Jamieson 1989. *Building partnerships with education*. Cambridge: Careers Research and Advisory Centre.

Boddy, M. 1992. Evaluating labour market policy: the case of TECs. *British Journal of Education and Work* **5**(3) 43–56.

Bostock, D. A. & L. J. Smith 1990. *Human resource development: education and training needs*. Birmingham: Educational Support Services.

Bowers, D. G. & S. E. Seashore 1966. Predicting organizational effectiveness with a four-factor theory of leadership. *Administrative Science Quarterly* **11** 238–63.

Brantwood 1992. *One stop shops: an overall assessment*. Report commissioned by DTI. Coventry: Brantwood Consulting.

Bridge Group 1991. *Contracts for success or failure*. London: Bridge Group.

Broadfoot, S. 1980. Assessment, curriculum and control in the changing pattern of centre–local relations. *Local Government Studies* **6**(6) 57–68.

Brown, A. & J. Fairley (eds) 1989. *The Manpower Services Commission in Scotland*. Edinburgh: Edinburgh University Press.

Brown, A. & J. Fairley (eds) 1990. *The Manpower Services Commission in Scotland*. Edinburgh: Edinburgh University Press.

Bryman, A. 1986. *Leadership and organisation*. London: Routledge & Kegan Paul.

BTEC 1991. *Common skills general guidelines*. London: Business and Technical Education Council.

Business in the Cities & Bennett, R. J. 1990. *Leadership in the community: a blueprint for the 1990s*. London: Business in the Community.

Callaghan, J. 1976. Ruskin College speech, *Times Educational Supplement* (22 October) 72.

Campbell, A., A. Sorge & M. Warner 1989. *Microelectronic product applications in Great Britain and West Germany: strategies, competence and training*. Aldershot: Gower.

Carr, C. 1990. *Britain's competitiveness: the management of the vehicle component industry*. London: Routledge.

Cassels, J. 1990. *Britain's real skill shortage: and what to do about it*. London: Policy Studies Institute.

CBI 1988a. *Building a stronger partnership between business and secondary education*. Report of task force, chaired by Sir Adrian Cadbury. London: Confederation of British Industry.

CBI 1988b. *Initiatives beyond charity*. Report of the CBI task force on business and urban regeneration. London: Confederation of British Industry.

CBI 1989a. *Towards a skill revolution*. London: Confederation of British Industry.

CBI 1989b. *Training and Enterprise Councils – the way forward*. London: Confederation of British Industry.

CBI 1991a. *World class targets: a joint initiative to achieve Britain's skills revolution*. London: Confederation of British Industry.

CBI 1991b. *Business success through competence: investors in people*. London: City & Guilds and Confederation of British Industry.

CBI 1992. *Focus on the front line – the role of the supervisor*. London: Confederation of British Industry.

CBI 1993a. *Routes for success: careership: a strategy for all 16–19 year old learning*. London: Confederation of British Industry.

CBI 1993b. *Survey of TEC board business members*. London: Confederation of British Industry.

CBI & Bennett, R. J. 1992. *Education–business partnerships: the learning so far*. London: Confederation of British Industry.

CEST 1991. *Attitudes to innovation in Germany and Britain: a comparison*. London: Centre for the Exploitation of Science and Technology.

Chandler, A. D. 1989. *Scale and scope: dynamics of industrial capitalism*. Cambridge, Mass.: Harvard University Press.

Chandler, J. A. & P. Lawless 1985. *Local authorities and the creation of employment*. Aldershot: Gower.

Clark, K. 1992. Speech to Royal Geographical Society. *Geographical Journal* **158**, 75–8.

CLD 1992. *London – a capital deficiency*. Report to London TECs. London: Coopers & Lybrand Deloitte.

CLES 1990. *Challenging the TECs*. Manchester: Centre for Local Economic Strategies.

CLES 1992. *Reforming the TECs: towards a new training strategy*. Manchester: Centre for Local Economic Strategies.

Cleverdon, J. 1988. *Report on education/employment links*. London: Industrial Society.

CMED 1988. *The management charter initiative*. London: Charter for Management Education.

Coldwell, B. 1989. A business view from a potential TEC in Teesside. *Regional Studies* **24**, 74–7.

Coffield, F. 1991. From the decade of enterprise culture to the decade of TECs. *British Journal of Education and Work* **4**(1), 59–78.

Commanor, W. S. & H. Liebenstein 1969. Allocative efficiency, x-inefficiency and the measurement of welfare losses. *Economica* **36**, 304–9.

Constable, J. & R. McCormick 1987. *The making of British managers*. London: British Institute of Management & Confederation of British Industry.

Corney, M. 1991. Credits, tax and partnership. *Training Tomorrow* (October), 15–16.

Curran, P. & K. Blackburn 1992. *Small business services*. Small business research programme. Kingston University.

Danson, N. W., M. G. Lloyd & D. Newlands 1992. Privatism in business development and training: a new approach. *British Journal of Education and Work* **5**(3), 7–16.

Davies, H. 1990. Mrs Thatcher's third term: power to the people or camouflaged centralization? In R. J. Bennett (ed.) (1990). Oxford: Oxford University Press.

Davies, H. & H. Powell 1993. Breaking up is hard to do: the impact of client enpowerment on local services in Britain 1987–1991. In R. J. Bennett (ed.) (1993b). Tokyo: United Nations University Press.

DE 1984. *Training for jobs*. Cmnd 9135. London: HMSO.

DE 1988. *Employment for the 1990s*. Cm 540. London: HMSO.

DE 1989. *TECs and their staff*. Sheffield: Department of Employment.

DE 1990/91. *TEC report*. Sheffield: Department of Employment.

DE 1991. *A strategy for skills*. Guidance from the Secretary of State for Employment on training, vocational education and enterprise. London: Department of Employment.

DE 1992a. *Review of the Employment Department's Training, Enterprise and Education Department*. Sheffield: Department of Employment.

DE 1992b. *TECs and national providers: a new partnership*. Report of Employment Department study team. Sheffield: Department of Employment.

DE 1992c. *Small firms in Britain*. London: Department of Employment.

DE 1992d. *Training credits: final report*. London: Coopers and Lybrand Deloitte.

DE 1992e. *People, jobs and opportunity*. Cm 1810. LONDON: HMSO.

DE/DTI 1992. *The strategy for skills and enterprise 1993–1994: Guidance for the Secretary of State for Employment and the President of the Board of Trade*. London: Department of Employment & Department of Trade and Industry.

DE and Kid's Club Network 1993. *Taking the initiative on out of school children: a guide for TECs*. London: Department of Employment.

DEG 1990a. *The partnership handbook*. Sheffield: Department of Employment Group.

DEG 1990b. *The partnership primer*. Sheffield: Department of Employment Group.

DES 1976. *A framework for expansion*. LONDON: HMSO.

DES 1987. *NAFE in practice*. London: Department of Education and Science.

DES 1988. *Report by HM Inspectors on the Youth Training Scheme in further education*. London: Department of Education and Science.

DES 1989. *Universities in the training market: an evaluation of the UGC PICKUP Selective Funding Scheme*. London: Department of Education and Science.

DES 1991. *Ordinary and advanced diplomas: a consultative document*. London: Department of Education and Science.

DES/DE/WO 1991. *Education and training for the 21st century*. [2 volumes] Cm 1536. LONDON: HMSO.

DFE 1993a. Survey of school–business links, DFE *Statistical Bulletin* **10/93**.

DFE 1993b. *Education*. White paper. Cmnd. ?? LONDON: HMSO.

Donovan, J. 1992. View from a TEC board. *Policy Studies* **13**(1), 40–5.

Dore, R. & M. Sako 1989. *How the Japanese learn to work*. London: Routledge & Kegan Paul.

Dornbusch, R. & R. Layard (eds) 1987. *The performance of the British economy*. Oxford: Oxford University Press.

DTI 1992. *A prospectus for One-Stop Shops for business*. London: Department of Trade and Industry.

DTI 1994. *Business link: a prospectus for One-Stop Shops for business*. London: Department of Trade and Industry.

EC 1990. *The role of the social partners in vocational education and training: summaries of the reports of the member states of the European Community*. Luxembourg: Commission of the European Communities.

Ernst and Young Accountants 1993. *TEC participation in relational development activity*. Research series no. 10. Sheffield: Department of Employment.

Esland, G. 1990. *Education, training and employment. Vol I: Educated labour – the changing basis of industrial demand*. New York: Addison-Wesley.

Fairholm, G. W. 1991. *Values leadership: toward a new philosophy of leadership*. New York: Praeger.

Fairley, J. 1992. Scottish Local Authorities and Local Enterprise Companies: a developing relationship? *Regional Studies* **26**, 193–9.

FEFC 1992. *Funding learning*. Coventry: Further Education Funding Council.

FEU 1989. *Planning a curricula response*. London: Further Education Unit.

Field, R. 1990. The business role in local economic regeneration: the Sheffield story. In *Local economic development in Britain and Germany*, Bennett et al. (eds), 49–64. London: Anglo–German Foundation.

Financial Times 1992. TEC survey of TEC directors (25 March).

Financial Times 1993. TEC survey of TEC directors (10 May).

Finegold, D. & D. Soskice 1988. The future of training in Britain: analysis and prescription, *Oxford Review of Economic Policy* **4**(3), 21–53.

Finegold, D. et al. 1990. A British Baccalaureate. *Education and Training Paper* **1**. LONDON: Institute for Public Policy Research.

Finegold, D. 1991. The implications of training in Britain for the analysis of Britain's skills problem: a comment on Paul Ryan's "How much do employers spend on training?". *Human Resources Management Journal* **2**(1), 110–15.

Fleishman, E. A., E. F. Harris & H. E. Burtt 1955. *Leadership and supervision in industry*. Bureau of Education Research, Ohio State University, Columbus.

Freeman, C., P. Patel & K. Pavitt (eds) 1991. *Technology and the future of Europe*. London: Francis Pinter.

Full Employment UK 1992. *TEC membership for local employers: report of a Windsor consultation for TECs*. London: Full Employment UK.

Fulton, D. & S. Ellwood 1989. *Admissions to higher education: policy and practice.* Sheffield: Training Agency.

G10 1992a. *Options for a new national body for training and enterprise; and briefing paper: option (IV), Development.* Redditch: Training and Enterprise Councils' Secretariat.

G10 1992b. *"osss": A submission to the DTI by the Training and Enterprise Councils.* Redditch: Training and Enterprise Councils' Secretariat.

Gibb, A. A. 1993. Key factors in design of policy support for the small and medium enterprise (SME) development process: an overview. *Entrepreneurship and Regional Development* **5**(1), 1–24.

Gleeson, D. 1989. *The paradox of training: making progress out of crisis.* Milton Keynes: Open University Press.

Graham, C. 1989. *After Lancaster House: a study of industry's plans for training and its use of further and higher education.* London: Department of Education and Science, PICKUP Programme.

Grayson, D. 1990. *Small business megatrends.* London: Business in the Community.

Green, A. & H. Steedman 1993. *Educational provision, educational attainment and the needs of industry: a review of research for Germany, France, Japan and Great Britain.* London: National Institute of Economic and Social Research.

Greenhalgh, C. & M. Stewart 1987. The effects and determinants of training, *Oxford Bulletin of Economics and Statistics* **49**, 171–90.

Greenleaf, W. H. 1983a. *The British political tradition 1: the rise of collectivism.* London: Methuen.

Greenleaf, W. H. 1983b. *The British political tradition 2: the ideological heritage.* London: Methuen.

Greenleaf, W. H. 1987. *The British political tradition 3: a much governed nation.* London: Methuen.

Gyford, J. 1985. *The politics of local socialism.* London: Allen & Unwin.

Halpin, A. W. & B. J. Winer 1957. A factorial study of the leader behaviour descriptions. In *Leader behaviour: its description and measurement.* R. M. Stogdill and A. E. Coons (eds). Columbus: Ohio State University Press.

Halsey, A., A. Heath & J. Ridge 1980. *Origins and destination: family, class and education in modern Britain.* Oxford: Oxford University Press.

Hampden-Turner, L. 1984. *Gentlemen and tradesmen: the value of economic catastrophe.* London: Gower.

Handy, C. 1985. *The future of work.* London: Penguin.

Handy, C. 1989. *The age of unreason.* London: Business Books.

Handy, C. & R. Aitken 1986. *Understanding schools as organisations.* London: Penguin.

Hargroves, J. S. 1987. The Boston compact: facing the challenge of school dropouts. *Education and Urban Society* **19**, 303–10.

Hausner, V. (ed.) 1986. *Critical issues in urban economic development*, VOL. I. Oxford: Oxford University Press.

Hendry, J. 1990. *Innovating for failure: government policy and the early British computer industry.* Cambridge, Mass.: MIT Press.

Heseltine, M. 1989. *The challenge of Europe.* London: Weidenfeld & Nicholson.

Heseltine, M. 1992a. Forging partnerships for world class support. *TEC Director* **15** (September/October), 8–9.

Heseltine, M. 1992b. Text of speech to TECs conference (10 July 1992).

HIE 1989. *A strategy for enterprise development in the highlands and islands of Scotland.* Inverness: Highlands and Islands Enterprise.

HIE 1990. *Board/HIE corporate plan 1990–95.* Inverness: Highlands and Islands Enterprise.

HIE 1991a. *A strategy for enterprise development in the highlands and islands of Scotland.* Inverness: Highlands and Islands Enterprise.

HIE 1991b. *The highlands and islands of Scotland: spreading their wings.* Inverness: Highlands and Islands Enterprise.

Himmelfarb, G. 1984. *The idea of poverty: England in the early industrial age.* New York: Alfred Knopf.

HM Government 1984. *Training for jobs*, Cmnd 9135. London: HMSO.

HMI 1990. *The teaching and learning of reading in primary schools.* London: Her Majesty's Inspectorate for Schools.

HMI 1991. *Report on NVQs.* London: Her Majesty's Inspectorate for Schools.

House of Lords 1990. A community framework for R&D. *House of Lords Papers* **66**, 1988–90. London: HMSO.

House of Lords 1991. Science policy and the European dimension. *House of Lords Papers*, 1990–91. London: HMSO.

IM 1989. *Raising the standard.* London: Industry Matters.

IMS 1993. *Progress in partnership: baseline study. National Evaluation of the Education Business Partnership Initiative.* London: Department of Employment.

Industry Department Scotland 1988. *Scottish enterprise: a new approach to training and enterprise creation*, Cm S34. EDINBURGH: HMSO.

Industry Department Scotland 1989. *Towards Scottish enterprise: "an inviation to play a vital part in stimulating enterprise and training in your locality".* EDINBURGH: HMSO.

Industry Department Scotland 1990. *Towards Scottish enterprise: the handbook.* Edinburgh: Scottish Office.

IPM 1981. *What do UK employers look for in school leavers?* London: Institute of Personnel Management.

IPM 1984. *TVEI: recommendations for an improved school/work liaison.* London: Institute of Personnel Management.

Jones, D. 1990. *The machine that changed the world.* London: Maxwell Macmillan.

Jones, I. 1988. An evaluation of YTS. *Oxford Review of Economic Policy* **4**(3), 54–71.

JURUE 1981. *Assessing the cost effectiveness of local economic initiatives.* Birmingham: Joint Unit for Research on the Urban Environment.

Katz, D., N. Maccoby & N. Morse 1950. *Productivity, supervision and morale in an office situation.* Ann Arbor, Michigan: Institute of Social Research.

Kaufman, H. 1971. *The limits of organizational change.* Alabama: University of Alabama Press.

Lane, C. 1989. *Management and labour in Europe: the industrial enterprise in Germany, Britain and France.* London: Edward Elgar.

336

Lawless, P. 1988. Enterprise Boards: evolution and critique. *Planning Outlook* **31**, 13–18.

Lawton, D. 1982. *The end of the "secret garden"?: a study in the politics of the curriculum*, 2nd edn. Institute of Education, University of London.

Lawton, D. 1989. *Education, culture and the national curriculum*. London: Hodder and Stoughton.

Layard, R. & S. Nickell 1985. The causes of British unemployment. *National Institute Economic Review* **III**, 62–85.

Layard, R. and Nickell, S. 1987. The labour market. In *The performance of the British economy*, R. Dornbusch & R. Layard (eds). Oxford: Oxford University Press.

Lickert, R. 1967. *The human organization: its management and value*. New York: McGraw Hill.

Lorenz, E. 1991. *Economic decline in Britain: the shipbuilding industry 1890–1970*. Oxford: Oxford University Press.

Lucie-Smith, E. 1981. *The story of craft*. Oxford: Phaedon.

Mackenzie, D. 1991. *Inventing accuracy: a historical sociology of nuclear missile guidance*. Cambridge, Mass: MIT Press.

Maclure, S. 1988. *Education re-formed: a guide to the Education Reform Act, 1988*. London: Hodder & Stoughton.

Main, B. & M. Shelley 1990. The effectiveness of the Youth Training Scheme on manpower policy, *Economica* **57**, 495–514.

Main, D. 1989. Training and Enterprise Councils: an agenda for action. *Regional Studies* **24**, 69–71.

Main, D, 1990. *Local economic development and TECs*. In *Local economic development in Britain and Germany*, Bennett et al. (eds), 85–90. London: Anglo–German Foundation.

Malinvaud, E. 1977. *The theory of unemployment reconsidered*. Oxford: Basil Blackwell.

Marquand, J. 1989. *Autonomy and change: the sources of economic growth*. London: Harvester Wheatsheaf.

Marquand, J. & K. Murphy 1990. *TECs and evaluation*. Paper delivered to OECD, ILE Seminar 27 (September).

Marsden, C. 1991. *Education and business: a vision for the partnership*. LONDON: BP Education Affairs.

Marshall, J. N., N. Alderman, C. Wong & A. Thwaites 1993. The impact of government-assisted management training and development on small and medium-sized enterprises in Britain. Environment and Planning C. *Government and Policy* **11**.

Mason, C. 1988. *Government restructuring of vocational education and training 1981–1987: local autonomy or dependence*. School of Advanced Urban Studies, Bristol.

Mawson, J. & D. Miller 1986. Interventionist approaches to local employment and economic development: the experience of Labour local authorities. In *Critical issues in urban economic development*, V. Hausner (ed.), 143–99. Oxford: Oxford University Press.

McCoshan, A. 1990. *Resources, unit costs and the curriculum: an analysis of changing priorities in local education authority secondary schools in England*. PhD thesis, London School of Economics.

McKleish, H. 1991. Labour's approach to TECs. *Training Tomorrow* (September) 5–8.

Meade, J. F. 1982. *Wage-fixing*. London: Allen & Unwin.

Metcalf, D. 1988. *Trade unions and economic performance: the British evidence*. Centre for Urban Economics, London School of Economics.

Middlemas, K. 1990. *Power, competition and the state*: Vol. 1: *Britain in search of balance 1940–61*; Vol. 2: *Threats to the postwar settlement in Britain 1961–74*; Vol. 3: *Power, competition and the state*. London: Macmillan.

Miller, A. 1993. *Building effective school–business links*. London: DE/DFE.

Minford, P. 1983. Labour market equilibrium in an open economy. *Oxford Economic Papers* 35, 207–44.

Moore, C. & S. Booth 1984. *Unlocking enterprise: policy innovation in Scotland*. Centre for the Study of Public Policy, University of Strathclyde.

More, C. 1980. *Skills and the English working class, 1870–1914*. London: Croom Helm.

Morris, A. 1991. Towards a unified 16+ curriculum. *Working Paper* 12. Institute of Education, University of London.

MSC 1985. *A challenge to complacency: changing attitudes to training*. Sheffield: Manpower Services Commission & National Economic Development Office.

MSC 1987. *The funding of vocational education and training: a consultation document*. Sheffield: Manpower Services Commission.

MSC 1988. *Compacts: guidelines for MSC support*. Sheffield: Manpower Services Commission.

MSC/NEDC/BIM 1989. *The making of managers: a report on management education, training and development in the USA, West Germany, France, Japan and the UK*. Manpower Services Commission, National Economic Development Council & British Institute of Management, London: NEDO.

Murray, C. 1984. *Losing ground: American social policy 1950–1980*. New York: Basic Books.

Murray, C. 1989. Underclass: a disaster in the making. *Sunday Times Magazine* (26 November), 26–45.

NATFHE 1993. *Credit limits: a critical assessment of the training credits pilot scheme*. London: National Association of Teachers in Further and Higher Education.

NCC 1990. *Core skills*. London: National Curriculum Council.

NCVQ 1990. *Core skills in NVQS. Response to the Secretary of State for Education*. London: National Council for Vocational Qualification.

NEDC 1991a. *Partners for the long term: lessons from the success of Germany and Japan*. London: National Economic Development Council.

NEDC 1991b. *What makes a supervisor world class?* London: National Economic Development Council, Engineering Skills Working Party.

NEDO 1991. *Training and competitiveness*. London: National Economic Development Office & Kogan Page.

NEDO/MSC 1984. *Competence and competition: training and education in the Federal Republic of Germany, the United States and Japan*. London: National Economic Development Office.

NFER 1990. *Standards of reading of seven year old children*. London: National Foundation for Educational Research for DES.

Nickell, S., S. Wadhwani & M. Wall 1991. *Productivity growth in UK companies 1975–86*. Centre for Economic Performance, London School of Economics.

Northcott, J., W. Kretsch, B. de Lestopis & P. Rogers 1985. *Micro-electronics in industry. An international comparison: Britain, France and Germany*. London: Policy Studies Institute.

NTTF 1992a. *The role of TECs in local economic development and enterprise*. Consultants report to NTTF panel. London: Coopers and Lybrand.

NTTF 1992b. *TECs and education*. Report of NTTF working party. London: Department of Employment.

NTTF 1993. *The role of TECs in enterprise and local economic development*. National Training Task Force. London: Department of Employment.

NTTF/LEG 1989. *London Employers Group report*. National Training Task Force. London: Department of Employment.

Oakley, B. & K. Owen 1990. *Alvey: Britain's startegic computing initiative*. Cambridge, Mass.: MIT press.

OECD 1975. *Education and working life*. Paris: Organisation for Economic Cooperation and Development.

Olson, M. 1982. *The rise and decline of nations: economic growth, stagflation and social rigidities*. New Haven: Yale University Press.

Osborne, D. & T. Gaebler 1993. *Reinventing Government*. London: European Policy Forum.

PA 1986. *Business results through training*. London: PA Management Consultants.

Parry, G., G. Moyser & N. Day 1992. *Political participation and democracy in Britain*. Cambridge: Cambridge University Press.

Payne, J. 1990. Adult off-the-job skills training: an evaluation study. *Research and Development Series* 57. Sheffield: Training Agency.

Peck, J. A. 1990. Post-corporatism in practice: TECs and the local politics of training. *SPA working paper* 9. University of Manchester.

Peck, J. A. 1991. Letting the market decide (with public money): TECs and the future of labour market programmes. *Critical Social Policy* 31, 4–17.

Perry, P. 1976. *The evaluation of British manpower policy*. London: British Association for Commercial and Industrial Education.

Peters, T. 1987. *Thriving on chaos*. London: Harper & Row.

Peters, T. 1990. Towards the entrepreneurial and empowering organisation. Lecture presentation at *The Economist*, London.

Peters, T. & R. H. Waterman 1982. *In search of excellence*. London: Harper & Row.

Pirie, M. 1988. *Privatisation: theory, practice and choice*. Aldershot: Wildwood Press.

Plummer, J. 1991. One-sided training contracts are obstacles to success. *Training Tomorrow* (December) 18–19.

Plummer, J. 1993. Training supplier's contracts with TECs, *TEC Director* 16 (February/March), 36–7.

Porter, M. E. 1980. *Competitive strategy: techniques for analysing industries and competitors*. New York: Free Press.

Porter, M. E. 1990. *The competitive advantage of nations*. London: Macmillan.

Prais, S. J. 1987. Education for productivity: comparisons of Japanese and English schooling and vocational preparation. *National Institute Economic Review* (February).

Price Waterhouse 1992. *Business support in the Thames Valley*. London: Price Waterhouse.

Rae, J. 1989. *Too little, too late? The challenges that still face British education*. London: Collier.

Randall, C. 1986. The nature of consultative arrangements of AMBs. *Research Working*

Paper. School of Advanced Urban Studies, University of Bristol.

Reid, R. P. 1989. "Management Charter Initiative – the way ahead". Speech at CBI conference (8 November).

Roberts, K. 1986. Firms' uses of the Youth Training Scheme. *Policy Studies* **6**(3), 37–53.

Roderick, G. & M. Stephens (eds) 1982. *The British malaise: industrial performance, education and training in Britain today*. Sussex: Falmer Press.

Rossano, K. R. 1985. *A partnership for excellence: the Boston public schools and Boston business community*. Boston, Mass.: Boston Chamber of Commerce.

Roussel, P., Saad, K. and Erikson, T. 1991. *Third generation R&D*. Cambridge, Mass.: Harvard Business School Press.

RSA/IM 1989. *Aim higher: widening access to higher education*. London: Royal Society of Arts & Industry Matters.

Rubinstein, W. D. 1986. Education and social origins of British elites, 1880–1970. *Past and Present* **112**, 163–207.

Rubinstein, W. D. 1993. *Capitalism, culture and the decline in Britain 1750–1990*. London: Routledge.

Ryan, P. 1991. How much do employers spend on training? An assessment of the "Training in Britain" estimates. *Human Resources Management Journal* **1**(4), 55–76.

Sako, M. & R. Dore 1986. How the Youth Training Scheme helps employers? *Employment Gazette* (June), 195–204.

Sampson, A. 1982. *The changing anatomy of Britain*. London: Hodder & Stoughton.

Sanderson, M. 1972. *The universities and British industry 1850–1970*. London: Routledge & Kegan Paul.

Sarup, M. 1982. *Education, state and crisis: a marxist perspective*. London: Routledge.

Scottish Enterprise 1990. *Statement of policy and operating principles*. Glasgow: Scottish Enterprise.

Sellgren, J. 1987. Local economic development and local initiatives in the mid-1980s: an analysis of the Local Economic Development Information Service. *Local Government Studies* **13**(6), 51–68.

Sellgren, J. 1989. *Local economic development in Great Britain: an evolving local government role*. PhD thesis, University of London.

Selznick, P. 1949. *TVA and the grass roots: a study in the sociology of formal organisations*. Berkeley: California University Press.

Selznick, P. 1957. *Leadership in administration*. New York: Harper and Row.

SI 1990. *Computer integrated manufacture for the engineering industry*. Glasgow: Strathclyde Institute.

Singleton, J. 1991. *Lancashire on the scrapheap: the cotton industry 1945–1970*. Oxford University Press/Pasold Research Fund.

Smithers, A. & P. Robinson 1989. *Increasing participation in higher education*. BP & University of Manchester.

Soskice, D. 1991. *The German training system: reconciling markets and institutions*. Mimeo. Wissenschaftzentrum Berlin.

SQW 1992. *The role of TECs in enterprise and economic development: the experiences of six TECs and one LEC*. Cambridge: Segal, Quince Wickstead for NTTF Panel.

Stanworth, P. & A. Giddens 1974. *Elites and power in British society*. Cambridge: Cambridge University Press.

Steedman, H., G. Mason & K. Wagner 1991. Intermediate skills in the workplace: development, standards and supply in Britain, France and Germany. *National Institute Economic Review* **136**(2), 60–76.

Steedman, H. & K. Wagner 1987. Machinery, production organisation and skills: kitchen manufacture in Britain and Germany. *Discussion Paper* **117**. NIESR, London.

Stogdill, M. & A. E. Coons (eds) 1957. *Leader behaviour: its description and measurement*. Columbus: Ohio State University.

Stratton, C. N. 1989. TECs and PICs: the key issues which lie ahead, *Regional Studies* **24**, 70–4.

TA 1989. *Training in Britain: a study of funding, activity and attitudes*. Training Agency. London: HMSO.

TC 1988. *The compacts development handbook*. Sheffield: Training Commission.

TEC guide 1989. *Guide to the development of TECs*. Sheffield: Training Agency.

TEC operating manual 1989. *TECs in England and Wales: operating manual*. Sheffield: Training Agency.

TEC operating manual 1991. London: Employment Department Group.

TECs prospectus 1989. *Training and Enterprise Councils: a prospectus for the 1990s*. Sheffield: Training Agency.

TEC WG 1992. *The future of adult training: a report to the Secretary of State by the TEC Working Group*. REDDITCH: TEC secretariat.

TEED 1991. *Recording achievement and planning individual development guidance on summarising the record and completing the National Record of Achievement*. Sheffield: Training, Enterprise and Education Directorate.

Thomas, H. (ed.) 1959. *The establishment*. London: Anthony Bland.

Thomas, I. C. 1993. *Friend or foe? Relations between metropolitan authorities and TECs*. London: Association of Metropolitan Authorities.

Thompson, F. M. L. 1990. *The Cambridge social history of Britain 1750–1950*: Vol. 1: *Regions and communities*; Vol. 2: *People and their environment*; Vol. 3: *Social agencies and institutions*. Cambridge: Cambridge University Press.

Thurley, K. & H. Wirdenius 1989. *Towards a European management*. London: Pitman.

TNPP 1992. *The way forward: prospectus for a national management agency*. Sheffield: TECs and National Providers Partnership Ltd.

Towler, D. 1993. Dancing lesson for giants and elephants: the TEED-TEC relationship: a study of network management. University of Buckingham, International Management Centres, *Design and Process Newsletter* **5** (July).

TVEL 1990. What do employers want from education? Summary of Thames Valley Enterprise Ltd report. *Skills and Enterprise Briefing* **3/91**.

Tyson, L. D. A. 1992. *Who's bashing whom? Trade conflict in high-technology industries*. Washington DC: Brookings Institution.

UDACE 1989. *Understanding competence*. Leicester: National Institute of Adult Continuing Education.

UDACE 1990. *An agenda for access*. Leicester: National Institute of Adult Continuing Education.

Vaughan, P. 1993. TECs and employers. Part 1: a survey. *Research paper series no. 12*. Sheffield: Department of Employment.

Wade, R. 1990. Stimulating "partnership" and leadership in a local context. In R. J. Bennett, G. Krebs and H. Zimmermann (eds) (1990a), 91–102. London: Anglo–German Foundation.

Walker, D. 1983a. *Municipal empire: the townhalls and their beneficiaries*. Hounslow: Maurice Temple Smith.

Walker, D. 1983b. Local interest and representation: the case of 'class' interest among Labour representatives in inner London, *Environment and Planning C. Government and Policy* 1, 342–6.

Warwick, D. (ed.) 1989. *Linking schools and industry*. Oxford: Basil Blackwell.

Warwick, D. (ed.) 1993. *The wealth of a nation: practical partnerships between industry and education*. London: Nicholas Brearley.

Wellington, J. (ed.) 1993. *The work related curriculum: challenging the vocational imperative*. London: Routledge.

Welton, J. & J. Evans 1986. The development and implementation of special education policy: where did the 1981 Act fit in? *Public Administration* 64, 209–27.

Whipp, R. & P. Clark 1986. *Innovation in the auto industry*. London: Francis Pinter.

Wiener, M. 1981. *English culture and the decline of the industrial spirit, 1850–1980*. Cambridge: Cambridge University Press.

Wicks, P. J. 1990. *Bureaucratic change in further education*. PhD thesis, London School of Economics.

Wicks, P. J., R. J. Bennett & A. McCoshan 1992. *Scotland's Local Enterprise Companies (LECs): an assessment*. Research Paper, Department of Geography, London School of Economics.

Wilkie, T. 1991. *British science and politics since 1945* Oxford: Basil Blackwell.

Willis, R. & S. Rosen 1979. Education and self-selection. *Journal of Political Economy* 87(5), pt 2, S7–S35.

Index

Index to anonymously cited TECs and LECs